SUPERVISION

A GUIDE TO PRACTICE

Third Edition

JON WILES
JOSEPH BONDI

University of South Florida

Merrill, an imprint of
Macmillan Publishing Company
New York

Collier Macmillan Canada, Inc.
Toronto

Maxwell Macmillan International Publishing Group
New York   Oxford   Singapore   Sydney

Editor: Linda A. Sullivan
Production Editor: Gloria Schneider Jasperse
Art Coordinator: Ruth A. Kimpel
Text Designer: Debra A. Fargo
Cover Designer: Robert Vega
Production Buyer: Pamela D. Bennett

This book was set in Trump Mediaeval

Macmillan Publishing Company
866 Third Avenue, New York, NY 10022

Collier Macmillan Canada, Inc.

Library of Congress Cataloging-in-Publication Data
Wiles, Jon.
    Supervision: a guide to practice/Jon Wiles, Joseph Bondi. —
3rd ed.
        p.   cm.
    Includes bibliographical references and index.
    ISBN 0-02-427635-9
    1. School supervision.   I. Bondi, Joseph.   II. Title.
LB2806.4.W55 1991
371.2 – dc20   90-21892
                                                    CIP

Printing: 1   2   3   4   5   6   7   8   9   Year: 1   2   3   4

*This book is dedicated to Kimball Wiles,
a pioneer in supervision.*

Preface

Now, in the 1990s, public education stands on the threshold of significant change. Innovations such as school-based management, new technology, and business-school partnerships promise to impact and alter forever the school form that we have known for nearly a century in America.

The prospect of such change is exciting for those in the education field. But along with great anticipation comes the realization of increasing and changing responsibility on the part of the supervisor. This new responsibility will bring with it the need for a cooperative style of leadership. More than ever before, supervisors will be required to be proactive while working cooperatively with teachers, administrators, parents, and community groups. Failure to do so will be to relinquish the leadership role.

At the same time, achieving success in such a role will require not only a positive attitude and a desire to succeed, but also the mastery of some very specific skills. *SUPERVISION: A Guide to Practice* is designed to provide a solid basis for identifying and developing these skills and for recognizing the changing nature of the supervisory role.

Text Organization

We bring six vital skill areas into focus in Part II of this text. Chapters four through nine, "Aiding Human Development," "Designing and Developing Curriculum," "Improving Classroom Instruction," "Encouraging Human Relations," "Providing Staff Development," and "Fulfilling Administrative Functions" represent major topics of interest for supervisors.

In contrast to the very specific treatment of skill areas, chapters 1 through 3 provide a general orientation to the field of supervision, along with an overview of the leadership role.

Part III (chapters 10 through 12) focuses on the problems of supervision in "Evaluating for Effectiveness" and "Politics in Supervision" and concludes with carefully selected case studies.

New to this Edition

This third edition of *SUPERVISION: A Guide to Practice* has been updated to reflect the newest trends and the most up-to-the-minute research available, including that in areas such as teacher induction, teacher empowerment, restructuring, technology, and teacher effectiveness.

An added feature titled "New Directions," appearing in chapters 1-11, offers a look at future trends and encourages the reader to set a course in acknowledging and managing the forces of the 1990s.

We believe this newest edition offers the reader a current and truly practical guide to supervision.

Acknowledgments

As ever, we are indebted to the many practitioners who have contributed ideas for this latest edition. We also thank the reviewers of this text for their comments and excellent suggestions: Gillian E. Cook, University of Texas at San Antonio; Albert J. Pautler, Jr., University of Buffalo; and Walter E. Sistrunk, Mississippi State University.

Jon Wiles
Joseph Bondi

Contents in Brief

Contents

THE WORLD OF SUPERVISION

CHAPTER 1

Orientation to Supervision

INTRODUCTION

Supervision is a complex and difficult leadership role in the field of education. Supervision occurs at many levels and supervisors hold many titles. In many school districts, the role of the supervisor is largely undefined and residual in nature. While historically a teacher-supporting role, supervision has recently become more administrative and managerial. Despite its lack of focus, supervision remains indispensable for the improvement of instructional programs in schools.

Supervision in the professional setting of a school is unique, and the recognition of this uniqueness is the beginning point for successful practice. Supervision in a school is not the same as supervision in a business. Even though many of the problems encountered in schools and industrial settings are similar, the responses to such problems must differ. Industrial supervisors gain their authority by decree such as found in the 1947 Taft-Hartley Act:

> those having authority to exercise independent judgment in hiring, discharging, disciplining, rewarding, and taking other actions of a similar nature with respect to employees.

School supervisors gain their authority by either borrowing the power of line administrators, exerting political influence in their relationship with others, or by demonstrating clearly superior competence in their knowledge and actions. In the professional environment of education, supervisors must use persuasive influence rather than authoritative influence in responding to problems and needs.

To fully understand the nature of supervision in an educational setting, it is useful to trace the historical factors that have shaped the role to this time. The reader will note that the definition of supervision in education, and the roles played by school supervisors, has changed dramatically in this century. It is expected that the role of the school supervisor will continue to evolve between the present and the year 2000 A.D.

HISTORY OF EDUCATIONAL SUPERVISION

The meaning of the term *supervision* and the role played by educational supervisors have evolved over time. Over time, school supervision has passed back and forth between a teacher-oriented role and an administrative role, with each swing redefining the function of supervision. The 1980s, for instance, witnessed a swing toward management while the 1990s, with the teacher empowerment movement, is seeing a move toward unions.

During most of the eighteenth and nineteenth centuries, supervision was a form of inspection. The earliest schools in America utilized appointed boards of lay persons or citizens to oversee the operation of schools. Records indicate that these lay boards would periodically review school facilities, equipment, and the progress of students attending the schools. This initial citizen assistance, fashioned after lay advisement in the churches, soon became a form of citizen inspection and control. The relationship of the inspectors and the teachers was often stern and punitive. Characterized by telling, directing, and judging, supervisory visits to schools sometimes led to the dismissal of teachers.

The following list of rules for teachers was posted in 1872 by a New York principal:

1. Teachers each day will fill lamps, clean chimneys, and trim wicks.
2. Each teacher will bring a bucket of water and a scuttle of coal for the day's session.
3. Make your pens carefully; you may whittle nibs to the individual tastes of pupils.
4. Men teachers may take one evening each week for courting purposes, or two evenings a week if they go to church regularly.
5. After ten hours in school, the teachers should spend the remaining time reading the Bible or other good books.
6. Women teachers who marry or engage in unseemingly conduct will be dismissed.
7. Every teacher should lay aside from each day a goodly sum of his earnings for his benefit during his declining years so that he will not become a burden on society.
8. Any teacher who smokes, uses liquor in any form, frequents pool or public halls, or gets shaved in a barber shop will give good reason to suspect his worth, intentions, integrity, and honesty.
9. The teacher who performs his labors faithfully and without fault for five years will be given an increase of twenty-five cents per week in his pay providing the Board of Education approves.

With the growth of individual schools and the formation of school districts in the late nineteenth century, the observation and inspection functions of the lay boards were taken over by an appointed supervisor. Serving as an adjunct of the superintendent, and working directly in the schools, this individual freed the board of lay advisors (later the school board) to deal with more global concerns such as the construction of buildings and the raising of school revenues.

By the early years of the twentieth century, lay inspections of schools had given way almost entirely to the supervisory inspection of teachers in the classroom. The redefining of supervision to deal almost exclusively with classroom instructional concerns resulted from the increased responsibilities of the superintendent. As the "span of control" (the manageable scope of responsibility) of the office of the superintendent grew, classroom visitations were no longer a practical matter. Supervisors assumed the tasks of visiting classrooms and assessing teachers as a representative of the superintendent. It was at this time that school supervision first "crossed over" from a role of direct authority (line position) to one of representative authority (staff position), borrowing its role and power from the office of the superintendent. From that time—around 1910 to the end of the 1980s—school supervision remained a primary extension of administration.

In the first third of the twentieth century American education was heavily influenced by models of industrial mechanization and the practices of so-called scientific management. The impact of an industrial orientation in education was pervasive and dominated supervision practices for nearly a quarter of a century. Writing of the period, Callahan observes:

> The procedure for bringing about a more businesslike organization and operation of the schools was fairly well standardized from 1900–1925. It consisted of making unfavorable comparisons between schools and business enterprise, of applying businesslike criteria (e.g., economy and efficiency) to education, and of suggesting that business and industrial practices be adopted by educators.[1]

For educational supervision the impact of the business age was the emergence of bureaucratic supervision. Supervision became tied to goals, objectives, and specifications. An orientation toward efficiency and economy led to divisions of labor, technical specialization, high organizational discipline, specific procedures for work situations, and a reliance on written communication.

Serious applications of empirical research accompanied the emphasis on rules and regulations, stratified authority, and the generation of comprehensive policy documents. Following the lead of industry, educators who served as supervisors conducted time and motion studies and looked for new ways to operate schools more efficiently. It was also during this period that instruction, and hence supervision, became specialized by subject area.

By the early 1930s educational supervision in the United States was becoming ineffective in its enforcement and inspector role. School supervisors, often called "snoopervisors" behind their backs, were able to work with classroom teachers in only the most mechanical ways due to the evaluative dimension of their observations and reports. Again, it was changes in the area of educational administration that altered the role of instructional supervision.

American education during the thirties entered a new era, a period to be labeled "progressive education" by later historians. A combination of rapid growth in school population, increasing diversity among school children, economic prosperity, mobility, and other socioeconomic factors temporarily released American education from its structured heritage. New school programs swept over the land. Schools became more personal, humane, and "child-centered."

For school administrators this new era meant increased responsibilities. Schools became more complex institutions, and even more complex management skills were needed. Early research on group dynamics indicated that a human element existed in organizations that administrators had not previously considered. School administrators, following the lead of business professionals, began to practice a more democratic style of leadership. By the 1940s such "human relations" behavior was common in schools and had become an emerging theme of educational supervision.

School supervision in the 1940s and into the middle of the next decade focused on processes rather than products. Supervisors spent more of their time helping teachers develop as instructors than judging teacher performance. Cooperative group efforts were maximized and democratic interaction practiced. During this period, supervision emerged as a recognized specialty area in education, and definitive texts were written on the subject.

The launching of Sputnik I by the USSR in 1957 altered the form and substance of American education. Overnight, old programs and goals were scrapped, and new educational plans and programs were designed. Curriculum development dominated the educational scene, and such development influenced the role of educational supervisors. In many school districts supervisors became curriculum developers and the lines of demarcation between these two specialized roles blurred.

In the early 1960s supervisors became subject matter field agents, and many large district supervisors today remain in this role. The tasks of the supervisor of the 1960s were a combination of interpreting curriculum projects, organizing materials, involving teachers in the production of school programs, and serving as a resource person to teachers in the classroom. As a sort of collateral duty, many supervisors found themselves entering into training and retraining of classroom teachers by organizing subject-focused inservice opportunities.

By the late 1960s, the goals of many school districts were no longer distinct. Too many program changes had occurred in a short period of time, leading to an overextended and crowded school curriculum. In addition, the first signs of declining achievement coupled with dramatically rising costs in education forced a reassessment of school programs as a matter of necessity. Administrators began to return to the traditional practices of making things orderly in schools. An evolution of events including performance contracts, behavioral objectives, standardization of curricula, testing, and legislated graduation requirements was set into motion and continued into the early 1990s.

The conditions during the late 1960s and the administrative responses in the 1970s and 1980s had an interesting effect on the field of supervision and the role of the school supervisor. As supervision was fighting for a clear identity in a time dominated by curriculum development, there was an effort to focus the role of supervisors in the instructional dimensions of school improvement. The supervision literature of the late 1960s and early 1970s was primarily concerned with the analyses of the teaching-learning process and the new concept of "clinical supervision." Supervisors followed this theoretical lead to become proficient in videotaping, the use of interaction analysis instruments, and the use of "action research" to explore new possibilities for instruction.

By the late 1970s, however, economic and political pressures on schools had become so great that administrators began returning to an industrial orientation reminiscent of the first quarter of the century. Supervisors, slow to assess the changes about them, continued to work with teachers and assume a support role even when unionization of teachers and movements such as "teacher centering" clearly established barriers to a supervisor-teacher relationship. In the process, many supervisors had their jobs abolished in negotiation sessions or saw their training roles usurped by classroom teachers in "centers." Those supervisors who did see the writing on the wall moved quickly to follow the line administrators into managerial roles.

Through the 1980s, supervisors held a strange assortment of jobs with titles such as Assistant Principal for Instruction or Program Manager. The deployment of supervisors at the district, school, and classroom level was too diverse to make a generalization about emerging patterns. Clearly, supervisors were speaking a management language and were on the "administrative team" in most districts. Also clear was the continued focus on improving instruction as the primary role of school supervision.

The 1990s have seen a shift from top-down management of schools through legislative, state, and district mandates to school-site

Table 1.1
The Evolution of Supervisory Roles

1850–1910	Inspection and enforcement
1910–1920	Scientific supervision
1920–1930	Bureaucratic supervision
1930–1955	Cooperative supervision
1955–1965	Supervision as curriculum development
1965–1970	Clinical supervision
1970–1980	Supervision as management
1980–1990	Management of instruction
1990–	Cooperative leadership

management. The idea of school-site management caught the attention of policy makers, researchers, and practitioners in the late 1980s. The 1986 Carnegie Task Force on Teaching as a Profession called on local school district administrators and supervisors to give teachers a greater voice in school decisions. This was followed by the 1987 task force of the National Governors' Association and the National Education Association Report of 1988, which called for school-site management.[2] Table 1.1 outlines the evolution of supervisory roles during the past 140 years.

School-site management was seen by some as just another way of using bureaucratic strategies to manage teachers. "Teacher Empowerment" extended school-site management to participatory school-site management, which allowed teachers equal access to decision making. Rochester, New York and Dade County (Miami), Florida provided early school district leadership in the teacher empowerment movement.

Supervisors have seen administrative authority, from which they borrowed power, being eroded by a shift of power to teachers at school sites. Supervisors have had to build new sets of relationships as they worked in schools. Helping teachers and administrators at school sites to achieve collegial and collective management will involve the best human relations skills of supervisors.

DEFINITIONS OF SUPERVISION

Another way to begin to understand the role and functions of supervision in schools is to review the various definitions as found in its literature. At least six major conceptualizations of supervision can be found in the leading texts on the subject during the past thirty years:

1. Supervision focused on administration
2. Supervision focused on curriculum

3. Supervision focused on instruction
4. Supervision focused on human relations
5. Supervision focused on management
6. Supervision focused on leadership

Some definitions of supervision follow a historic thread and link administration and supervision. Eye, Netzer, and Krey, for instance, define supervision as "that phase of school administration which focuses primarily upon the achievement of the appropriate instruction expectations of the educational system.[3] Harris and Bessent also define supervision as an administrative action:

> Supervision is what school personnel do with adults and things for the purpose of maintaining or changing the operation of the school in order to directly influence the attainment of major instructional goals of the school.[4]

Another frequent definition found in supervision literature sees the supervisor as a curriculum worker. Cogan, as an example, gives the following definition of general supervision work:

> General supervision, therefore, denotes activities like the writing and revisions of curriculums, the preparation of units and materials of instruction, the development of processes and instruments for reporting to parents, and such broad concerns as evaluation of the total educational program.[5]

Writing with the same orientation, Curtin observes:

> Curriculum practices can exist without supervision, although one would scarcely wish to vouch for their vitality. However, it is so blatantly obvious that supervision is utterly dependent on concern for curriculum that one need hardly bring up the matter at all. That is, if the newer concept of supervision is accepted. Of course, supervisors can 'do' things that are not related to curriculum and instruction, just as they have in the past. They can gather statistics and information to no avail; they can observe teachers for no good reason; they can confer with teachers about irrelevancies; and they can conduct staff meetings that are unrelated to the imperatives of teaching. Enough of this exists today to make one uneasy. The only comfort that one can draw is that these activities are not supervisory at all. They are called 'supervisory,' and this tends to give the whole concept of supervision a bad name. Supervision must find meaning in curriculum. If it does not, it has no meaning.[6]

A third definition of supervision focuses squarely on instruction. An early example of this definition of supervision was provided by the Association for Supervision and Curriculum Development (ASCD), the major professional organization for school supervisors:

> Since the titles "supervisor" and "curriculum director" are often used interchangeably as to function, the terms might be used to indicate a person who, either through working with supervisors, principals, or others at the central office level, contributes to the improvement of teaching and/or the implementation or development of curriculum.[7]

The definition of supervision in terms of instruction continues today in the works of Marks, Stoops, and King-Stoops: Supervision is "action and experimentation aimed at improving instruction and the instructional program."[8]

A fourth definition of supervision found in the literature sees the supervisor in terms of human relations, working with all persons in the educational environment. The earliest proponent of this definition was Kimball Wiles:

> They [the supervisors] are the expediters. They help establish communication. They help people hear each other. They serve as liaison to get people into contact with others who have similar problems or with resource people who can help. They stimulate staff members to look at the extent to which ideas and resources are being shared, and the degree to which persons are encouraged and supported as they try new things. They make it easier to carry out the agreements that emerge from evaluation sessions. They listen to individuals discuss their problems and recommend other resources that may help in the search for solutions. They bring to individual teachers, whose confidence they possess, appropriate suggestions and materials. They sense, as far as they are able, the feelings that teachers have about the system and its policies, and they recommend that the administration examine irritations among staff members.[9]

A definition provided by Sergiovanni and Starrett follows this same theme:

> Traditionally, supervision is considered the province of those responsible for instructional improvement. While we hold this view, we add to this instructional emphasis responsibility for all school goals which are achieved through or dependent upon the human organization of the school.[10]

Finally, a draft from the 1982 ASCD Yearbook on supervision continues the human relations theme:

> By 'supervisor' we mean not only those who have the word in the title, but also principals, superintendents, department heads—all those whose responsibilities include helping other staff members improve their performance.[11]

Supervision has also been defined as a form of management. Illustrating this position is a definition by Alfonso, Firth, and Neville:

> Supervision is found in all complex organizations. This is so because organizations are determined to maintain themselves and are sometimes concerned about their improvement or refinement. The connection between supervision and organizations is clear and direct. Organizational resources must be applied to the analysis of efficiency and effectiveness. . . . These descriptions of supervision within organizational production systems have implications of significant consequence to the educator engaged in instructional supervision. The school is a production system.[12]

The sixth definition of educational supervision is as a leadership function. According to Mosher and Purpel:

> We consider the tasks of supervision to be teaching teachers how to teach, and the professional leadership in reformulating public education—more specifically, its curriculum, its teaching, and its forms.[13]

It is our observation that all six definitions of educational supervision are valid and meaningful in the context from which they are drawn. If schools in the 1960s were frantically updating curriculum, then supervision had a strong curriculum orientation. Likewise, supervision in the 1970s and 1980s was primarily managerial. Definitions are obviously influenced by social and economic conditions during the times in which they were formulated.

We see supervision as a *general leadership function that coordinates and manages those school activities concerned with learning.*

Our definition is dynamic rather than static. We can envision a time in the near future when social, economic, and political conditions in the United States would allow schools to redefine their mission and enter another developmental stage. If this should occur, supervision and the role of supervisors would once again be transformed to meet the changing conditions in schools. Whatever the format, however, supervisors will be leaders who are striving to improve learning experiences for students.

DIMENSIONS OF SUPERVISION

The role of the supervisor has many dimensions or facets, and for this reason supervision often overlaps with administrative, curricular, and instructional functions. Because supervision is a general leadership role and a coordinating role among all school activities concerned with learning, such overlap is natural and should be perceived as an asset in a school setting.

Supervision leadership involves thinking, planning, organizing, and evaluating processes. The thinking and planning phases of improving instruction are most like policy formation and administration. Organizing instructional programs is most like those functions of curriculum where a translation of ideas into programs occurs. The evaluation functions of supervision are usually directed toward the instructional activities of the educational institution. Each of these three dimensions – administration, curriculum, and instruction – is treated below in terms of typical supervision tasks to be accomplished.

Administration

Among the many administrative supervision tasks usually encountered are:

1. *Setting and prioritizing goals* – Helping others in the school district focus on ends for schooling and establishing priorities among the many possible programs available to schools.
2. *Establishing standards and developing policies* – Translating goals into standardized levels of expectation, complete with rules and regulations to enforce such performances.
3. *Providing long-range planning* – Designing expectations in terms of actions and activities to be accomplished over time.
4. *Designing organizational structures* – Establishing structural connections between persons and groups within school districts.
5. *Identifying and securing resources* – Locating applicable resources and seeing that they are available to various organizational structures.
6. *Selecting personnel and staffing* – Identifying personnel needed to implement programs and assignment to organizational structures.
7. *Providing adequate facilities* – Matching available facilities with program needs; developing new facilities where needed.
8. *Securing necessary funding* – Raising the monies needed to adequately finance programs.
9. *Organizing for instruction* – Assigning staff and other instructional and support personnel to organizational structures.
10. *Promoting school-community relations* – Establishing and maintaining contact with those who support educational programs.

Curriculum

Curriculum-oriented supervision tasks are:

1. *Determining instructional objectives* – Translating goals into specific objectives for instruction.
2. *Surveying needs and conducting research* – Assessing present conditions to determine how school programs can effectively meet learner needs.
3. *Developing programs and planning changes* – Organizing the instructional content and reviewing existing programs for greater relevance.
4. *Relating programs to various special services* – Tying together the many instructional components both within the school and in the community.
5. *Selecting materials and allocating resources* – Analyzing available instructional materials and assigning them to appropriate programs.
6. *Orienting and renewing instructional staff* – Introducing the school program to new teachers and assisting regular staff in upgrading their capacity.
7. *Suggesting modification in facilities* – Designing a plan to restructure facilities to fit the instructional program and, where appropriate, suggesting the need for new facilities.
8. *Estimating expenditure needs for instruction* – Cost-estimating program development and making recommendations for the application of existing and anticipated funding.
9. *Preparing for instructional programs* – Forming various instructional units and teams; providing inservice opportunities for instructional development.
10. *Developing and disseminating descriptions of school programs* – Writing accurate descriptions of school programs and informing the public of successful activities.

Instruction

Some supervision tasks that are instructional in nature are:

1. *Developing instructional plans* – Working with teachers to outline and implement instructional programs.
2. *Evaluating programs* – Conducting testing and other types of evaluation to determine if instructional programs are meeting standards.
3. *Initiating new programs* – Demonstrating new techniques and otherwise establishing the groundwork for new programs.
4. *Redesigning instructional organization* – Reviewing existing instructional organization for effectiveness and, where appropriate, making alterations.
5. *Delivering instructional resources* – Being sure that teachers

have necessary instructional materials and anticipating future material needs.

6. *Advising and assisting teachers* – Being available to teachers in a consulting, helping role.

7. *Evaluating facilities and overseeing modifications* – Assessing educational facilities for instructional appropriateness and making on-site visits to ensure that modifications are as designed.

8. *Dispersing and applying funds* – Following the flow of monies to ensure their application to intended programs.

9. *Conducting and coordinating inservice programs* – Guiding inservice programs so that they are applied to instructional needs.

10. *Reacting to community needs and inquiries* – Receiving community feedback about school programs and sending information to parents of school children where appropriate.

While all of these tasks are supervisory in nature, they do intersect with administrative, curricular, and instructional domains. The unique role of supervisors is to bridge or coordinate these other areas as they conceptualize, plan, organize, and evaluate instructional programs. Like an engineer overseeing a construction project, the supervisor follows and directs the work flow in instructional improvement efforts (see Table 1.2).

CONCEPTIONS OF SUPERVISION

Due to the situational nature of the job, no two supervisors are likely to do the same thing on a day-to-day basis. This differentiation of roles means that job descriptions for supervisors are likely to be nebulous and, to a great degree, the supervisory role may be self-defined. A 1978 study of instructional supervisors conducted by the Association for Supervision and Curriculum Development (ASCD) sought to clarify the role through a survey of 1,000 school leaders. The study found:

> The data gathered by the survey substantiated the thesis that there was great confusion and little agreement when it comes to defining the distinct roles of supervisors and curriculum directors.[14]

That same study seemed to project a clear role for supervisors if they can free themselves from environmental constraints:

> The instructional supervisor should be more in the role of decision maker with authority than in an advisory one; should be more of a subject matter specialist in the supervised area than a generalist; should be more capable of planning and conducting research than merely an

Table 1.2

Administration Tasks	Curriculum Tasks	Instructional Tasks
1. Set and prioritize goals	Determine instructional objectives	Develop instructional plans
2. Establish standards and policies	Survey needs and conduct research	Evaluate programs according to standards
3. Provide long-range planning	Develop programs and plan changes	Initiate new programs
4. Design organizational structures	Relate programs to special services	Redesign instructional organization where needed
5. Identify and secure resources	Select materials and allocate resources	Deliver instructional resources
6. Select personnel and staff	Orient and renew instructional staff	Advise and assist teachers
7. Provide adequate facilities	Suggest modifications in facilities	Oversee modifications in facilities
8. Secure necessary funding	Estimate expenditure needs for instruction	Disperse and apply funds
9. Organize for instruction	Prepare instructional programs	Coordinate inservice activities
10. Promote school-community relations	Disseminate descriptions of school programs	React to community inquiries about school programs

————————— THE SUPERVISION FLOW OF ACTIVITY —————————→

Note: Supervisory activity overlaps and coordinates administrative, curricular, and instructional concerns and tasks.

interpreter of research; should be more involved in the improvement of instruction than in curriculum development; should work with the teaching staff more in a directive fashion with authority than in a permissive manner; should be less involved in staff evaluation than responsible for such evaluation; and should exercise more budgetary or fiscal management control responsibility than no control over the budget.[15]

This same ASCD study, noteworthy because so many practicing supervisors contributed to the findings, did identify a number of tasks felt to be "more supervisory than curricular" in nature. Among those tasks identified as strong for supervision were:

1. Developing standards of effectiveness
2. Evaluating instructional performance

3. Observing teaching in the classroom
4. Conducting staff development activities
5. Conducting inservice programs

There was also an attempt to define the knowledge base that should be possessed by practicing supervisors as well as some guidelines for their selection. Among the most important college courses in a preparatory program for supervisors, in rank order, were the following:

1. Supervision of Instruction
2. Group Processes and Human Relations
3. Curriculum Theory and Development
4. Educational Measurement and Evaluation
5. Educational Psychology
6. Organization and Administration of Schools
7. Educational Research
8. Philosophy of Education
9. Media and Technology
10. Sociology of Education
11. History of Education
12. Anthropology of Education

Selection criteria for supervisors, based on their training and experience, were recommended by the study participants:

I. Experience
   A. Minimum of two years of classroom teaching experience
   B. Minimum of one year of leadership experience (such as department chairperson, principal, internship, laboratory school researcher)
II. Preparation
   A. Certification as a teacher (assumes competence in the science of teaching and conditions of learning)
   B. Completion or equivalent of an educational specialist degree leading to certification as an instructional leader with courses and experience in:
      1. Supervision, including:
         a. Knowledge regarding the principles and nature of supervision, trends, and issues in supervision and models of staff development
         b. Ability to apply communication and group development skills
         c. Ability to evaluate staff personnel and to design improvement programs

2. Curriculum, including:
   a. Knowledge regarding curriculum programs and processes of curriculum development
   b. Ability to evaluate curricular programs and plan appropriate strategies for their improvement
   c. Understanding of curriculum theory and design of various curricular models
3. Instruction, including:
   a. Knowledge regarding principles and concepts, trends, issues, and models of instructional strategies
   b. Ability to design, develop, implement, and evaluate various instructional systems
   c. Understanding of instructional theory, utilization of media, and analysis of instructional factors
4. Educational psychology, including:
   a. Ability to conduct appropriate research for determining teaching and learning problems
   b. Understanding of adult learning and the teaching/learning process
5. Leadership, including:
   a. Processes and purposes of organizations
   b. Skills to organize and coordinate perceived resources for facilitating operations of and changes in curriculum and instruction
   c. Understanding of the function of supervision as provided by other educational leaders such as college professors, principals, and district curriculum leaders

Regardless of the relative emphasis given to administrative, curricular, or instructional roles, it is clear that the modern supervisor must perform many acts to fulfill the role function. An important distinction is provided by Harris concerning the "patterns" of supervisory behaviors. Harris distinguishes between a "tractive supervisor" and a "dynamic supervisor" claiming that each would combine his or her skills and roles for different ends:

> Tractive Supervision gears activities to continuity, to maintaining the existing level of instruction, to promoting minor changes in the program, to supporting or enforcing existing relationships, and to resisting pressures for change from various sources.[16]

Examples of tractive or static supervisory activities are:

Enforcing statutory requirements
Evaluating semester course outlines

Holding enrollments to correct ratios

Approving daily class schedules

Final editing of curriculum guides

Enforcing legal requirements in schools

Regulating visitors to the district

In contrast, Dynamic Supervision promotes activities that are designed to change the program . . . with emphasis on discontinuity, the disruption of existing practice, and the substitution of others.[17]

Examples of dynamic supervisory activities are:

Planning programs for staff development

Working with teachers to apply research

Initiating pilot curriculum programs

Revising the philosophy of a school district

Evaluating various media

Demonstrating new instructional techniques

Obviously, supervisors must choose not only a pattern of activities from among administrative, curricular, and instructional domains, but also the orientation of their pattern of behavior. These choices result from a personal conception of the role of the practicing school supervisor. More than tasks encountered, the selection of an appropriate balance between reinforcing activities and change-oriented activities will define the role of the supervisor.

EIGHT SPECIAL AREAS OF SUPERVISION COMPETENCE

The authors, in consulting with educational supervisors in some forty states, have had ample opportunity to observe supervision in action. From such experience has come a belief that the best supervisors, regardless of their title, orientation, or job requirements, possess special areas of competence. Eight skill areas are identified that allow supervisors to range from thinking about desired programs to evaluating operational instruction. Introduced on the following pages, these same skill areas are the subject of entire chapters in Part Two of this book.

1. Supervisors Are Developers of People. The best educational supervisors never forget that schools are learning environments designed to help children grow up. The global task for all educators is to study the subjects of planning and children and to design the best possible learning experiences for those clients. Such a sensitivity to the growth of children requires a thorough knowledge of the development process as well as the special character of various groups of children in school.

All children in the United States spend better than a decade in schools enroute to becoming an adult citizen. Those children come to school with varying degrees of readiness to learn, and they leave the school with varying degrees of competence. The patterns of development among children are predictable and have been outlined in any number of models, hierarchies, and taxonomies. All students must master certain "developmental tasks" to grow up successfully.

There are differences as well as similarities among children in school and these, too, must be accommodated by school leaders. Children differ in the backgrounds and social experiences they have had prior to school. They differ in their natural capacities to learn in school. They differ in their values, as those values often reflect the values of their parents. Some children are stronger than others and more able to tolerate failure or success.

There are some children in schools who are so "different" that they wear the label "special." This specialness comes from their being unable to adjust to a norm-based instructional program. For these students—the handicapped, the gifted, the disturbed—unique programming is required.

The danger for any educator, but particularly for someone with as much influence as a supervisor, is to become "prison dumb," or unable to remember what schools are all about. A special type of competence for supervisors, then, is never to forget why we operate schools and for whom the curriculum and the instructional program is planned.

2. Supervisors Are Curriculum Developers. It has been observed time and again that the "real" curriculum is what is experienced by students at the classroom level. While various district documents, textbooks, and guides tell us what should be taught, the actions of the teacher delivering the curriculum actually define the study program. Because they work directly with teachers on instructional problems, supervisors have the best opportunity to influence the development of curriculum.

Curriculum development can be conceptualized as a cycle that begins with the analysis of purpose for schooling. Clarifying philosophy and goals, pinpointing priorities, and extracting program concepts form this stage of development. The cycle continues with the design of the curriculum including developing standards and objectives and considering the approach to improvement. A third step in the curriculum development cycle is to implement or manage the proposed changes. Here, the direction of staff development and material up-grading is critical. Finally, the cycle concludes with evaluation of the effort and the identification of further needs.

Supervisors, working with both administrators and teachers, also have a birds-eye view of the curriculum development process. Because they work in classrooms with teachers to deliver the "real" curriculum, they are the primary quality control agents in most districts. The ability of supervisors to meld practices with general policy formation makes them the purveyors of critical information about curriculum improvement.

3. Supervisors Are Instructional Specialists. Most supervisors are se-lected for their position because they are excellent teachers. The his-tory of teaching in the United States suggests that good teachers be-come leaders, and rightly so. The primary task for anyone in a supervisory role is to improve learning opportunities for students.

Specifically, the instructional role of supervision has at least three dimensions: research, communication, and teaching. In the re-search role, the supervisor must know the meaning of the many stud-ies conducted in the area of teaching during the past thirty-five years. Recent studies of teacher and school effectiveness, learning styles, and the physiology of learners suggest many changes in the classroom. In this role, the supervisor is an analyst of instruction and a resource to relevant knowledge about the area of instruction.

Supervisors, as instructional specialists, are also communicators. As the supervisor moves among the rooms in a school building, he or she gains a unique perspective of the "whole" in the instructional program. Assisting with articulation (coordination) among grade levels or between levels of schooling, putting subject area teachers in touch with one another across subject lines, or enriching the offerings of a single subject at a single grade level are among the supervisor's natural communications. Equally important is the ability of the supervisor to convey what is observed to those who plan school operations or to link teachers with larger resources available outside of the school site.

Finally, as instructional specialists, supervisors are teachers, most of whom were excellent in the classroom. Their expertise proves invaluable in helping novice teachers or in actually demonstrating new techniques to experienced teachers. Despite the sophistication of many school systems today, most real learning by classroom teachers still takes place by demonstration.

Helping classroom teachers by being knowledgeable, by sharing with and among teachers a host of new ideas, and by actually going into classrooms to demonstrate or model teaching are roles of the supervisor as the instructional specialist.

4. Supervisors Are Human Relations Workers. Most supervision work is informal and person-to-person, whether supervisors are working with individual teachers or in group settings. Supervisors are also communicating with the teaching staff and the administrative staff. For these reasons and others, supervisors must be specialists in basic human relations.

The human relations skills called for in daily supervision are multiple. Supervisors must be sensitive to the needs of various client groups with whom they interact. They must employ diplomacy in their language usage, assuming that what they say will be heard and conveyed to others. Supervisors must be particularly good listeners, hearing not only what is said but also what is not said.

Supervision also includes a special capacity to motivate others. Often, the task of translating a policy or decision into behavior will fall to the supervisor because he or she is "on the line." Understanding what motivates people in a profession like teaching is very important, and connecting such motivation to the tasks of the school as an organization requires skill.

Supervisors, too, must possess a special series of conferencing abilities as they work in small groups to improve education. Like the building administrator, the typical supervisor's day is usually a series of meetings in small groups to attack problems and provide solutions. Knowing how to manage such meetings effectively and how to actually accomplish tasks are primary human relations skills.

Finally, supervisors are regularly public relations specialists in schools. While their work is not always dealing directly with media personnel or speaking for the school district to large groups, the trouble-shooting nature of the job requires constant interface with important audiences who demand competence. Supervisors are always engaged in public relations activities as they go through the workday.

5. Supervisors Are Staff Developers. If the primary task for instructional supervisors is to improve learning opportunities for students, and if supervisors work most often in the classroom with teachers, then a major role is that of staff development or inservice specialist. Planning staff development activities is the major method of improving instruction for the supervisor.

Because schools are human organizations, improving performance by teachers is more difficult than simply providing skill-development training. There is always an affective, or feeling, dimension to the area of staff development, and each supervisor must have ready a model of training in his or her head as inservice experiences for teachers are planned. Much staff development, for instance, deals with the teacher as a person as a prerequisite to improving the teacher as an instructor.

Supervisors need the skill of being able to "see" teachers in planning staff development. There must be some way to profile the development of individual teachers so that growth can be continuous and directional. Some method must be used to make staff development respectable, overcoming a historic model of inservice to correct deficiencies in teachers.

Finally, supervisors must scout for talent when it comes to identifying and scheduling inservice assistance. Because much staff development in the past was irrelevant to the direct needs of classroom teachers, supervisors often find a basic skepticism among teachers about such assistance. Quality help must be found and the delivery of that help must be linked to the improvement of classroom instruction. Making inservice work is a skill of the instructional supervisor.

6. Supervisors Are Administrators. One of the most difficult tasks for the teacher-turned-supervisor is to accept an administration role in education. While historically supervisors have been supervising teachers, this role has changed during the past fifteen years. Heavy union activity and the resulting collective bargaining have pushed the field of supervision into a management posture. The supervisor who does not perceive his or her job as a subset of administration in the 1990s is apt to find tenure in the role short-lived.

As an administrator, the supervisor can expect to spend a major portion of the workday interacting with other administrators. This is not due to the location of problems as much as the location of solutions to instructional problems. The interrelatedness of a school "system" makes any decision a team decision. While not yet a full-fledged member of the administrative team, the supervisor has become more administrative during the past five years.

As administrators, supervisors need basic administrative skills. They need to be able to manage assistants and secretaries. They should be able to manage information and establish effective recordkeeping in the instructional areas. They should become skilled at the use of administrative influence. To work effectively with other administrators, they must be able to think like an administrator.

There are many serious work issues that will define the meaning of the term *professional in supervision.* Women in supervision must be able to resolve a traditional male/female role dichotomy in working as an administrator. The supervisor-as-teacher may have difficulty in posing as an administrator. The degree of manipulation and politics may shock many new supervisors as they learn of the school-community relationship and power structures. In short, the supervisor as an administrator is an attitude as well as a set of skills.

7. Supervisors Are Managers of Change. Twenty years ago, many supervisors conducted much of their business on an interpersonal basis, improving instruction by working directly with people. The size of today's school districts plus the pressures of accountability have diminished that interpersonal role. Today's supervisor is often perceived as a manager of meaningful change and is certainly held accountable for his or her actions.

Throughout the United States, state legislatures acted during the 1980s to legislate quality control in education. Testing programs, graduation requirements, and instructional competencies are only a few of the signs of the times. Most of this legislation enforces account-ability that holds educational programs up to public scrutiny in the area of performance. Because of this, educational supervisors are under some degree of pressure to get results. Instructional engineering has resulted in some school districts.

Even without the pressures of state law, a general systems men-tality has taken hold in the area of instruction. Text series, work-sheets, media, and computer programs are tied directly to performance, making the cycle of curriculum development also a cycle of account-ability. Monitoring these results and making adjustments in the sys-tem is now a regular part of supervision. The management of budgets through the use of categorical funding (for certain uses only) has fur-thered this mechanical approach to instructional improvement.

Overall, this management function of supervision means that the instructional supervisor must be sharp with numbers, organized, and able to see all the pieces as an interacting whole.

8. Supervisors Are Evaluators. The previously stated roles, collec-tively, place the supervisor in a constant evaluation position. Assess-ing teacher performance, program outcomes, texts and materials, con-sultant performance, and analysis of testing results — all are part of the evaluation role.

Supervisors are regularly expected to initiate general needs as-sessments and to conduct community surveys and follow-up studies of graduates. The organization of this information and the translation of this data into curriculum management plans or school improvement plans are expected roles for an instructional supervisor.

Finally, supervisors are expected to keep up with overall research in education and to translate these findings for other administrators and teachers. In some smaller districts, supervision is linked to eval-uation directly in writing grants and in designing studies of student achievement.

These eight skill areas, then, form the foundation for supervisory competence in today's modern educational systems. Each of these skill areas will be treated in depth in Part Two of this book so that the reader can understand how these general competencies are applied on the job. Before addressing those areas, however, we need to gain a global perspective of the general leadership function in school super-vision and how that leadership role operates at each level of schooling.

NEW DIRECTIONS

Supervision in the last decade of the 20th century has entered an era of participatory school-site management where the bureaucratic mode of management no longer works. Supervisors formerly could borrow authority from administrators at the district or school level. Now supervisors must borrow authority also from their client group, teachers at school sites. The role of teacher unions is evident in the birth of teacher empowerment, but what role unions will play in school-site management is still not clearly defined.

Other issues must be addressed, including: With which decisions will professional teachers become involved? Who will make what decisions in school-site management? What are the basic tasks of teachers and administrators in the context of decentralized decision making?

Helping establish specific relationships between teachers and administrators by redesigning managerial structures and processes will require new skills for supervisors.

Restructuring of schools is a term of the 1990s that is drawing increasing attention in the literature. The 1990 annual conference theme of the Association for Supervision and Curriculum Development (ASCD) focused on this issue. The semantics of restructuring schools signals an end to the code word of the 1980s — reform. Restructure replaced reform and while few ventured to define what that meant, there was a growing consensus that the managerial style of top-down leadership in schools had to change.

Accountability is another term which is suffering from overuse. The paperwork and test scores prevalent in the accountability movement of the 1980s has been replaced by a "get tough" accountability that tells school bureaucracies to shape up in the interest of children or get out of business. Calls for voucher plans and implementation of school site school boards are evidences of dissatisfaction with school bureaucracies.

Parent advocacy groups have demanded more parent involvement in schools. Rather than being relegated to advisory — and essentially powerless — positions, parents, as organized school-based groups, are demanding involvement as full partners in decisions about curriculum and organization. After two decades of the Federal Chapter 1 program, a program to help disadvantaged children, Congress switched parent emphasis there from parent advisors to parent educators. Parents are treated as equal partners in the instructional effort.

School business partnerships have arisen out of the realization that business should not merely criticize the products of schools but should become active partners in determining what these products should be. The shortage of young workers, along with a growing technology that requires highly skilled workers, is helping to accelerate the partnerships between schools and business.

The growing number of minorities in this country has brought on a realization that our schools are the melting pot of a culturally pluralistic nation. The 1990 census revealed startling increases in the number of Hispanic and Asian students in our schools. African-Americans are facing the reality that after they have experienced two decades of gaining power as a minority group, other minority groups may assume as much or more power in the 1990s.

Changes in Europe and Asia in the early 1990s also signaled new challenges for Americans and America's schools. A growing interdependence among nations will require new understandings on the part of our youth. Only our schools can provide that understanding.

The scourges of drugs, AIDS and family breakup have shaped a new curriculum for our youth. Basics now include sex education, health and nutrition, and family life education. The growing number of service jobs requiring "people skills" is forcing a new look at areas such as self-concept, school retention, and testing programs that measure little more than low-level cognitive information. Moral education is receiving new attention as a recycled concept that may now be ready for the times.

After two decades of top-down regulations and legislative mandates, a bottom-up teacher empowerment movement has become the focus of the 1990s. The early part of the decade of the 1990s has seen middle managers such as supervisors and district and school administrators caught in the squeeze between leftover mandates of the 1970s and 1980s and the growing power of teachers and parents in the decision-making process. A basic question might be: Will the empowerment of teachers make supervision and school administration obsolete?[18]

A final area of change has been the move toward cooperative learning in many classrooms. In a culturally pluralistic society, cooperative learning methods offer alternatives to ability grouping, special programs for the gifted, Chapter I pull-outs, and even special education. Rather than isolating children, cooperative learning builds collaborative skills necessary for living in an increasingly interdependent society. Cooperative learning also serves to improve relationships among students of different racial or ethnic backgrounds.[19]

Three major approaches to cooperative learning appear frequently in the literature. The first is the "Learning Together" model developed by Roger and David Johnson, professors at the University of Minnesota.[20] The model emphasizes the six essential elements of cooperative learning: heterogeneous grouping, positive interdependence, individual accountability, monitoring, interpersonal skills, and processing/

feedback. Cooperative learning can be applied to any subject area at any grade level. Social skill development is also stressed in group work.

The second model is a "structural approach" developed by Spencer Kagan, a psychologist at the University of California, Riverside. This approach emphasizes the use of structures which can be integrated into any existing curriculum in all content areas. Structures used in the lessons include group discussion, interview, brainstorming, round robin, and roundtable. All structures have a "domain of usefulness" (the most effective place in the lesson in which to use the structure).[21]

The third model is the "package approach" created by Robert Slavin, a leading researcher from Johns Hopkins University. Cooperative learning is applied to a specific content area. Task and reward structures are provided. Improvement scoring, team recognition, and group competition are stressed. Slavin has also discovered, through extensive research, that positive interdependence and individual accountability are the keys to boosting student achievement. This means that groups must help each other learn the material, not just do the assignment. Learning, instead of just doing, is stressed throughout all of the lessons.[22]

SUMMARY

Supervision is a complex role in professional education. With an all-important mission of improving the learning experiences for students, that role remains constant despite changes in schools. Over time, supervision has been altered by certain social, political, and economic conditions, and with those changes have come changes in the definition of instructional supervision. Six separate definitions from the professional literature of supervision have been identified for the reader.

In the 1980s, supervision seemed to be focused on the management of instruction. Meeting state mandates and legislation for minimal quality control measures, promoting achievement in testing, and otherwise working with materials and teachers to improve "systems" of education defined the current role. After two decades of top-down management of schools, the 1990s were ushered in by a bottom-up teacher empowerment movement. Middle managers, including supervisors, are now challenged to build a collegial relationship with teachers and school administrators.

The next section views supervision and its mission through the lens of leadership. This general orientation, it is felt, provides a way of understanding how the competencies of supervision are applied in a professional setting.

NOTES

1. Raymond E. Callahan, *Education and the Cult of Efficiency* (Chicago: University of Chicago Press, 1962), p. 6.

2. Sharon Conley and Samuel Bacharach, From School-Site Management to Participatory School-Site Management, *Kappan* 78(7) (March, 1990), pp. 539–541.

3. Glen G. Eye, Lanore A. Netzer, and Robert D. Krey, *Supervision of Instruction* (New York: Harper & Row, 1971), p. 31.

4. Ben Harris and Wailand Bessent, *In-service Education: A Guide to Better Practice* (Englewood Cliffs, NJ: Prentice-Hall, 1969), p. 11.

5. Morris Cogan, *Clinical Supervision* (Boston: Houghton-Mifflin, 1973), p. 9.

6. James Curtin, *Supervision in Today's Elementary Schools* (New York: Macmillan, 1964), p. 162.

7. Association for Supervision and Curriculum Development, *Role of the Supervisor and Curriculum Director in a Climate of Change*, 1965 Yearbook (Washington, DC: Association for Supervision and Curriculum Development, 1965), pp. 2–3.

8. James R. Marks, Emery Stoops, and Joyce King-Stoops, *Handbook of Educational Supervision: A Guide for the Practitioner*, 2nd ed. (Boston: Allyn & Bacon, 1978), p. 15.

9. Kimball Wiles, *Supervision for Better Schools*, 3rd ed. (Englewood Cliffs, NJ: Prentice-Hall, 1967), p. 10.

10. Thomas Sergiovanni and Robert Starrett, *Emerging Patterns of Supervision: Human Perspectives* (New York: McGraw-Hill, 1971), p. 3.

11. Draft statement, ASCD 1982 Yearbook Committee, *Supervision* (working title).

12. Robert Alfonso, Gerald Firth, and Richard Neville, *Instructional Supervision: A Behavior System* (Boston: Allyn & Bacon, 1975), p. 3.

13. Ralph Mosher and David Purpel, *Supervision: The Reluctant Profession* (Boston: Houghton-Mifflin, 1972), p. 4.

14. Allan Sturges, ed. *Certifying the Curriculum Leader and Instructional Supervisor*, (Washington, DC: Association for Supervision and Curriculum Development, 1978), p. 28.

15. Ibid., p. 29.

16. Ben Harris, *Supervisory Behavior in Education* (Englewood Cliffs, NJ: Prentice-Hall, 1963), pp. 18–19.

17. Ibid.

18. Vicki Knight, "Supervision in the Age of Empowerment," *Educational Leadership*, Association for Supervision and Curriculum Development (May 1989), pp. 27–28.

19. David T. Johnson and Roger T. Johnson, *Cooperative, Competitive and Individualistic Learning* (Englewood Cliffs, NJ: Prentice-Hall, 1987), pp. 20–21.

20. Ibid.

21. Spencer Kagan, *Cooperative Learning Resources For Teachers* (Riverside, CA: University of California Press, 1987), pp. 60–61.

22. Robert E. Slavin, "Cooperative Learning and Student Achievement," *Educational Leadership*, 46(3) (October, 1987), pp. 31–34.

SUGGESTED LEARNING ACTIVITIES

1. Identify major forces that have changed the definition and role of supervision in the past fifty years.
2. Describe why the role of the supervisor in education is not more clearly defined.
3. Develop a list of those things that make supervision a unique area of specialization in education.
4. Develop a conceptual model showing the relationship of the supervisor to those persons serving in administration, curriculum, and support roles.
5. Study a school district familiar to you to assess how supervisors are deployed within the administrative hierarchy.

BOOKS TO REVIEW

Association For Supervision and Curriculum Development. *Changing School Through Staff Development*. Alexandria, VA: 1990.

Callahan, Raymond. *Education and the Cult Of Efficiency*. Chicago: University of Chicago Press, 1962.

Glickman, Carl. *Supervision of Instruction: A Developmental Approach*. Boston: Allyn and Bacon, Inc., 1990.

Glasser, William. *Control and Theory in the Classroom*. New York: Harper and Row, 1986.

Joyce, Bruce and Weil, Marsha. *Models of Teaching*. Englewood Cliffs, NJ: Prentice-Hall, Inc., 1986.

Sergiovanni, Thomas and Starratt, Robert. *Supervision: Human Perspective*, 4th Ed. New York: McGraw-Hill, 1988.

Tanner, Daniel and Tanner, Laura. *Supervision in Education: Problems and Practices*. New York: Macmillan Publishing Company, 1989.

Wiles, Kimball and Lovell, John. *Supervision For Better Schools*, 5th Ed. Englewood Cliffs, NJ: Prentice-Hall, Inc., 1983.

CHAPTER **2**

Leadership in Supervision

INTRODUCTION

Leadership in supervision is not simply a series of competencies enacted by a person in a role. Rather, leadership is an approach, a way of working with people within an organization to accomplish a task. Persons in supervisory leadership roles must understand the conditions of an organization, and interlock the behaviors of others with that organization's structure. To lead, the supervisor must have a theory of leadership.

Administrative leadership theory, in its literature, has traditionally followed one of four major threads. The oldest viewpoint is one concerning the structure or bureaucracy of an organization. From this vantage point, the control and organization of schools can be seen as a major means of improving instruction. Supervisors can "organize" instructional improvement by structuring the way schools work and the relationships among people.

A second major approach to understanding leadership is the study of process or the way organizations work. How are decisions made? What is the communication pattern? What is the relationship between line officers (superintendent, principals) and staff personnel (supervisors)? These processes can be altered to improve the way a school works and, therefore, to improve instructional efficiency.

A third thread found in the literature of administration and supervision is a study of relationships—informal as well as formal. Here the supervisor may be concerned with one-on-one human relations, group work within organizations, or even climate control in the school environment. Such human interaction is a constant theme of supervision books because schools are so directly perceived as "human organizations."

Finally, a more recent theory is one dealing with the use of influence in organizations. Who, in schools, is really powerful and influ-

29

ential? How are decisions really made? This political area of organizational theory is dealt with in a later chapter.

Collectively or individually these approaches form the beginnings of a way of seeing how schools or school districts work. It is the job of the supervisor to understand these things and to work *within* that organization to improve instruction. The deliberate mismatch of a supervisor's style with the organization and purpose of an educational institution has led to a majority of failures in supervision.

Once the supervisor knows the environment and understands how it works, he or she must then compare that purpose with his or her own conception of what schools should be doing. Using the overlap between these two realities, the supervisor should set a course to improve instructional experiences for learners. Viewing the process in the long run, as opposed to day-to-day, will help eliminate minor frustrations and improve job efficiency. The evolution of a clear theory, one that works, may take a considerable time.

ORIGINS OF ADMINISTRATIVE THEORY

The evolution of leadership theory began thousands of years ago. The Egyptians, for example, demonstrated complex organizational skills in constructing pyramids in 5000 B.C. The Babylonians created the highly sophisticated Code of Hammurabi sometime between 2000–1700 B.C. Thousands of years ago, the Chinese had complex training programs for training leaders and scholars. The bases of leadership theory are ancient.

In the United States, the Industrial Revolution spurred the study of leadership behavior. By the early nineteenth century the mechanization of industry led to classic problems of organization and role delineation among workers. By the first years of the twentieth century, ideas about leadership and administration were being catalogued, and the first operational theories developed. We review these theories in order to provide the reader with four perspectives available to supervisors who work in schools.

Organizational Structures

The concern of leaders with organizational structure evolved from the managerial complexities found in the mechanization of industry. Relationships among men and between men and machines were in transition because of increased industrial productivity and the need for greater efficiency of operation. Practice evolved to the theory stage at the close of the nineteenth century, and found outlet in the writings of men such as Frederick Taylor, Max Weber, and Henri Fayol. These writers and others approached administration and management as a scientist might, using the scientific tools of research, measurement, and analysis.

Based on his extensive field experimentation, Frederick Taylor launched the serious study of organizational structure with his book *Principles of Scientific Management* (1911), in which he advocated meticulous observation and study of the work process and reordering of organizations along functional lines.[1] Modern concepts such as specialization and standardization of work, use of mathematical models for production, the piece-rate system, and time standards for production were major contributions to the budding science of management. Other writers, such as Frank and Lillian Gilbreth[2] and Henry Gantt[3], filled in specific techniques of the scientific method by perfecting systems and record-keeping procedures for monitoring organizational productivity. Most of the work of this period focused squarely on the operation of the organization and ignored the human factors related to productivity.

Paralleling the scientific management movement around the turn of the century was an attempt by some practicing industrial managers to uncover general principles of organizations: to develop theory based on the structure of organizations. The best-known writer of this "universals" school of thought was Henri Fayol, a French engineer, whose book *General and Industrial Management* was translated into English in 1929.[4] Fayol contended that management was general to all human endeavors, and developed a set of principles applicable to all management activities. His fourteen principles included the concepts of division of labor, unity of command, subordination, remuneration, and esprit de corps.

Major concepts of the traditional monocratic, bureaucratic organization were

1. *Administrative efficiency* — the ultimate purpose of an organization is to establish conditions that will help it achieve its goals
2. *Unity of purpose* — the effectiveness of any organization is enhanced when it has clearly defined goals and purpose.
3. *Standardization* — an organization is more effective when there exists a regular routine for all administrative operations.
4. *Stability* — the effectiveness of an organization is enhanced when policies and procedures are maintained until results are evaluated.
5. *Single executive* — central coordination of activities provides for greater effectiveness in achieving the purposes of the organization.
6. *Unity of command* — the organization defines the role of each individual, and everyone knows to whom and for what they are responsible.
7. *Division of labor* — labor and task division or specialization enhance productivity.

8. *Delegation of authority/responsibility*—delegation of both responsibility and the authority to carry out tasks improves the effectiveness of the organization.
9. *Span of control*—effectiveness is enhanced when each administrator is assigned only the number of persons that can be directly supervised.
10. *Security*—the organization is more effective when it provides for the security of its members.[5]

Early theorists thus recommended a pyramidal, hierarchical organizational structure that constrained power for decision making from superordinates downward to subordinates. The principles and practices that characterize this traditional structural pattern are known as "formal organization." The most thorough analysis of these elements of structural theory was developed by the German sociologist Max Weber, who fully defined the concept of a bureaucracy and adapted an administrative system to the needs of large and complex organizations.

In *The Theory of Social and Economic Organizations*,[6] Weber outlined the ideal bureaucratic structure in terms of components such as (1) fixed jurisdictional areas enforced by rules and regulations; (2) hierarchies of graded authority, assuring clear relationships between superordinates and subordinates; (3) authority derived from written documents and vested in offices, not men; (4) administration by fully trained and competent officials; and (5) the use of comprehensive planned policies to guide change. According to Weber, wide application of such characteristics produced the highest degree of efficiency and predictability in large, complex organizations.

The scientific management advocated by Taylor, the universal principles of Fayol, and the bureaucracy designed by Weber culminated in an administrative arrangement dominated by its concern for structure. The least complex formal organization was the line organization, so named because of the direct lines of authority between administrative officers. Line organizations have no staff, advisory, or auxiliary officers. A second type of formal organization has line relationships as well as staff members who are not links in the chain of authority. A third, and more complex, type of formal organization might have both line and staff personnel, plus technical (functional) specialists, who service several layers of the administrative hierarchy. Where there are many layers of hierarchy in an organization, it is known as "tall," while an organization with few layers and wide spans of control is known as a "flat" organization. Figure 2.1 shows the various organizational styles.

During the early years of this century, most school districts in the United States were organized in a highly structured manner, according to the best available administrative theory. Today, most

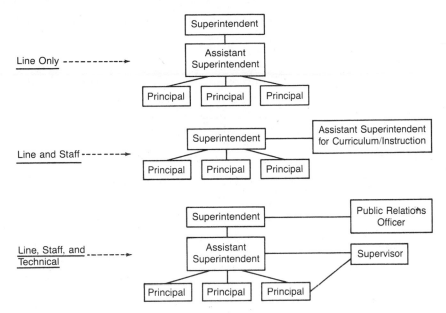

Figure 2.1
Formal Organizations

school districts employ a modified bureaucracy, which they find more flexible and responsive to a changing educational environment. Even in the large city systems, where bureaucracies are still entrenched, we see the emergence of technical specialists (such as computer programmers) who break down the monocratic structure with the influence of their expertise rather than political influence. Perhaps the greatest conflict for an individual administrator in a bureaucratic educational structure is that between loyalty to administration and professional loyalty to issues and products.

Organizational Processes

A second focus in the study of organizations is the processes by which they function. Most contributions to this approach have come from the social and behavioral sciences. Collectively, the input from these fields make up organizational theory and its derivative, general systems theory.

A theory of leadership concerned with functional operation of an organization as an integrated whole evolved because of the inability of monocratic structures to change. In the 1920s, organizations underwent drastic changes because of the increasing scope and complexity of operations and advances in technology. The piecemeal evolution of major organizations in the face of such comprehensive change resulted in dysfunctions and imbalance. During this period of change, organizations needed the capability of responding to their environment through self-regulation, self-adaptation, and self-renewal.

Organizations are social units purposefully constructed, and sometimes reconstructed, to meet goals. Those goals provide an identity to the organization, and communicate the organization's mission to the environment. In times of substantial change, organizations that do not maintain goal-clarity, or fail to see themselves as a functioning whole, soon become obsolescent.

In this respect, the study of organizational processes emerged from need, because bureaucratic organization proved unable to monitor and accommodate major changes in the environment. In educational organizations, the highly structured bureaucracy had trouble dealing with a number of forces, including a changing mission with expanding boundaries, control of school resources by varying levels of government, and growing public access to educational decision making. Educational organizations responded by creating specialists and staff officers to perform the many peripheral roles associated with running the schools. Supervisors are one such role.

Organizational processes encompass a cycle for dealing with change, the steps of which include: analyzing, planning, implementing, and evaluating. Social science investigations have uncovered a staggering variety of specialized inquiry areas in analyzing the processes of organization. As Table 2.1 shows, each area of specialization includes many tasks.

Theorists of educational administration often selected various processes to explain the complexity of school operations. Griffith, for example, sees the specific function of administration as the development and regulation of a decision-making process.[7] According to Griffith, decision making follows identifiable steps:

1. Recognize, define, and limit the problem.
2. Analyze and evaluate the problem.
3. Establish standards by which the solution will be evaluated.
4. Collect data.
5. Formulate and select preferred solutions.
6. Put into effect the preferred solution.

Other theorists throughout the 1960s and 1970s have selected variables such as management techniques, fiscal analysis, and performance evaluation as handles for describing the processes of school administration.

By the early 1960s, the myriad variables represented by the various organizational processes found focus in general systems theory. Systems theory, a product of the physical sciences, provided the concept of interdependence in organizations and explained why changes

Table 2.1
Specialized Areas of Organizational Process

Area	Tasks
Planning	Forecasting
	Planning cycles
	Work flow analysis
	Fiscal projections
	Management techniques (management-by-objectives)
Decision making	Operations research
	Management information systems
	Cost benefit analysis
Project management	Task analysis
	Communications systems
	Long-range planning (program evaluation and review technique/critical path method)
Personnel administration	Job analysis
	Manpower recruitment
	Testing/classification
Accountability and control	Fiscal projection
	Internal auditing
	Long-range budgeting (program planning budgeting system)

in one part of an organization affected other parts or the whole of the organization. A system is simply a group of objects treated as a unit. With the adoption of systems theory in educational administration, all the important processes of operating a school or school district could be seen holistically.

In modern organizational theory, the systems concept describes administration as the central force in organizations—a force that co-ordinates and relates activities. Such a role calls for insight by the administrator and skill in conceptualizing relationships. Robert Katz refers to conceptual skill as:

> The ability to see the organization as a whole; it includes recognizing how . . . the various functions of the organization depend on one another, and how change in any one part affects all the others. Recognizing these relationships and perceiving the significant elements in any situation, the administrator should then be able to act in a way which advances the overall welfare of the organization.[8]

In school settings, a system might be defined as any set of com-ponents organized in such a way as to result in accomplishment of a goal. Thus, school programs are systems comprised of facilities, materials, funds, teachers, testing, and a host of other contributing variables for the purpose of educating children. The real value of a systems perspective for supervisors is as a means of identifying non-contributing conditions or bottlenecks in the flow of activity. Once identified, the system deficiencies can be targeted for redesign. Systems can also help the educator build models of preferred conditions for learning.[9]

Perhaps the high point in the study of organizational processes is the concept of Organization Development (O.D.), a planned and sustained effort to apply behavioral science for system improvement.[10] Organization Development consists of data gathering, organizational diagnosis, and action intervention. The fulfillment of the O.D. program is, in a real sense, changing the way a school works. The three elements of organizational process that appear important for meeting change are the roles people play, the goals of the organization, and the operational procedures already in place. In effect, Organization Development is a people-involving approach to systematic analysis. Through analysis, it is hoped, the members of the organization will become committed to the efficacy of the systems function.

The other key to the success of Organization Development methodology in improving institutional process is the commitment to deal with change over an extended period of time, and to use some of the resources of the organization to maintain, rebuild, and expand its structure. Organization Development technology approaches the goal of a self-renewing school.

Organizational Relationships

While the study of organization structure and process has been a convenient way to look at supervision, another focus has been the relationship among people in organizations. Approached from a number of variables, such as communication, individual needs, morale, motivation, and small group work, the study of organizational relationships has enriched the study of leadership and given us clues to organizational function.

It was, in fact, a study of efficiency that ushered in the human relations era of organizational analysis. During the 1920s, researchers at Western Electric's Hawthorne Plant were attempting to determine the relationship between illumination and production. The chief investigator, F.J. Roethlisberger, was surprised to find that production increased with every change in the experimental condition; whether illumination was increased or decreased, productivity went up. A mysterious force, later labeled the "Hawthorne Effect," was eventually determined to be a human attitudinal factor.

An early proponent of the human relationship approach to the study of leadership, Elton Mayo, proposed that an overemphasis of scientific method studies had alienated workers and led to a form of psychological deterioration in organizations. Mayo recommended more small group interaction and face-to-face communication to overcome these dehumanizing forces.[11] The early concern of Mayo and others for attention to the psychosocial dimensions of an organization soon led to extensive application of social science research to leadership theory.

One of the first major theories in this area was Kurt Lewin's "field theory." Lewin held that causal relationships in organizations, or cause and effect, could be explained in terms of: (1) the psychological environment as it exists for groups or individuals; (2) the needs, values, and desires of individuals in that environment; and (3) the variables of life space, such as functions, behaviors, and flexibility. Lewin mentioned a "force field," where certain driving or restraining forces competed to raise or lower productivity. His basic formula, $B = F(PE)$ (behavior is a function of the person and the environment), introduced an entirely new element into the concept of management.[12]

Later work in the social sciences focused more specifically on the nature of man and human behavior. An early contribution was the work of psychologist A.H. Maslow, who proposed that man's needs are arranged in hierarchical order. According to Maslow, these needs had a prepotency effect, so that as one level of needs was satisfied, the next level was activated. Maslow's model proposed five levels of need: (1) physiological needs; (2) security or safety needs; (3) social, belonging, or membership needs; (4) esteem needs, including autonomy; and (5) self-actualization, or self-fulfillment needs. The value of Maslow's hierarchy for administration was in providing an explanation of worker behavior and motivation.

One piece of social science research that built on Maslow's work was Frederick Herzberg's "job enrichment" model.[13] Through extensive interviews with workers, Herzberg determined that some job characteristics led to job satisfaction, while others led to job dissatisfaction. Characteristics that led to job dissatisfaction were called "hygiene factors" (salary, work conditions, job security), because they were contextual and always in need of replenishment. Contrasted with hygiene factors were "motivators" (recognition, responsibility, possibilities for growth), which satisfied the individual's need for self-actualization at work. Herzberg's work approached prescription for administrators working in organizations with the so-called "human factor." Maslow's and Herzberg's models appear in Figure 2.2.

By the 1950s, management theorists began to speak of the lack of congruence between the tasks of organizations and the needs of

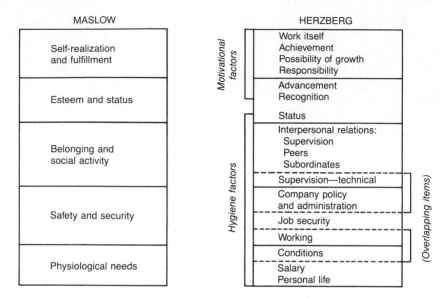

Figure 2.2
Maslow's Need-Priority Model Compared with Herzberg's Motivation-Hygiene Model

Source: Adapted from K. Davis, *Human Relations at Work.* New York: McGraw-Hill, 1967, p. 37.

individuals. Argyris stated the condition in these three propositions:

1. There is a lack of congruence between the needs of healthy individuals and the demands of formal organizations.
2. The result of this disturbance is frustration, failure, short-term perspective, and conflict.
3. The nature of the formal principles causes the subordinate, at any given level, to experience competition, rivalry, insubordinate hostility, and a focus on the parts rather than the whole.[14]

Another theorist, Likert, called for management to modify the rigid communication patterns of many organizations and link formal and informal groups for greater productivity and effectiveness. Suggesting that people with membership in overlapping groups with an organization can play a critical role in promoting better communication, Likert developed his *linking pin theory* for modifying formal organizations.[15] Blau and Scott illuminated the role of informal groups:

The fact that an organization has been formally established does not mean that all activities and interactions of its members conform strictly to the official blueprint. In every organization there arise informal organizations ... [which] develop their own practices, norms, and social relations ...[16]

Finally, Douglas McGregor made the direct connection between leadership style, organization, and the individuals in the organization. McGregor suggested that underlying assumptions of the leader about human behavior were instrumental to both the design and operation of an organization. McGregor characterized two different styles of leadership, each of which would elicit different responses from individuals in the organization. One style, called "Theory X leadership," assumes a posture of distrust in viewing workers in the organization. The opposing style, "Theory Y leadership," believes in the capacity of workers to grow and contribute. This work of McGregor's provided new insights into how organizations might be operated to integrate individual needs with institutional tasks.[17] Figure 2.3 compares the characteristics of the two leadership styles.

Overall, the study of organizations from the perspective of relationships supplied practicing supervisors with many insights about their role in influencing human behavior. The study of relationships also opened a fourth approach to inquiry, the study of influence in the operation of an organization.

Figure 2.3
Organizational View of People

Theory X Assumptions	Theory Y Assumptions
People by nature:	People by nature:
1. Lack integrity	1. Have integrity
2. Are fundamentally lazy and desire to work as little as possible	2. Work hard toward objectives to which they are committed
3. Avoid responsibility	3. Assume responsibility within their commitments
4 Are not interested in achievement	4 Desire to achieve
5. Are incapable of directing their own behavior	5. Are capable of directing their own behavior
6. Are indifferent to organizational needs	6. Want their organization to succeed
7. Prefer to be directed by others	7. Are not passive and submissive
8. Avoid making decisions whenever possible	8. Will make decisions within their commitments
9. Are not very bright	9. Are not stupid

Source: Reprinted by permission of the publisher, from Douglas McGregor, "The Human Side of Enterprise," MANAGEMENT REVIEW (Nov/1957), 22–28, 88–92, American Management Associations, Inc., New York.

Organizational Influence

A final avenue, and the most recently explored, evolved because the study of structure, process, and relationships failed to explain completely the operation of an organization. The study of influence in organizations has its origins in sociology and political science, and speaks in terms of power, authority, and persuasion. Emergence of this perspective has hastened since 1960 because of the issues of community pluralism, governance, and control brought about by shrinking resources and increased legalism in our schools.

The study of influence is comprised of at least four subareas: studies of change, of leadership, of decision making, and of the role of politics. These subareas break down into more specialized studies, such as the influences of finance, media, technology, and other variables that can alter an organization's operation.

The literature on change includes studies of types of change, models of change, strategies of changing, and barriers to change. One major distinction in the literature is the difference between planned change and evolutionary or natural change. Guba identifies three types of change: evolutionary (natural change), homeostatic (reactive change), and neomobilistic (planned change).[18] Bennis lists eight types of change, including planned change, indoctrination, coercive change, technocratic change, interactional change, socialization change, emulative change, and natural change.[19]

There are both adopted models and developed models of change. Stereotypic models include those of agriculture (change agent), medicine (action research), business (incentives), and the military (authority). Most models build on an original conception of five stages of change: awareness, interest, evaluation, trial, and adoption.[20] A more sophisticated version of the basic model focuses on the relationship between the change agent and the client system:

1. The development of a need for change
2. The establishment of a change relationship
3. The diagnosis of the client system's problem
4. The examination of goals and alternative routes of action.
5. The transformation of intentions into action
6. The generalization and stabilization of change
7. The achievement of a terminal relationship[21]

Chin offers the most general conceptualization of strategies of change, under the headings (1) rational-empirical, (2) normative-reeducative, and (3) power-coercive. The rational-empirical strategy is based on the assumption that people will follow their rational self-interests once they are revealed to them. The normative strategy recognizes change as a sociocultural phenomenon that is reinforced by group values and attitudes. The power-coercive strategy, obviously, is based upon the application of influence through position or some other irrefutable source.[22] Bennis identifies eight other traditional strategies of change: exposition and propagation, elite corps, human relations training, scholarly consultation, circulation of ideas to influentials, use of staff, developmental research, and action research.[23]

Finally, the literature on organizations points to a number of persistent barriers to change, including a lack of understanding of the change, human nature's tendency to favor the status quo, lack of skills for implementing change, poor leadership, and absence of precise goals for assessing the impact of change. Klein observes, however, that barriers to change are not all bad, because they:

1. Protect the organization from random change which may be harmful;
2. Protect the system from takeover by vested interests; and
3. Insure that unanticipated consequences of a change be spelled out and possibly avoided.[24]

Another area of study in the broad area of influence is that of leadership, that intangible driving force in planned change. Attempts to study and analyze leadership have evolved through three stages of inquiry: a study of leadership traits; an analysis of situation or environment affecting leadership; and a study of exchange or transactions between leaders and followers.

Although many traits have been considered unique to leaders (height, persistence, imagination), none has withstood objective analysis as an absolute predictor of leadership style or capacity. Stogdill suggested that leadership is linked to situations, and identified six factors associated with leadership: achievement, responsibility, participation, capacity, status, and the situation. Stogdill stated, "A person does not become a leader by virtue of the possession of some combination of traits, but the pattern of personal characteristics of the leader must bear some relevant relationship to the characteristics, activities, and goals of the followers."[25]

Further research on leadership revealed another important factor in the formula of leadership: the follower. The follower is crucial in determining leadership because this person *perceives* the leader and the situation, and reacts according to that perception. With this observation, leadership research emerged into the "exchange theory" stage, focusing on how leaders motivate groups to accept their influence and the processes underlying the prolonged exertion of that influence.

Other focuses of study in the area of leadership have included small group management,[26] communications,[27] and perceptual psychology.[28] Collectively, these inquiries have led to the understanding that to be a leader, in the real sense of the word, a person must be perceived as a leader by the groups that make up an organization. The leader can have an impact on the perceptions of the organization's members by being aware of their needs and structuring the organization to meet their needs. Specific acts of leadership may include selectively applying roles and tasks to problems, encouraging desirable communication patterns, changing individual perceptions with information and experience, and tailoring rewards to motivational levels. Collectively, the leader's actions to influence the organization can be seen as the establishment of an environment to control transaction.[29]

A third area of study relating to influence has concentrated on decision making and policy formation. A pervasive element of administration is the need to coordinate activities; coordination is the bridge between planning and action. Policies facilitate coordination by providing a detailed conception of the method for accomplishing tasks and encouraging delegation of both authority and responsibility in organizations. The study of policy formation and implementation becomes particularly important in organizations such as schools that are open and subject to input from diverse sources.

Agger, Goldrich, and Swanson provide a six-step model of policy development that helps us understand this complex area. They refer to:

1. Policy formation
2. Policy deliberation
3. Organization of policy support
4. Authoritative consideration (support endorsement)
5. Policy promulgation
6. Policy effectuation[30]

Developing policy, or authoritative decisions for guiding other decisions, provides supervisors with a way of governing and stabilizing organizations through times of change. Specialized areas in the study of policy include policy formation, access to decision making, influence of external bodies on policy formation, and conflict resolution. Interest in policy and decision making in schools is likely to continue and expand. As Campbell observes:

> The traditional belief is that education is a profession in which policy decisions are made by a representative board of lay persons and implemented by professionals. This ideology has been challenged on two grounds which, taken together, provide the rationale for new efforts in citizen involvement. The public has challenged (1) the effectiveness of schools and (2) the representativeness of the school policymakers.[31]

A final area of study for understanding the concept of influence has been the politics of education. Politics can be defined as the art or science of governing, but the concerns of inquiry have focused on the application of power to influence organizations. An early definition by Goldhammer and Shils held that "a person is said to have power to the extent that he influences the behavior of others in accordance with his own intentions."[32] Inquiry has delineated specialized study in areas such as power structures, passing bond issues, and budget control.

According to Nunnery and Kimbrough, "The power structure of the community is the systematic, relative distribution of social power among citizens in determining the kind of community they want and the kind of institutional arrangement that will best serve them. The exercise of power by citizens is not equal; there is an unequal distribution of influence in the system.[33]

Hunter's study found a pyramidal type of informal power structure that included: (1) the policymakers; (2) leaders who established policy positions; (3) those who implemented policy; and (4) the professional educator and lay board. In other words, Hunter stated, "Those who held the formal power to make decisions tended *not* to appear in the policy-making group."[34]

Writing on this topic, Kimbrough observes, "The entrenched power group is usually lodged deep in the socioeconomic fabric of the human group. Students who for the first time do empirical analyses of power in administration units in which an informal power group is predominant are awed by the extent to which its leaders are embedded in community affairs.[35]

In 1971, Nunnery and Kimbrough revealed the full extent of political activity in schools and their influence on the operation and administration of school districts:

> The school system is administered within a complex power structure. The typical board of education does not exercise final authority over educational policies. In reality it exercises power only to the extent that it can legitimize its decisions (make them acceptable) in the political system. It cannot enforce a policy that is unacceptable to the people it serves and retain power. Thus, schoolmen must continually seek public affirmation of operating policies.[36]

Inquiry into the functioning of organizations has been comprehensive and continuous in this century. Four main focuses—structures, processes, relationships, and influence—have served as organizers for this inquiry, as shown in Figure 2.4.

ROLES AND TASKS OF LEADERSHIP

Leadership in supervision is not a function of title or appointed position. Titles may legitimize formal authority, but they do not ensure

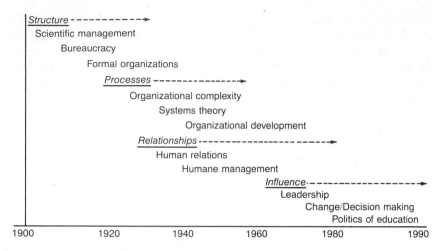

Figure 2.4
Study of Organizations 1900–1990

leadership capacity. True leadership is a function of four complex variables: the character of the leader, the character of those being led, the character of the organization, and the character of the environment.

Leadership in educational organizations is a situational phenomenon. It is determined by the collective perceptions of individuals, is related to group norms, and is influenced by the frequency of interaction among members of the organization. Before leadership can be effective in an open organization such as a school, it must be acknowledged as a group activity.

To some extent, leadership is a product of the leader's vision. The way in which the leader conceives of the group's tasks, and the policies and practices to successfully achieve those ends, defines leadership. In the words of management specialist Douglas McGregor, "The theoretical assumptions management holds about controlling human resources determines the whole character of the enterprise."[37]

The way in which the leader sees the organization and its needs, when formalized, sets the foundation for a theory of leadership. Without such a theory, leadership behaviors will be little more than a series of activities and projects that have little relationship to one another. Most often, conceptions of leadership are developed in terms of what the leader is to be and do, in terms of roles and tasks.

Leadership roles in supervision are multiple due to the numerous environments in which the supervisor operates and due to the supportive role of most supervisory positions. Here is a list of common leadership roles that can be applied to various situations:

> *Expert*—sometimes the consultant is the source of knowledge or skill in an area.

Instructor—the consultant may take the role of instructing about an area of knowledge.

Trainer—a trainer goes beyond instruction in that he helps people master "do it" behavioral skills in performing actions.

Retriever—the retriever brings what is needed to the client system.

Referrer—the referrer sends the client system to a source where it can find what it needs.

Linker—the linker provides a bridge to parties, or parts of a system, that need to be in contact.

Demonstrator—the demonstrator shows the client system how something is done, but does not necessarily show him how to do it for himself.

Modeler—the modeler provides an example of how to do, or be, something by evidencing it as his (the consultant's) own behavior.

Advocate—there are times when a consultant can best facilitate an intention by taking the role of advocate for a goal, value, or strategy.

Confronter—when the client system needs to be confronted with awareness of a discrepancy.

Counselor—the role of the counselor generally includes listening, acting as a sounding board, and raising awareness of alternatives. It is a non-directive effort in helping the client think through issues.

Advisor—the advisor role differs from the counselor in being more directive about what the client might do and how to do it.

Observer—the observer comments on the things that exist and how things are being done.

Data Collector—the data collector gathers information about what exists and how things are being done.

Analyzer—the analyzer interprets the meaning of data found in the system.

Diagnoser—the diagnoser uses analyses, data, and observations in determining why things happen the way they do in the system.

Designer—the designer develops action strategies, training programs, and management models for use by the system.

Manager—the manager takes charge of the development process by ordering events to achieve accountability.

Evaluator—the evaluator serves to feed back information that will make the system more effective in its task.[38]

Like the roles of supervision, the tasks associated with successful practice are numerous. The tasks performed and the task pattern for any one supervisor will vary from organization to organization and work situation to work situation. However, some generic tasks are found in most supervision leadership opportunities.

Developing an Operating Theory. Leaders must be able to conceptualize tasks and communicate the approach to those tasks to others in the organization. The pattern of task identification and response forms the basis of an operating theory.

Developing Organization and a Work Environment. Supervision tasks are often nonpermanent responses to needs. In such cases, the way in which people, resources, and ideas are organized is left to the leader. An important task is to structure an organization and work environment that can respond to those needs.

Setting Standards. Because supervision problems often involve diverse groups of individuals with different needs and perceptions, an important task for a curriculum leader is to set standards and other expectations that will affect the resolution of problems. Such standards may include work habits, communication procedures, time limitations, or a host of related planning areas.

Using Authority to Establish an Organizational Climate. Persons assigned to leadership positions generally are able to structure organizations by suggesting changes and initiating policies. One of the most important tasks for a supervision leader is using such authority to establish a desirable work climate. Such a climate, discussed later in this chapter, is made up of the collective perceptions of persons affected by the structure of the organization.

Establishing Effective Interpersonal Relations. Since leadership is a product of human exchanges or transactions within organizations, it is essential that interpersonal relationships contribute to the attainment of desired ends. The way in which a supervision leader interacts with others in the organization can assist in the establishment of a pattern of effective interpersonal relationships.

Planning and Initiating Action. The supervision leader is sometimes the only person with the authority to plan and initiate actions. Deciding when and how to initiate action is a strong leadership activity. Failure to lead planning or initiate action can undermine other leadership functions.

Keeping Communication Channels Open and Functioning. Many times the supervision leader is in a unique position of being able to communicate with others in an organization when lateral and horizontal communication is limited for most members. The leader can use his or her position to facilitate the matching of persons who need to communicate with one another. The leader can also make changes in communication patterns, where necessary, to ensure that such communication channels are functioning.

These tasks, in combination, are used to improve instructional programs in schools by supervisors in leadership roles.

STYLES OF LEADERSHIP

As the reader will note, the study of leadership is a far-ranging inquiry characterized by sometimes conflicting expert opinion and a rich body of literature. There are some 130 different definitions of leadership in today's educational literature, a sample of which is provided for review:

> A leader is best when people barely know he exists. When our work is done, his aim is fulfilled, they will say, "We did this ourselves." Lao-Tsu, *The Way of Life*, 6th Century, B.C.

> Love is held by a chain of obligation ... but fear is maintained by the dread of punishment which never fails.... A wise prince must rely on what is in his power and not on what is in the power of others ... Niccolo Machiavelli, *The Prince*, 1500 A.D.

> Leadership is the art of imposing one's will upon others in such a manner as to command their obedience, their respect and their loyal cooperation. *G-I Manual*, Staff College, United States Army, 1947

> Leadership is the ability to get a man to do what you want him to do, when you want it done, in a way you want it done, because he wants to do it. Dwight Eisenhower, 1957

> Leadership is the human factor which binds a group together and motivates it toward a goal. K. Davis, *Human Relations at Work*, 1962

> Leadership is the process of influencing the activities of an individual or group in efforts toward goal achievement in a given situation. Hersey and Blanchard, *The Management of Organizational Behavior*, 1977[39]

In addition, the literature on leadership often defines it by what it does or in how it is applied:

> *Leadership as the focus of group process:* the leader is the nucleus of social movement. By control of social processes (structure, goals, ideology, atmosphere), the leader becomes the primary agent for group change.

> *Leadership as personality and its effects:* the leader possesses the greatest number of desired traits. Using these, the leader exerts a degree of influence over those about him.

> *Leadership as the art of inducing compliance:* the leader, through face-to-face control, causes the subordinate to behave in a desired manner.

> *Leadership as the exercise of influence:* the leader establishes a relationship and uses this interpersonal influence to attain goals and enforce behavior beyond mechanical compliance.

Leadership as a power relationship: the leader is perceived as having the right to prescribe behavior patterns for others. Sources of power include referent power (liking), expert power, reward power, coercive power, and legitimate (authority) power.

Leadership as the initiation of structure: the leader originates and structures interaction as part of a process to solve problems.

Leadership as goal achievement: the leader is perceived as controlling the means of satisfying needs as the group moves toward definitive objectives.[40]

There have also been attempts in educational supervision literature to "prescribe" leadership under certain conditions. Wiles and Lovell attempt to state such "principles of leadership" in stating how leadership works in a school environment where multiple group needs are present:

1. Leadership is a group role . . . he is able to exert leadership only through effective participation in groups.
2. Leadership, other things being equal, depends upon the frequency of interaction between the leader and the led.
3. Status position does not necessarily give leadership.
4. Leadership in any organization is widespread and diffused . . . if a person hopes to exert leadership for everybody, he is doomed to frustration and failure.
5. The norms of the group determine the leader.
6. Leadership qualities and followership qualities are interchangeable.
7. People who give evidence of a desire to control are rejected for leadership roles.
8. The feeling that people hold about a person is a factor in whether they will use his behavior as leadership.
9. Leadership shifts from situation to situation.[41]

Finally, leadership in supervision is sometimes portrayed by simple models that enable us to see the various options available in leading others (Figure 2.5).

The reader is encouraged to begin thinking about his or her own leadership style by completing the following assessment questionnaire. There are no right or wrong responses, only choices.

Leadership Style Questionnaire

Following, you will find ten statements or situations that are common in supervision practice. Place a check beside your favored response in each of the ten areas. What does the sum of your responses suggest concerning your supervisory style?

1. In leading a meeting, it is important to:

Keep focused on the agenda at hand   1. _____

Focus on each individual's feelings and help people express their emotional reactions to the issue   2. _____

Focus on the differing positions people take and how they deal with each other   3. _____

Figure 2.5
Leadership Styles

1. "TELLS" Leadership
    A. Seeks unquestioning obedience
    B. Sometimes relies on fear, intimidation
    C. Gives orders
    D. Relies heavily on authority
    E. Sets all goals and standards
    F. Makes all decisions without consulting the group

2. "SELLS" Leadership
    A. Work assignments are allotted to workers
    B. Assignments are sometimes arbitrary
    C. Tries to persuade the group to accept assignments
    D. Seldom builds teamwork
    E. Does not motivate worker involvement
    F. Makes decisions without consulting the group

3. "CONSULTS" Leadership
    A. Does not rely on authority
    B. Develops considerable worker loyalty
    C. Does not hesitate to delegate
    D. Will usually explain why a task is to be performed in a certain way
    E. Takes time to inform his group what he thinks may be a solution

4. "JOINS" Leadership
    A. Builds teamwork by group involvement
    B. Accepts suggestions from the work group
    C. Treats each worker as an individual
    D. Helps workers achieve their potential
    E. Uses the decision of the group

5. "DELEGATES" Leadership
    A. Turns the decision-making process over to the group
    B. Accepts all group decisions that fit within accepted parameters
    C. Encourages subordinate participation in many activities
    D. Stimulates creative thinking in employees

Source: Michael C. Giammatteo, "Training Package for a Model City Staff," Field Paper no. 15 (Portland, Oreg.: Northwest Regional Educational Laboratory, 1975), 30. Used with permission.

2. A primary objective of a leader is:

Maintaining an organizational climate in which learning and accomplishment can take place   4. _____

The efficient operation of his organization   5. _____

To help members of the organization find themselves and be more aware of who they are   6. _____

3. When strong disagreement occurs between a group member and yourself about work to be done, would you:

Listen to the person and try to uncover where he might have misunderstood the task   7. _____

Try to get other people to express their views as a way of involving them in the issue   8. _____

Support the person for raising his question or disagreement   9. _____

4. In evaluating a group member's performance, the leader should:

Involve the entire group both in setting goals and in evaluating one another's performance   10. _____

Try to make an objective assessment of each person's accomplishments and effectiveness   11. _____

Allow each person to be involved in determining his own goals and performance standards   12. _____

5. When two groups members get into an argument it is best to:

Help them deal with their feelings as a means of resolving the argument   13. _____

Encourage other members to respond to the argument and try to help resolve it   14. _____

Allow some time for expression of both sides, but keep in focus the relevant subject matter and the task at hand   15. _____

6. The best way to motivate someone who is not performing up to his ability is to:

Point out to him the importance of the job to be done and his role in it   16. _____

Try to get to know him better so you can understand why he is not realizing his potential   17. _____

Show him how his lack of motivation is ad-   18. _____
versely affecting other people

7. The most important element in judging a person's performance is

His technical skills and ability   19. _____

How he gets along with his peers and how he   20. _____
helps others learn and get work done

His success in meeting the goals that he has   21. _____
set for himself

8. In dealing with minority group issues, a leader
should:

Deal with such issues as they threaten to dis-   22. _____
turb the atmosphere of his group

Be sure that all group members understand the   23. _____
history of racial and ethnic minorities in this
country and the community

Help each person achieve an understanding of   24. _____
his attitude toward people of other races and
cultures

9. A leader's goal should be to:

Make sure that all of his group members have   25. _____
a solid foundation of knowledge and skills that
will help them become effective, productive
people

Help people learn to work effectively in groups,   26. _____
to use the resources of the group, and to understand their relationships with one another
as people

Help each person become responsible for his   27. _____
own education and effectiveness and take the
first step toward realizing his potential as a
person

10. The trouble with leadership responsibilities is:

They make it very difficult to cover adequately   28. _____
all the details that must be attended to

They keep a leader from really getting to know   29. _____
her/his group members as individuals

They make it hard for a leader to keep in touch   30. _____
with the climate and pulse of the group

Supervisors, like other leaders in education, are formally evaluated each year. The reader may be interested to see the relationship between style and evaluation on the following "real world" form:

Supervisor Evaluation Form

Individual Being Rated _____

This form has been designed to give the individual named above information that might assist him to focus more clearly on those things that will help him to become more effective.

Instructions: for each numbered item, select two statements:
  (M) place an M before that statement that seems *most like* this individual's typical behavior.
  (L) place an L by the statement that is *least like* his typical behavior as you know him/her.
  Please give examples to clarify your selections.

<table>
<tr><td align="center">*Items*</td><td align="center">*Examples*</td></tr>
</table>

1. Listening:
   a. _____ Draws other people out
   b. _____ Gives no indication that he/she hears what is said
   c. _____ Hears content but not feeling
   d. _____ Blocks people out
   e. _____ Hears and interprets communications from sender's point of view
   f. _____ Hears words but does not comprehend them

2. Expressing Ideas to Others
   a. _____ Comes across clearly to individuals
   b. _____ Comes across clearly to both individuals and groups
   c. _____ Uses words well but doesn't convey ideas clearly
   d. _____ Is not easily understood
   e. _____ Conveys ideas but does so awkwardly
   f. _____ May not try sufficiently hard to get his ideas across

3. Influences:
   a. _____ By weight of ideas and logic
   b. _____ By force of personality
   c. _____ By being friendly
   d. _____ By scheming and manipulation
   e. _____ By involving others in the issue
   f. _____ By status and/or position

4. Decision Making:
   a. _____ Focuses primarily on keeping people happy
   b. _____ Tries to get job done through getting people involved
   c. _____ Believes in making important decisions by himself/herself
   d. _____ Works for compromise between productivity and morale
   e. _____ Focuses primarily on getting job done
   f. _____ Follows leads of other people

5. Relationships with Others:
   a. _____ Harmonizes and compromises differences in the group
   b. _____ Doesn't see need for supporting others
   c. _____ Keeps others involved
   d. _____ Insensitive to feelings of others
   e. _____ Supports associates right or wrong
   f. _____ Tolerant of differences in others
   g. _____ Doesn't support things in which he/she doesn't believe
   h. _____ Puts others down with value judgment

6. Task Orientation:
   a. _____ Works on task only if he is personally interested

   b. _____ Procrastinates in getting job done

   c. _____ Works on task only in spurts

   d. _____ Encourages involvement of others in work tasks

   e. _____ Works equally hard on important and unimportant tasks

   f. _____ Constantly presses to get job done

7. Handling of Conflict:

   a. _____ Readily engages in conflict when it presents itself

   b. _____ Doesn't recognize any conflict

   c. _____ Tends to smooth or gloss over conflicts

   d. _____ Stirs up conflict for its own sake

   e. _____ Uses and works through conflict openly

   f. _____ Goes out of way to avoid conflict

8. Willingness to Change:

   a. _____ Defends his ideas against all comers

   b. _____ Mulls ideas over thoroughly before committing himself/herself to something new

   c. _____ Values change for change's sake

   d. _____ Quick to utilize new ideas

   e. _____ Will try new things only if he/she thinks of them himself/herself

   f. _____ Usually thinks things through until it is too late to change

9. Problem Solving:

   a. _____ Sets goals and keeps them in mind

   b. _____ Slows down groups by going off on tangents

c. _____ Considers all pertinent
information
d. _____ Jumps to conclusions
quickly
e. _____ Doesn't recognize existing
problems
f. _____ Utilizes resources of others

10. Self-development:
a. _____ Understands why he/she
does what he/she does
b. _____ Is not critical of himself/
herself
c. _____ Blames others for his/her
own shortcomings
d. _____ Encourages comments on
his/her own behavior
e. _____ Doesn't realize how others
see him/her
f. _____ Is growing and developing
in work effectiveness

11. Expressing Emotions to Others:
a. _____ Clearly and frequently
verbalizes his/her emotions
b. _____ Acknowledges emotions
only when asked by others
c. _____ Has difficulty stating
emotions clearly to others
d. _____ Uses emotional words but
does not act/live out his
feelings
e. _____ Uses only global words
("good," "comfortable,"
etc.) to describe emotions

Name of person doing the rating: _____
Date _____

As a conclusion to this chapter on leadership, the reader is presented with information about some new conditions affecting school leadership and a number of issues to be considered.

FACTORS AFFECTING LEADERSHIP

As recently as 1970, educational texts dealing with leadership began to describe a number of new conditions affecting leader performance.

These new "descriptive studies" did not fit neatly within the confines of the traditional "prescriptive theories" of leadership, and led to a real dichotomy for preparation programs in education. In effect, theory did not fit practice in many educational settings. It is important that the reader know of these new forces so that they can be incorporated in the development of any leadership theory.

One of the most subtle, but important, changes in American education has been the continuous consolidation of school districts during the past fifty years. In 1933, there were over 127,000 independent school districts in the United States. In 1990, there are about 13,500 districts. Such consolidation has resulted in larger and vastly more complex school districts and has caused many administrative roles to become more bureaucratic. Obviously, this force has affected supervision by moving the supervisor out of the "independent operator" role in schools and into the "management team" position in a bureaucracy.

A second major change has been the development of specialization in professional education. During the past thirty years, each new mission for the school, each new learner discovered, has required additional knowledge by those in leadership roles. Today, areas such as funded projects, contracted settlements, and technical education programs (computers) present schools with a complex layer of administrative authority and responsibility. Supervisors, without a clear job role, must pick their way through this complex series of relationships.

A third major force that has entered professional education in recent years is the rise of unionism and the new power relationships that have come with collective bargaining. Collective bargaining in education, first seen in 1963, has produced a classic labor-management conflict in many school districts. The legalities of standard grievance procedures have produced restrictions for classroom supervision and, in many cases, a dispiriting climate for supervisor-teacher communication. Teacher empowerment in the 1990s has created additional challenges for supervisors as they work at school sites.

A final change that has altered the traditional leadership role of supervision is the sheer volume of tasks required to operate today's schools. Whether at the district or building level, supervisors have been hampered by the little jobs that must be done on schedule and that cause the postponement of more important long-term tasks.

Collectively, these four factors have changed the nature and role of leadership in schools. Many of the previous theories of leadership, as well as the styles of leading, have been challenged by this new practice environment. Completing our picture of leadership in supervision, the reader is next presented with a number of classic issues that must be resolved by anyone providing leadership in a school environment.

Issues of Leadership

As we have seen, the leadership style of a supervisor will be dependent on his or her vision of the job, the type of organization leadership is practiced in, and the underlying philosophy of the supervisor. Certainly, the task of bringing together these elements in a rapidly changing educational environmment presents a challenge. It is the authors' contention that looking at leadership in terms of five key issues may assist readers in clarifying their own portrait of leadership in supervision.

The School Mission Issue. There is a wide range of opinions among Americans about the purpose of schools. Specific arguments may revolve around buzz words such as "basics" or "cooperative learning," but the issues underlying these concerns are foundational. Schools in the United States initially adopted an educational pattern found in Europe in the seventeenth century: a system of education rationalized by the mastery of specific content. In the nineteenth century, a different conception of educating was imported from Europe—a child-centered program drawing its rationale from the needs of growing children. Both of these purposes of educating have been preserved in the American system, and exist today.

An important philosophical question underlying the design of school curricula, however, is whether the intention of the program is to: (1) "round out" the student so that all graduates possess common knowledge and attributes, or (2) whether the schooling experience should "accentuate the uniqueness" of the individual in an effort to gain the full potential of the student for society. The issue of the school's mission is best seen in the competition between goals of the school: learning competencies and graduation requirements on the one hand, and efforts to serve special students and find unique characteristics (gifted, talented, special education) on the other.

While both goals are worthy, a school would be organized in different ways to accomplish these different ends. To encourage sameness and uniformity of graduates, the school would employ high degrees of structure so that students would experience nearly identical programs. To encourage uniqueness, flexibility would be encouraged, so that each student could have the freedom to develop to his capacity, whatever that capacity. Arguments over course materials, teaching methods, building designs, etc., spring from this key difference in the intention of the program. Supervisors need to know which of these purposes seems more important to them, because they have an unusual degree of control over these variables.

The Scope of Responsibility Issue. An issue that separates many supervisors is the perceived scope of their responsibility. Few job descriptions are meant to be comprehensive or restrictive in nature, and the residual dimensions of school leadership (the assumed duties) will provide supervisors with many choices beyond that which is identified as their direct responsibility. For example, is the supervisor responsible for helping a teacher who has a problem outside of school that is affecting school performance? Or, is the supervisor responsible for providing a quality school program for students who are beyond the benefit of the standard school curriculum?

In many cases, the nature of what constitutes the job of supervisor—even what is meant by the term itself—will be decided by the person who fills the position. Defining the scope of the job will, of course, reflect a larger definition of the purpose of schooling and the nature of leadership in education.

Focus of Leadership as an Issue. It is evident that supervisors can and will significantly influence how educational programs are organized and how they will operate. By the control of task focus, communications, resource allocation and evaluation, the supervisor will set a tone for working. In channeling activities, the supervisor will focus more on either tractive (static) or dynamic (change oriented) operations.

Within this choice of tractive or dynamic leadership style lies the supervisor's definition of professionalism in education. For some leaders, professionalism is the efficient application of administrative skills to operate an educational program. A model for this type of supervisor might be an engineer who keeps the machinery operating efficiently. A different conception of leadership and professionalism could be a supervisor who constantly improves schools, using as a model the architect who is always in the process of enacting a vision.

Public Involvement as an Issue. A third issue that regularly separates school leaders is whether the public should be directly involved in school operations. While reason would seem to prevail on a case-by-case basis, involvement or noninvolvement of citizens actually constitutes an entire operational strategy for some administrators.

Many districts conduct assessments of need to gain information for use in making decisions about school programs. Whether the public should be involved in gathering and analyzing such information and whether the public should be involved in the actual decision making resulting from that analysis, is an administrative issue. One argument for public involvement is that the public sponsors the schools with its tax dollars and entrusts its children to their educational programs. By this argument, involvement in decision making is only natural, and almost a right of every interested parent. On the other hand, many school administrators feel there is no clear consensus on many educational issues, and public involvement in decision making only polarizes the many public groups that support the schools. Those who take this position draw an analogy to representative government or refer to professional judgment to support their feeling that the school administrator has no real obligation or mandate to involve the public in the daily decision making operation of the schools.

In truth, this issue revolves around the concept of trust and democratic principles. It is also true that the issue has never been satisfactorily resolved by the courts, so it remains both recurrent and pressing.

Use of Influence as an Issue. One of the most difficult issues for new supervisors is the use of influence. Most new supervisors like to think of public school leadership as a democratic process where they, as professionals, oversee many competing forces in the formulation of ideas and policy. In reality, things are not always so simple.

A school supervisor is a highly trained professional, more knowledgeable about the field of education than most persons. Such knowledge should mean that the supervisor has information and skills that the average teacher or citizen does not possess. The issue in the use of influence arises when the supervisor knows that teachers or the public are making a poor choice from among limited alternatives. At what point does the supervisor offer professional expertise that may not have been solicited? By the same token, when does the sharing of such knowledge become a form of manipulation? An honest supervisor will acknowledge that even methods of leadership (how a committee is formed) constitute a degree of manipulation.

Obviously, to lead a public institution such as a school, the supervisor needs a clear conception of democratic principles and their use. But, it makes a tremendous amount of difference whether the leader considers himself or herself a controller of events by virtue of position, or simply one more force or influence in a democratic arena.

Moral Integrity as an Issue. A final issue, which some would call an imperative, is moral integrity in supervision. Unlike supervisors in other professions, school supervisors carry a special burden stemming from the value-laden nature of education and schooling. The public holds special expectations for schools, due to the special nature of the commodity that is the subject of educational influence. For this reason, supervisory behavior will be monitored constantly by a number of concerned groups.

Not only must the school supervisor be exemplary in his or her own behavior, but they also insist that others around them hold high standards for performance. If there is a breakdown in the quality control of instruction, it is the responsibility of the supervisor of instruction. If materials are less than adequate, it is the responsibility of the supervisor of instruction. If there is a problem in a school under the

Directions: Mark an X over that number which best describes your current
feelings about each issue. (1 = strong feeling; 3 = no opinion.)

Schools should round out pupils and promote commonality				Schools should accentuate the uniqueness of pupils
1	2	3	2	1

Supervisors should stick to their appointed roles and duties				Supervisors should pursue whatever duties necessary to succeed
1	2	3	2	1

Supervisors should not allow extensive public involvement				Supervisors are obligated to involve the public extensively
1	2	3	2	1

Supervisors should not use their position to influence the public				Supervisors must use their position to influence the public
1	2	3	2	1

School supervisors are much like other supervisors in terms of moral integrity				School supervisors must possess an exceptional moral integrity in leading
1	2	3	2	1

Figure 2.6
Defining Supervisory Values

supervision of a district leader called the supervisor, it is the responsibility of the supervisor and no one else. In short, the buck stops at the level of the supervisor, and the integrity of that person must be impeccable because the nature of school work is too important for him not to be. Supervision is the critical link between the classroom teacher and the administration; it is the primary quality control agency in schools.

In Figure 2.6, the reader is encouraged to react to these issues as a matter of personal feeling.

NEW DIRECTIONS

School/Business Partnerships

Business will be heavily involved in schooling throughout the 1990s, because it perceives schools as the key to American survival in a world economy. Each year, American business spends an estimated 25 billion dollars to train and educate their workers with skills—skills they might have learned during twelve years of formal schooling.

It is estimated that by the year 2000, 75% of all new employees will be deficient in reading, writing, and verbal skills. Of the 20 million new jobs created from 1980 to 2000, fully 82% will be filled by female, non-white, and immigrant workers, but only 22% of these workers will be able to function at required reading levels, and only 5% will have the skills to read journals, write reports, and understand complex technology. That top 5% will be "stolen" from one business to another, forcing higher costs for products because of salaries and constant recruiting.[42]

In a nutshell, businesses are going to have to live with the best of the worst, and they will pressure schools for any help they can find in combating these conditions.

Restructuring

Restructuring is an active participatory process that seeks to enhance leadership in schools, professionalize the teaching profession, and invigorate the learning process for students. Major tenets of restructuring include:

1. Recognizing the school as a unit of collaborative decision making.
2. Establishing trust and respect among all parties active in school operation.
3. Establishing responsible management practices in order to best meet student needs.

Restructuring is not the same as educational reform. Reforms, over this century, have sought new ends for education. Restructuring, by contrast, is a means for making fundamental changes in the way schools operate; it is a process and a commitment to a way of working.

Target areas for restructuring efforts might include:

1. Restructuring for more effective teaching and learning.
2. Restructuring for more effective leadership patterns.
3. Restructuring to redefine teaching and professional roles in schools.
4. Restructuring for more effective use of resources in schools.

The primary changes in any restructuring effort are in the roles of persons in the school. The school principal's role, for example, would be transformed from that of the traditional authority figure to one of facilitator and manager. Teachers, rather than being autonomous professionals who deliver content in a classroom, would become instructional managers who are part of an instructional team.

Limitations on this concept in practice environments (such as Dade County [Miami], Florida) have centered around the differentiation of teacher roles, and the problem of gaining full support from all members of a teaching faculty for such changes.

SUMMARY

Leadership in supervision is more than the selected use of administrative skills; it is an approach to working with people within an organization to get a job done. Persons in educational leadership roles must see their behaviors as influencing the behaviors of others, and develop an approach to leading that brings desired results.

Organizational theory undergirds all leadership in supervision, and that theory is organized around four themes: structures, processes, relationships, and use of influence. Alone, or in combination, these historic organizers suggest an approach or style in leadership.

Definitions of leadership are multiple, depending on the setting in which leadership is practiced. Styles of leadership, too, are varied, according to a blend of leadership assumptions and organizational realities.

Recent factors that are influencing the practice of leadership in school settings include consolidation of districts, role specialization, unionization and collective bargaining, and an increasing work load in administration.

Finally, all supervisors must clarify issues that influence practice including defining the mission of schools, the supervisor's responsibility, the focus of practice, the degree of public involvement, and the moral integrity of the leader.

NOTES

1. Frederick W. Taylor, *Principles of Scientific Management*, 2nd ed. (New York, Harper and Row Publishers, 1947).
2. Frank B. Gilbreth, *Field Systems* (New York: Myron C. Clark Publishing Company, 1908).
3. Henry L. Gantt, *Organizing For Work* (New York: Harcourt, Brace and Howe, 1919).
4. Henri Fayol, *General and Industrial Management* (Geneva: International Management Institute, 1929).
5. The reader is encouraged to review a later attempt to codify these prin-

ciples in Lyndall Urwick, *Elements of Administration* (London: Pittman, 1947).

6. Max Weber, *The Theory of Social and Economic Organizations*, trans. A.M. Henderson and T. Parsons, ed. T. Parsons (New York: Free Press, 1947).

7. Daniel E. Griffith, "Toward a Theory of Administrative Behavior," in *Administrative Behavior of Education*, ed. Roald Campbell and Russell T. Gregg (New York: Harper and Row, 1957), p. 368.

8. Robert Katz, "Skills of an Effective Administrator," *Harvard Business Review* (January/February 1955), pp. 35–36.

9. For a complete coverage of systems application in education see Kathryn Feyereisen et al., *Supervision and Curriculum Renewal: A Systems Approach* (New York: Appleton-Century-Crofts, 1970).

10. See Richard Schmuck and Matthew Miles, *Organization Development in Schools* (Palo Alto, CA: National Press, 1971).

11. Elton Mayo, *The Human Problems of an Industrial Civilization* (New York: Macmillan, 1933).

12. Kurt Lewin, *Field Theory in Social Science* (New York: Harper Torch Books, 1951).

13. Frederick Herzberg, *Work and the Nature of Man* (Cleveland: World Publishing Company, 1966). Used by permission.

14. Chris Argyris, "The Individual and the Organization: Some Problems of Mutual Adjustment," *Administration Science Quarterly* 2 (1957), pp. 327–38.

15. Rensis Likert, *New Patterns of Management* (New York: McGraw-Hill, 1961).

16. Peter M. Blau and W. Richard Scott, *Formal Organizations* (San Francisco: Chandler, 1962).

17. Douglas McGregor, *The Human Side of Enterprise* (New York: McGraw-Hill, 1960).

18. Egon Guba, "The Role of Educational Research in Educational Change" (Bloomington, IN: National Institute for the Study of Educational Change, 1967).

19. Warren G. Bennis, *Changing Organizations* (New York: McGraw-Hill, 1966).

20. H. Lionberger, *Adoption of New Ideas and Practices* (Ames, IA: Iowa State University Press, 1961).

21. R. Lippitt, J. Watson, and B. Westley, *The Dynamics of Planned Change* (New York: Harcourt, Brace, and World, 1958).

22. W. Bennis, K. Benne, and R. Chin, *The Planning of Change* (New York: Holt, Rinehart and Winston, 1969), pp. 34–35.

23. Bennis, *The Planning of Change*, pp. 67–68.

24. D. Klein, "Some Notes on the Dynamics of Resistance to Change," in *Concepts For Social Change*, ed. G. Watson (Washington, DC: Coopera-

tive Project for Educational Development, National Training Laboratories, 1967).

25. R.M. Stogdill, "Personal Factors Associated With Leadership," *Journal of Psychology* 25(1948), p. 64.

26. See M. Sherif and C.W. Sherif, *Reference Groups* (New York: Harper and Row, 1964).

27. See Bryce Ryan, "A Study of Technological Diffusion," *Rural Sociology* (September 1948), pp. 273–85.

28. See Arthur Combs and Donald Snygg, *Individual Behavior: A Perceptual Approach to Behavior* (New York: Harper and Row, 1949).

29. Jon Wiles and Joseph Bondi, *Curriculum Development: A Guide to Practice* (Columbus, OH: Merrill, 1989), pp. 213–51.

30. Robert Agger, Daniel Goldrich, and Bert Swanson, *The Rulers and the Ruled* (New York: John Wiley, 1964).

31. Roald Campbell et al., *The Organization and Control of American Schools* (Columbus, OH: Merrill, 1980), p. 340.

32. Herbert Goldhammer and Edward A. Shils, "Types of Power and Status," *American Journal of Sociology* 95 (September 1939), p. 171.

33. Michael Nunnery and Ralph Kimbrough, *Politics, Power, Polls, and School Reform* (Berkeley, CA: McCutchan Publishing, 1971), p. 8.

34. Floyd Hunter, *Community Power Structure* (Chapel Hill, NC: University of North Carolina Press, 1953).

35. Ralph Kimbrough, *Political Power and Educational Decision Making* (Chicago: Rand McNally, 1964), p. 144.

36. Nunnery and Kimbrough, *Politics, Power, Polls, and School Reform*, p. 7.

37. Douglas McGregor, *The Human Side of Enterprise* (New York: McGraw-Hill, 1960).

38. Ronald Havelock, Institute for Social Research, University of Michigan, 1969.

39. J.M. Burns, *Leadership* (New York: Harper and Row, 1978), p. 66.

40. Ralph M. Stogdill, *Handbook of Leadership* (New York: Free Press, 1974).

41. Kimbal Wiles, John Lovell, *Supervision for Better Schools*, fifth edition. Englewood Cliffs, NJ, Prentice-Hall, 1983.

42. Harold Hodgekinson, *The Same Client: The Demographies of Education and Service Delivery Systems.* Washington DC: 1989.

SUGGESTED LEARNING ACTIVITIES

1. Develop a list of your own assumptions, principles, and observations about the leadership process. Can these statements be presented in the form of a theory of leadership?

2. Make a list of adjectives to characterize the desirable school supervisor.

3. Identify from the list in item 2 those things that make the supervisor different from the line administrator in schools.

BOOKS TO REVIEW

American Association of School Administrators. *Challenges For School Leaders*. Arlington, VA: AASA, 1988.

Blumberg, Arthur. *School Administration As a Craft: Foundations and Practice*. Boston: Allyn and Bacon, 1989.

Burdin, Joel. *School Leadership: A Contemporary Reader*. Newbury Park, CA: Sage Publications, Inc., 1989.

Griffith, Daniel et al. *Leaders For America's Schools*. Berkeley, CA: McCutchan, 1988.

Kotter, John. *The Leadership Factor*. New York: Macmillan Publishing Company, 1988.

Smith, Stuart. *School Leadership: Handbook For Excellence*. Eugene, OR: Eric, 1988.

Wiles, Jon and Bondi, Joseph. *Curriculum Development: A Guide to Practice*. Columbus, OH: Merrill, 1989.

CHAPTER 3

Supervision in Practice

INTRODUCTION

Supervisors operate at many levels of education under varying titles. Their role and tasks often overlap those of administration, support staff, and even teachers in the classroom. Despite this variety of identities, supervisors are usually positioned at the critical junction of leadership. More than other leadership roles in schools, supervisors have the opportunity to tie together all actions that improve learning experience for students.

To help the reader understand what supervisors really do in practice, this chapter looks at some of the activities of supervision at three levels: district, school, and classroom. While this vantage point is necessarily cursory, it should indicate that the skills of supervision are constant despite the changing roles and tasks. We have attempted to organize efforts at each level according to three roles: to assist, to link together, and to develop. Hence, the reader is provided a simple three-by-three grid in which to begin plotting the various actions of supervisors in practice (see Figure 3.1).

SUPERVISION AT THE DISTRICT LEVEL

The size of the school district, more than any other single variable, determines the placement of the supervisor. As the reader can see from Table 3.1, there are few large school districts in the United States, but they enroll the majority of pupils. This means that one common pattern of supervision would be a placement at the district level with various responsibilities.

In the largest districts, supervisors would probably be specialized, holding titles such as Mathematics Supervisor, Program Manager, or Instructional Coordinator. If the district was midsized (2500–5000 pupils) the title would be broader, such as Supervisor or General

Figure 3.1
Various Tasks of Instructional Supervision

Assisting	Linking	Developing
District		
1. Serving as resource person	1. Interpreting laws	1. Recruiting teachers
2. Serving as major committee member	2. Adopting texts	2. Interpreting research
3. Managing special projects	3. Hiring consultants	3. Planning inservice
4. Maintaining resources	4. Conducting public relations	4. Seeking other resources
School		
1. Involving others in instruction	1. Communicating policy	1. Developing school improvement plans
2. Overseeing visitations	2. Reviewing discipline	2. Initiating new programs
3. Supervising testing	3. Coordinating special services	
4. Overseeing budgeting		
Classroom		
1. Orienting new teachers	1. Observing and evaluating teachers	1. Finding lighthouse classes
2. Resolving crisis	2. Demonstrating teaching	2. Gathering information about students for teachers
3. Interpreting instructional materials		

Supervisor, or Elementary Supervisor. The six common types of districts in the United States are presented in Figure 3.2.

Activities at the district level can be roughly divided into those that assist the superintendent and other district officials, those that link the district with school-level operations, and those in which the supervisor is actually developing instructional programs. The following activities are offered as examples of supervision work and should not be construed as comprehensive in nature.

Assisting Tasks

1. Serving as a Resource Person. Supervisors are always on duty to assist the superintendent and staff at a variety of functions. You will find supervisors at school board meetings providing information, you will find them in community meetings representing the district, and sometimes you will find the supervisor meeting with the public to interpret school district policy or procedures.

2. Member of Major Committees. Because the supervision role does cut across layers of bureaucracy and functions of other leaders, the supervisor tends to be a member of most major committees at the district level. Curriculum committees, instructional resource committees, and special program committees are examples of memberships held by the supervisor. It is quite common for the supervisor to chair many of these committees as a technique of facilitating vertical communication in the district.

3. Managing Special Projects. On an ad hoc (temporary) basis, school

Table 3.1
Size of School Districts in the United States

| Enrollment Size | School Systems | | Pupils Enrolled | |
	Number	Percent	Number (in thousands)[a]	Percent
1	2	3	4	5
Total	13,500	100.0	42,944	100.00
25,000 or more	201	1.5	11,984	27.9
10,000 to 24,999	561	4.2	7,435	17.3
5,000 to 9,999	1,505	11.0	7,698	17.9
2,500 to 4,999	2,088	15.5	7,194	16.8
1,000 to 2,499	2,400	18.0	5,670	13.2
600 to 999	1,800	13.5	1,442	3.4
300 to 599	2,214	16.4	1,014	2.4
1 to 299	2,434	18.0	508	1.2
None[b]	298	2.0	0	.0

Source: U.S. Department of Health, Education, and Welfare, National Center for Education Statistics, *Education Directory, Public School Systems, 1989-90.*
[a]Enrollment data are not strictly comparable from state to state.
[b]Systems not operating schools.
Note: The above data on school systems and enrollment differ slightly from those published in *Statistics of Public elementary and Seconday Day Schools, Fall 1989.* Because of rounding, details in columns 4 and 5 do not add to totals.

districts deploy themselves to handle special events or projects. A bond issue campaign, the United Way drive, or an exchange program with a sister school district in a foreign nation are all examples of special projects that might be managed by a supervisor at the district level.

Figure 3.2
Common School Districts in U.S.

State Districts. Hawaii is the only state that has only one school district for the entire state. Alaska's District One, the largest geographical school district in the country, contains all the schools in the state except a few in cities and villages that are controlled partially by city councils.

County Districts. In some southeastern states and in Nevada, Utah, and Louisiana, the county is the operating unit for both elementary and secondary school districts. Florida, for example, has sixty-seven counties and sixty-seven school districts.

Common Districts. Most western states and New York, Ohio, Michigan, South Carolina, and Mississippi have common school districts. Common districts are often small, and are often in rural areas. A recent trend has been to combine such districts into larger units.

City Districts. Many states permit large cities to operate their own school systems because larger cities present unique problems of organization and governance.

Town and Township Units. Many school districts in New England, Indiana, New Jersey, and Pennsylvania are organized on a town or township basis. Towns usually comprise a village and the rural area surrounding it, while townships often do not seem to be logical natural units.

Regional Districts. California, Illinois, New Jersey, and New York have local school districts that have combined to form regional high school districts, while the local districts continue to operate separate elementary schools. A parent may have children who attend school in two separate districts. In a few areas of the country, a superintendent may oversee both an elementary and a high school district at the same time, and have to deal with two separate school boards.

Pennsylvania has a unique school unit called the Intermediate Unit (I.U.). The I.U. is governed by an appointed school superintendent and a school board along with superintendents of the member school districts it serves. The I.U. serves as a resource unit for special programs for exceptional children and as a source for inservice training of teachers and administrators. Although it does not operate any schools, it does provide special teachers, materials, and even bus service to students in the districts it serves.

Other states, such as New York, Nebraska, Michigan, Washington, and Wisconsin, have established special purpose or supplementary service districts that serve a number of local school districts.

Obviously, such projects are seen as collateral duties rather than primary responsibilities by a supervisor's superiors.

4. Maintenance of Resources. Medium and large school districts tend to have considerable resources in the district offices of the school system and someone must be responsible for these items. Seeing that a television studio or professional library is maintained is often part of the written or "understood" job description of a supervisor.

Linking Tasks

1. Interpreting Laws and Regulations. A common task of supervision in the 1990s is keeping others informed of new laws and regulations that affect practice at the district, school, and classroom level. Almost every state in the nation has recently enacted legislation to ensure greater accountability in schools, and this has meant increased regulation in the schools. Coordination of activities within the district to comply with these mandates is an example of a linking function at the district level.

2. Adopting Textbooks. In most states, textbooks are screened at the state level and placed on an acceptable adoption list. Districts then select from these acceptable texts those that meet their instructional needs. Supervisors, representing the districts, are often on these state committees that select books. Supervisors are also in school buildings working with teacher committees to identify instructional needs that would guide selection.

3. Hiring Consultants. One of the most important duties of the instructional supervisor is to find adequate help for teachers who need remediation or are trying to expand their capacities in the classroom. Supervisors are often sent to state and national meetings to find a consultant to help the district with a problem area. Knowing the real needs of the schools and finding the kind of consultant who can be useful for those needs represents another example of a linking task.

4. Conducting Public Relations. Supervisors are often the representative of the superintendent in school buildings. They also bring back information from the field about what is working and what needs fixing. Because of this district office/field pattern, the supervisor is strategically placed to recognize public relations opportunities and to pursue them for the district. By the same token, when there is an inquiry to the district from the media or concerned community members, supervisors are often asked to field the questions because they "know what's happening" in the schools.

Development Tasks

1. Recruiting and Selecting Teachers. While larger school districts have personnel offices that recruit and select teachers, many smaller districts (those under 5,000 students) leave this task to supervisors. The rationale for this delegation is, of course, that the supervisors know the needs of schools and are often available to "break away" for recruitment activities. This task is probably one of the most important given to the supervisor because, in the long run, he or she can place a large number of quality teachers in the right spot.

2. Interpreting Research. Supervisors are "information addressees" on nearly all paperwork going through the school district. They have a need to know what is happening in other areas, and many actually have a broader "routing slip" list than even the superintendent. Part of this constant information flow is educational research coming from both inside the district and from the outside. It is the supervisor's task to be alert to changes that might contribute to improved instruction and to translate that incoming information into a form useful to teachers.

3. Planning Inservice Activities. An area where supervisors can truly influence the classroom instructional program is in the selective application of inservice for teachers. Many supervisors let this key leadership behavior become a monotonous and routine activity, while the best supervisors see inservice as a prescriptive activity to overcome diagnosed problem areas.

4. Seeking Additional Resources. One of the most developmental tasks of supervision is to identify and secure additional resources for schools. Most school districts in the United States have less than 5 percent discretionary funds after taking away salaries and operating costs. This means, frankly, that instructional improvement can be a slow process due to the unavailability of funding for planned change. The alert supervisor looks for resources, writes grant proposals, and otherwise sees additional resources as the means of accelerating instructional improvement. During the past twenty years, this quality in supervision behavior has distinguished many practicing supervisors.

SUPERVISION AT THE SCHOOL LEVEL

While most supervisors, by title, are found in the district offices, they obviously go into schools to practice their roles. In the very largest and the very smallest districts, for different reasons, supervisors may be physically located in the school building. If the district is large, this building supervisor may be called Instructional Coordinator or Assistant Principal for Instruction. In districts with only one or two schools, the supervisor, the principal, and even the superintendent may reside in the same building. Although most of America's 100,000 buildings do not have a resident supervisor, almost all have the services of supervisors who visit classrooms.

The organization of school buildings has a lot to do with how supervisors work to improve instruction. Some buildings are organized by subject areas (departments). Others utilize a "team of teachers" approach across a grade level or across subjects. Still others have individual teachers who are generalists. Regardless of the internal organization, supervisors perform certain assisting, linking, and development tasks, some of which are outlined here.

Assisting Tasks

1. Involving Others in Instructional Improvement. Because the number of teachers in a single school building may range from ten to well over 100, it is inconceivable that one supervisor could upgrade instruction alone. A task that remains challenging is to involve others in assessing, designing, implementing and evaluating instruction. Making this task more difficult in the 1990s is the degree of restriction to such a process found in collective bargaining agreements.

Of particular importance in any school is helping the teaching staff understand and select an approach to instruction that can be refined. Without the direction coming from a philosophy and goals, school programs meander, become targets of social pressure, and often operate in a state of programmatic contradiction.

2. Overseeing Visitations to the School. Any number of groups may wish to visit schools during a school year. Some will be on official business such as accreditation teams or consultants from the state department of education. Others may wish to study the school (researchers) or observe the school (citizen groups) or to see special aspects of the program (other schools). Because the contact point for such visits is usually at the district level, supervisors often assist in the scheduling and coordination of visitations.

3. Supervising Testing. Testing of students is usually organized at the building level and reported on a building-by-building basis. It often falls to the supervisor, however, to plan, schedule and coordinate the testing programs. In small districts, the supervisor may even physically administer standardized tests as one means of ensuring uniform testing conditions throughout the district. In this role, the supervisor merely assists the building principal who is ultimately responsible for carrying out a testing program in his or her building.

4. Overseeing Instructional Budgeting. In most school districts, principals are given a budget for the year that has been developed by the superintendent and adopted by the Board. Supervisors play an important role in budgeting by helping principals develop a list of instructional needs and then serving as an advocate for those needs during the development of the districtwide budget. In the absence of an active supervisory role, the budget development process can become mechanical with all schools — for instance, getting last year's budget plus 5 percent, regardless of needs.

Linking Tasks

1. Communicating District Policy. Under the United States Constitution, education is a state right. In most states, however, the implementation of law and regulations is delegated to local school districts. With the myriad of federal programs and state laws initiated since 1980, most local districts have been very busy updating policies by which they operate.

Translating Board decisions and interpreting state and federal laws affecting instruction are often left to the school supervisor. In this role the supervisor meets with the local administrator and key personnel to outline changes that are mandated. The supervisor is also responsible to see that these policies are being implemented at the building level. Examples that might fall into this task area would be special education requirements, gifted program regulations, or state laws affecting time-on-task.

2. Reviewing Discipline Decisions. Schools vary tremendously on how they work with students to maintain discipline. Almost always, local administrators implement discipline programs that fit within district guidelines. As a safeguard against abuse, particularly in the case of paddlings or suspensions, the supervisor may be assigned to routinely review discipline decisions. If there is an excessive pattern of some form of discipline at the building level, the supervisor would meet with the principal to clarify the condition.

3. Coordinating Special Services. In districts with more than one school, the coordination of special services is an important task sometimes served by supervisors. Special services are those things that districts do for students that fall outside the normal classroom teaching.

Examples of special services would be linkage with outside agencies (social workers, health agencies, law enforcement), special resources for students (handicapped facilities), and coordination of special services provided by community groups (the Lions Club's vision programs or the Shriners' treatment centers).

While many of these services are handled directly through programs such as Special Education, it is the coordination of these services that concerns the supervisor. Are services available to all students in the district? Is there a duplication of services? Are there additional services that might be made available to students?

Development Tasks

Even though much of the work of the supervisor at the building level is concerned with tying school programs to district policy, supervisors do engage in activities that help schools improve their overall programs. We call these "development tasks" because they provide the supervisor with the opportunity to advocate new directions as well as maintain existing programs.

1. School Improvement Plans. Because of the cyclical nature of the school year in the United States (nine months on, three months off), many schools simply reinvent the same program each year. If the staff turns over or the principal leaves, there can be an erosion of instructional quality. One way to overcome this condition is through the School Improvement Plan, a long-range effort to develop desired programs.

Supervisors usually implement School Improvement Plans by leading the faculty through a series of steps to clarify the goals of the existing program and identify the discrepancies between what is desired and what currently exists. The difference between this ideal and reality then becomes a series of instructional targets scheduled over several years' time. This topic, called a Curriculum Management Plan at the district level, is the subject of a section in Chapter Ten.

2. Initiation of New Programs. Supervisors often bring new ideas to the local school because they have a greater opportunity to learn what is going on in other schools within and outside the district. As these new ideas are gathered, the supervisor initiates a novel program. This "pollination" role is one of the most important played by the instructional supervisor. Examples of new programs might include gifted education, classroom management, or programs to increase critical thinking and creativity.

SUPERVISION AT THE CLASSROOM LEVEL

Historically, the heart of supervision is what the supervisor does with the teacher in the classroom. You will remember that the "real" curriculum is what teachers do with students, as opposed to the "planned" curriculum that may be found in guides or even school-based plans. It is important, then, that supervisors get into classrooms to see what is really going on and to ensure that what is "intended" is, in fact, delivered.

In contrast to the work at the district and school level, where the supervisor may be seen as a kind of technician, supervisory work in the classroom is always interpersonal. Supervisors in classrooms are dealing with the most "human" organization in the adult world, where supervisor power and teacher rights are a gray area still being defined in the 1990s. To be effective, the supervisor must have special "people" skills that precede the more technical skills.

Assisting Tasks

1. Orienting New Teachers. A task that falls to supervisors in most districts is orienting new classroom teachers. This can be as superficial as a one-day meeting to tell them about paperwork to an intense year-long evaluation-guided process such as the Florida Beginning Teacher Program.

Even though it can be expected that principals will work with new teachers to make them feel comfortable in their buildings, the supervisor should not assume that new teachers will clearly understand the larger instructional picture on the job. Since teacher isolation in a contained classroom is a classic problem in most school buildings, supervisors should press vigorously for a district-level training program during the teachers' first year.

2. General Crisis Resolution. Teachers have needs, both in and out of their classrooms, and one of the most important tasks for supervisors is to be available to troubleshoot problems and help teachers to be effective. The resolution of teachers' personal and professional crises can ultimately be rationalized as contributing to the improvement of classroom conditions.

The supervisor's advantage in this crisis resolution role, over the building principal, is the "general understanding" of conditions he brings to the setting. The supervisor, for example, knows of similar situations in other buildings. The supervisor may actually recognize a pattern from a larger experience background. The supervisor may also be aware of a resource beyond the school to help solve the existing problem.

3. Interpreting Instructional Materials. During the past twenty-five years there has been a significant change in the way curriculum development occurs in American schools. Prior to 1960, teachers developed instructional materials and used textbooks, where appropriate, as a back-up instructional resource. Today, due to the complexity of the media, most curriculum development comes from publishing companies who hire curriculum experts to design and develop "programs." These curricula generally combine text, worksheets, and media and are often tied to a testing program so that results can be calculated for the sake of accountability.

The supervisor, in leading instructional improvement, spends much time helping teachers understand and use such materials. In particular, the supervisor must ensure that if an instructional "system" is in place it is being used as designed by the publisher.

Linking Tasks

1. Observing and Evaluating Teachers. The most historic role of supervision is to observe and judge teachers. In the old days, supervisors conducted such inspections according to a picture in their heads of what a "good" teacher should be. Today, school districts are much more concerned that the teacher be "effective," achieving desired results as the curriculum is delivered.

Supervisors today should enter classrooms to look for those skills that, according to research, contribute to instructional effectiveness. Their task in this role is to link the performance of the teacher with the expectations of the instructional program. Seen in this light, there are no "good" or "bad" teachers, only "effective" or "ineffective" ones. Evaluation should be a measure of how effective a teacher is in doing what is intended by the instructional plan.

2. Demonstration Teaching. The ultimate accountability for a supervisor, from a teacher's standpoint, is the ability to practice what is preached. Teachers repeatedly have observed that a supervisor "preaches" at them, but rarely can deliver whatever is asked for in a live classroom environment.

As a linking task, demonstration teaching seeks to close the gap between the desired and the actual condition of teaching. Some of the generic skills that might be demonstrated to any teacher in any subject are addressed in Chapter Six.

Development Tasks

1. Finding Lighthouse Classrooms. The mobile supervisor will soon notice that some teachers are mediocre, some are strong, and some are truly outstanding. A task that leads to an improved instructional program is the identification and spotlighting of the best classrooms in the district. These classrooms, when identified, serve as a "lighthouse" to other teachers who are struggling or who are at rest in their instructional patterns.

Once these model classrooms have been identified, the supervisor should initiate a process that enables other teachers to observe the procedures or skills of the best teachers. This process, of course, must be handled tactfully so that those teachers who lack the skills of others will remain openminded to the experience.

2. Gathering Information About Students. The authors believe that one of the most important tasks fulfilled by a supervisor is gathering information to help teachers "see" the students they are teaching. It is a reality of teaching that people tend to get into a pattern of behavior and stick to it. When a routine becomes so ingrained that teachers no longer remember the ultimate purpose of a general education, or are unable to recognize unique differences among students, the teacher becomes ineffective.

An example of providing information to teachers is one commonly found at the high school level today. Because of the mobility of students and their parents in the 1990s, high school faculties sometimes fail to realize that, for instance, a college-bound curriculum no longer effectively serves a student body where the majority of graduates no longer go to college.

SUPERVISION IN PRACTICE

As we have seen in this chapter, supervisors operate in a number of different environments to improve the instructional experience for students. Some of these environments are impersonal and some are quite personal. Most supervisors operate in both a managerial and an interpersonal setting and must be able to apply skills selectively to be effective.

We have also noted that supervision tasks can be thought of as either supporting (assisting), coordinating (linking), or building (developing) school programs. The degree of emphasis on any or all of these three tasks is often a matter of philosophy and role-definition by the supervisor or his or her superiors.

What is clear is that it is very difficult to describe *the* supervisor in American education or even to describe realistically the job role unless we consider environment and the general orientation toward the position in a district. We can, however, begin to see supervision as a role, clearly, if we focus on the skills that are employed by the supervisor. Regardless of the level of operation, the title of the supervisor, or whether the supervisor is tractive or dynamic, the skills of supervision are constants.

The authors have identified eight key skills of supervision that will become the focus of the second section of this book:

Aiding Human Development

Designing and Developing Curriculum

Improving Classroom Instruction

Encouraging Human Relations

Providing Staff Development

Fulfilling Administrative Functions

Managing Change for Accountability

Evaluating for Effectiveness

Each of these areas is explored in depth to assist the reader in learning how the skill affects the quality of classroom instruction. From this review of each area it is expected that the reader should apply these skills to the environment in which he or she practices or hopes to practice.

NEW DIRECTIONS

Supervision in this decade will mean more than improving schools. Harold L. Hodgkinson in his 1989 study "The Same Client: The Demographics of Education and Service Delivery Systems," pointed out that while it is true that schools could do a better job of educating students, many other systems also affect the kind of education students receive: housing, transportation, and health care.[1] Albert Shanker, in his December 31, 1989 *New York Times* column, also pointed out the impact of lack of services on poor children in American schools.[2]

Housing is critical to school-age children. With no place to study and a noisy environment, there is little chance that a child could succeed in school. Being evicted or living on the streets can be so demeaning to a child that her self-concept is destroyed.

Without public transportation, poor parents cannot get to work. Not getting to work on time can result in losing a job, not paying the rent; this in turn affects the relative stability needed by children.

Health care is another area that affects children. Pregnant women who receive no prenatal care or who take drugs are likely to increase the number of handicapped students in our schools.

Supervision in the new age of social services may involve inter-action with many social agencies, both private and public. It may well involve a new kind of political involvement on the part of supervisors as they become advocates for at-risk children both inside and outside school settings.

SUMMARY

Supervisors operate at many levels under many titles. The tasks of supervision often overlap other roles in a school setting. Nonethe-less, supervisors are usually positioned at the junction of leadership. Their mobility within the three levels of practice—the district, the school, and the classroom—give them a unique perspective of school operations.

In this chapter we have looked at each level of operation in terms of tasks that assist, link, or develop school programs. These examples are not intended to include all of the tasks of supervision, but rather to suggest that supervisors will operate in all three levels with various orientations. The ultimate choice of where to apply supervisory skills and whether the intent of those skills is to support or change existing programs is usually up to the supervisor. That choice is philosophical and is related to how the supervisor sees the mission of the school.

Ultimately, the authors believe that the skills of supervision, rather than the tasks or titles, provide a way of understanding the field. They present the reader in the following chapters with eight general skills that have multiple applications in the schools of the United States.

NOTES

1. Harold L. Hodgkinson, "The Same Client: The Demographics of Education and Service Delivery Systems," Center for Demographic Policy Institute for Educational Leadership, Washington, D.C., September, 1989.
2. Albert Shanker, "Educating Poor Children: It's More Than Fixing Schools," *New York Times*, December 31, 1989, 7E.

SUGGESTED LEARNING ACTIVITIES

1. Develop a conceptual model showing the relationship of supervi-sion at the district, school, and classroom levels.
2. Identify why, in your own words, supervision is so difficult to de-scribe and define.
3. List six events in education today that will have an impact on the tasks of supervision at either the district, school or classroom level.

BOOKS TO REVIEW

Harris, Ben. *Supervisory Behavior In Education*, 3rd ed. Englewood Cliffs, NJ: Prentice-Hall, Inc., 1985.

Hyman, Ronald. *School Administrator's Faculty Supervision Handbook.* Englewood Cliffs, NJ: Prentice Hall, Inc., 1986.

Krey, Robert and Burke, Peter, *Design For Instructional Supervision.* New York: Charles Thomas, 1989.

Marks, James. *Handbook For Educational Supervision: A Guide For The Practitioner.* New York: Longwood Division Of Allyn And Bacon, Inc., 1985.

Maeroff, Gene. *The Empowerment Of Teachers.* New York: Teachers College Press, 1988.

Oliva, Peter. *Supervision For Today's Schools*, 3rd ed. New York: Longman Inc., 1988.

Wood, John. *The Secondary School Principal: Manager And Supervisor*, 2nd ed. Boston: Allyn And Bacon, 1985.

PART TWO

SKILL AREAS OF SUPERVISION

CHAPTER 4

Aiding Human Development

INTRODUCTION

Supervision, as a leadership specialty in professional education, is first about helping people grow and develop. Schools are human organizations; their ultimate product is an adjusted and knowledgeable young adult. It is the job of the supervisor in schools to work with people to improve the educational process and to aid the growth and development of students. In working with teachers, supervisors must never forget that the improvement of teaching is a means, not an end. The end to which all supervision contributes is a better learning experience to aid human development.

Having made this observation, it follows that all supervisors must know how children grow and develop. They must possess some conception or model of normal development, and they must fully understand patterns of deviation in growth and development. Finally, supervisors must possess a skill that allows them to clearly link the development of students to the instructional programs and behaviors of teachers. Without such an understanding of development and the linking of instruction to development outcomes, the schooling experience is reduced to a mindless process based on the historical repetition of academic activity.

A good starting place for the development of such a skill in supervisors is to look comprehensively at the growth and development of school students, using as a tool some of the better known models of growth.

MODELS OF HUMAN GROWTH

The past twenty-five years have seen many contributions to our understanding of how humans develop. While statistical summaries have been available throughout the century, the patterns of growth are now much clearer thanks to the contribution of many "models" of development. These models are not certain prescriptions of how each person will develop, but they do provide us with a way of "seeing" the entire process of development. Some of these models focus on physical growth, some on social and emotional development, and some on intellectual growth. The utility of these models for supervisors is that they provide the "big picture" of the unfolding process of student development, thereby organizing the many isolated pieces of information encountered in school environments.

Models of physical development are plentiful in the literature of education and psychology. For nearly ninety years educators have measured and charted growth patterns of infants and children. It is possible to predict with considerable precision the normal course of motor development from birth to three years of age:

Birth	Exhibits reflex behavior Motor behavior highly variable Head sags when not supported
3 months	Holds head erect and steady Reaches for objects but misses Steps when held erect
6 months	Bears weight when in standing position No thumb apposition yet Can follow distant object with eyes
12 months	Can walk with support Can sit up alone, pull self upright Places objects on top of one another
24 months	Walks well Can kick large ball Can turn pages of book one at a time
36 months	Rides a tricycle Can button and unbutton Walks down steps with alternative footing.[1]

Most models of physical development are constructed from statistical averages gleaned from studies of large numbers of children. Information from the studies is useful to the supervisor in planning physical education programs, developing facility specifications, analyzing art curricula, and a lot of other everyday instructional tasks.

Another set of models (Figure 4.1) available to supervisors traces the growth and development patterns in terms of social progression. Probably the best-known of these models are the "Developmental Tasks" first suggested by sociologist Robert Havighurst.[2]

The developmental tasks focus on those things that children must master to grow up in American society. These maturation

Figure 4.1
Aiding Human Development

Examples of Developmental Tasks

Adolescence
Emancipation from parent-dependency
Occupational projection-selection
Completion of value structure
Acceptance of self

Preadolescence
Handling major body changes
Asserting independence from family
Establishing sex role identity
Dealing with peer group relationships
Controlling emotions
Constructing a values foundation
Pursuing interest expression
Utilizing new reasoning capacities
Developing acceptable self-concept

Late Childhood
Mastering communication skill
Building meaningful peer relations
Thinking independently
Acceptance of self
Finding constructive expression outlets
Role projection

Middle Childhood
Structuring the physical world
Refining language and thought patterns
Establishing relationships with others
Understanding sex roles

Early Childhood
Developing motor control
Emerging self-awareness
Mapping out surroundings
Assigning meaning to events
Exploring relationships with others
Developing language and thought patterns

measures occur both in and outside of school. For supervisors they indicate student interests and potential sources of motivation for classroom teachers at various levels of development.

Still another model of social development is provided by Abraham Maslow in his Hierarchy of Needs:

Self-Realization and Fulfillment

Esteem and Status

Belonging and Social Activity

Safety and Security

Physiological Needs

According to Maslow, human beings tend to their personal/social needs in a specified order of development. At the bottom of this list, and always satisfied first, are physiological needs (food, sleep). The most sophisticated human needs concern finding meaning in life. According to Maslow, an individual cannot satisfy higher needs until lower needs have been met.

This single model could go a long way toward explaining student behavior in school. Children who are hungry are poor students. Students who are insecure at home or in school are poor students. Students who need attention or friends are rarely good students. Even students who are "hung up" on being recognized (grade chasing) are not good students. Helping students clear out those lower level needs that retard academic performance is a worthy task for any teacher who wants discipline in the classroom and students fully engaged in the learning process.

One of the most interesting models of emotional development to be contributed during the last twenty years is the Stages of Moral Development by Lawrence Kohlberg.[3] Kohlberg's concern with how children gain self-control resulted in a six-tier model:

Levels	*Stages*
1. Preconventional	1. The punishment and obedience orientation
	2. The instrumental-relativist orientation
2. Conventional	3. The interpersonal concordance orientation
	4. The "law and order" orientation
3. Postconventional	5. The social-contract legalistic orientation
	6. The universal ethical-principle orientation

In his model, Kohlberg sees little children behaving because of a fear of punishment by larger authority figures. At some point around the middle school age, however, the student must assume an internal code of behavior if he or she is to behave moralistically as an adult. It is interesting to think about the discipline programs of schools and their contribution, if any, to this transition by the student. It is equally interesting to think about the consequences for a society if the student does not assume responsibility for his or her behavior in growing up.

Finally, there are a number of models of intellectual growth available to supervisors, the best-known of which is Jean Piaget's Theory of Intellectual Development.[4] According to this model, the development of the mind occurs in four distinct stages, somewhat related to chronological age, and the pattern of development is a defined path that never varies:

Age 0–2	Sensorimotor stage–	Trial and error learning based on organized motor activity.
Age 2–7	Preoperational stage–	Use of symbols to represent objects. Development of language and use of dramatic play.
Age 7–11	Concrete Operations–	Use of concepts. Logical thinking.
Age 11–15	Formal Operations–	Use of abstract as well as concrete thinking.

Piaget's model, while badly overextended by many educators, does provide a way of thinking about mental maturation. Questions, such as when a young person becomes capable of abstract thinking, have tremendous implications for academic programming in areas like math and science. Supervisors need to see this development as one measure of the appropriateness of content and instructional methodology.

Models such as those outlined direct our understanding of the quantitative growth and development of students in school. It is helpful to know, for instance, that first graders are about forty-six inches tall and weigh just under fifty pounds while sixth graders should approach five feet in height and weigh about ninety-plus pounds. These data and these models, then, speak to us about normal development and what we can anticipate in working with children. They also should alert us to "qualitative" growth, leaps in functioning, intelligence, creative capacity and such, that make individuals distinct and unique.

Supervisors can easily organize their thinking about school programs in terms of four general stages of development: early childhood (grades K–3), late childhood (grades 4–5), preadolescence (grades 6–8), and adolescence (grades 9–12). They should not, however, lose sight of the fact that the normal range of development at any stage is a wide spectrum of differences. See, for instance, the portrait of a thirteen-year-old eighth grader as described by this anonymous student:

PORTRAIT OF A THIRTEEN YEAR OLD

6 ft. 2 inches in height	OR	4 ft. 7 inches
So awkward that she trips going up the stairs	OR	Olympic gold medal winner with a perfect 10.0 in parallel bar competition
Alcoholic, drug addict	OR	Sunday school leader, Little leaguer
Wears mouth braces	OR	Competes in Miss Teenage America
Curious and enthusiastic learner	OR	Turned off and looking forward to quitting school
Unable to read the comic page	OR	Reads The Wall Street Journal
Has trouble with whole numbers	OR	Can solve geometry problems
A regular in juvenile court	OR	An Eagle Scout
Already a mother of two	OR	Still plays with dolls

If supervisors understand these models for the normal development of students in school, they can better identify abnormal deviations from healthy growth—a key role for supervision. Table 4.1 illustrates a checklist used in one school district to identify students in need of assistance.

THE GROWTH ENVIRONMENT

In addition to knowing about how growth occurs in students, it is also important to recognize fully the environment in which development occurs. No other single factor has so influenced the planning of school programs in the past two decades as the changing milieu of the American society.

It is not an overstatement to say that the traditional American society as we have known it for two hundred years is in the process of reformation. Once a nurturing environment characterized by strong institutions and a nuclear family structure, the American society of the 1990s is splintered into a new series of arrangements that reflect an adjustment to an emerging economic order. The following statistics are offered for the reader's consideration:

- □ The divorce rate in the United States has increased 121 percent in twenty years.
- □ The combined total of stepfamilies and single-parent families exceeds the number of "intact" families in America.
- □ For the first time in our history, the typical school child has a mother in the work force.
- □ Many children are unattended during the work day including some 50,000 children under age 8 who are alone at home most of the day.
- □ One-half of the children living in a family where the mother is the primary support live in poverty as compared with 8 percent of "traditional" families. The average income for female households with children is one-third that of married couples.
- □ The average American family will move ten times in its lifespan.
- □ It is estimated that as many as 30 percent of all girls and 10 percent of all boys experience some form of child abuse before age 18.
- □ Children ages 5–14 are being killed at triple the rate of 1950 in the United States.
- □ Illegitimate births among teens age 15–19 have increased dramatically since 1960. Abortions by unmarried girls in the same age group have also increased dramatically.
- □ Preschool children spend one-fourth of their waking hours in front of the television. Elementary school children spend more time on TV than on homework, reading and chores combined.
- □ Less than 20 percent of households have children in them.[5]

These figures, while shocking, only tell part of the story. For most black schoolchildren, the plight is even more acute. In 1990, in households headed by a female, 71 percent are below poverty. Only 40 percent of black children live with their natural parents. Today, over one-half of all black children are born out of wedlock, and the infant mortality rate for those infants is twice that of white babies.[6]

As shocking as these statistics are, they reveal only the tip of the iceberg in terms of the impact of these conditions on schooling. What was once considered "normal" readiness for the school experience is being reconsidered. The "typical" family support for schooling is being redefined. And, the role and tasks for education at all levels has been called into question. Supervisors need to be familiar with local conditions in their communities to assist principals and teachers in considering these environmental concerns.

Table 4.1
Checklist for Identifying Students Who May Need Educational Therapy

1. Gross motor and motor flexibility
   _____ incoordination and poor balance
   _____ difficulty with jumping—skipping—hopping (below age 9)
   _____ confusion in games requiring imitation of movements
   _____ poor sense of directionality
   _____ inept in drawing and writing at chalkboard
   _____ inaccuracies in copying at chalkboard
   _____ eyes do not work together
   _____ eyes lose or overshoot target

2. Physical fitness
   _____ tires easily
   _____ lacks strength

3. Auditory acuity, perception, memory—speech
   _____ confuses similar phonetic and phonic elements
   _____ inconsistent pronunciation of words usually pronounced correctly by
           peers
   _____ repeats, but does not comprehend
   _____ forgets oral directions, if more than one or two

4. Visual acuity, perception, memory
   _____ complains that he cannot see blackboard
   _____ says that words move or jump
   _____ facial expression strained
   _____ holds head to one side while reading

5. Hand-eye coordination
   _____ difficulty in tracing—copying—cutting—folding—pasting—coloring at
   _____ desk; lack of success with puzzles—yo-yo's—toys involving targets,
           etc.

CATEGORIES OF SPECIAL LEARNERS

If there is a single major difference between schools of the 1960s and 1990s, it would be that the impact of our knowledge of human development has caused specialization in designing educational programs. Schools of the 1990s are characterized by the labeling of learners according to special needs and the development of curriculum programs to accommodate individual differences. It is essential that supervisors master the many categories of students to help teachers understand and respond to the many needs found in schools.

As sensitive people, educators have a long history of working with students having special needs. Until 1975, most of these efforts in public school settings were carried out in special rooms within

6. Language
   _____ has difficulty understanding others
   _____ has difficulty associating and remembering
   _____ has difficulty expressing himself

7. Intellectual functioning
   _____ unevenness of intellectual development
   _____ learns markedly better through one combination of sensory avenues than another

8. Personality
   _____ overreacts to school failures
   _____ does not seem to know he has a problem
   _____ will not admit he has a problem

9. Academic problems
   _____ can't tolerate having his routine disturbed
   _____ knows it one time and doesn't the next
   _____ writing neat, but slow
   _____ writing fast, but sloppy
   _____ passes the spelling test, but can't spell functionally
   _____ math accurate, but slow
   _____ math fast, but inaccurate
   _____ reads well orally, but has poor comprehension
   _____ does poor oral reading, but comprehends better than would be expected
   _____ lacks word attack skills
   _____ has conceptual—study skill—organizational problems in content areas

10. Parents
   _____ seemingly uninformed about nature of learning problem
   _____ seemingly unrealistic toward student's problems

Source: Jon Wiles and Joseph C. Bondi, *Curriculum Development: A Guide to Practice,* 3rd ed. (Columbus, OH: Merrill), 1989. Used with permission.

school buildings or in special schools for categories of students like the physically handicapped. However, the many kinds of learners with special needs and the expense of serving these learners sometimes caused service to be less than uniform. Three laws enacted at the federal level between 1965 and 1975 sought to organize all of the existing programs and spell out, legally, what the rights and obligations of special education were.

   P.L. 89-313 (1965)—This law amended Title I legislation to provide funds to state agencies for supplementing education for handicapped children in state-operated schools.

   P.L. 93-112 (1973)—This law (section 504) first provided that handicapped persons could not be discriminated against due to their handicap. Architectural barriers for handicapped persons were also eliminated by regulations under this law.

P.L. 94-142 (1975) — This law authorized a series of grants to state agencies to "initiate, expand, and improve" educational programs for the handicapped. The law also established the Bureau of the Handicapped in the U.S. Office of Education.

Unlike previous laws, Public Law 94-142 (Education For All Handicapped Children Act) promoted regular education for handicapped children at full public expense. The bill called for the identification of handicapped children, a thorough evaluation of their needs and a developed Individual Education Plan (IEP), free appropriate public education in the "least restrictive environment," and procedural safeguards for the process. It was the least restrictive environment clause (known as "mainstreaming") that provided the greatest challenge to schools in implementing this benchmark legislation, but fifteen years after passage the bill is fully implemented. (Table 4.2 outlines the major principles of Public Law 94-142.)

The result of the various laws and regulations concerning special students led to some specific definitions of categories that are closely adhered to in today's schools:

Trainable mentally handicapped — A moderately mentally handicapped person is one who is impaired in intellectual and adaptive behavior and whose development reflects his reduced rate of learning. The measured intelligence of a moderately handicapped person falls approximately between 3 and 4 standard deviations below the mean (51–36 on the Stanford Binet, and 54–40 on the Wechsler), and the assessed adaptive behavior falls below age and cultural expectations.

Severely mentally handicapped — A severely mentally handicapped person is one who is impaired in intellectual and adaptive behavior and whose development reflects his reduced rate of learning. The measured intelligence of a severely handicapped person falls approximately between 4 and 5 standard deviations below the mean (35–20 on the Stanford Binet, and 39–25 on the Wechsler), and the assessed adaptive behavior falls below age and cultural expectations.

Profoundly mentally handicapped — A profoundly mentally handicapped person is one who is impaired in intellectual and adaptive behaviors and whose development reflects his reduced rate of learning. The measured intelligence of a profoundly handicapped person falls approximately five standard deviations below the mean (below 25 on the Stanford Binet) and there is limited or no adaptive behavior.

Educable mentally handicapped—An educable mentally handicapped student is one who is mildly impaired in intellectual and adaptive behavior and whose development reflects a reduced rate of learning. A student's performance on an individual psychological evaluation that indicated an approximate intellectual ability between 2 and 3 standard deviations below the mean (68–52 on the Stanford Binet, and 69–55 on the Wechsler, plus or minus 5).

Students with communicative disorders—Students with a communicative disorder may have trouble speaking, understanding others, or hearing the sounds of their world. They may have difficulty saying specific sounds or words, using words correctly, using the voice correctly, or speaking clearly and smoothly. Some students are unable to make muscles needed for speech work adequately. Other students may have a hearing problem that prevents them from understanding the teacher and others around them. Some students need help in learning words and in understanding how to put them together into sentences. To be considered for speech, language or hearing therapy services, the student should be referred to the speech, language, and hearing clinician for testing, with written permission from parent or guardian. After all testing (speech, hearing, language and any others as appropriate), a staffing committee meets to discuss the student's problem and to decide how best to help the student.

Hearing-impaired students—Students who are born with a severe hearing loss (70 dB or greater in better ear in speech frequencies), or who acquire a loss before learning language and speech, are considered deaf by state Department of Education definition. These students will be unable to learn language and speech unless they receive special education instruction. To be considered for enrollment in the Hearing Impaired Program, the student must have a medical evaluation that would include a general physical examination and an evaluation by an ear specialist (otologist) and complete hearing evaluation by an audiologist. After all testing is completed, a staffing committee meets to discuss the student's problem and to decide how best to help the student.

Specific learning disabilities—A student with specific learning disabilities has a disorder in one or more of the basic psychological processes involved in understanding or in spoken and written language. These may be manifested in disorders of listening, thinking, reading, talking, writing, spelling, or arithmetic. They include conditions that have been referred to as perceptual handicaps, brain injury, minimal brain dysfunction, dyslexia, and developmental aphasia. They *do not* include learning problems due primarily to visual, hearing, or motor handicaps, mental retardation, emotional disturbance, or an environmental disadvantage.

Table 4.2
Major Principles of Public Law 94-142

P.L. 94-142 was enacted by Congress in November, 1975. Its major purpose, as stated in the act, is as follows:

It is the purpose of this Act to assure that all handicapped children have available to them . . . a free, appropriate public education which emphasizes special education and related services designed to meet their unique needs, to assure that the rights of handicapped children and their parents or guardians are protected, to assist States and localities to provide for the education of all handicapped children, and to assess and assure the effectiveness of efforts to educate handicapped children. (Sec. 601(c)).

There are six major principles of P.L. 94-142:

1. *Principle of Zero Reject*
   This principle, simply stated, requires that *all* handicapped children be provided with a free, appropriate public education. States are required to provide full educational opportunities to all handicapped children in the age range of 3–18 by September 1, 1978 and to all handicapped children in the age range of 3–21 by September 1, 1980. This principle is implemented by conducting a child fund program on an annual basis to locate, identify and evaluate all handicapped children who reside in the jurisdiction of each public agency. If local agencies comply with this principle, they become eligible to receive federal funds based upon the number of handicapped children being served, not to exceed 12% of the school population.
   In addition to providing an educational program to all handicapped children, the public agency must insure that handicapped children have equal opportunities with nonhandicapped children to participate in nonacademic and extracurricular services. In addition, physical education must be provided to every handicapped child.

2. *Principle of Nondiscriminatory Evaluation*
   A handicapped child must receive a full individual evaluation prior to placement in a special education program. A placement decision should be made by a group of persons knowledgeable about the child, the meaning of the evaluation data, and the placement options. The placement recommendation may be suggested by the evaluation team and finalized by a committee who has the responsibility for writing the Individual Educational Plan. All handicapped children must be completely re-evaluated every three years.

3. *Individualized Educational Programs*
   The legislative approach for insuring that educational programs are tailored on an individual basis to the needs of handicapped students is through the requirement of providing individual educational plans for all handicapped students. The IEP must contain the following essentials:
   a. Current level of student's educational performance.

b. Annual goals.
c. Short-term objectives.
d. Documentation of the special education services to be provided.
e. Time the student will spend in special education and related services.
f. Time student will spend in regular education.
g. Dates for initiating service and anticipated duration.
h. Evaluation procedures and schedules for determining mastery of the objectives.

Members required to be in attendance at the IEP meeting must include the following:
a. Representative of the public agency.
b. The child's teacher.
c. Child's parents.
d. The child, when appropriate.
e. Other individuals at the request of the parents.
f. Individuals who provided the evaluation.

4. *Least Restrictive Environment*
   To the maximum extent appropriate, handicapped children should be educated with children who are not handicapped. The removal of handicapped children to special classes and separate facilities should occur only when the nature or severity of their handicap prevents them from successfully being educated in regular classes with the use of supplementary aids and services.

5. *Due Process*
   Due process is a procedure which seeks to insure the fairness of educational decisions and the accountability of both the professionals and parents making these decisions. It can be viewed as a system of checks and balances concerning the identification, evaluation, and provision of services regarding handicapped students. It may be initiated by the parent or public agency as an impartial forum for presenting complaints regarding the child's identification, evaluation, and placement or for challenging decisions made by another party.

6. *Parent Participation*
   Each of the principles has either the direct or indirect implications for parental participation. At the local level, parents should be permitted to review any educational records on their child which are used by the agency before the meeting to develop the IEP and within a 45-day period after receipt of the request.
   These six principles of P.L. 94-142 provide the basis for the legislative definition of free, appropriate public education.

To be considered for placement in a specific learning disabilities program, the student must have average to near average mental abilities, normal visual and hearing acuity, and no evidence of a primary physical handicap. Standardized achievement test scores would indicate difficulty in the basic academic areas of reading, writing, arithmetic, and/or spelling. Specialized test scores would show student difficulty in handling information received by sight and/or by hearing, in language usage and/or in fine motor skills.

Emotionally handicapped—An emotionally handicapped student is one who exhibits consistent and persistent signs of behaviors, such as withdrawal, distractibility, hyperactivity, or hypersensitivity, that disrupt the learning process.

Emotionally handicapped students show the following behaviors to the extent that they may not be served in the regular school program without at least part-time special placement or consultative services: learning problems that are not due primarily to mental retardation; severe behavior disorders that cannot be controlled or eliminated by medical intervention; inability to build or maintain satisfactory interpersonal relationships with adults and peers.

Physically handicapped—A student who has a crippling condition or other health impairment that requires an adaptation to the student's school environment or curriculum is considered physically handicapped. The student may have an impairment that interferes with the normal functions of the bones, joints, or muscles to such an extent that special arrangements must be made to provide an educational program.

The student may have a special health problem such as cardiac disorders, diabetes, epilepsy, cystic fibrosis, hemophilia, asthma, leukemia, or nephritis, that would require special arrangements to provide an educational program.

Multi-handicapped students whose primary or most severe disability is a crippling condition or other health impairment may be included in this program.

In addition to these many legal classifications and definitions, other special categories of students include gifted, talented, and creative students, disadvantaged and culturally different students, non-English speaking and bilingual students.

Gifted, talented, and creative—For years teachers have had to contend with students who, because of superior intellectual development, are capable of high academic performance. In 1972, Congress acted to establish the Office of Gifted and Talented, an act resulting in the establishment of gifted programs in schools in all fifty states. While funding for this office has been meager, identifying this special group of learners spurred research efforts that continue today. The result of such inquiry, however, has been to discredit many of the identification schema based solely on I.Q. (intelligence quotient) scores and to present a unique profile for gifted, talented, and creative thinking.

Disadvantaged and culturally different—By design our schools are the melting pot of the American society. Court decisions as well as federal and state law have mandated that children of different races and cultures be provided the opportunity to learn. In fact, the courts have even defended the rights of children who are not United States citizens to have a free public education. Among major legislation that has directly sought to aid these special learners in school are The Civil Rights Act of 1964, The Elementary and Secondary Education Act of 1965, and the Bilingual Education Act of 1968.

Cultural differences present a special problem for supervisors due to the rapidly changing ethnic ratios in some parts of the country. Maintenance of a monocultural curriculum in an all-black city system or a majority-Hispanic district of the southwest is challenging to say the least.

Non-English speaking and bilingual—The United States has always been a country that receives and assimilates new citizen groups. Recent years have brought many such groups to our shores: the Cuban influx in the 1960s, Vietnamese refugees in the 1970s, Haitian "boat people" in the 1980s, plus a continuous influx of Mexican immigrants throughout the period. Accommodating these sometimes non-English speaking students and honoring their native languages in schools has been difficult.

One other special group that presents cultural as well as language difficulties has been the mainstreaming of the Native American populations. During the 1970s and into the 1990s, Bureau of Indian Affairs schools have closed and public schools have assumed the duty of providing a public education to Indian youth. In many districts of the west, preservation of language and heritage is a primary issue of curriculum development and teacher training.

The critical concern about all of these special groups of students is that they must be served by the school programs. The practices of ignoring the needs of these students becomes impossible as their number quickly approaches one-third of all students attending school. On the other side of the coin is the danger of fragmenting the school program by placing all of the emphasis on exceptionality. A balance of general and specialized programs must be maintained.

Table 4.3
National Organizations and Agencies Concerned with Special Needs Children

ACLU Juvenile Rights Project
22 East 40th Street
New York, NY 10016

**American Academy for
Cerebral Palsy**
University Hospital School
Iowa City, IA 52240

**American Association for the
Education of Severely and
Profoundly Handicapped**
1600 West Armory Way
Garden View Suite
Seattle, WA 98119

**American Association for
Gifted Children**
15 Gramercy Park
New York, NY 10003

American Epilepsy Society
Department of Neurology
University of Minnesota
Box 341, Mayo Building
Minneapolis, MN 55455

American Foundation for the Blind
15 West 16th Street
New York, NY 10011

American Medical Association
535 North Dearborn Street
Chicago, IL 60610

**American Psychological
Association**
1200 17th Street, NW
Washington, DC 20036

**Association for the Aid of
Crippled Children**
345 East 46th Street
New York, NY 10017

**Association for Children with
Learning Disabilities**
2200 Brownsville Road
Pittsburgh, PA 16210

**Association for Education of the
Visually Handicapped**
919 Walnut
Philadelphia, PA 19107

**Bureau for Education
of the Handicapped**
400 6th Street
Donohoe Building
Washington, DC 20202

SERVICES FOR SPECIAL STUDENTS

In addition to the regular and special curricula provided for students in school, a large number of special services are provided that can be the concern of supervisors. Among these services are transportation, food provision, tutoring, and guidance. It is the area of guidance that illustrates the degree to which schools have become service industries. The reader will find here some of the specialists that interact with supervisors each day to serve students:

Counselors   deal with academic, vocational, and personal
                  problems of students.
Psychometrists   are the personnel who administer tests and
                  make interpretations and diagnoses for
                  instruction.
Psychologists   administer special tests and give individual and
                  group therapy.

Council for Exceptional Children	National Institutes of Health
1920 Association Drive	United States Department of Health,
Reston, VA 22091	Education, and Welfare
Institute for the Study of Mental Retardation and Related Disabilities	Washington, DC 20014
	National Rehabilitation Association
130 South First	1522 "K" Street, NW
University of Michigan	Washington, DC 20005
Ann Arbor, MI 48108	**President's Committee on Employment of the Handicapped**
Muscular Dystrophy Association of America	U.S. Department of Labor
810 7th Avenue	Washington, DC 20210
New York, NY 10019	**President's Committee on Mental Retardation**
National Association for Retarded Citizens	Regional Office Building #3
2709 Avenue E, East	Room 2614
P.O. Box 6109	7th and D Streets, SW
Arlington, TX 76011	Washington, DC 20201
National Association of Social Workers	
2 Park Avenue	
New York, NY 10016	
National Committee for Multi-Handicapped Children	
239 14th Street	
Niagara Falls, NY 14303	

Psychiatrists	provide help to students with deep-seated problems.
Attendance Personnel	help enforce compulsory school attendance laws.
Social workers	are also known as visiting teachers; facilitate home-school communication about student needs.
Classroom Teachers	are involved in low-level guidance functions such as advisor-advisee activities.

In providing services for students in school the supervisor needs to be aware of national organizations and agencies concerned with special needs students (Table 4.3) as well as the wide range of professional publications that specialize in providing information about these students (Table 4.4).

Finally, supervisors must make a special effort to begin to learn of the various professional examiners who may be involved in the

Table 4.4
Periodicals and Journals of Special Education

AAESPH Review (American Association for the Education of the Severely and Profoundly Handicapped)	Journal of Creative Behavior
	Journal of Learning Disabilities
	Journal of Negro Education
American Educational Research Journal	Journal of Nervous and Mental Disease
American Journal of Mental Deficiency	
American Journal of Psychology	Journal of Psychology
Aviso (Journal of Special Education)	Journal of Social Psychology
Childhood Education	Journal of Special Education
Child Welfare	Journal of Teacher Education
The Deaf American	Perceptual and Motor Skills
Developmental Psychology	Personnel and Guidance Journal
Exceptional Children	Phi Delta Kappan
Gifted Child Quarterly	Psychology in the Schools
Harvard Educational Review	Rehabilitation Digest
Journal of Abnormal Child Psychology	Review of Educational Research
Journal of Abnormal Psychology	Teacher of the Deaf
Journal of Child Psychology and Psychiatry	

identification and treatment of school children. Some of those specialists are found in Table 4.5.

ISSUES FOR INSTRUCTIONAL SUPERVISORS

This chapter has focused on the development of human beings in an institution called a school. All modern societies maintain some form of schooling to help young people develop and enter the society as a productive member. The conception of a healthy and productive citizen, more than anything else, should define the program of the school and, consequentially, the role of the supervisor. Human development, and our recent knowledge of how it occurs, raises some serious issues for all instructional supervisors.

At the general level is the issue of scope of responsibility. For what is the school responsible? We have seen that children who come to school are vastly different. Do we wish to encourage those differences or reduce them? Is there a desired pattern of development? Can we expect the same performance of all students in school? What is a comprehensive program of education to assist the growing up process? How can we maintain a balance in school programs? What is an ade-

Table 4.5
Recommended Professional Examiners for Certifying Students
for Special Education Programs

Classification	Recommended Professional Examiner
Crippled and Special Health Problems	Heart Specialists Orthopedist Pediatrician Neurologist Physician
Deaf and Hard-of-Hearing	Audiologist Othologist Otolaryngologist
Neurologically Impaired	Physician
Learning Disabled	Neurologist Psychologist
Visually Handicapped	Ophthalmologist Optometrist

quate educational offering? The instructional supervisor, more than anyone else in school leadership, will answer these very important questions.

In addition, there are a host of instructional issues tied directly to human growth and development. They are, in a sense, dilemmas for the supervisor because they present value-laden choices that can only be answered in terms of a conception of what education is for. The authors identify here a dozen of these issues as representative of the many other decision areas:

Testing. In order to meet individual needs of students, it is first necessary to assess them in a meaningful way. Schools rely heavily on testing to achieve this insight, measuring everything from personality to intelligence. In schools throughout the nation, for instance, psychometrists regularly administer the Stanford-Binet, Wechsler (WISC), and Otis-Lennon tests to identify the "intelligence" of students. These scores are interpreted as in Table 4.6, and given to teachers as one source of information for planning instruction.

The problem with such "scores" is that they depend heavily on verbal skills, hearing, vocabulary, and syntax, and can be culturally biased. They also can easily lead to a simplistic labeling of students — redbirds, bluejays, and buzzards.

How much testing should be done with students? How should testing and the results of testing be utilized? What safeguards can be built in for error or rapid changes in the developmental pattern of the

Table 4.6
The Meaning of I.Q. Scores (Stanford-Binet)

The Child Whose IQ Is:	Equals or Exceeds (percent)	The Child Whose IQ Is:	Equals or Exceeds (percent)
136	99	112	77
135	98	111	75
134	98	110	73
133	98	109	71
132	97	108	69
131	97	107	66
130	97	106	64
129	96	105	62
128	96	104	60
127	95	103	57
126	94	102	55
125	94	101	52
124	93	100	50
123	92	99	48
122	91	98	45
121	90	97	43
120	89	96	40
119	88	95	38
118	86	94	36
117	85	93	34
116	84	92	31
115	82	91	29
114	80	90	27
113	79	89	25

student? These are fair questions for any supervisor and possible sources of concern by classroom teachers.

Grouping/Placement. In most elementary, middle, and secondary schools teachers group students in order to provide more meaningful instruction. As a rule of thumb, for each year in school the range in a given class is one year (e.g., a sixth grade class will have a six year range in reading). Grouping is generally thought to be a sound educational practice.

There are, of course, real problems with grouping students. Most school schedules, for instance, are static. Once a student is grouped for two or more subjects, he or she is automatically sectioned for others. Grouping also fails to acknowledge change in students such as those proposed by Piaget for the middle years. Low achievement grouping can often cause disruptive and emotional behavior problems among students. Finally, the Federal District Court of Washington,

Table 4.6
(Continued)

The Child Whose IQ Is:	Equals or Exceeds (percent)	The Child Whose IQ Is:	Equals or Exceeds (percent)
88	23	74	6
87	21	73	5
86	20	72	4
85	18	71	4
84	16	70	3
83	15	69	3
82	14	68	3
81	12	67	2
80	11	66	2
79	10	65	2
78	9	65	2
77	8	64	1
76	8	63	1
75	6	62	1
160	1 out of 10,000		
156	3 out of 10,000		
152	8 out of 10,000		
148	2 out of 1,000		
144	4 out of 1,000		
140	7 out of 1,000		

Source: Reproduced with the permission of the publishers from *Supplementary Guide for the Revised Stanford-Binet Scale* (L) by Rudolph Pinter, Anna Dragositz, and Rose Kushner. Stanford: Stanford University Press, 1944, p. 135.

D.C. ruled in 1976 that ability grouping was unconstitutional because it was discriminatory against students of certain racial and socioeconomic backgrounds.

Obviously, the practice of grouping students found in over 80 percent of all districts in the United States is laden with issues. The validity of grouping students depends heavily on the supervisor's definition of education and the mission of the school in question.

Pull-out Programs. A phenomenon of the past twenty years has been the "pull-out" program—a special program superimposed over regular class time and characterized by students leaving and returning during the regular class period. Without question, pull-out programs for special students is one way to meet the real needs of those children. What concerns supervisors, however, is the effect of that program on those who remain.

If, for example, students are pulled out of a junior high math class twice a week for a gifted program, should the teacher stall and await their return before introducing new material or simply hold the gifted students responsible for getting the new material themselves? This type of situation, incidently, has done more to harm gifted education than any other the authors have witnessed.

The supervisor, in dealing with pull-out programs, is wrestling with the concept of the majority program — what every student should experience. If pull-outs are so frequent that they totally disrupt the continuity of the majority program, then there ceases to be a majority program. In too many schools today, there is no common denominator in the curriculum. Supervisors, as instructional designers, must confront this issue in meeting the needs of both special students and regular students.

Mainstreaming. Since the passage of P.L. 94-142, mainstreaming is not an issue, per se, it is the law. Still, as supervisors sit in on staffings and develop I.E.P.'s for handicapped students, they do have a great deal of input in defining mainstreaming. Supervisors must have a concept of education in order to keep mainstreaming as a contributing factor in providing quality education.

At stake in all mainstreaming is the placement of a child into an environment to impose his or her educational experience. The "least restrictive environment" clause of P.L. 94-142 was intended to produce the most normal situation for any child who suffered a handicap. The definition of benefit to the student and normal condition for learning is widely open to professional interpretation. Mainstreaming is a good example of how our knowledge of human development directs our definition and design of classroom learning.

Subsidized Care Programs. Few programs sponsored by the federal government in the 1960s received as much attention as the "free" breakfast and lunch programs for indigent children. These highly visible educational programs were begun because of the belief that a student with an empty stomach cannot be a good student. Much was made of the fact that taxpayers were feeding children in the name of education, and it should be noted that almost anyone who went to public school in the United States during the 1940s and 1950s was also subsidized every time he or she bought a school lunch.

At stake in all of these care programs, programs involving food, health care, school supplies, medical care, and other assistance, is the notion of the scope of the school's responsibility. If human development research tells us that children come to school unequal, is it not dishonest to treat them as equals? And if they are recognized as unequal, does the school have a responsibility to provide minimum assistance to them in their growing up? This question is very important to the design of curriculum and instruction and is one that all supervisors must satisfy prior to assisting other teachers in improving instruction.

Compensatory Programs. During the early days of school desegregation in the 1960s, a revolutionary concept was proposed that has since had a major impact on all school programming. The major theme was that some children would need more assistance from the school than others to compensate for environmental deficiencies in their home life. From this idea came massive federal programs such as Title I, Head Start, and Follow Through. From these legislated programs came a variety of novel initiates to compensate including small teacher-pupil ratios, special materials, teacher aides, and parent helpers.

For supervisors, the notion of compensation and purposeful favoring of some students over others, for whatever reason, is a powerful one. At issue is the notion of fairness, access to educational experience, and school mission. It may be easier for the reader to understand this issue by looking at gifted programs that obviously provide those students with a superior learning environment, special materials, and a more highly trained teacher. Supervisors, because of their role, have the potential to define this balance between the regular offering and the compensated programs of the school.

Gifted Education. In the 1990s, no program in school is quite as controversial as the gifted education programs. On the positive side of these programs is the provision of a curriculum for an obviously superior group of students who would otherwise suffer in the regular classroom. On the negative side of many gifted programs is the use of superficial intelligence tests for identification, tremendous social pressure from parents to have their child in such programs, and the possible misuse of educational resources to favor a small minority of students.

The gifted education program raises questions about the obligation of the public school to educate and what the core of the general program should be. Many parents of nongifted students have argued since 1972 that their children are also special, and that if there is a better instructional program for the gifted it should be the program available to all students. While finance is a critical variable in this instance, supervisors must be able to rationalize "plus" experiences for a limited number of students at public expense.

Health and Sex Education. The AIDS problem has resulted in most school districts in the United States teaching health education and sex education to students in some form. Because of the controversy over defining morality, these programs are often masked by euphemisms: life education, family living, growing up in America. Schools teach this information to students because social statistics indicate it is sorely needed and because educational philosophy has generally accepted human development as a critical planning variable. This is also one of the most dangerous areas of the curriculum in terms of public opinion.

Supervisors regularly encounter citizen groups who oppose part of the school program. A label like *sex education* or even *humanism* can be a tinderbox for controversy. The supervisor who does not have command of the facts about human development and the ability to use them to rationalize health education programs will soon experience an unpleasant encounter.

Punitive Discipline. An area of widespread disagreement among teachers and educational theoreticians concerning human development is the area of discipline. In particular, the use of punitive discipline measures such as paddling and social isolation highlights questions about normal development and the influence of certain adult behaviors on child growth. Nationally, 4 percent of all students in public schools are paddled each year.

Arguments against paddling, offered by the National Center for the Study of Corporal Punishment at Temple University, include "an increase in the amount of disruption and aggression, a decrease in genuine learning time, and a decline in school morale."[7] School supervisors should see all forms of student punishment in terms of the school program rather than historical precedent. A wealth of literature exists from which to form an educated opinion on this important question.

Grading Policies. In working with classroom teachers, a ticklish area is grading. Grades mean different things to different people, and school attempts to experiment with new grading patterns have not been widely successful. Ultimately, grading is a human development question because grades assess growth. At issue in the area of grading is the question of student capacity, fairness, and the effect on subsequent student learning.

In many school districts, grading is like Pandora's box; open up the question and the whole program comes apart. Supervisors should be knowledgeable about what educational research says about grading in schools and should be able to clarify issues about grading for teachers. Ultimately, the supervisor's position on how grading should be handled will reflect his or her understanding of human development and the purpose of schooling.

Language Usage. A sleeping controversy exists in the question of the role of language in schools. We know, for a fact, that most school learning is directly dependent on the use of words to form thoughts and to communicate. Small children with big vocabularies, for instance, score higher on I.Q. tests and therefore receive preferred placement in learning groups. We also know that a degree of cultural bias exists in language use, since most school districts demand that only standard English be used to communicate in learning.

Supervisors must wrestle with this instructional problem because many of today's students do not speak standard English. In many parts of the United States in the 1990s, Spanish is the majority language. In addition, dialects and social class language patterns dominate some communication in certain school districts. The effects of language on school achievement, and the role of language in learning, can only be clarified in terms of the larger question of growth and development in students and the role of the school in providing an adequate education for the future.

Cultural and Sex Bias. An issue area related directly to human development is the question of cultural and sex bias found in schools. Traditionally, schools have taught students a set of values that are Anglo-Saxon, Protestant, and white in their orientation. Additionally, many of the values taught in schools possess a degree of sexism in defining roles and relationships. Supervisors should view these historical precedents critically to clarify their relationship to growing up in today's American society.

During the past two decades much has been done to remove obvious cultural and sex bias from school books and other learning materials. Less has been done to work with teachers in recognizing and combatting these conditions. Supervisors must first be aware of these human development questions before they can adequately work with teachers in the classroom to improve instructional opportunities for students.

Retention. New studies have indicated that retention does nothing to increase student achievement, and in reality results in lower self-concepts and greater failure rates. In the early 1990s Florida and California introduced legislation to eliminate retention in lower grades.[8]

THE ROLE OF THE SUPERVISOR

In concluding this chapter on Aiding Human Development, it is important to review the role of the supervisor. We have defined supervision as a leadership role that is concerned with improving learning experiences for students. We have observed that this important educational role sits at the juncture of most communication and decision making in school settings. Supervisors link district offices with schools and classrooms. They also represent a highly educated professional who can provide resources and knowledge to teachers and other leaders in the school system.

Having said all this, it is clear that the supervisor must be knowledgeable to be useful to others. The area of human development is the base of all educational planning since schools exist to assist learners in growing and developing. To define the appropriate school experience, supervisors must understand how humans grow and develop and they must possess some vision of what a healthy and educated adult is like.

Armed with this knowledge and that conception, the supervisor works with others to raise awareness levels, provide decision-making data, and clarify issues about school practices. The degree to which the supervisor attempts to influence policy and practice in a school setting will be defined by his or her own conception of leadership.

NEW DIRECTIONS

Family. In the 1980s the American nuclear family continued to decline. Only 27% of our 91 million households consisted of a married couple with children. Of the others, 50% of the white children will live with a mother who is divorced; 54% of the black children will live with a mother who has never married; 33% of the Hispanic children will live with a mother who has never married. This condition alone is creating a social underclass of massive proportions where the average income is $11,000 as compared to $36,000 for other households. Entering the 1990s, 40% of all poor in America are children.

Age. By the turn of the century, one third of America will be age 55 or older. In 1990, the 50 million people aged 55 or older comprised 22% of the population.[9]

The balance of governmental power has begun to shift from youth to old age, and it will not return to the more familiar pattern in our lifetimes. Gaining support for schools will be an increasing problem.

We are also going to have to change our expectations for what 70-year-old people look like and act like, what choices they have, and what healthy, normal aging means.

Children with Special Needs. Our conception of specialness is changing daily, the best example being babies born with a substance dependence on cocaine or "ice." In the United States today, 5000 persons become new users of cocaine each day, resulting in an estimated 375,000 drug-exposed babies born in 1990 alone. For some states, such as Florida, this translates into 12,000 cocaine babies each year (the size of an entire school district in many cases).

The manifestations of this "social force" is a child born with a defective central nervous system characterized by hyperactivity, numerous deformities, tremors, poor reflexes, abnormal sleep and eating patterns, high-pitched screaming, and an inability to "bond" with other humans. A curriculum for such students would have to include nutrition/health, affective education, enrichment, language/motor development, academic readiness, and a supplemental program in parenting for the natural parent or guardian. Institutional care for one such child is estimated to cost $100,000 per year.

SUMMARY

Supervision is first about helping people grow and develop. It is the job of the supervisor in education to work with others to provide an improved process for aiding the growth and development of students.

To be effective in this role, supervisors must be generally knowledgeable about how humans develop. They must develop and possess a model or conception about growth and use that "big picture" in reviewing practice. Supervisors must be able to see student development in terms of physical, social, emotional, and intellectual maturation.

A special skill that the supervisor must possess is distinguishing between normal and unique development in students. In cases of human specialty, the supervisor must be able to design educational experiences that promote growth without undermining the basic program of schooling. A knowledge of resources to assist such students is a valuable asset for supervisors.

Supervisors must be aware of the issues in education that are directly tied to their conceptions of human development. A dozen such issues were provided to the reader as examples of how knowledge about human growth can be interpreted in the public school classroom.

The role of the supervisor is to help teachers and other educational leaders understand issues and make wise decisions affecting student education. The force with which the supervisor pursues this role is dependent upon his or her conception of leadership in education.

NOTES

1. An excellent resource for supervisors in understanding physical development is David Elkind's *A Sympathetic Understanding of the Child: Birth to Sixteen* (Boston: Allyn and Bacon, 1971).
2. Adapted by Jon Wiles and Joseph Bondi in *The Essential Middle School* (Columbus, Ohio: Merrill, 1981).
3. For an in-depth discussion see L. Kohlberg and E. Turiel "Moral Develop-

ment and Moral Education," in G. Lesser, *Psychology and Educational Practice* (Chicago: Scott, Foresman, 1971), pp. 410-465.

4. For further reading see Richard M. Gorman, *Discovering Piaget, a Guide for Teachers* (Columbus, Ohio: Merrill, 1972).

5. Statistics cited in items 1-6, 11 from U.S. Dept. of H.E.W., "Annual Summary for the United States: Births, Marriages, Divorces and Deaths," National Center for Health Statistics, PHS, 28 (March 1990) No. 12, 80-1120; in item 7 from U.S. Dept. of H.E.W., National Clearinghouse for Mental Health Information, Annual Report, 1990; in item 8 from U.S. Dept. of H.E.W., National Institute of Mental Health, Annual Report, 1990; in item 10 from U.S. Dept. of H.E.W., National Institute of Child Health and Development, Annual Reports 1990.

6. United States Department of Education, National Institute for Child Health and Development, Annual Report, 1990.

7. For further information, contact the National Center for the Study of Corporal Punishment, 833 Riffer Annex, Temple University, Philadelphia, Pa., 19122.

8. *Grade Level Retention, A Position Paper of the Florida Department of Education*, March, 1990. See also Irving Balow and Mahna Schwager, *Retention in Grade: A Failed Procedure*, California Educational Research Cooperative, USC, Riverside, February, 1990.

9. Harold Hodgkinson, "The Same Client: The Demographics of Education and Service Delivery Systems," Center for Demographic Policy, Washington, DC 1989.

SUGGESTED LEARNING ACTIVITIES

1. Trace the development in the past thirty years of legislation and court decisions that protect and guarantee the rights of special students in school.
2. Outline a parent awareness program to help parents understand and support special programs in a school building.
3. Develop a set of procedures to assess the instructional contribution of special programs to the regular or general curriculum in a school.
4. Develop a one-paragraph position statement on each of the twelve issues areas presented. (Example: I believe that discipline. . . .)

BOOKS TO REVIEW

Acheson, Keith and Gall, Meredith. *Techniques in the Clinical Supervision of Teachers*. White Plains, NY: Longman, 1990.

Association For Supervision And Curriculum Development. *Toward The Thinking Curriculum: Current Cognitive Research*. Alexandria, VA: ASCD, 1989.

Bloom, Benjamin, *Developing Talent In Young People*. New York: Ballantine Books, 1985.

Carnegie Council On Adolescent Development. *Turning Points—Preparing American Youth For The 21st Century*. Washington, DC: Carnegie Corporation, 1989.

Chalofsky, Neal And Reinhardt, Charlene, *Effective Human Resource Development*. San Francisco: Jossey-Bass, 1988.

Oakes, Jennie. *Keeping Track: How Schools Structure Inequality*. New Haven, CT: Yale University Press, 1987.

Nucci, Larry, Ed. *Moral Development And Character Education*. Berkeley, CA: McCutchan Publishing Co., 1989.

Riordan, Cornelius. *Girls And Boys In School*. New York: Teachers College Press, 1990.

Titmus, Colin, *Lifelong Education For Adults: An International Handbook*. Elmsford, NY: Pergamon Press, Inc. 1989.

Steinberg, Robert. *Beyond I.Q.: A Triarchic Theory Of Human Intelligence*. New York: Cambridge University Press, 1985.

CHAPTER 5

Designing and Developing Curriculum

INTRODUCTION

The word *curriculum* comes from the Latin word *currere* which means "to run." With time, the course of the race became the course of study, and in schools the curriculum is the means by which the purpose of education is enacted. Supervisors are regularly involved in curriculum design and development both by the decisions they make, and by the decisions they fail to make. An understanding of this critical framework of all education is a necessary skill for successful supervisory practice.

Various modern definitions of curriculum have been offered, and the wording differs according to the philosophical orientation of the person defining the term. Some see the curriculum as a static document (course of study, syllabi, or text), some see it as a process or structure for educating (opportunities, plans), and some see it as a product (outcomes, performance). For our purposes, we shall focus not on curriculum per se, but on the design and development of curricula, thus presenting it as a process carried out by educators including instructional supervisors.

In its simplest form, curriculum development is a cycle of activity. First, there is an analysis of existing conditions and a search for purpose. Second, there is a design stage where the plan is activated. Finally, completing the cycle, there is an evaluation phase in which results are assessed and the analysis begins anew.

Looking at these stages more carefully, we can see that each step contains a series of actions that would naturally involve a school supervisor.

ANALYSIS

Often in school planning there is an absence of philosophic consensus that detracts from the spirit and efficiency of curriculum development efforts. Because the goals of American education are dynamic and ever-changing, maintaining a public consensus for school programs is difficult. The process of clarifying values and establishing themes, because of its regularity, can be perceived as both time-consuming and redundant. Yet, without such a basic operation, curriculum development remains largely unstructured and directionless. The school supervisor is in a key position to work with citizens, administrators, and teachers to find those common areas of support.

Design

Once the intentions of the curriculum improvement effort are clear, relevant data about desired changes must be organized and placed into the form of an action plan. Such a plan clearly identifies what is to be done, the order of changes to be made, a time estimate for changing, various responsibilities for parts of the plan, and the anticipated results of these efforts. Collectively, these parts of the plan serve to communicate to all persons involved what is to happen. Supervisors are in a position to help establish the tasks, to define the outcomes, and to communicate the plan to others.

Implementation

The activation of the curriculum design often calls for some sort of management system that takes the basic plan for changing or improving the curriculum and "drives" it toward completion. Involved in this step are things such as the application of resources and training for those in need of skills. Most curriculum development efforts at this stage are a basic "time, distance, and rate" problem with the resources applied being the primary variable.

Supervisors, in many districts, are the linkage between the desired ends identified in a district plan and the delivered curriculum as found in the classroom.

Evaluation

The evaluation of curriculum development efforts includes both monitoring progress and validating achievements. Supervisors, because they operate at the district, school, and classroom level, are perfectly positioned to observe curriculum planning and implementation. They also are positioned to ensure that the desired change is occurring, that improvements are directional, and that the results obtained are those projected in the planning process.

The reader can easily see that supervisors are involved in curriculum development, and that the four steps of changing provide many opportunities for application of general supervisory skills. We now look more carefully at the practice environment.

CURRICULUM DEVELOPMENT IN PRACTICE

Except in the smallest districts where the supervisor is also the curriculum development specialist, supervisors will rarely see the development of school programs in a pure form. Rather, supervisors will witness curriculum development in terms of daily decisions and actions carried out at the district, school, and classroom levels. In the school setting, the basic curriculum cycle is translated into questions concerning philosophy, goals, objectives, themes, and content. The supervisor should seek to see these events holistically, and understand their significance in terms of the general purpose of schooling.

A beginning point in any school district for improving the curriculum is to establish a philosophy of education. A philosophy — the clarification of beliefs about the purpose and goals of education — is essential to any form of improvement. Without philosophic direction, school programs meander, become targets for social pressure, and sometimes operate in a state of philosophic or programmatic contradiction.

Supervisors can assist others with whom they work in the clarification of their beliefs and goals in at least three ways:

1. Others can be asked to review existing statements of philosophy or related documents and restate them in terms of desired changes.
2. Others can be asked to transfer their own personal philosophy of living into a school context, setting goals for school from general life goals.
3. Others can be asked to look for patterns in current behavior in society that might suggest goals for schools.

Examples of reviewing existing statements might be the study of previous philosophy statements (Figure 5.1) or by survey method (Figure 5.2).

One widely practiced method of clarifying philosophic positions is to have persons develop belief statements. These statements rest on a simple premise: each time a person acts, there is a rationale for action. Without a formalization of such rationales, it is impossible to coordinate or manage individual activities.

Belief statements can be organized in numerous ways, and the correct way for any individual district is dependent upon the planning format. On the next page are examples of belief statements organized

Figure 5.1
Finding Consensus by Reviewing Previous Statements

Education in Los Alamos Schools must entail the acquisition and dissemination of knowledge, the cultivation of intellect, an introduction into the uses of reason, the development of abilities to solve problems and make decisions, and an understanding of what it means to be human.

As educated individuals, the graduates of the Los Alamos Schools must be able to appreciate, respect, and by action and words, communicate with people of widely varying backgrounds. The programs through which the education of the students is presented should reflect the world of the late 20th century and the 21st century and the program goals should be based on that which will be required of them to function during that period of time.

Significant emphasis should be placed on "how to learn," in the development of educational programs for the Los Alamos Schools. Opportunities will be provided for students to participate to the extent feasible in planning total learning experience.

The family and other social institutions bear a major responsibility for the moral growth of youth. Therefore, attitudes, habits, and knowledge that support the family as the basic institution of society will be presented in the schools, and specific moral and religious training will be left with the home.

Note: A Statement of Philosophy and Goals, Los Alamos, New Mexico, School District, 1984. Permission granted.

around students, learning, teaching roles, grouping of students, and educational programs in general. The generic philosophy from which these are drawn is that the school exists to meet the needs and interests of students:

Students

1. WE BELIEVE that students are individuals with unique characteristics and interests.
2. WE BELIEVE that each student should have an equal opportunity to learn, based on his/her needs, interests, and abilities.

Learning

1. WE BELIEVE that students learn best when content is relevant to their own lives.
2. WE BELIEVE that students learn best in an environment that is pleasant and one in which the democratic process is modeled.

Figure 5.2
Finding Consensus by Surveying Community Members

THE GRADUATING SENIOR ...	How important is it for...						
	STUDENTS TO LEARN?			SCHOOLS TO TEACH?			Should it be REQUIRED for GRADUATION? (Circle)
	Low Medium High (Circle)			Low Medium High (Circle)			
SAMPLE: Knows what action to take as a consumer when cheated	0 1 2 3 4 ⑤ 6 7			0 1 2 ③ 4 5 6 7			ⓃⓄ YES
1 Reads to learn	0 1 2 3 4 5 6 7			0 1 2 3 4 5 6 7			NO YES
2 Computes accurately (adds, subtracts, multiplies, and divides)	0 1 2 3 4 5 6 7			0 1 2 3 4 5 6 7			NO YES
3 Listens carefully	0 1 2 3 4 5 6 7			0 1 2 3 4 5 6 7			NO YES
4 Can think scientifically — hypothesize, experiment, analyze, and reach conclusions	0 1 2 3 4 5 6 7			0 1 2 3 4 5 6 7			NO YES
5 Knows the rights and responsibilities of employees	0 1 2 3 4 5 6 7			0 1 2 3 4 5 6 7			NO YES
6 Appreciates music	0 1 2 3 4 5 6 7			0 1 2 3 4 5 6 7			NO YES
7 Drives defensively	0 1 2 3 4 5 6 7			0 1 2 3 4 5 6 7			NO YES
8 Can describe the role of the United States in world affairs	0 1 2 3 4 5 6 7			0 1 2 3 4 5 6 7			NO YES
9 Recognizes the consequences of his/her own behavior	0 1 2 3 4 5 6 7			0 1 2 3 4 5 6 7			NO YES
10 Can read and write a second language	0 1 2 3 4 5 6 7			0 1 2 3 4 5 6 7			NO YES

Teaching

1. WE BELIEVE that the role of the teacher in the classroom is primarily that of a facilitator of learning.
2. WE BELIEVE that student learning may be affected more by what teachers do than by what they say.

One more common method of establishing a consensus of beliefs about school programs is to conduct a needs assessment where all of the ideas and issues can be reduced to planning information. From such information, priorities and concerns emerge to focus improvement efforts. An outline of a basic needs assessment is provided in Figure 5.3.

Finally, most school districts periodically review their statements of philosophy as they renew their state or national accreditation on a scheduled basis. Figure 5.4 illustrates the type of questions that must be answered in self-study prior to a school going through the accreditation process.

Once these philosophic concerns have been reviewed during the analysis stage of curriculum development, they must somehow be translated into a design or general framework for planning. Goals, objectives, and general conceptions of organization are used to formulate the design.

Educational goals are statements of the outcomes of education. The scope of the entire educational program of a school can be found in the goals of that school. Goals are the basic elements in educational planning. The reflection of societal needs in educational goals usually results in statements describing categories of human behavior. Goals relating to "maintaining health," and "carrying out the activities of a citizen in a democratic society" are examples of societal needs.

Goals may be stated at several levels of generality or specificity. Goals that are general or broad reflect a philosophical base and are not concerned with a particular achievement within a period of time.

Perhaps the most familiar goals were defined by the Commission on Reorganization of Secondary Education in 1918. Those goals were (1) health, (2) command of fundamental processes, (3) worthy home membership, (4) vocation, (5) citizenship, (6) worthy use of leisure time, and (7) ethical character. These became widely known as the Seven Cardinal Principles of Secondary Education.

Another attempt at defining the purposes of secondary education was expressed in 1938 by the Educational Policies Commission of the National Education Association and the American Association of School Administrators. The group developed a number of goals under the four headings of (1) self-realization, (2) human relationships, (3) economic efficiency, and (4) civic responsibility.

More recently, the ASCD Working Group on Research and Theory identified a set of valued learning outcomes "that reflected the 'holistic' nature of individuals." Hundreds of organizations, including state departments of education and regional research and development centers, were requested to share their goals with the group. The group identified ten major goals for youth:

1. Self-Conceptualizing (Self-Esteem)
2. Understanding Others
3. Basic Skills

Figure 5.3
Finding Consensus by Conducting a Needs Assessment

The Needs Assessment Framework
I.   General Information
   a. Location of school district
   b. Demographic characteristics of immediate area
   c. Natural resources of region
   d. Commercial—industrial data
   e. Income levels of area residents
   f. Special social-economic considerations
II.   General Population Characteristics
   a. Population growth patterns
   b. Age, race of population
   c. Educational levels of population
   d. Projected population
III. School Population Characteristics (Ages 3-19)
   a. School enrollment by grade level
   b. Birth rate trends in school district
   c. In-migration, out-migration patterns
   d. Race/sex/religious composition of school district
   e. Years of school completed by persons over 25 years of age
   f. Studies of school dropouts
IV.   Programs and Course Offerings in District
   a. Organization of school programs
   b. Programs' concept and rationale
   c. Course offerings
   d. Special program needs
V.   Professional Staff
   a. Training and experience
   b. Awareness of trends and developments
   c. Attitudes toward change
VI.   Instructional Patterns and Strategies
   a. Philosophical focus of instructional program
   b. Observational and perceptual instructional data
   c. Assessment of instructional strategies in use
   d. Instructional materials in use
   e. Decision-making and planning processes
   f. Grouping for instruction
   g. Classroom management techniques
   h. Grading and placement of pupils
   i. Student independence
   j. Evaluation of instructional effectiveness
VII. Student Data
   a. Student experiences
   b. Student self-esteem
   c. Student achievement
VIII. Facilities
   a. Assessment of existing facilities and sites
   b. Special facilities
   c. Utilization of facilities
   d. Projected facility needs
IX.   Summary of Data

4. Interest and Capability for Continuous Learning
5. Responsible Member of Society
6. Mental and Physical Health
7. Creativity
8. Informed Participation in the Economic World of Production and Consumption
9. Use of Accumulated Knowledge to Understand the World
10. Coping with Change

The scope of all of the above goals indicates that they are general goals aimed at an entire unit of organization such as the elementary school, middle school, or senior high school.

Goals are generally broken down into objectives as schools attempt to more clearly define their priorities and desired ends. The authors project such objectives at three levels: very general (level 1), specific (level 2), and behavioral (level 3).

Level 1 objectives are really goals and are usually related to a policy statement or a philosophy statement. The eighteen goals in Figure 5.5 are general, making no attempt to define what is meant by "a good citizen" or the "use of leisure time."

Level 2 objectives are more specific than Level 1 objectives and usually "break down" Level 1 objectives into defined parts. Thus, a good citizen is, for example, someone who votes regularly, follows mutually agreed upon rules, and so forth.

Level 3 objectives, or behavioral objectives, are usually found at the classroom level and describe an anticipated outcome of learning.

Figure 5.4
Philosophy Questions During Self-Study for Accreditation

1. What are the central purposes of this school within its community?
2. What are the responsibilities of the school to the community; of the community to the school?
3. What are the common concerns of students, regardless of the differences among them?
4. How does the school identify individual differences, abilities, and capacities, and how does it adjust methods, materials, and programs to foster individual development?
5. What is a desirable relationship between student and student, student and teacher, teacher and administrator, administrator and community?
6. How does the school identify the changes occurring in American society? How does it best equip students to understand and react to them now and in the future?
7. What specific commitments has this school made for educating its students for a pluralistic society?

Figure 5.5
Level 1 Objectives (Goals)

The Goals of Education

---

1. Learn how to be a good citizen
2. Learn how to respect and get along with people who think, dress, and act differently
3. Learn about and try to understand the changes that take place in the world
4. Develop skills in reading, writing, speaking, and listening
5. Understand skills and practice democratic ideas and ideals
6. Learn how to examine and use information
7. Understand and practice the skills of family living
8. Learn to respect and get along with people with whom we work and live
9. Develop skills to enter a specific field of work
10. Learn how to be a good manager of money, property, and resources
11. Develop a desire for learning now and in the future
12. Learn how to use leisure time
13. Practice and understand the ideas of health and safety
14. Appreciate culture and beauty in the world
15. Gain information needed to make job selections
16. Develop pride in work and a feeling of self-worth
17. Develop good character and self-respect
18. Gain a general education

Source: As outlined in a speech by Harold Spears, George Peabody College for Teachers, 1975.

Popular since the early 1960s, behavioral objectives provide the specificity to allow the certain assessment of learning. The relationship of the three levels is shown in Table 5.1.

Table 5.1
Levels 1, 2, and 3 Objectives Compared

Level of Objective	Type	Origin	Features
Level 1	Broad goals or purposes	Formulated at district level by councils or school board	Seldom revised
Level 2	General but more specific than Level 1	Formulated at school or department level	Contain an outline of process to accomplish Level 1 objectives
Level 3	Behaviorally-stated	Formulated by teams of teachers or single teacher	Describe expected outcome, evidence for assessing outcome, and level of performance

Table 5.2
Graduation Requirements Structure the Secondary Curriculum

	Graduation Standards	Credits
4 Years of English	Major concentration: composition and literature	4
3 Years of Mathematics	Including one semester in micro-computer literacy at the 9th grade level	3
3 Years of Science	Two courses must have a laboratory component	3
3 Years of Social Science	1 year-American History	1
	1 year-World History	1
	1 semester-Economics	½
	1 semester-American Government	½
1 Semester of Practical Arts	Selected from the following: typing, business, industrial arts, home economics, vocational education	½
1 Semester of Fine Arts	Selected from the following: music, dance, theater, painting, sculpture	½
1 Semester of Personal Health	Including nutrition, parenting, drug education	½
1 Semester of Physical Education		½
	Requirements	15
	Electives	9
	Total Credits	24

Source: Secondary Education: A Report to the Citizens of Florida (Governor's Commission on Secondary Schools for the State of Florida, 1990).

The philosophy, goal statements, and objectives weave together a general pattern of expectation for school programs. Superimposed over these statements may be state laws, graduation requirements, testing areas, or other constraints that more clearly define what is to be found in the curriculum. Table 5.2 shows how precisely the secondary program is defined by state law in Florida schools. In some school districts, the amount of time allocated to each subject is even spelled out (see Figure 5.6).

All of these expectations for the curriculum rest in a historic framework that artificially divides schooling into three distinct levels: the elementary school, the middle school, and the high school. A brief explanation of each level follows.

The Elementary Program

The modern elementary school in the United States is the result of over 200 years of evolution. Originally a narrow curriculum devoted to teaching reading, writing, arithmetic, and religion, today's program is very broad, seeking to educate the "whole child." Programs contain not only academic subjects but a wide variety of personal development components to assist learner growth.

The two major change periods in the development of the elementary school in America were the 1930s and the 1960s. In the 1930s the so-called "progressive education era" witnessed an expansion of the curriculum beyond the academics as well as a methods change toward more experience learning. The 1960s, by contrast, was a period of immense effort to individualize the curriculum of elementary school. Innovations such as nongradedness, team-teaching, and prescribed instruction found their way into the school program only to fade during the 1970s and 1980s. Today's elementary school continues to rationalize the curriculum on the growth and development of the students, but standardizes the curriculum. Elementary schools in the 1990s reflect movements toward integrated curriculum and cooperative learning on one hand, while including earlier deparmentalization on the other.

The Middle School Program

The newest of the established levels of education in the United States—intermediate education—developed around 1910 because the students did not seem to fit well into the elementary or high school programs. For fifty years the dominant intermediate program was the junior high school, a school form that gave way to the "middle school" during the mid-1960s.

Like the elementary school, today's middle school uses human development to identify a special group of learners, the preadolescent. Encompassing all those students in transition from childhood to adulthood, the middle school attempts to guide the passage through a broadly focused curriculum that includes academics, skill development, and personal development activities. In the 1990s, the middle school is still reminiscent of the junior high school in many ways, unable to shake off the historical influence of the high school programs.

Here the reader will find ten functions of the intermediate school as perceived by those advocating a middle school design:[1]

1. A unique program adapted to the needs of the pre- and early-adolescent student.

Figure 5.6
Defining the Curriculum by Time

REDEFINED SCHOOL DAY
SUGGESTED PRIMARY TIME FRAME
Minimal Time Allotments

Weekly Time Allotments	Daily Time Allotments	Teacher Activities	
1 hr. & 15 min.	Planning 15 min.	Organizing and planning the day with students	
13 hrs & 20 min.	LANGUAGE ARTS 2 hrs. 40 min.	*1 hour and & 30 min.—Directed instruction in basal developmental reading skills.	30 min. of directed reading with teacher.
			30 min. of basal related skill activities, follow written assignments and/or learning centers reinforcing the reading instruction.
			30 min. to continue the above or reading labs, enrichment centers, creative writing, free reading.
		*1 hour & 10 min.—Instruction in handwriting, oral and written language, spelling and listening. Library experience to reinforce reading, reference skills, and literary appreciation.	1 hour & 10 min.—Part of time will be spent receiving instruction from teacher in these language related skills. Part of time will be spent doing reinforcement activities such as written assignments, learning centers, or language games.
		*A combination of these language skills will be taught within the 5 hours and 50 min. weekly. However, all skills may not be taught daily.	

2 hrs. & 30 min.	PHYSICAL ED 30 minutes	30 min.—Directed instruction in physical education with P.E. Teacher or Classroom Teacher.	30 min. of physical education skills.
5 hrs. & 45 min.	45 minutes	45 min.—Lunch, restroom breaks, and movement to and from activities throughout the day.	
5 hrs.	MATHEMATICS 1 hour	1 hour—Directed instruction in mathematics: computation, problem solving, measurement, and geometry.	1 hour—Part of this time will be spent in directed math instruction with the teacher. Part of this time will be spent doing reinforcement activities such as written assignments, learning centers, and math games.
5 hrs. & 25 min. *A combination of these content areas will be taught within this weekly time allotment. However, all areas will not be taught.	MUSIC AND *CONTENT AREAS 1 hr. & 5 min. *science social studies health humanities art	30 min. twice a week—Directed instruction in music with Music Teacher, with the additional 35 min. for directed instruction in applying and reinforcing reading and study skills in the content areas. 1 hour and 5 min.—three days a week for instruction in applying and reinforcing reading and study skills in the content areas. Art should be considered as part of all disciplines.	1 hour and 5 min.—Directed instruction in music skills and applying and reinforcing study skills in the content areas. Science-a-Process Approach should be alloted one hour per week. A portion of this time will also be used to evaluate the day with students.
WEEKLY TOTAL 31 HRS. & 15 MIN.	DAILY TOTAL 6 hrs. & 15 min.		

Source: Hillsborough County Schools, Tampa, Florida. Used with permission.

127

2. The widest possible range of intellectual, social, and physical experiences.
3. Opportunities for exploration and development of fundamental skills needed by all, with allowances for individual learning patterns. An atmosphere of basic respect for individual differences should be maintained.
4. A climate that enables students to develop abilities, find facts, weigh evidence, draw conclusions, determine values, and that keeps their minds open to new facts.
5. Staff members who recognize and understand the student's needs, interests, backgrounds, motivations, goals, as well as stresses, strains, frustrations, and fears.
6. A smooth educational transition between the elementary school and the high school that allows for the physical and emotional changes of transescence.
7. An environment where the child, not the program, is most important and where the opportunity to succeed is ensured for all students.
8. Guidance in the development of mental processes and attitudes needed for constructive citizenship and the development of lifelong competencies and appreciations needed for effective use of leisure.
9. Competent instructional personnel who will strive to understand the students whom they serve and will develop professional competencies that are both unique and applicable to the transescent student.
10. Facilities and time to allow students and teachers an opportunity to achieve the goals of the program to their fullest capabilities.

The High School Program

Most unchanging of all programs in American education is the secondary curriculum that appears today much as it did a century ago. Most high school curricula are, in reality, a series of unrelated courses that must be passed to meet graduation requirements. In some states in the 1990s, a graduation exam has been added to ensure that key competencies are addressed by the program. Unlike the programs of the elementary and middle school, the high school programs rarely incorporate knowledge of human development and therefore tend to be more standardized and less accommodating than the lower programs.

To the academic, social, and personal dimensions of the lower programs the high school adds a fourth area—vocational education. Since the high school is the last of formal education for the majority of American students, the high school attempts to offer courses leading to immediate employment upon graduation. This task has become more difficult in recent years since fewer than one-third of the jobs of the early 1990s will exist in the early 2000s.

A final task for the secondary school is to polish whatever skills of citizenship the graduate will possess. This task is a vital one in a nation practicing participatory democracy. The secondary school remains the major social instrument in the United States for protecting human rights and maintaining access to the free enterprise system.

The authors wish to note in leaving this review of elementary, middle, and secondary programs that a new division of the school ladder appears to be forming in the 1990s. As the research on human development becomes more accessible, some school districts are beginning to view the organization of schools in four tiers: early childhood, late childhood, preadolescence, and adolescence. If this trend continues, it is likely that a new school form will evolve serving grades four and five within the coming decade.

SUPERVISORS AS CURRICULUM DESIGNERS

For supervisors, structure provided by philosophy statements, goals, learning objectives, laws and regulations, and organizational patterns are a "given." These things provide a framework within which the curriculum is designed and developed at the classroom level. Where most supervisors engage curriculum design and development is in the implementation and evaluation stages of the curriculum development cycle. It is a role of the supervisor to ensure that what is taught is, in fact, what is intended by school planners.

Hilda Taba, an early curriculum theorist, provides a list of seven steps that would guide the supervisor in implementing the planned curriculum in a school setting:[2]

1. diagnosis of needs
2. formulation of objectives
3. selection of content
4. organization of content
5. selection of learning experiences
6. organization of learning experiences
7. determination of what to evaluate and means of doing it

Looking most closely at steps three through six, it can be seen that the supervisor often assists the teacher in the "translation" of the intentions of the curriculum into a delivered product in the classroom. The primary tools of this translation are the identification of program "standards" and the establishment of a "curriculum management" system in the classroom.

Curriculum standards are benchmarks of excellence in the program being taught and differ from goals or objectives in that they are often quantitative measures of conditions in that classroom. The

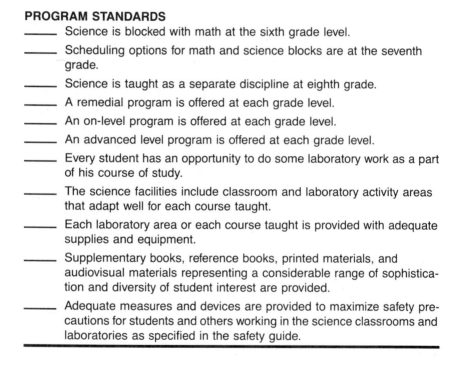

Figure 5.7
Science Standards as a Checklist

PROGRAM

Science

It is the concern of science education that the science program reflects the character of science, becoming a program exploratory in nature; fostering the development of scientifically and technologically knowledgeable citizens; furthering the students' general education; and providing content commensurate with the level of cognitive readiness of students. Further, it is highly desirable that the science program be composed of a variety of components, each designed to meet the varied needs and interests of the students.

PROGRAM STANDARDS

_____ Science is blocked with math at the sixth grade level.

_____ Scheduling options for math and science blocks are at the seventh grade.

_____ Science is taught as a separate discipline at eighth grade.

_____ A remedial program is offered at each grade level.

_____ An on-level program is offered at each grade level.

_____ An advanced level program is offered at each grade level.

_____ Every student has an opportunity to do some laboratory work as a part of his course of study.

_____ The science facilities include classroom and laboratory activity areas that adapt well for each course taught.

_____ Each laboratory area or each course taught is provided with adequate supplies and equipment.

_____ Supplementary books, reference books, printed materials, and audiovisual materials representing a considerable range of sophistication and diversity of student interest are provided.

_____ Adequate measures and devices are provided to maximize safety precautions for students and others working in the science classrooms and laboratories as specified in the safety guide.

standards seek to guide the design of instruction by informing the teacher of what is expected in any learning experiences. In Figure 5.7, the reader will see how an intermediate science program is delineated by observable criteria, i.e., every student has an opportunity to do some laboratory work as a part of his course of study. In Figure 5.8, schoolwide standards for math are identified in terms of present status, needs to meet standards, and priority in program development.

Establishing program standards at the district or school level enables the supervisor to then measure the programs in the classroom

Figure 5.8
Math Standards for a District

Program Standards	Status				Needs					Specifics	Priority		
	Below	Mark all that apply			Mark all that apply								
Mathematics													
Provides sequential development of skills that enable students to comprehend our number system, to perform mathematical calculations, and to use mathematical thinking in solving problems.													
• Sufficient classroom quantity of durable, accurate, manipulative materials	—	46	33	13	13	—	4	17	—	4	4	63	17	—
• Developmental program provided	—	88	13	—	—	—	—	—	4	4		67	17	—
• Remedial program provided	—	71	13	—	13	8	4	4	—	8	—	67	8	—
• Enrichment program provided	—	29	20	13	20	29	13	17	—	29	4	67	13	—
• Opportunities to apply computation skills in daily living situations	—	79	17	4	—	—	—	—	—	4	4	71	4	4
• Variety of practice materials for basic skills	—	63	38	4	—	—	—	8	—	8	4	58	13	4
• Supplemental materials	—	67	25	8	—	—	—	—	—	4	—	58	20	4
• Opportunity to practice creative problem-solving	—	71	20	8	—	4	4	—	8	—		71	17	4
• Opportunity to practice solving word problems	—	79	17	4	—	—	—	—	—	—	8	71	4	4

against expectation. If the standards established are being met in all classrooms, the supervisor can rest assured that all students are receiving at least a minimum program with an established level of quality control.

A second tool for working with the curriculum at the classroom level is curriculum management planning, a process where the supervisor helps the teacher map out his or her curriculum. One of the most severe instructional problems today in many schools is that the general curriculum plan (intentions) of the school has been allowed to become stagnant. At the same time, many teachers have come to view the textbook as "the curriculum." It should be obvious to the reader that a textbook is *not* the curriculum, and to allow these instructional materials to serve as the curriculum is to create a disjointed plan for learning (see Figure 5.9).

Unless a single text series is adopted throughout the school district and during an entire level of schooling, the district allows the many unrelated texts to create gaps and redundancy in the program experienced by school children (see Figure 5.10).

If the text or learning series is not to be the curriculum, it is vital that teachers identify the essential structure or what they intend to teach. The authors have developed a relatively simple series of steps that could be led by the supervisor to achieve clarity of intention at the classroom level.

A first step in mapping the curriculum[3] is to have teachers develop an outline of the major concepts, content, and skills that they intend to teach (see sample for Figure 5.11). At first, teachers will simply want to list chapters in the available textbook, but addressing concepts or big ideas will open fully the question of intent. Why do we teach the wars of the United States in American history? It is recommended that these maps correspond to grading periods so that the "time flow" of the curriculum becomes more visible to the teacher.

Figure 5.9
An Elementary School with Textbook Curriculum

Grade	Reading	Math	Science
1	Lippincott '71	Addison '78	Silver-Burdette '72
2	Lippincott '75	Addison '78	Charles Merrill '82
3	Macmillan '79	Addison '78	Silver-Burdette '72
4	Macmillan '79	Addison '78	Silver-Burdette '72
5	Macmillan '79	Addison '78	Merrill '82
6	Macmillan '79	Addison '78	Merrill '82
7	Harcourt '77	Addison '78	Merrill '79
8	Harcourt '77	Addison '78	Merrill '79

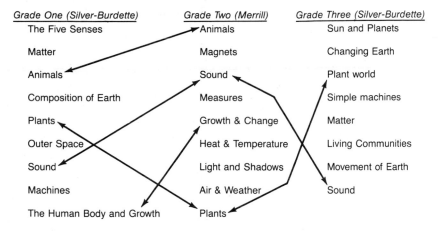

Grade One (Silver-Burdette)	Grade Two (Merrill)	Grade Three (Silver-Burdette)
The Five Senses	Animals	Sun and Planets
Matter	Magnets	Changing Earth
Animals	Sound	Plant world
Composition of Earth	Measures	Simple machines
Plants	Growth & Change	Matter
Outer Space	Heat & Temperature	Living Communities
Sound	Light and Shadows	Movement of Earth
Machines	Air & Weather	Sound
The Human Body and Growth	Plants	

Figure 5.10
Redundancy in an Elementary Science Curriculum with Textbook
Structure (Topics)

A second step is for the supervisor to assist the teachers in looking at the curriculum vertically or from grade-to-grade in one subject.
Where are there gaps in the subject matter taught? Where is there
redundancy? This vertical look should be followed by a horizontal look
across subjects. Which subject area, for instance, is responsible for
teaching metrics? Human development?

Following this weeding out or clearance process, attention should
then focus on learning materials. What texts seem best to contribute
to this set of learning objectives? What other non-text learning materials (worksheets, visuals, films) can assist the teacher in presenting
these ideas and concepts?

The emerging map may now be compared and contrasted with
external expectations for the curriculum. What do state or district
guidelines call for? What is currently being tested at this level by both
norm-based and teacher-made tests?

Finally, the teacher and supervisor may wish to look at student
needs and interests, as well as performance, to see if this plan is practical and relevant to the student.

What emerges from the effort to manage the curriculum is a total
visual that maps out what each teacher at each grade level is actually
teaching. Through schoolwide or departmental committee work, the
map can be smoothed out and overlaps and gaps eliminated. The plan
can be tied to testing or state requirements. At this point, the supervisor and the classroom teacher can fully communicate on a daily,
weekly, or quarterly basis about what is or is not happening in the
classroom and why. Such a communication about the curriculum can
lead to realistic evaluation criteria for assessing teacher performance.

Figure 5.11
Sample Curriculum Map in Social Studies

| GRADE LEVEL: | Third | SUBJECT: | Social Studies |
| GRADING PERIOD: | 1st Nine Weeks | TEACHER: | Smith |

CONTENT	CONCEPTS	GENERAL SKILLS	SPECIFIC SKILLS/ OBJECTIVES	TEXTS/* MATERIALS
1. National resources of the United States. 2. Major topographical classifications—desert, forest, ocean, river. 3. Climate regions of the United States. 4. States and topographs in the United States. 5. Major water masses in the United States. 6. Peoples and cultures in the United States.	1. American culture is a composite of many cultures. 2. American cultures have shaped American behavior (freedom, individualism, equaling). 3. People of different cultures have different points of view. 4. Cultural ways are influenced by physical environment. 5. Florida and the United States are populated by people of different cultures and different points of view.	1. Collecting and organizing information. 2. Mapping 3. Relating 4. Thinking 5. Comparing 6. Communication 7. Drawing conclusions 8. Determining sequence.	1. The student names the States and water masses that border/ surround Florida. 2. The student locates the boundaries of the United States. 3. The student locates a specific geographical region of the United States. 4. The student locates and names the state and geographic region in which he lives. 5. The student interprets information from a map legend.	*Florida Handbook* 1983-84 Rand McNally Atlas, 1983—Map of growing seasons *National Geographic* Film *The United States,* U.S. Dept. of Interior *Textbook would appear in this column. Page and chapter numbers should be appropriate.

6. The spread of cultural characteristics takes place more readily along established trade routes.
7. Our national resources are limited.

6. The student matches products with regions in the United States in which they are found.
7. The student discusses how holidays are celebrated in different regions of the United States.
8. The student identifies leaders in the United States.
9. The student compares seasonal changes and weather patterns in the United States.

Source: Glades County Schools, Florida.

Figure 5.12
A Curriculum Based on Concept Development

Level/Subject	Concept
HEALTH	Growth and Development follows a predictable sequence and is unique for each individual
I (Grades K–3)	a. Cite examples showing how persons of the same age differ and yet are the same while growing and developing. b. Describe how each person becomes unique. c. Explain why differences in the rate of growing among children of the same ages can be expected.
II (Grades 4–6)	a. Describe how growing and developing occurs for body parts, systems, functions. b. Identify different ways children grow physically, mentally, socially. c. Predict the kind of changes that will occur during preadolescence.

From this point on in curriculum development, the supervisor and teacher will be communicating about methodology because the "what" question will be settled. Without standards and curriculum management, no logical discussion about methodology can occur because the "what" of the curriculum is being assumed by both the teacher and the supervisor or drawn from a nebulous source such as district goals, testing expectations, or textbook coverage.

Using the curriculum map, instruction can move in many directions. The curriculum may take on a structure based on the mastery of concepts (Figure 5.12). The curriculum might be organized around basic skills in a subject (Figure 5.13). The curriculum might also be deployed into a minicourse format to meet student interests and attention levels (Figure 5.14). Finally, the curriculum may cross subject lines to become an interdisciplinary theme curriculum where all subjects contribute to common ideas (Figure 5.15).

As the supervisor uses the tools of standards and maps to engage the teacher in the classroom, a relationship based on tasks rather than personality will evolve. Further communication about instruction and evaluation will become reality-based. These topics are treated fully in later chapters in this book.

CURRICULUM ESSENTIALS FOR SUPERVISORS

All supervisors, regardless of their role and title, should work to ensure that a minimal level of quality control exists in the program of studies

Figure 5.13
A Curriculum Based on Skill Continuums

DIRECTIONS TO THE TEACHER: This chart contains those objectives from the complete *K-8 Scope and Sequence of Mathematics Objectives* that are designated *promotion objectives*.

CODE: Three columns are provided for marking in the event the objective is marked more than once in a given year, or is marked in a preceding or following year. *Objectives are numbered as they appear in the complete K-8 Scope and Sequence.*

"+" - Objective mastered by the pupil
"√" - Objective partially mastered by the pupil
"−" - Objective *not* mastered by the pupil

GRADE 3			
SETS: The student will . . . 1. name the members of a set.			
3. identify equivalent sets.			
NUMBER AND NUMERATION: The student will . . . 2. count by 2's, 5's and 10's to 100.			
9. using a reference point, identify the ordinal position of any object in a set of no more than 10 objects.			
10. put in order any three whole numbers less than 100.			
WHOLE NUMBERS: The student will . . . 1. add three 3-digit numbers, *without* regrouping.			
4. subtract two 3-digit numbers, *without* regrouping.			
5. subtract two 3-digit numbers, with *only one* regrouping.			
7. write basic multiplication facts, products through 45.			
10. write basic division facts, products through 45.			
NUMBER THEORY (No promotion objectives)			
FRACTIONS: The student will . . . 1. identify halves, thirds, fourths, or fifths of a region and write the fraction.			
GEOMETRY (No promotion objectives)			
MEASUREMENT (No promotion objectives)			
TIME (No promotion objectives)			
MONEY: The student will . . . 1. identify a set of coins equivalent in value to a given set of coins with the value not to exceed 99¢.			
GRAPHS: The student will . . . 2. read and make horizontal and vertical pictographs, and bar graphs.			
GRADE 4			
SETS (No promotion objectives)			
NUMBER AND NUMERATION: The student will . . . 1. identify the number of objects in a set of no more than 1000 objects.			

Source: Palm Beach County Schools, Florida.

Figure 5.14
A Curriculum by Minicourse (Science)

Anatomy
This course covers cellular structure, organization of the body in terms of cells, tissues, organs and systems, and anatomical terminology. Special attention will be paid to the effects of alcohol, drugs, and tobacco on the systems of the body.

Ecology
This course studies man's relationship to the total environment. Students will learn how man has changed his environment and the type of actions needed to preserve our environment.

Rocks and Minerals
This course will help the student understand the materials that make up the earth's crust. The actual identification of rocks and minerals will be accomplished through field study. .

Microbiology
This course is designed to study all microscopic forms of life such as algae, fungi, mold, bacteria, and protozoans. With the aid of the teacher all students will grow their own cultures for study.

experienced by students. There are certain essential indicators of a complete curriculum, and these are offered to assist readers in assessing a school or district in which they work. We present them in the form of questions that could easily be answered yes or no.

1. The program has a clearly identified mission that focuses on the learners being served?
   a. A philosophy state exists and is endorsed by Board?
   b. The philosophy is up-to-date, being reviewed annually?
   c. The philosophy includes standards that identify general quality control criteria for all educational programs?
2. The program has comprehensive goals and objectives that are known to all persons implementing the curriculum?
   a. Goals and objectives are available for all subjects taught?
   b. Teacher lesson plans are monitored for congruence with the stated goals and objectives?
   c. There is active administrative involvement in continuously updating the written plans for instruction?
3. The curriculum is current and reflects what is actually taught?
   a. A systematic procedure exists to regularly upgrade the curriculum?
   b. Curriculum maps are used to communicate planned lessons?
   c. Classroom supervision includes monitoring content as well as methods?

Figure 5.15

A Curriculum Based on Interdisciplinary Concepts

Concept	Kindergarten Through Grade Three	Grades Four Through Six
MULTIPLE CAUSATION	Students will demonstrate a knowledge of housing patterns (on their block, in their neighborhood, and in their community) that are changing for a variety of reasons.	Students will understand that the United States government is the product of numerous factors, including colonization, constitutionalization, protection of individual rights, participation in a world community, and development as an industrial nation.
NEEDS	Students will be able to tell how people meet their need for food, clothing, shelter, love, and security.	Students will compare their own ways of meeting needs with the ways in which others meet their needs.
PROPERTY	Students will be able to identify some common forms of ownership, including individual, communal, and state ownership.	Students will be able to describe attitudes toward property and ownership in specific situations and to identify and explain some of the factors that may affect those attitudes, including individual psychology, experience, and culture.
AUTHORITY/ POWER	Students will demonstrate a knowledge of the need for order in the classroom when certain tasks are to be performed.	Students will be able to analyze situations in which authority exists and to identify its intermediate and alternate sources; for example, the authority of teachers, which is based upon custom, tradition, law, need, and consent.
OOANOITY	Oludenls will practice economical use of school materials and will develop an understanding that these materials are provided by tax money paid by their parents.	Sludents will understand that all the countries of the Western Hemisphere must be concerned with the use and misuse of resources as attempts are made to fulfill the wants of growing populations.
SOCIAL CONTROL	Students will understand that they are members of many groups (family, school, and so forth) at the same time. They will understand that groups have some rules that are common but that some rules are unique to a particular group.	Students will understand that laws that serve the total U.S. population have been designed to protect certain individual rights of all citizens and that such laws are open to continuing interpretation and implementation.

4. Classroom instruction follows the written or planned curriculum?
   a. There is balance in the curriculum by subject emphasis?
   b. Content, teaching strategies, and resources are directly related to the written objectives of the curriculum?
   c. Instructional decision making is tied formally to student learning outcomes:
5. Teacher evaluation is a logical extension of the implemented curriculum?
   a. Student testing is analyzed according to instructional objectives?
   b. Teacher evaluation is "outcome" oriented?
   c. Staff development is planned according to needs for instructional improvement?

If the supervisor can answer yes to these questions and finds most of the indicators in place, then it is likely that the curriculum is at least sufficient. Another area worthy of inspection in most districts is the long-range plan or subject renewal.

In many school districts, textbook salespeople are the chief curriculum developers. They come to the district with various incentives for adopting their product, some subtle and some not so subtle, and put in place the major organizer of learning. At a minimum, this adoption process should be logical and controlled by the school district. A supervisor can begin to gain such control by establishing a schedule of text renewal as shown in Figure 5.16.

The reader will note that the actual adoption process should come only after the curriculum has been evaluated and the faculty has had an opportunity to study that evaluation through staff development programs. If these preliminary steps are taken, the faculty or textbook

Figure 5.16
A Schedule for Textbook Renewal

LONG-RANGE PLAN FOR SUBJECT AREA RENEWAL							
Subject	1983 –84	1984 –85	1985 –86	1986 –87	1987 –88	1988 –89	1989 –90
Science	R					E	SD
Reading	E	SD	R				E
Lang. Arts	E	SD	R				E
Mathematics		E	SD	R			
Social Studies			E	SD	R		
Health/PE				E	SD	R	
Music					E	SD	R
Art					E	SD	R

E = Evaluation of area by administration/Board
SD = Applied staff development in areas of need
R = Renewal of subject area/text adoption

committee will view each vendor's product in terms of the curriculum planned and the results obtained by the present program.

In conclusion, the reader is directed to Figure 5.17 which provides a set of questions relevant to most curriculum decisions.

Figure 5.17
How Many of These Questions Were Answered *Before* You Made Your Last Curriculum Decision?

Should you build your *own* curriculum or adopt one that is already well developed?

Are learner behaviors specified in terms of instructional objectives?

How do you define *goals* and *objectives?*

Which is the more *economical*—your current curriculum or one of the new instructional systems?

Will *replacement* and equipment costs make adoption prohibitive?

Do the new instructional materials really fit your students' *needs?*

Do the teaching methods include *discovery* or inquiry?

Are the salesman's *claims* completely accurate?

Can the new materials be used with "disadvantaged" children?

What about *process* versus content?

What about *personnel,* time, and space?

Will special kinds of multi-media *hardware* be needed?

Should teachers use only a *textbook?*

Will the new elementary curriculum match your secondary program?

Will the new curriculum be *flexible* enough for your teachers' individual styles?

How do the alternative models compare in terms of cost?

Do local *budget* restrictions eliminate any consideration of certain curricula?

What *advertising* claims can be refuted after using one of these units?

How much *evaluation* time can your staff save by using an information unit?

Is the prospective new program really based on *well-researched* learning theories?

Are methods for *individualizing* provided?

What about *individual* differences, levels of abilities, readability, etc.?

How was *content* selected and how is it organized?

What are the anticipated *cognitive,* affective, or psychomotor outcomes?

What kind of staff *training* will be necessary?

NEW DIRECTIONS
Technology

Technology accelerates change in society. Today, the changes in daily life are occurring faster than ever before. For example, the microcomputer, now in widespread use, was virtually unheard of at the beginning of the last decade. Ten years later, the microcomputer assists or complicates our daily experiences. By contrast, the refrigerator took nearly 30 years to develop during the first three decades of this century.

As we develop faster and faster means of communicating and manufacturing, the future worker must be educated in at least some part of this technology. As a result, technology will soon foster a partnership between schools and industries from which both will profit. During this decade, workers will continue to lose permanent jobs to new computerized equipment. Car manufacturing is an example where computerized machines, "robots," are now performing many of the assembly line jobs formerly performed by workers. These displaced workers require retraining to re-enter the job market. Therefore, there will be two major groups who will require technological training: the high school or college graduate first entering the job market, and the displaced worker trying to re-enter the job market. This is a massive job—one which government, business, and education must address.

As technology—and teleconferencing in particular—increases, teachers may meet the need to develop specific programs to retrain adult workers who may or may not be located in their own communities.

A survey conducted by *Inc. Magazine,* listing America's fastest growing, small, publicly-held companies, disclosed the following data: of the top 100 companies, 55 were engaged in the business of one product—the development and sale of software/hardware for computers.[4] Several other categories were health-care diagnostics and health-care cost containment, financial management services, food franchises, and child-care services. All of these ventures will require workers who have a minimal understanding of computer technology. As an example, Mrs. Field's Cookies gives each new employee their own disk with four computer games to get the new employee comfortable using the extensive Mrs. Field's interactive computer system. After the employee is comfortable with the computer, a peer employee trains the new employee on basic operations of the system. This training continues until the new employee is proficient on the system and can run it without the help of management. An interesting sidenote: the Field's organization notes that employees learn faster with peer "teachers" rather than formal "teachers" or managers looking over their shoulders.

Technology will force educators to become proficient with some aspects of computers, their uses in school settings, and their future use in the careers of their students. Teachers are comfortable with text books and television because that is what they have used up to the present. Educators will have to "educate" themselves in the untapped resources of technology, and sift through what will work and what will not work for them.

The future generation of computers will open new areas of where and how students will study. Socialization is an important part of education. However, with the advent of interactive teleconferencing, students of the future may study independently at home, in a library, or in a museum for one or two days per week. Student work will be sent on-line, immediately ready for feedback from a school based instructor. The range of educational possibilities using interactive computers and teleconferencing is just starting to dawn on forward-thinking educators and business people alike.

Currently, educational software is in its infancy stage. As more educators become involved in the development of the software, the quality will increase and teachers will begin to use the more effective products. Educators have the knowledge of how students learn and the experience of curriculum development. These two elements should be incorporated into educational software. The technology exists today for the programming of educational software; what's missing is the educational experience. Therefore technology will spin off another career path for educators: that of software advisor/developer.

Students have always learned at their own pace. Educators have taken this fact into consideration with many attempts at addressing differences in student ability. In addition, educators in the United States now address differences in culture and language. Computers are capable of instructing in many languages from the beginning grades. The future student could be gradually weaned from his native language and begin instruction in English. There is currently a debate over bilingual education in the United States. Perhaps using existing and emerging technology will help resolve this discussion.

The future is exciting. Technology will be one force changing our schools and the way education is administered in the coming decades.

Technology, talked about for thirty years as a coming force, has arrived. By the year 2000, over 50% of all industrial jobs in the United States will be eliminated and replaced with technology service representatives, creators, and technical manufacturers due to the use of robotics.[5]

In particular, interactive technologies are being introduced to schools sooner than anyone expected. The success of such technological application is based on a need in education to individualize, accommodate learning and teaching styles, and contend with a rapidly changing data base. Television came into being in the 1940s; transistors and computers in the 1950s; video cassette recorders and compact disc players in the 1970s and the compact disc-read only memory (CD-ROM) in the 1980s. Together, these technologies make possible a tailor-made "hyper-media interactive communication."

Schools in the 1990s will be a mix of traditional teacher lecture side-by-side with LANs (local area networks) where teachers monitor and prescribe an individualized program of education, via computers, for up to sixty students at once. It is highly likely that the entire traditional curriculum will be available on software and accessible at home for those who so desire. A standard CD-ROM stores about 550 million characters of information (equivalent to 1000 floppy disks), so most school libraries will be available on just two CD-ROMs. With lasers, "frame freezing," "blow-ups," "slow motion," and "reverse replay" teachers will have an arsenal of information at their fingertips.

Life in the 1990s will be fun! At home there will be temperature-check pajamas for kids, holograph bifocal contact lenses for Mom and Dad, deodorant underwear for teenagers, and video telephones for the whole family. The supervisor who isn't fully engaged in this future technology will be both dysfunctional and a dinosaur.

The Japanese Model

Americans are very impressed with the Japanese and their ability to pursue a "high-tech" future. From a war-torn economy of the 1940s, Japan has emerged as a world leader in industry and commerce. Many businesspeople believe that the Japanese education system is responsible, since it regularly outperforms the American system in various measures of achievement.

The Japanese education system has the same curriculum as the American system, with modifications added. Among the major differences are: the Japanese believe in preschool (70% in nursery school); involve parents throughout the school years; use tutors extensively; go to school more days per year; do not fail or retain pupils extensively; have a respectable vocational track for those not going to college; have mostly nuclear families with the mother free to support learning (not working outside the home); and have a reinforcing moral education program at home and school which encourages persistence, self-discipline, group values, and reflection.

America cannot borrow the virtues of Confucian principles, as Japan has, or turn back the clock to the social conditions of the 1950s. We are not a homogenous culture, pressed for personal space, as Japan is. On the other hand, we do have enormous natural resources (Japan doesn't), and we use personal technology more than Japan (only .58%

of Japanese children have a personal computer, compared to 22% of American children with some easy access). In short, Japan has adapted our education system to their social and cultural needs.

There is one last observation worth noting. Almost all of the achievement studies comparing grade level achievement fail to ac- knowledge that Japanese 5th graders have attended school almost 300 days longer than American 5th graders. Perhaps achievement should compare their 5th graders to our 7th graders? At any rate, this model will continue to dominate our thinking about education as long as American industry seeks to become competitive through the work- force as opposed to the organization and objectives of our major companies.

SUMMARY

Supervisors in schools are regularly involved in basic efforts to im- prove the curriculum. The authors feel that knowledge of this critical framework for instruction is a necessary skill for any practicing supervisor.

Curriculum development is a recurring cycle that includes an analysis step, a design step, an implementation step, and an evaluation step. All of the skills of supervision will be employed in working with others through this basic cycle.

The actual practice of curriculum design and development by the supervisor will focus on the construction of a philosophy, the estab- lishment of goals, the delineation of objectives for learning, and the design of an instructional approach.

Supervisors can assist teachers and principals in the structuring of the curriculum through the use of standards, by establishing a cur- riculum management system (mapping), and by controlling textbook adoption procedures.

There are, clearly, essential indicators of a satisfactory curricu- lum development process in schools. Among those major indicators are a clear mission statement, goals and objects known to all involved, a curriculum that is current and reflects what is actually taught, class- room teaching that is based on the planned curriculum, and a system of teacher evaluation that is a logical extension of the curriculum.

NOTES

1. Jon Wiles and Joseph Bondi, *The Essential Middle School* (Columbus, OH: Merrill, 1981), p. 8.

2. Hilda Taba, *Curriculum Development: Theory and Practice* (New York: Harcourt, Brace, Jovanovich, 1962), p. 12.

3. A more complex version of curriculum mapping is presented by Fenwick English in *Quality Control in Curriculum Development* (Arlington, VA: American Association of School Administrators, 1978), pp. 35–45. See also Duval County, Florida, *Mapping Efforts in the Middle School*, 1990.
4. Sara Baer-Sinndh, Editor, *Inc Magazine*, May 1990, pp. 32–44.
5. *Report on the NEA Special Committee on Technology*, 1990.

SUGGESTED LEARNING ACTIVITIES

1. Write your own personal definition of curriculum development. Is it a dynamic or static definition?
2. Identify ways in which supervisors would be involved in the analysis, design, implementation, and evaluation of the curriculum.
3. Develop an outline of events that would lead a school district with no philosophy to one with a clear and consistent curriculum development process.
4. Develop a teacher evaluation instrument to be used by a supervisor that would reflect curriculum development at the classroom level.
5. Develop an operational definition of leadership in curriculum development.
6. Identify the five most important skills a supervisor must possess to be effective in school curriculum development efforts.

BOOKS TO REVIEW

Association for Supervision and Curriculum Development. *Toward The Thinking Curriculum: Current Cognitive Research*. Alexandria, VA: Yearbook, 1989.

Bell-Gredler, Margaret. *Learning And Instruction: Theory Into Practice*. New York: Macmillan Publishing Company, 1986.

Brandt, Ronald, Ed. *Content Of The Curriculum*. Alexandria, VA: Association For Supervision And Curriculum Development, 1988.

Clark, Barbara. *Optimizing Learning*. Columbus, OH: Merrill, 1986.

Connelly, F. Michael and Clandinin, Jean. *Teachers As Curriculum Planners*. New York: Teachers College Press, 1988.

Gagne, Robert. *Instructional Technology's Foundations*. Hillsdale, NJ: L. Erlbaum Assocs., 1987

Slavin, Robert. *Cooperative Learning*. New York: Longman, 1986.

Walker, Decker. *Fundamentals of Curriculum*. New York: Harcourt Brace Jovanovich, 1990.

Wiles, Jon and Bondi, Joseph. *Curriculum Development: A Guide to Practice*, 3rd ed. Columbus, OH: Merrill, 1989.

CHAPTER **6**

Improving Classroom Instruction

INTRODUCTION

The primary job of a school supervisor is to improve the instructional experience of students. This task includes many dimensions including the organization of schools and staff, the selection of learning materials, developing methodology, and conducting evaluation to insure that the intentions of the curriculum are being met. The way in which this task is carried out is situationally determined by the size of the school district, the interpersonal relationships that exist, and the job description of the supervisor.

In this chapter we will focus squarely on the classroom and the individual teacher, for this is where instructional accountability takes place. To insure effective instruction for students, the supervisor must follow the intended curriculum into the classroom setting and work with the teacher. To assume that the teacher will follow the planned curriculum simply because it exists is just unrealistic, given the many variables in today's classroom. The role of the supervisor is to work with the teacher in the classroom to minimize distortions in the delivered curriculum and to synchronize the instructional methodology with the curricular intent.

A beginning point for such practice is the recognition that there is no "teacher" per se, but rather many individuals trying to teach. Recognizing the diversity of background, experience, training, and expectation of each school faculty suggests that how the supervisor works with the individual teacher in a single classroom may be unique to that classroom. The supervisor, armed with a knowledge base about teaching and an understanding of the curriculum, works with the individual teacher to produce the best possible delivery of the planned curriculum. A conception of teaching and a model for improving instruction establish a point of departure for practicing supervision.

147

TEACHING — ART OR SCIENCE?

Supervisors need a way of thinking about teaching in order to develop a model for instructional improvement. There is not widespread agreement about the nature of teaching, and, in fact, something of a schism exists among professional educators: Is teaching an art or a science? During the past decade, a heavy research emphasis appears to have tipped the balance momentarily in the favor of a science; most of today's literature suggests that teaching is a series of highly integrated skills. The authors believe that the supervisor must clarify this dichotomy of opinion, in his or her mind, prior to entering into a classroom to work with the teacher.

The basic argument for the "art of teaching" perspective is that teaching is a complex act, incorporating the "persona" of the individual teacher. Areas that are difficult to assess — such as asking quality questions, openness to student inquiry, or the ability to establish a "climate" for learning — may be the distinguishing characteristics of the successful teacher.

In considering the many choices faced daily by the classroom teacher, some researchers feel that teaching requires an artistic judgment. It has been estimated that there are about 200–300 personal interactions each hour in the standard classroom. Such decisions about content, sequence, and emphasis can't be made with exactness.

Those who favor the "science of teaching" point to the many studies of the 1970s and 1980s that statistically isolated the critical variables of instruction. Rosenshine, for example, prescribes specific steps to be taken by an "effective" teacher:

- ☐ Begin the lesson with a short statement of goals.
- ☐ Begin the lesson with a short review of the previous prerequisite learning.
- ☐ Present new material in small steps with student practice after each step.
- ☐ Ask many questions, check for student understanding, and obtain responses from students.
- ☐ Provide systematic feedback and correction.
- ☐ Provide explicit instruction and practice for seatwork exercises.
- ☐ Continue practice until students are independent and confident.[1]

The authors see the question of "art versus science" not as an absolute position, but as a continuum where various types of teaching can be constructed to achieve certain purposes. McNeal and Wiles, for instance, present three models of teaching: Direct, Indirect, and Self-Directed.[2]

The Direct Model of teaching emphasizes teacher control of learning and high degrees of structure to maintain such control. This teacher would be lecturing to rows of students in a traditional fashion.

The rationale for this pattern may rest with the belief that "teachers know best," but more commonly the direct model advocates the need for structure in order to insure logic and sequence in the presentation of complex material.

The Indirect Model of teaching is interactive, with teacher and student sharing input into instructional procedures. There is a belief that students are different and that their experience is valuable to the learning process. Cooperative learning, for example, is based on this model.

The Self-Directed Model of teaching sees the student as increasingly capable of guiding his or her own instruction. This type of teaching acknowledges the universe of information made available to students by, for example, the recent impact of technology on teaching.

These three models, then, begin to suggest that there are many legitimate patterns or styles of teaching, and that a supervisor should be able to see teaching as a subset of the objectives of the curriculum. Most of the research covered in the following section focuses on "direct" teaching, but before moving on, the authors present a few caveats concerning what is known:

1. Almost all of the available research on teaching is concerned with one approach to teaching, subject mastery. It is not directed toward social interaction, information processing, or non-directive growth of students.
2. Most of the research that makes up the "science of teaching" was conducted on one type of learner, the disadvantaged.
3. Most of the primary research that supports a scientific approach to teaching was directed toward achievement in reading and mathematics as measured by standardized tests.
4. Most of the conclusions about such primary research have been reached by synthesis of previous studies rather than further research.

TEACHING: THE STATE OF THE ART

The period between 1980 and 1990 has been an interesting one in terms of the metamorphosis of teacher/learning research. In this period there has been a constant synthesizing and consolidating effect as original studies of the 1970s have been analyzed and rethought. This reexamination has taken place under an immense pressure of "accountability" where school districts have been asked to document their achievements and rationalize their programs. Pushing the process along have been the findings of numerous blue-ribbon committees and the numerous bills of state legislatures.

Figure 6.1

Processes and Measures Associated with School Outcomes

School Processes	Measures
Academic Emphasis	Is homework frequently assigned?
	Do administrators check that teachers assign homework?
	Do teachers expect students to pass national exams?
	Is work displayed on classroom walls?
	Is a large proportion of the school week devoted to teaching?
	Do a large proportion of students report library use?
	Is course planning done by groups of teachers?
Skills of Teachers	Do teachers spend a large proportion of their instruction with students involved?
	Do inexperienced teachers consult with experienced teachers about classroom management?
Teachers' Actions in Lessons	Do teachers spend a large proportion of time on the lesson topic?
	Do teachers spend less time with equipment, discipline, and handing out papers?
	Do most teachers interact with the class as a whole?
	Do teachers provide time for periods of quiet work?
	Do teachers end lessons on time?
Rewards and Punishments	
Punishment	Are there generally recognized and accepted standards of discipline uniformly enforced by leaders?
Rewards	Do teachers praise students' work in class?
	Is there public praise of pupils at assemblies?
	Is students' work displayed on walls?
Pupil Conditions	Is there access to telephone and provisions for hot drinks?
	Is care in decoration of the classroom evident?
	Is there provision for school outings?
	Do students approach staff members about personal problems?
	Do teachers see students at any time?
Responsibility and Participation	Do a large proportion of students hold leadership positions?
	Do students participate in assemblies?
	Do students participate in charities organized by the school?
	Do students bring books and pencils to class?
Staff Organization	Do teachers plan courses together?
	Do teachers report adequate clerical help?
	Does the principal check to see that teachers give homework?
	Is administration aware of staff punctuality?
	Do teachers feel their views are represented in decision making?

Source: Effective Schools and Classrooms, ASCD, 1984, pp. 57–58.

Working backwards, researchers in the 1980s looked at effective schools—those that were working—and tried to verify their success with the findings of the original studies on teacher effectiveness. Evolving from this synthesis of literature and practice came the early foundations of prescription. Key variables that emerged and were formalized include the degree of academic emphasis in schools, the skills of the teacher, how the teacher delivers the lesson, rewards and punishments for students, the various conditions of pupils themselves, responsibility and participation of teachers, and staff organization. Some of the questions related to this inquiry are presented in Figure 6.1.

In particular, researchers have attempted to focus the improvement of instruction at the classroom level by asking questions about the teacher. What should the teacher know about students? What skills should he or she possess? Are there desirable sequences of behavior in the teaching act? What happens to students because of these teacher actions? Emerging from the study of teaching are general categories of competence (see Figure 6.2) and the rudiments of an outline for successful teaching.

One highly developed example of such a prescription can be drawn from the Florida Beginning Teacher Project, a culminating program of the Florida Accountability Act of 1976. This program, mandated for all new teachers in the state, requires training and evaluation according to a set of sequential skills. For the sake of clarity, indicators of these behaviors are listed in the comments section of Figure 6.3.

As the reader can observe, a prescriptive pattern emerges for teacher behavior based on available studies. The effective teacher enters the room and quickly gets down to business (time-on-task). Stu-

Figure 6.2
General Competency Areas for Teachers

1. Oral Communication	13. Presents Directions
2. Written Communication	14. Test Construction
3. Listening Comprehension	15. Establishes Routines
4. Reading Comprehension	16. Behavior Standards
5. Fundamental Math Skills	17. Management Techniques
6. Human Growth, Development	18. Record Keeping System
7. Entry Level Diagnosis	19. Human Growth, Development
8. Long Range Goals	20. Cultural Awareness
9. Lesson Objectives	21. Student Self Concept
10. Instructional Materials	22. Positive Interaction
11. Select/Develop, Sequence Activities	23. Values Clarification
12. Establishes Rapport	24. Special Needs Children

Source: Florida Beginning Teacher Program, 1985. Reprinted with permission.

Figure 6.3
Florida Teacher Assessment Instrument with Sample Concerns (pp. 152–155)

PHASE I OBSERVATION INSTRUMENT

	FREQUENCY	COMMENTS	FREQUENCY	
1. Begins instruction promptly/maintains instruction				Delays/interruptions
2. Handles materials in an orderly manner		Punctuality Management transition Wait time avoidance Controlled interruptions		Does not organize materials systematically
3. Orients students to classwork		Lesson initiation Academic transition signals		
4. Conducts beginning/ending review		Lesson-initiating review Topic summary within lesson Lesson-end review		
5. Maintains academic focus				Uses talk/activity unrelated to subject
6. Modulates speech				Uses loud-grating/high pitched/monotone/low inaudible
7. Utilizes verbal-nonverbal behavior to show interest/enthusiasm				Uses sarcasm/frowns/humdrum/glares/shows disgust

PHASE II OBSERVATION INSTRUMENT

	FREQUENCY	COMMENTS	FREQUENCY
8. Treats concepts-definitions/examples/non-examples			Gives definitions or examples only
9. Applies laws, rules, principles			
10. Uses linking words (thus, therefore, etc.)			
11. Emphasizes important points			

Figure 6.3
(continued)

PHASE III OBSERVATION INSTRUMENT

	FREQUENCY	COMMENTS	FREQUENCY	
12. Asks questions — single factual				Uses multiple questions asked as one
requires analysis/ reasons				Uses non-academic/ procedural questions
13. Recognizes/ amplifies/corrective feedback		Acknowledges a student response Extension of student response by probing (amplifying)		Ignores/harshly responds to student talk
		Discussion of student response by peer involvement		
14. Gives specific academic praise				Overuses general praise/ non-specific
15. Provides for practice and checks for academic comprehension				Extends lecture/changes topics/no practice

154

PHASE IV OBSERVATION INSTRUMENT

FREQUENCY		COMMENTS	FREQUENCY	
	16. Utilizes correct spelling/grammar/ mathematics/etc.			Makes academic errors— spelling/grammar/ mathematics/etc.
	17.			Uses vague/scrambled discourse
	18. Gives directions/ assigns/checks comprehension of homework/ assignment/ feedback			Gives inadequate directions/no homework check/feedback
	19. Circulates and assists students consistently			Remains at desk/ inappropriate circulation/ assistance
	20. Stops misconduct and maintains instructional momentum	Reacting to an irrelevant stimulus Flip-flop Dangles		Delays/does not stop misconduct
				Stops misconduct/loses momentum

Source: Florida Beginning Teacher Program, 1985. Reprinted with permission.

155

dents are given the big picture (advanced organizers) and the teacher enthusiastically begins coverage of the lesson. Students are given the opportunity to ask relevant questions and the teacher reinforces correct answers with praise. Throughout the lesson the teacher moves about the room and systematically redirects irrelevance and misconduct back to the focus of the lesson. Homework is recognized in this model as an integral part of the instructional process.

What such a model of teaching suggests is that the teacher be extremely directive during instruction. It assumes that the purpose of the instructional process is mastery of the lesson. It focuses time and teacher behavior toward lesson learning. It should be recalled that most of the research for such a model comes from studies of disadvantaged students who were scoring poorly on national standardized tests.* This is one conception of teaching and learning.

The important point to be remembered about the current research-based prescription for teaching is that it represents only one of many conceptions of the learning process. If the supervisor's job is to synchronize the objectives of the curriculum with the methodology of the teacher, then a review of the purpose and objectives of the curriculum is the beginning point for improvement of the instructional process. Stated another way, the supervisor must be careful to draw the connection between what teachers are being asked to do in the classroom and the global intentions of the learning plan.

THREE MODELS OF TEACHING

While much of what we know about teaching was summarized in the late 1970s and early 1980s, we have continued to gain understanding about other possible prescriptions for teachers and learners. McNeil and Wiles[3] have suggested the three basic patterns outlined below:

The Direct Teaching Model

The Direct Teaching Model is characterized by predetermined learning outcomes and high degrees of teacher control (structure) over the learning process. In this model, the teacher structures the learning process heavily, thus narrowing the teaching-learning focus, and enforces this focus on student learning.

The Indirect Teaching Model

The Indirect Teaching Model is characterized by a greater sharing of control over the teaching-learning process by the teacher. Learning

---

*Research on teaching has tended to follow the funding available for research. Studies of disadvantaged learners bring prescriptions for disadvantaged students.

intentions are more general and the teacher allows greater flexibility (more intervening variables) in the learning environment. This pattern is also known as interactive teaching.

The Self-Directed Model

The Self-Directed Model is characterized by the teacher relinquishing significant control over the learning process and allowing greater flexibility (student choices) in the process of learning. Learning in this model is accomplished primarily through small group work and independent study, and the teacher serves as a facilitator in order to maximize each student's growth.

RESEARCH ON TEACHER EFFECTIVENESS

Research since 1980 on teacher effectiveness has been clustered in each of these areas, producing for the first time a "technical" prescription for different kinds of learning outcomes. Outlined below are three examples in each model for the reader's consideration:

Direct Model Research

A. Mastery Learning (Bloom, Burkey, Gates)
   1. Preassessment of student
   2. Instructional objectives (behavioral)
   3. Criterion-referenced expectation for student learning
   4. Drill and practice methodology
   5. Accepted levels of performance
   6. Summative tests of mastery

   Findings: Positive achievement results, greater benefit at the elementary level, more engaged (time-on-task) learnings.
B. Direct Questioning Techniques (Rosenshine)
   1. Short questions and answers (narrow focus drill)
   2. Focus on answers (pause-prompt-praise)
   3. Immediate reinforcement by teacher (select praise)
   4. Higher level cognition for some students

   Findings: Effective with disadvantaged learners, best with skill mastery, increases textbook learning, higher cognitive functioning with better students.
C. Use of Programmed Computer-aided Instruction
   1. Drill and practice formats
   2. Teaching of programming skills

   Findings: More engaged learning time, improved motivation with disadvantaged learners, improved logical thinking.

Indirect Model Research

A. Interactive Questioning Procedures (Rowe, Swift, Gooding)
   1. Extended "wait time" for student answers
   2. More open-ended questions
   3. Involves more students in formulating answers
   4. Builds on student responses—related questions
   5. Prevents teacher bias in questioning

   Findings: Longer verbal responses by students, more student engagement in learning, more high-level student learning exhibited, increased achievement, increased minority participation.
B. Grouping Practices—Cooperative (Slavin, Palincsar)
   1. Mixed ability at appropriate levels
   2. Reciprocal student teaching—framing questions, predicting, summarizing etc.

   Findings: High achievement in reading and math, increased achievement in all areas grades 3–12, increased reading comprehension.
C. Teacher Expectation (Dusek, Good)
   1. Higher and preconceived expectations for students
   2. Low and preconceived expectations for students.

   Findings: High expectation brings initial achievement gains, low expectation brings significantly lower achievement gain.

Self-Directed Model Research

A. Use of small groups in instruction (Swing, Lucker)
   1. Placing students in small learning teams

   Findings: Higher gains for low achievers, better minority performance, better conflict resolution.
B. Teaching Meta-Cognition (Perkins, Marzano)
   1. Teaching "learning to learn" skills
   2. Teaching tactical intelligence (thinking frames)

   Findings: Increases student independence in learning, promising increases in creative thinking.
C. Self-Concept Development (Gerlach, Bayer, Yawkey)
   1. Proving experience in skill enhancement
   2. Instilling pride in learners

   Findings: Effective only if tied to certain levels of task orientation.

In summary, research since the early process-product studies in the 1970s seems to suggest that achievement can be gained by a number of different teaching patterns. While these findings should be viewed as tentative, the true message appears to be that teaching can produce varied outcomes in learners. As we focus more on the purpose of teaching and learning, we will have an increased capacity to prescribe style and technique for teachers in order to be effective.

WORKING IN CLASSROOMS WITH TEACHERS

Armed with a conception of teaching and the latest knowledge of what research says about effective instruction, the supervisor enters the classroom to work directly with the teacher. Regardless of the level of experience of that teacher, there are three basic tasks to be accomplished through supervisory activity: (1) to help the teacher develop an intellectual understanding of the scholarly, psychological, and professional dimensions of teaching, (2) to develop and apply the relevant skills of teaching in the classroom, and (3) to coordinate the delivery of the curriculum as it was intended by those who planned the program.

One of the first tasks for the supervisor is to gain a shared perception of what is supposed to be happening in the classroom with the teacher. Most teachers carry in their heads a picture of "teacher" and that picture may or may not correspond with the view held by the supervisor or district leaders. Less common is a teacher who can envision the entire curriculum as a planned experience. The supervisor, by the nature of the job, has such a global perspective and sharing it with a teacher constitutes a beginning point. In the words of Charles Silberman in his classic book, *Crisis in the Classroom:*

> If mindlessness is the central problem, the solution must be in infusing the various educational institutions with purpose, more important, with thought about purpose and the way in which techniques, content, and organization fulfill or alter purpose.[4]

There are many ways to go about this first important task. Curriculum mapping (see chapter five) may reveal the relationship of the teacher's subject to all other content being taught in the school. The supervisor may provide the teacher with "facts" about schoolwide problems (see Figure 6.4) to initiate a discussion of purpose. A third method of gaining the attention of the teacher concerning the role of instruction is to provide assistance in seeing the kind of instructional variables that are more obvious to the supervisor. Simply talking about the organization of a classroom (see Figure 6.5) reveals a great deal about what is and is not happening in the teacher's room:

1. What kind of instruction does the organization of the room suggest?

Figure 6.4
Common Schoolwide Problems

Student Attendance, Behavior and Discipline
Attendance
☐ Frequent truancy.
☐ Frequent tardiness.
☐ Frequent class-cutting.
☐ High absentee rate.
☐ High dropout rate.
☐ High rate of student mobility.

Behavior and Discipline
☐ Vandalism.
☐ Violence.
☐ Disruptive classroom behavior.
☐ Students' use of illegal drugs.
☐ Disruptive behavior on campus or playground.
☐ Frequent referrals of students to office for disciplinary action.
☐ Disruptive behavior caused by outsiders.
☐ Excessive noise level and confusion throughout the school.
☐ Disrespect for authority.

Improvement of Basic Academic Achievement
☐ Pupils perform below real ability.
☐ Students not prepared for grade level.
☐ Students consider curriculum irrelevant.
☐ Instructional materials are too difficult.
☐ Advanced course offerings not available in some subjects.
☐ Low standardized test scores.
☐ Students do poorly on daily work.
☐ Graduates seem unprepared for job market or higher education.
☐ High rate of student failure.
☐ Students can't apply basic skills.

Continued Commitment to Reduction of Racial Isolation
☐ Student polarization along racial lines.
☐ Division among faculty along racial lines.
☐ Student-teacher antagonism along racial lines.
☐ Racially-motivated hostility in the community.
☐ Unequal status roles for minorities in curriculum materials.
☐ Transported students feel unwelcome.
☐ Racial groups establish certain areas of the school as their "territory."
☐ School lacks unified approach to reducing racial isolation.
☐ Parents of transported students are not involved in the school.
☐ Avoidance of problem situation by school personnel.

Figure 6.5
Two Contrasting Classroom Organizations (pp. 161–162)

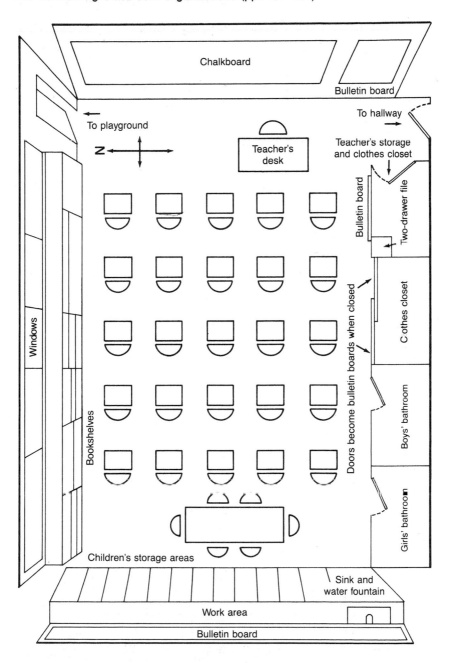

A typical arrangement for direct teaching.

Figure 6.5
(Continued)

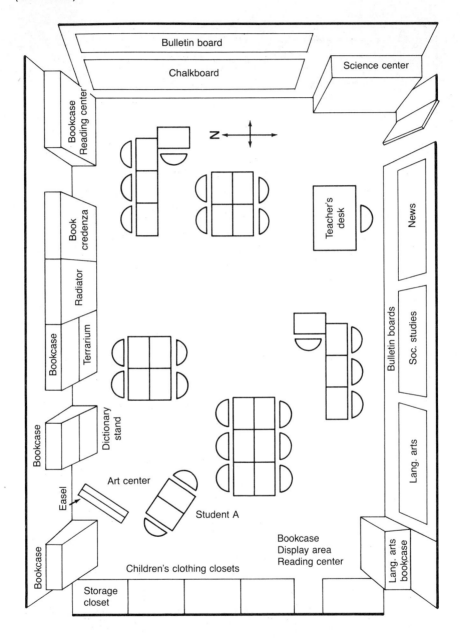

Sample arrangement of a small classroom to accommodate
indirect teaching.

2. What kind of space priorities are there in this room? To whom does the space belong?
3. What kind of movement is suggested in this room? How does this pattern fit with the type of instruction that the teacher or curriculum intends?
4. Where are the learning materials in this room? Are they accessible to students? To the teacher?
5. Does the arrangement of furniture in this room allow the type of learning intended (lecture, independent study, small group)?
6. Does this arrangement allow for climate setting objects such as student work, plants, or personal objects to be displayed?
7. What is the effect of this arrangement on discipline? How far away is the most distant student? Do students have lateral vision (can they see others besides the teacher) in this room?

Regardless of the technique for establishing communication about the classroom, it is essential that the supervisor and the teacher develop a shared reality that can become the basis of professional dialogue. Without this point of origin, the supervisor will remain an outsider who has come to judge the teacher. A typical response heard from teachers in schools where good communication is lacking is that the supervisor "doesn't know what's happening in my room."

A second stage to the improvement of instruction through supervision is to become more clinical in viewing the processes and procedures of the classroom. Once the supervisor and the teacher reach an agreement upon the intent of the curriculum and begin to share a reality about conditions in the classroom, an organized way of seeing is needed. Fortunately, the field of supervision has made dramatic breakthroughs in this realm since 1960. Two areas, interaction analysis and the analysis of classroom questioning, serve as examples.

Interaction Analysis

During the past thirty years, the concept of systematic classroom observations has been fully developed.* By its very nature, an observational system represents an effective means of providing objective and empirical data describing specific teacher and student variables that are found to interact in a given teaching-learning situation. Data of this sort can help reinforce previously held conceptions of reality or call into question stereotypic perceptions held by either the supervisor

---

*For a thorough treatment of these changes, see C.M. Galloway, "Non-Verbal and Teacher-Student Relationships," in Aaron Wolfgang (ed.), *Non-Verbal Behavior* (New York: C.J. Hogrete, Inc., 1984), pp. 411–430.

or the teacher. Systematic observation reduces global perceptions or feelings to a data state that can be analyzed and fully interpreted.

Currently, a number of manageable observational systems are available for teacher use. Each is specifically designed to assess a different and particular dimension of the classroom situation. Originally developed by Flanders, interaction analysis is designed to assess the verbal dimension of teacher-pupil interaction in the classroom.

Flanders developed a category system that takes into account the verbal interaction between teachers and pupils in the classroom. The system enables one to determine whether the teacher controls students in such a way as to increase or decrease freedom or action. Through the use of observers or audio or videotape equipment, a teacher can review the results of a teaching lesson. Every three seconds an observer writes down the category number of the interaction he or she has just observed; the numbers are recorded in sequence in a column. Whether the observer is using a live classroom or tape recording for observations, it is best that he or she spend ten to fifteen minutes getting oriented to the situation before categorizing. The observer stops classifying whenever the classroom activity is inappropriate as, for instance, when there is silent reading or when various groups are working in the classroom, or when children are working in their workbooks.

Table 6.1

Description of Categories for a Thirteen-Category Modification of the Flanders System of Interaction Analysis

	Category Number	Description of Verbal Behavior
	1.	*Accepts Feeling:* Accepts and clarifies the feeling tone of students in a friendly manner. Student feelings may be of a positive or negative nature. Predicting and recalling student feelings are also included.
T E A C H E R I N D I R E C T	2.	*Praises or Encourages:* Praises or encourages student action, behavior recitation, comments, ideas, etc. Jokes that release tension not at the expense of another individual. Teacher nodding head or saying "uh-huh" or "go on" are included.
	3.	*Accepts or Uses Ideas of Student:* Clarifying, building on, developing, and accepting the action, behavior, and ideas of the student.
	4.	*Asks Questions:* Asking a question about the content (subject matter) or procedure with the intent that the student should answer.
	5.	*Answers Student Questions: (Student-Initiated Teacher Talk):* Giving direct answers to student questions regarding content or procedures.

Table 6.1
(Continued)

	Category Number	Description of Verbal Behavior
T A L K — D I R E C T	6.	*Lecture (Teacher-Initiated Teacher Talk):* Giving facts, information, or opinions about content or procedure. Teacher expressing his or her own ideas. Asking rhetorical questions (not intended to be answered).
	7.	*Gives Directions:* Directions, commands, or orders to which the student is expected to comply.
	8.	*Corrective Feedback:* Telling a student that his answer is wrong when the correctness of his answer can be established other than opinions (i.e., empirical validation, definition, or custom).
	9.	*Criticizes Student(s) or Justifies Authority:* Statements intended to change student behavior from a nonacceptable to an acceptable pattern; scolding someone; stating why the teacher is doing what he is doing so as to gain or maintain control; rejecting or criticizing a student's opinion or judgment.
S T U D E N T — T A L K	10.	*Teacher-Initiated Student Talk:* Talk by students in response to requests or narrow teacher questions. The teacher initiates the contact or solicits student's statements.
	11.	*Student Questions:* Student questions concerning content or procedure that are directed to the teacher.
	12.	*Student-Initiated Student Talk:* Talk by students in response to broad teacher questions which require judgment or opinion. Voluntary declarative statements offered by the student, but not called for by the teacher.
	13.	*Silence or Confusion:* Pauses, short periods of silence, and periods of confusion in which communication cannot be understood by an observer.

Indirect-Direct Ratio — categories 1, 2, 3, 4, 5; categories 6, 7, 8, 9

Revised Indirect-Direct Ratio = categories 1, 2, 3; categories 7, 8, 9

Student-Teacher Ratio = categories 10, 11, 12; categories 1, 2, 3, 4, 5, 6, 7, 8, 9

Source: John B. Hough, "A Thirteen Category Modification of Flanders' System of Interaction Analysis," mimeograph (Columbus: The Ohio State University, 1965).

A modification of the Flanders system of ten categories is a system developed by Hough and used by Bondi in research studies.[5] This system provides three more categories of behavior than the Flanders system. In the thirteen-category system, teacher statements are classified as either indirect or direct. This classification gives central attention to the amount of freedom a teacher gives to the student. In a given situation, the teacher can choose to be indirect, maximizing

Table 6.2

Summary of Categories for the Bondi and Ober Reciprocal Category System

Category Number Assigned to Party 1*	Description of Verbal Behavior	Category Number Assigned to Party 2+
1	"WARMS" (INFORMALIZES) THE CLIMATE: Tends to open up and/or eliminate the tension of the situation; praises or encourages the action, behavior, comments, ideas, and/or contributions of another; jokes that release tension not at the expense of others; accepts and clarifies the feeling tone of another in a friendly manner (feelings may be positive or negative; predicting or recalling the feelings of another are included).	11
2	ACCEPTS: Accepts the action, behavior, comments, ideas, and/or contributions of another; *positive reinforcement* of these.	12
3	AMPLIFIES THE CONTRIBUTIONS OF ANOTHER: Asks for clarification of, builds on, and/or develops the action, behavior, comments, ideas and/or contributions of another.	13
4	ELICITS: Asks a question or requests information about the content, subject, or procedure being considered with the intent that another should answer (respond).	14
5	RESPONDS: Gives direct answer or response to questions or requests for information that are initiated by another, includes answers to one's own questions.	15
6	INITIATES: Presents facts, information, and/or opinion concerning the content, subject, or procedures being considered that are self-initiated; expresses one's own ideas; lectures (includes rhetorical questions— not intended to be answered).	16
7	DIRECTS: Gives directions, instructions, order, and/or assignments to which another is expected to comply.	17
8	CORRECTS: Tells another that his answer or behavior is inappropriate or incorrect.	18
9	"COOLS" (FORMALIZES) THE CLIMATE: Makes statements intended to modify the behavior of another from an inappropriate to an appropriate pattern; may tend to create a certain amount of tension (i.e., bawling out someone, exercising authority in order to gain or maintain control of the situation, rejecting or criticizing the opinion or judgment of another).	19
10	SILENCE OR CONFUSION: Pauses, short periods of silence, and periods of confusion in which communication cannot be understood by the observer.	20

Source: From Joseph Bondi, "The Reciprocal Category System—A System for Assessing Classroom Verbal Interaction" (Tampa: University of South Florida, 1988). Used with permission.

*Category numbers assigned to Teacher Talk when used in classroom situation.

+Category numbers assigned to Student Talk when used in classroom situation.

freedom of a student to respond, or direct, minimizing the freedom of a student to respond. Teacher response is classified under the first nine categories.

Student talk is classified under three categories and a fourth category provides for silence or confusion where neither a student nor the teacher can be heard. All categories are mutually exclusive, yet include all verbal interaction occurring in the classroom. Table 6.1 describes the categories in the thirteen category modification of the Flanders System of Interaction Analysis. Table 6.2 describes the Reciprocal Category System. This system, developed by Bondi and Ober, is an elaboration of the ten and thirteen category systems of interaction analysis. Utilizing the Flanders system and its other modifictions, teachers and supervisors can begin to isolate the essential elements of effective teaching by analyzing and categorizing the verbal behavioral patterns of teachers and students.

Four classroom patterns that particularly affect pupil learning are thrown into sharp relief when verbal patterns are identified and revealed by these techniques. The first pattern can be labeled "the excessive teacher-talk pattern." This occurs when teachers talk two-thirds or more of the time in the classroom. Obviously, if teachers are talking that much, there is very little time for students to get in the act. In classrooms where teachers talk this much, pity the curriculum approaches that emphasize extensive student participation in learning. Yet such a percentage of teacher-talk is found in many classrooms today. Teachers can become aware of and able to control the amount of time they spend talking in the classroom through the use of feedback from interaction analysis.[6] This finding alone makes interaction analysis an effective teaching and supervisory tool.

Classroom Questions. In the Flanders or Modified System of Interaction Analysis, only one category of behavior deals with questions. That category concerns a teacher asking questions about content or procedure in order to elicit a student response. For a teacher to encourage greater understanding of her or his questions, other types of feedback instruments must be used.

Questioning is probably the most ancient pedagogical method. The Socratic dialectics and Plato's dialogues have been used throughout history as models for teachers. As pointed out when we discussed recitation, unfortunately most of the questions asked by teachers require little thinking on the part of students. A number of reports in recent years have confirmed the high frequency of teacher questions that require little more than the recall of memorized material.[7]

Perhaps these reports of the low level of teachers' questioning are the result of a tradition of asking set questions requiring memorized answers. In improving classroom instruction, we must examine

Table 6.3
Classifying Classroom Questions

Category	Key Word	Typical Question Words
1. KNOWLEDGE (Any question, regardless of complexity, that can be answered through simple recall of previously learned material.) e.g., "What reasons did Columbus give for wanting to sail west to find a new world?"	Remember	1. Name 2. List; Tell 3. Define 4. Who? When? What? 5. Yes or No questions: e.g., "Did . . . ?" "Was . . . ?" " Is. . . ?" 6. How many? How much? 7. Recall or identify terminology. 8. What did the book say . . . ?
2. COMPREHENSION (Questions that can be answered by merely restating or reorganizing material in a rather literal manner to show that the student understands the essential meaning.) e.g., "Give the ideas in your own words."	Understand	1. Give an example . . . 2. What is the most important idea? 3. What will probably happen? 4. What caused this? 5. Compare. (What things are the same?) 6. Contrast. (What things are different?) 7. Why did you say that? 8. Give the idea in your own words.
3. APPLICATION (Questions that involve problem solving in new situations with minimal identification or prompting of the appropriate rules, principles, or concepts.) e.g., "How big an air conditioner?"	Solve the problem	1. Solve 2. How could you find an answer to . . . ? 3. Apply the generalization to . . .
4. ANALYSIS (Questions that require the student to break an idea into its component parts for logical analysis: assumptions, facts, opinions, logical conclusions, etc.)	Logical Order	1. What reason does he give for his conclusions? 2. What method is he using to convince you? 3. What does the author seem to believe? 4. What words indicate bias or emotion?

Table 6.3
(Continued)

Category	Key Word	Typical Question Words
e.g., "Are the conclusions supported by facts or opinion?"		5. Does the evidence given support the conclusion?
5. SYNTHESIS	Create	1. Create a plan . . .
		2. Develop a model . . .
(Questions that require the student to combine his ideas into a statement, plan, product, etc., that is new for him.)		3. Combine those parts . . .
e.g., "Can you develop a program that includes the best parts of each of those ideas?"		
6. EVALUATION	Judge	1. Evaluate that idea in terms of . . .
(Questions that require the student to make a judgment about something using some criteria or standard for making his judgment.)		2. For what reasons do you favor . . .
		3. Which policy do you think would result in the greatest good for the greatest number?

Source: Rosemarie McCartin, "Raising the Level of Teacher Questions by Systematic Reinforcement" (Paper read at the annual meeting of the American Educational Research Association, Los Angeles, February, 1969).

ways teachers' questioning ability can be developed. One of the most frequently used guides to the cognitive level of teachers' questions has been Bloom's *Taxonomy of Educational Objectives.*[8] A report of studies conducted by Farley and Clegg indicated that training in the knowledge and use of Bloom's taxonomy helps teachers increase their use of questions at higher cognitive levels.[9] Table 6.3 illustrates the use of Bloom's taxonomy in classifying teacher questions.

A final system of analyzing and controlling classroom questioning techniques that has been used extensively in training teachers is the Gallagher-Aschner method. Shown below in Table 6.4, the Gallagher-Aschner system easily displays the "level" of questioning used by the teacher.

Together, these examples of systems to assess interaction and questioning in the classroom suggest that there are tools now available to supervisors to help focus perceptions of classroom instruction. The

Table 6.4
The Gallagher Aschner System—A Technique for Analyzing
and Controlling Classroom Questioning Behavior

1. *Cognitive-Memory:* calls for a specific memorized answer to response; anything which can be retrieved from the memory bank.

    1a. What is 2 × 3?
    1b. When did Florida become a state?
    1c. What is a noun?
    1d. At what temperature Centigrade does water boil?

2. *Convergent:* calls for a specific (single) correct answer which may be obtained by the application of a rule or procedure; normally requires the consideration of more than a single quantity of information and/or knowledge.

    2a. What is 30.5 × 62.7?
    2b. How many years was the U.S. under the Prohibition Law?
    2c. Diagram this sentence.
    2d. How many calories are required to melt 160 grams of ice at 0 C?

3. *Divergent:* allows the student a choice between more than one alternative or to create ideas of his own; more than a single answer is appropriate and acceptable.

    3a. What is 10 to three other bases?
    3b. What might have been the effects on the growth of the United States had there not been a Civil War?
    3c. Write a short story about Halloween.
    3d. Design an apparatus that will demonstrate the Law of Conservation of Matter.

4. *Evaluative:* the development and/or establishment of relevant standard of criteria of acceptability involving considerations as usefulness, desirability, social and cultural appropriateness, and moral and ethical propriety, then comparing the issue at hand to these; involves the making of value judgments.

    4a. Is 10 the best base for a number system?
    4b. Was the Civil War defensible?
    4c. Is English the best choice for a universal language?
    4d. Should we continue our space program now that we have landed on the moon?

Source: J.J. Gallagher and Mary Jane Aschner, "A Preliminary Report: Analyses of Classroom Interaction," *Merrill-Palmer Quarterly of Behavior and Development* 9 (1963): 183–94.

reduction of "opinion" by the teacher and supervisor to the study of "data" is an important step in building the case for specific skill development through inservice activities regardless of the experience level of the teacher. The integration of individual teacher inservice needs into a staff development plan are addressed fully in chapter eight.

    The final step of supervision to improve instruction in the classroom is to begin to coordinate the delivery of the curriculum by re-

Figure 6.6
An Instructional Paradigm

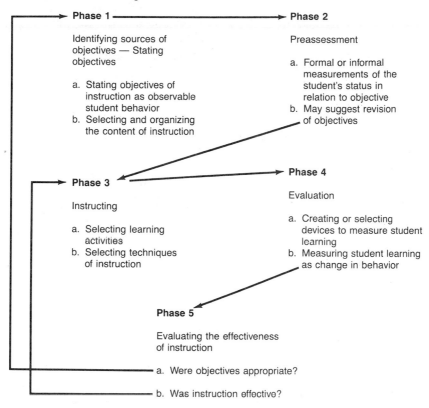

vealing the curriculum-instruction interface and by removing the detrimental conditions identified by the teacher.

THE CURRICULUM INSTRUCTION INTERFACE

Having classroom instruction subsumed within curriculum is made easier if the supervisor has previously implemented a district-wide curriculum development effort. The reader will recall that in chapter five that type of planning was constructed around a cycle of development and included items such as needs assessments, goal statements, a map of the total curriculum, textbook analysis and other related steps. If the teacher has been involved in such a process, repeating such a cycle at the classroom level will come easily. Shown above in Figure 6.6 is an instructional paradigm that illustrates the connecting steps to improving the classroom program. It begins with a review of what the general purpose of the program is, as derived from the district plan, and ends with an assessment of whether the outcomes of the classroom teaching contributed to those purposes.

The classroom teacher may have difficulty translating the more global goals at the district level to his or her grade level and subject. For the most part, such translation will be a matter of how to teach rather than what to teach. The supervisor should encourage the teacher to gather more information about the target of instruction so that an approach can be devised. Listed here are some common methods of gathering information about students:

Informal Observation. Teachers can become more aware of a student's interests, physical and mental sets, and potential for learning by informal observations of students in instructional settings. Supervisors can sit with teachers as they observe a child and help teachers identify behaviors that will enhance or inhibit learning. Informal observation is a particularly helpful technique in diagnosis because it allows teachers to see a child as a person rather than a statistic.

Experienced supervisors can use observations to point out patterns of student behavior that teachers can use to determine readiness for learning. Teachers looking for reading readiness often rely solely on formal testing when they could just as easily determine readiness through informal observations.

Interest Surveys. Supervisors can suggest a variety of interest surveys for teachers to use in determining student interests. Most surveys utilize the "what I like most or least" technique. Students like to respond to these surveys and teachers can find the information they are seeking about student interests.

Time Samplings. Teachers can use time samplings in observing individuals or groups. In this method, teachers jot down entries on a card every few minutes during a portion of the school day. The information recorded describes the exact behavior of a student or a group of students and can yield useful information about work habits and group interaction.

Anecdotal Records. A more formal record of observations of student behavior can be obtained by recording descriptions of student behavior in various situations over a number of weeks or months. Anecdotal records give important clues to a child's self-concept and personal or intellectual needs. An evaluation of the records is not made until behavioral patterns can be identified by the teacher.

Sociometric Anaylsis. Sociometric studies can help teachers study interpersonal relationships in a group setting. The social structure of a class can be determined by asking students to list classmates they would prefer to work with on a project or identify the students they would like for class leaders.

The teacher uses the information to plot a sociogram that graphically depicts the social pattern of a class; cliques, social stars, class leaders, and isolates can be identified. Teachers can use this information to structure situations that will allow greater student interaction. New friendships and a greater sense of belonging will hopefully evolve as students form new social relationships.

Standardized Tests. Supervisors need to help teachers understand not only the potential but also the limitations of tests in providing information about students. Group tests generally are not as definitive as tests administered individually. Students with special problems, therefore, need to be tested individually by the teacher or a specialist.

Supervisors should help teachers in interpreting test results. Many times a teacher will use test results as the sole criterion for determining a pupil's abilities. This often leads to stereotyping a child as "bright" or "not so bright." Test results should be used as information, not judgment. Information gathered through informal observations can help teachers interpret test data relating to a given student more accurately.

Files and Cumulative Records. Cumulative folders and files may contain samples of a student's work, test results, and other descriptive information. Supervisors must help teachers apply the same principles used in writing anecdotal records to these data; descriptive rather than interpretive information should be recorded. Comments that are judgmental have no place in a student's file or cumulative folder. Professional access to student files should be carefully controlled.

Teacher-prepared Diagnostic Materials. Supervisors can help teachers prepare diagnostic materials that identify a child's reading level, mastery of a math skill, or other areas of performance. Often, the best diagnostic materials are those prepared by a teacher rather than those prepared by a person unfamiliar with the student.

Parent Conferences. The parent conference can be helpful to the teacher in providing information about family expectations, home environment, and quality of family relationships. Parents many times inform teachers about unique home problems that may be affecting school work.

Pupil Conferences. Student conferences can provide teachers with information that cannot be obtained elsewhere. As with parent conferences, there must be a feeling of mutual trust during the conference. Comfortable settings and a friendly, open atmosphere contribute to that feeling of trust. Supervisors can use a variety of techniques (e.g., modeling and role playing) to help teachers develop good conference skills.

Using this local input the teacher begins to ask the question, "How can I teach what is intended to the students in my class in a manner that will be both honest and effective?" Such a question may call for different instructional techniques or even a new organizational pattern in the school itself.

Another place that many teachers bog down in planning instruction is with the basic lesson plan for the day. Somehow, in many schools, there is an idea that lesson plans are for student teachers and not for veterans of the classroom. Yet, in reviewing the literature on effective teaching, goal-clarity is an essential skill regardless of the method employed. Lesson plans can be simple (see Figure 6.7), but should reflect a deductive logic from the annual plan, the quarterly (grading period) outline, this week's goals and objectives, and today's tasks. It is interesting to report that research suggests that listing the goals for the week on the bulletin board or similar place will greatly increase goal-focus each day.

Still another place that teachers may need assistance in. linking the curriculum with their instruction is in the selection of materials. It is a fact that in many districts, the textbook is the curriculum. But what happens, for instance, if the text is unreadable or overly difficult for students? Supervisors should be familiar with the following readability formulas and be able to assist teachers in using them to analyze their primary instructional materials:[10]

1. Flesch Reading Ease Score – Grades 5–12. Involves checking word length and sentence length. Source: Flesch, R.F. *How to Test Readability.* New York: Harper & Brothers, 1959.

2. Wheeler and Smith – Index Number. Involves determining sentence length and number of polysyllabic words. Grades: Primary–4. Source: Wheeler, L.R., and Smith, E.H. "A Practical Readability Formula for the Classroom Teacher in the Primary Grades." *Elementary English* 31 (November 1954); 397–99.

3. The Cloze Technique. The readability of two pieces of material can be compared by the Cloze technique. Measures redundancy (the extent to which words are predictable) while standard readability formulas measure the factors of vocabulary sentence structure. It can be used to determine relative readability of material, but cannot predict readability of a new sample. It does not give grade level designations. Source: Taylor, W.C. "Cloze Procedure: A New Tool for Measuring Readability." *Journalism Quarterly* 30 (Fall 1953): 415–33.

4. Lorge Grade Placement Score – Grades 3–12. Uses average sentence length in words, number of difficult words per 100 words not on the Dale 769-word list, and number of prepositional

Figure 6.7
Lesson Plan Form

_____

                                    Teacher _____

                                    Lesson Title _____

                                    Unit _____

GOAL(S):

OBJECTIVE(S):

PROCEDURES AND MATERIALS:

EVALUATION:

_____

    phrases per 100 words. Source: Lorge, I. _The Lorge Formula for Estimating Difficulty of Reading Materials._ New York: Teachers' College Press, 1959.
  5. The Fry Graph. Method is based on two factors: average number of syllables per 100 words, and average number of sen-

tences per 100 words. Three randomly selected 100 word samples are used. Source: Fry, Edward. "Graph for Estimating
Readability." *Journal of Reading* (April 1968): 513–16, and
Reading Teacher (March 1969): 22–27.
6. SMOG Grading Plan—Grades 4–12. Involves counting repetition of polysyllabic words. Source: McLaughlin, Harry G.
"SMOG Grading—A New Readability Formula." *Journal of
Reading* 12 (1969): 639–46.
7. Spache Grade Level Score—Grades 1–3. Looks at average sentence length and number of words outside Dale list of 769
words to give readability level. Source: Spache, G. "A New
Readability Formula for Primary Grade Reading Materials."
Elementary School Journal 53 (March 1953): 410–13.

A final area that will help the teacher link instruction with the
planned curriculum is assessing student performance. A beginning
point for such work is the observation that instruction is designed to
bring about the achievement of selected learning objectives. Learning
other than that which is planned occurs, of course, but the purpose of
formal instruction is to bring about learning that might not occur in
a less organized fashion. Conferencing with the teacher about the following types of assessment may help focus the teacher's classroom
behaviors.

The Concept of Mastery. The topic of learning outcomes mastery
introduces a need for a change in how we think about instruction as
well as assessment. In conventional instruction, students and teacher
expect few students to master all objectives so as to receive an A in a
course. When test scores are plotted as frequency distributions, a "normal curve" is formed, with students ranging in grades from A to F.
Such a system tends to fix academic goals of both students and teachers at low levels, thus reducing student and teacher motivation. Bloom
has proposed the concept of mastery learning where 90 to 95 percent
of students can actually master objectives now reached by only "good
students." This concept requires an effort by teachers to determine
why certain students fail to reach mastery and requires teachers to
remedy the situation through more time for learning, different materials, or diagnosis to determine what prerequisite skills are missing.
Thus, the mastery learning concept abandons the concept of students
learning more or less well.

Criterion-referenced Testing. An approach in assessing student performance that is receiving increased attention is that of criterion-
referenced testing. This technique of testing involves an interpretation
of test results in terms of the types of learning tasks students achieve

in some clearly defined area (e.g., that a student can define 90 percent of the terms in a social studies unit).

Supervisors must help teachers with the theory and research necessary for the preparation and use of criterion-referenced tests in the classroom.

Realiability of Objective-referenced Measures. Selecting criteria for items and tests designed to accomplish objective-referenced measurement requires standards of performance appropriate for the stated objective. The items used for assessment must also have reliability. The term *reliability* refers to consistency of measurement from one item to the next or one test to another.

Norm-referenced Measures. Tests that yield scores that compare one student's performance with that of a group are called "norm-referenced." These tests generally measure student achievement over relatively large segments of instructional content rather than specific objectives. The selection and interpretation of norm-referenced tests is a major task in instruction.

Supervisors are often called upon to answer parents' questions about results of norm-referenced tests. They must assist teachers in interpreting test results and provide guidance in strengthening segments of the instructional program where achievement is low.

Standardized Tests. Norm-referenced tests designed for large numbers of students in a region, or nation as a whole, may have norms that are standardized.

Standardized tests are not appropriate for us in assessing learning outcomes from lessons having specifiable objectives. They can be used to provide information about the effects of total instructional programs.

Teacher-designed Tests. Tests designed by teachers may be objective or norm-referenced tests. Norms generally refer to class norms.

Objective-referenced tests allow teachers to assess for attainment of specific objectives. They are more valuable to the classroom teacher than norm-referenced measures because they can provide the possibility of diagnostic help for students in overcoming specific learning deficiencies.

Alternatives to Grades. Wherever teaching and learning go on, grades usually become the end product of assessment of student learning. Recently, alternatives to grading have been proposed by those concerned with the effects grading has had on student attitudes toward learning and self. Computerized reporting systems, contract methods, and performance evaluation have been suggested as alternatives for traditional grades.

If supervisors are to help students and teachers realize the extent of their creative capacities, they must provide leadership in changing the grading game played in the classrooms.

In summary, the supervisor can assist the teacher in drawing the necessary connection between the planned curriculum of the district and the classroom instruction of that teacher by:

1. learning how to assess fully and interpret the needs of the learners in that classroom;
2. placing greater emphasis on objectives to be accomplished through instruction;
3. looking at the relevance and accessibility of instructional learning materials; and
4. becoming more comfortable with alternative measures of student learning.

The following general learning principles are presented for the reader's study:

1. One thing we are sure about in education is that no two learners and/or learning situations are alike. A learner is first of all an individual with unique needs, preferences, abilities, and so on. A teacher needs to recognize this and consider it carefully when carrying out his or her role as a "facilitator of learning."
2. The same set of stimuli is perceived differently by two different learners. Both the amount and the quality of learning that takes place are dependent upon how the learner perceives the available stimuli.
3. Learning objectives should be stated precisely and clearly so that both the learner and the teacher are aware of and in agreement with what is expected. When learning objectives are unclear and ambiguous, the learner becomes overly dependent upon the teacher. Moreover, ambiguous learning objectives create problems for the teacher when it comes time to measure the learning that has taken place — valid final evaluation may be impeded or impossible.
4. The teacher is an agent of instruction. As an agent of instruction, his or her role is one of "facilitating learning."
5. Teachers need to be capable of controlling their teaching behavior. They must learn how to plan and control their teaching behavior in order to facilitate the most effective learning.
6. It is quite likely that a teacher is unable to teach a learner

anything. In all probability a teacher can only hope to aid (facilitate) the student in learning.

7. A teacher must develop a sensitivity to and an ability for assessing a given learning situation. Sensing the situation, he or she must make accurate analyses and competent judgments about instructional methods and techniques that will result in maximum effective learning. To carry out this role effectively, the teacher should have available an adequate number and variety of tested instructional methods and techniques from which to draw.

8. To create an atmosphere conducive to learning, the teacher needs to display toward the learner the personal qualities of empathy, congruency, unconditionality of regard, and a willingness to be known. In such an atmosphere both the teacher and the learners are free and better able to communicate within the learning situation at hand. The relationship now becomes one of cooperation rather than competition and/or compliance.

9. Teachers need to learn to be "good listeners." Through careful listening practices the teacher becomes aware of the learner's feelings, needs, abilities, weaknesses, and so on. This awareness of the learner's nature enables the teacher to make proper analyses and plans to aid learning.

10. Neither indirect teaching behavior nor direct teaching behavior is to be preferred over the other. Rather, the proper use of each in a learning situation for which it is best suited is the optimum choice. This sensitivity of when and how to incorporate either direct or indirect teaching behavior is termed "control" or "flexibility."

NEW DIRECTIONS

The 1970s and 1980s became the decades of increased accountability, regulations, and statutes aimed at improving student performance. The top-down nature of those changes came into sharp conflict with the bottom-up teacher empowerment movement of the late 1980s and 1990s. Teachers were asked to make more instructional decisions while still attempting to meet numerous state and local regulations. Deciding what to teach, when to teach it, and who would teach it became new roles for teachers and administrators who were accustomed to following state instructional frameworks, defined instructional time, and "teach to the test" skills programs.

Bridging the gap between the decades of accountability and the decade of empowerment will largely fall to the instructional supervisor. Supervisors will work with groups of administrators and teachers, sharing responsibility for curriculum, instruction, and organization. At the same time, they will be responsible for making sure regulations and accountability measures still on the books will be met.

Cooperative learning among students will require retraining of teachers who are comfortable with whole group instruction. The growing number of students with social problems brought on by drugs, breakdown of the family, and other problems will require an affective dimension of the instructional program that is missing in many schools. These factors, coupled with an increasingly pluralistic society, require cooperative behavior among teachers, among students, and among teachers and students.

Year round schools is an idea that has re-emerged in the 1990s, especially in growth states like California and Florida. New demands on time and resources will tax supervisors as they work in schools operating on year round schedules.

SUMMARY

The primary job for a school supervisor is to improve the instructional experience for students in a school. To insure that the program planned in a district is actually taught, the supervisor must go into the classroom and work directly with teachers.

The question of whether teaching is an art or a science is important for it both rationalizes the supervisory presence in the classroom and prescribes how the supervisor can assist the teacher. In the 1980s the emphasis was on teaching as a science because of the many skills identified by teacher effectiveness research. The authors warn that these skills are, at best, guidelines for one type of learning. It is important that the supervisor see that the skills prescribed for the teacher in carrying out the curriculum are, in fact, skills that will contribute to the objectives of the curriculum.

In working with classroom teachers the supervisor has three tasks: (1) to help develop a fuller understanding of the teaching act itself, (2) to develop and apply the relevant skills of teaching to the curriculum, and (3) to coordinate the delivery of the curriculum in a form intended by the planners. Developing a shared perception of reality is a beginning point for dialogue regarding the match of curriculum and instruction. Specific instruments, such as those of interaction analysis, can be used to verify perceptions of reality.

Helping teachers to connect curriculum and instruction, and assisting teachers in trouble shooting instructional problems is the heart of supervisory behavior in the classroom. With the more experienced teachers today, the latent desire to be effective can be used as a motivator to foster high growth conditions for learning.

NOTES

1. Barak Rosenshine, "Synthesis of Research on Explicit Teaching," *Educational Leadership*, 43 (April 1986), pp. 61–69.
2. John McNeil and Jon Wiles, *The Essentials of Teaching* (New York: Macmillan, 1990), pp. 30–33.
3. Ibid.
4. Charles Silberman, *Crisis in the Classroom* (New York: Random House, 1970), p. 11.
5. Joseph Bondi, "The Effects of Interaction Analysis Feedback on the Verbal Behavior of Student Teachers" (Paper presented at the annual meeting of the American Educational Research Association, Los Angeles, February 1969).
6. Joseph C. Bondi, Jr., "Feedback in the Form of Printed Interaction Analysis Matrices as a Technique for Training Student Teachers" (Paper read at the annual meeting of the American Educational Research Association, Los Angeles, February 1969).
7. Ambrose A. Clegg, Jr., et al., "Teacher Strategies of Questioning for Eliciting Selected Cognitive Student Responses" (Report of the Tri-University Project, University of Washington, 1970), p. 1.
8. Benjamin S. Bloom, ed., *Taxonomy of Educational Objectives: Handbook I — Cognitive Domain* (New York: Longman, Inc., 1956).
9. George Farley and Ambrose Clegg, Jr., "Increasing the Cognitive Level of Classroom Questions in Social Studies" (Paper read at the annual meeting of the American Educational Research Association, Los Angeles, February 1969).
10. For a thorough treatment of this important topic see Joan Nelson, "Readability: Some Cautions for the Content Teacher," *Journal of Reading* 21 (April 1978), pp. 620–25.

SUGGESTED LEARNING ACTIVITIES

1. As a supervisor visiting a school, what are some of the more common distortions of the curriculum that might be found in the classroom?
2. How can a supervisor effectively apply the "budding science" of teaching research?
3. How could an evaluation system, like that used in the Florida Beginning Teacher Project, be used in a classroom with a single teacher?
4. How does the supervisor establish a "shared reality" with a teacher? Develop a sequence for such a contact.
5. List some of the limitations on the use of interaction analysis instruments in the classroom.
6. Outline how teacher needs have changed in the period from 1970–1990.

BOOKS TO REVIEW

Acheson, Keith and Gall, Meredith. *Techniques in the Clinical Supervision of Teachers,* 2nd ed. White Plains, NY: Longman, Inc., 1987.

Bigge, Morris. *Learning Theories For Teachers,* 6th ed. New York: Harper and Row, 1985.

Beach, Don And Reinhartz, Judy. *Supervision: Focus On Instruction.* New York: Harper and Row, 1989.

Buxton, Thomas (Ed.). *The Many Faces of Teaching.* Lanham, MD: University Press of America, 1987.

Duckworth, Eleanor. *The Having Of Wonderful Ideas And Other Essays On Teaching And Learning.* New York: Teachers College Press, 1987.

Dunn, Rita And Griggs, Shirley. *Learning Styles: Quiet Revolution In American Schools.* Reston, VA: NASSP, 1988.

Good, Thomas and Brophy, Jere. *Looking In Classrooms,* 4th ed. New York: Harper and Row, 1987.

Jackson, Philip. *The Practices Of Teaching.* New York: Teachers College Press, 1986.

McNeil, John and Wiles, Jon. *The Essentials of Teaching: Decisions, Plans, Methods.* New York: Macmillan Publishing Company, 1990.

Wigginton, Eliot. *Sometimes a Shining Moment: The Foxfire Experience.* New York: Anchor Press, 1985.

Wittrock, Merl (Ed.). *Handbook Of Research On Teaching,* 3rd ed. New York: Macmillan Publishing Company, 1986.

Zumwalt, Karen (Ed). *Improving Teaching.* Alexandria, VA: Association For Supervision And Curriculum Development, 1986.

CHAPTER 7

Encouraging Human Relations

INTRODUCTION

Of all the skills of supervision, none is cited as often in the literature as human relations. In fact, most supervision activity is just that! Supervisors are communicators and connectors in the human network of the school. Most supervisory activity is face-to-face. Supervision is not a role for someone who is shy or unwilling to relate to others in a positive and outgoing manner. Supervisors, as people, should be humane, "self-actualized" individuals who establish a cooperative climate by their very presence.

THE SUPERVISOR AS A PERSON

Because supervision is a "people position," it is helpful if the individual in that role relates naturally to others with an out-going personality. The supervisor should be *self-actualized,* which means that he or she should hold a positive view of self, have the capacity to identify with others, and have a rich experience base from which to provide an understanding of events in which he or she is involved. If these characteristics do not come naturally to the supervisor, they should be seen as behaviors that must be mastered as quickly as possible on the job.

Supervisors must strive to be humane in their work because they often serve as the linkage between the goals of the organization and the needs of the individuals in it. A task-directed supervisor is unable to bridge the sometimes enormous gap between the job to be done and the persons who must do it. Things that contribute to a humanized organization are:

1. Permitting free expression.
2. Placing the individual above the organization.

3. Seeing each person as unique.
4. Providing for the right to make mistakes.
5. Allowing individuals to assume responsibility.

Supervisors must realize the power of being positive in their language patterns. The words of the supervisor are important because they are the words of the person in charge of the schools. Figure 7.1 displays a list of positive and negative expressions that, in fact, say the same thing.

Supervisors should become familiar with the concept of a work climate which is often a critical factor in teacher motivation. The climate is a perceived reality that is shared by all those working in a school. While this reality is not necessarily factual in nature, it is the basis for teachers' behavior. Research has identified nine organizational variables that make up the climate or feeling of an institution:

1. *Structure* — The feelings that employees have about the constraints in the group, how many rules, regulations, procedures there are; is there an emphasis on red tape and going through channels, or is there a loose and informal atmosphere.
2. *Responsibility* — The feeling of being your own boss; not having to double-check all of your decisions; when you have a job to do, knowing that it is your job.
3. *Reward* — The feeling of being rewarded for a job well done; emphasizing positive rewards rather than punishments; the perceived fairness of the pay and promotion policies.
4. *Risk* — The sense of riskiness and challenge in the job and in the organization; is there an emphasis on taking calculated risks, or is playing it safe the best way to operate.
5. *Warmth* — The feeling of good fellowship that prevails in the work group atmosphere; the emphasis on being well-liked; the prevalence of friendly and informal social groups.
6. *Support* — The perceived helpfulness of the managers and other employees in the group; emphasis on mutual support from above and below.
7. *Standards* — The perceived importance of implicit and explicit goals and performance standards; the emphasis on doing a good job; the challenge represented in personal and group goals.
8. *Conflict* — The feeling that managers and other workers want to hear different opinions; the emphasis placed on getting problems out in the open, rather than smoothing them over or ignoring them.
9. *Identity* — The feeling that you belong to a company and you are a valuable member of a working team; the importance placed on this kind of spirit.[1]

Such research has also led to a series of hypotheses about the relationship between a person in an organization and the climate:

Figure 7.1
The Use of Positive Language in Working with Teachers

Negative Expressions	More Positive Expressions
Must	Should
Lazy	Can do more when he tries
Trouble maker	Disturbs class
Uncooperative	Should learn to work with others
Cheats	Depends on others to do his work
Stupid	Can do better work with help
Never does the right thing	Can learn to do the right thing
Below average	Working at his own level
Truant	Absent without permission
Impertinent	Discourteous
Steal	Without permission
Unclean	Poor habits
Dumbbell	Capable of doing better
Help	Cooperation
Poor	Handicapped
Calamity	Lost opportunity
Disinterested	Complacent, not challenged
Expense	Investment
Contribute to	Invest in
Stubborn	Insists on having his own way
Insolent	Outspoken
Liar	Tendency to stretch the truth
Wastes time	Could make better use of time
Sloppy	Could do neater work
Incurred failure	Failed to meet requirements
Mean	Difficulty in getting along with others
Time and again	Usually
Dubious	Uncertain
Poor grade of work	Below his usual standard
Clumsy	Not physically well-coordinated
Profane	Uses unbecoming language
Selfish	Seldom shares with others
Rude	Inconsiderate of others
Bashful	Reserved
Show-off	Tries to get attention
Will fail him	Has a chance of passing, if

1. Individuals are attracted to work climates that arouse their dominant needs.
2. Such on-the-job climates are made up of experiences and incentives.
3. These climates interact with needs to arouse motivation toward need satisfaction.
4. Climates can mediate between organizational tasks requirements and individual needs — it is the linkage.

5. Climates represent the most powerful leverage point available to managers to bring about change.[2]

Collectively, these research observations suggest that the way a supervisor acts and how he or she works with others have a major influence on the effectiveness of any organization or school.

Finally, related research in the field of perceptual psychology[3] has suggested that people, as individuals, always perceive selectively — that is, they discriminate in their vision and tend to see what they are seeking if it is present in the environment. The supervisor who knows and understands this phenomenon of "selective perception" can use it to communicate with others. It is actually possible to send signals to others to establish an image of what supervision is or can be. To illustrate, let us focus on three possible images: physical appearance, environment, and roles.

Physical appearance or image is made up of two major categories: our dressing pattern and our body language. Both are critical to the success or failure of a school administrator. While each individual must work with what he has in looks, it is possible to dress up the image of any individual.

Men and women in school supervision today are generally appearance-conscious. Gone are the days of the *nerd* who wore white socks, showed a T-shirt at the neck, and wore pleated, out-of-style pants. Still, all of us should acknowledge that some school administrators look the role while others lack pizzazz. The following are some observations on dress:

Hair length is generally a good indicator of personality — at least in terms of uptightness or easy-goingness. Hair that is loose (not plastered) and medium-long (not out of control) suggests a growing, open personality.

Eyeglasses can be useful in projecting an image. Large, heavy glasses can mask youthfulness. Tortoise shell or rimless glasses may indicate a studious or intellectual person whereas tinted glasses or dark colored styles may suggest playful or shy personalities.

The discreet use of men's and women's jewelry as well as ties for men and printed scarves for women are dress opportunities that promote visual values. As college professors have for years used the Phi Beta Kappa key to send a message to their colleagues, it is possible to speak quite clearly with symbolic ties or printed scarves, medallions, or bracelets. Jewelry itself is probably important in establishing social contact and initiating communication with strangers. In general dress, color is extremely important. Color speaks a universal language, and people respond to it even before they do symbols (for instance, stop signs). Additionally, we live in a color-coded world. Color is used to cue us, warn us, and encourage us. Three primary colors make up the spectrum—red, blue, and yellow, and these are the most easily grasped colors visually. They are also the least intriguing and most easily forgotten. In dress, the importance of colors is in choosing the right one to fit the occasion. White shirts, for instance, suggest tidiness. Yellow is a transitory color used in society to warn or caution. Blue is a softer, less alert color.

Dress for the school supervisor sets an initial impression of the role image. The supervisor who anticipates the type of day he or she will have (budget sessions all afternoon) and dresses accordingly (conservative brown or grey suit, white shirt, solid or print tie of soft color) will find his or her image matching the role task. Or, for a special meeting with an important superior, the choice of a symbol-projecting device such as a sail tie or special medallion can ease initial conversation and establish common values beyond the immediate meeting.

The reader may wish to review the contrasting images below and attempt to visualize dressing specifically to reinforce the image:

Aggressive	Retiring
Changeable	Constant
Secure	Insecure
Bold	Timid
Articulate	Inarticulate
Careless	Particular
Serious	Frivolous
Overconfident	Hesitant

Even more important than the supervisor's attire is the way in which it is worn and the general body language that is communicated to others. Years of investigation in the social sciences have led to a subspecialization labeled *kinesics:* the study of movement and gesture. So powerful is this science in interpreting facial gestures, walking gestures, and body posture, that it is used regularly by professional labor negotiators to assess openness, defensiveness, readiness, suspicion, confidence, nervousness, and a host of other telltale traits in communication. School supervisors can use a knowledge of kinesics both to project and image and to interpret the behaviors of others.

Over 135 distinct gestures and expressions of the face, head, and body have been recorded in American society. With so many cues, discovering the meaning of gestures may prove difficult. However, as Edward T. Hall has observed in his classic book *The Silent Language,* people are "constantly striving to discover the meaning of relationships between individuals and groups of individuals. The professional scholar soon learns to disregard the immediate explicit meaning of the obvious and to look for a pattern."[4] Gestures, then, come in clusters, and by watching we can understand more clearly what is being expressed verbally. The supervisor can use such gestures and posturing to reinforce what he or she wishes to communicate.

Through nonverbal feedback the supervisor can learn whether what is said is being received or rejected. Nonverbal behaviors can indicate a need to change the subject, withdraw, or try something different to facilitate the communication. An old Cantonese proverb warns, "Watch out for the man whose stomach doesn't move when he laughs." An Apache adage states, "Speak with your deeds, listen with your eyes."

In general, the openness or tightness of body limbs tells a lot about the person being studied. Crossed arms or legs, limbs pulled tightly against the body, and tucked chins are sure signs of discomfort. A reception cluster, by contrast, might involve unbuttoning a coat, uncrossing legs, leaning forward toward you or otherwise not blocking you off from the body trunk.

Eyes and face also tell a lot about the individual being studied. Ralph Waldo Emerson once observed the following: "The eyes of men converse as much as their tongues, with the advantage that the ocular dialect needs no dictionary, but is understood the world over." Studies reveal that the amount of eye contact is significant. Normally, when two people are talking they look at each other about 60 percent of the time. Eye contact greater than 60 percent indicates an interest in the other person beyond what is being said.

Eye *aversion* in face-to-face communication is generally taken to be a sign of disinterest or avoidance. Read with other signs, such aversion indicates poor communication. A tightening jaw muscle or pursed lips can indicate antagonism. A frown can mean confusion or, in some cases, disapproval. Raised eyebrows often indicate envy or disbelief.

Gestures add another dimension to the ability to read a person or at least to send a person a nonverbal message. Classic evaluation or judging gestures are a finger pointing to the temple, a finger alongside the nose, a stroking of the chin or beard, or a slight quizzical tilt of the head. Frustration may be indicated by clenching or wringing the hands. A pointing finger is a powerful message. As the Jamaican proverb observes, "A pointing finger never says 'look here,' it always says 'look there.' "

A person who speaks with a hand in front of the mouth, as children often do, or through clenched teeth, often reveal a lack of certainty about what he or she is saying. By the same cultural cues, a person who scratches behind his ear or wipes his eye with the back of his knuckles is signaling disbelief.

Physical image or appearance, then, is influenced by both the dress of the supervisor and his or her body language. Careful study of these phenomena will help the supervisor assess the intent or actions of others about him, reinforce communication to others, and project an image appropriate to the occasion.

The supervisor's environmental image is one that can be created even without the benefit of poise or contributing physical appearance. Environmental image consists of on-the-job things that others recognize as a style. Examples of this might be the attractiveness of the supervisor's office, how he or she uses media for communicating, how time is manipulated and used, and the associations the supervisor maintains.

The office of supervisor reveals a great deal about the individual's personality, role image, work habits, and aspirations. Even in a sterile government office, with government-issued furniture, wall plaques, and name plates, individuality is evident. The school supervisor who is aware of this can dress the office to improve an image.[5]

When entering an office, the observer gains an overall impression of neatness or clutter. If the supervisor works in a school district with a heavy theme of management and efficiency, it is advantageous to project the "clean desk" to visitors. This can be done as simply as having one drawer in which everything is placed whenever the supervisor is out of the office. Much like the clothes-under-the-bed routine that children use to fool their moms, the work drawer leaves an unexpected visitor with the unmistakable impression that this person is really on top of things.

The location of furniture within an office is also important. An authority figure trying to intimidate others will place his or her desk in the center of the room, leaving only boundary areas for visitors. On the other hand, if the supervisor wishes to appear friendly and warm and as a trusted confidant, the desk should be pushed against a side wall to open up an intimate reception area. A throw rug, comfortable chairs, and a low coffee table help create the illusion of a place to relax and discuss.

The office walls and what is on them are also important to image. Charts (preferably with a line indicating upward progress) are useful to create the "manager" image or that of an efficient, on-top-of-the-numbers type person. Pictures and photographs are useful for drawing associations (isn't that you with the mayor?). Plaques and inscribed certificates can be used for an "achiever" image. Books with the "accepted" titles can reinforce the image of scholarship and intellectualism. Finally, the little knickknacks on top of the desk are symbolically useful. The hole-in-one mounted golf ball tells about your hobby, as does the fishing fly cleverly tucked in the little plant. Like the jewelry discussed in the section on dress, conversation openers can be planted or even tailored for the special occasion.

Another contributor to an environmental image is the careful choice of an appropriate communication medium. Most individuals regularly use the medium they feel most comfortable with, be it a telephone, letter/memo, or personal visit. The error in this way of doing things is failure to consider the receiver of the message. All of us are like school children in that we are either better readers or listeners, or prefer to be shown. The understanding supervisor knows how and when to deliver his or her message in the *receiver*'s favorite medium. As McLuhan has observed, "the medium can be the message." McLuhan continues, "The first item in the press to which all men turn is the one about which they already know. Why? The answer is central to any understanding of the media . . . Experience translated into a new medium literally bestows a delightful playback of earlier awareness."[6]

The supervisor must also think of the purpose of the message. Is it to expedite communication or to store information? Should the communication be exact or just leave an impression? Is this a public-type communication or does it contain some degree of confidentiality? Answers to these questions might determine whether a memo will suffice or whether a face-to-face meeting is needed.

Two other observations might be made about communication in general and specifically in organizations. First, before communicating it is necessary to get the attention of the receiver. Everyone has heard the story about the man who got the donkey's attention by cracking it over the head with a two-by-four. While this degree of force is usually not called for, it is important to understand the receiver's frame of reference or experience. That is why platform speakers use jokes to warm up audiences or, in casual conversations, why banal observations are made about the weather. Finding common values or experiences helps the listener focus on your communication, whatever the medium.

A second observation is a true phenomenon that simply exists: most people respond to a telephone more readily than to a live person. Again McLuhan observes, "Anybody can walk into any manager's office by telephone. The telephone is an irresistible intruder in time or place. In its nature the telephone is an intensely personal form that ignores all the claims of visual privacy."[7] If a supervisor needs communication access to a superior in a hurry, thirty seconds on the phone can open the door for thirty minutes.

Like the office image and the way the supervisor uses the various communication media, the use of time establishes an image or symbolic identification. Each occupation has a "time sense" that results from the nature of the work. The scientist, for instance, is, as a rule, a precise person who jealously guards that precious attribute. Bankers are punctual by nature. Educators, and especially school administrators, also have a time sense, but it differs from organization to organization. The supervisor who can assess the relationship between the use of time and the organizational mission can use time to create an image.

One thing that has happened in school work during the past twenty years is that supervisors have experienced a form of knowledge implosion. There are simply too many things to know or attend to, and the job has become overwhelming. For that reason, the administrator who wishes to appear anything but the image of Chicken Little must learn to make selective responses to the variables. This is known as "managing time" or otherwise described as bunching up related events.

Because "administrivia" tends to fritter away time, the school supervisor must recognize how his or her time is allocated from day to day. Some sort of time diagnosis, like keeping a record at fifteen minute intervals of how time is used during a week, is revealing. From such an analysis can come the identification of obvious time-wasters that might be delegated or simply abandoned. A second step in effective time use is to analyze that time in the work day that is discretionary, such as the lunch hour, and try to combine it with other such times during the day. This gives the supervisor several large blocks of thinking time to decide how to attack the many events in the day. A final step in good time usage is to do important things first and do them one thing at a time. By focusing on what is really important, freeing up time to work on them in concentrated doses, and knocking them off one at a time, the supervisor can show what has been accomplished each day. With considerable practice, the supervisor will discover that by putting together patterns of products he or she can begin to project an image by how time is spent. The type of time-use image required or destined (creative, efficient, or report-producers) depends on the environment. Monochronism pays big dividends.

A second time concern worth attending to is the organization's time orientation. Depending on the age of the organization, the age of its chief administrators, and the scarcity or abundance of resources, every organization will have a dominant time orientation. In general, this time orientation can be categorized as past-oriented, present-oriented, or future-oriented.

While most organizations in the United States are either oriented toward the present or future, thereby diminishing the importance given to what has occurred in the past, schools are something of an exception. Because of the curriculum that often consists of knowledge put together by the last generation regarding the previous generation's efforts, schools rarely live only in the present or future. For this reason, few totally future-oriented changes stick in schools. The supervisor should be aware of the relative emphasis given to the past, present, and future in his district and draw the connection to his own image and behavior.

Singer speaks of this time orientation as a Future-Focused-Role-Image.[8] This image consists of self-projection into the future linking self, time, and change. Singer observes that when the future is questionable, the present expands. If both the future and the present are bleak, then the past is embraced and glorified. If, however, the future is perceived as promising, the individual or organization can disregard tradition and downplay the present. A future-focused role image provides a motive for achievement and is a determiner of social conduct.

The school supervisor must assess his district and determine whether the future is seen as bright and promising. This will become an increasingly rare phenomenon in the 1990s in the public school sector. If there is a strong hope factor about the future but no clear vision related to such hope, the district will be living a day-to-day existence waiting for better times. However, if the general vital signs are in an overall downspin, with linear curves projecting more bad times ahead, the school district can be expected to embrace the past and exhibit hard-core conservatism. The important point of all this is for the supervisor to synchronize time orientation with the organization. To do otherwise is to invite a collision course.

The final contributor to the supervisor's overall environmental image is his or her associations. It is the pattern of associations in work, not the position title, that tends to define the job. The supervisor must give thought to the question, "How do you wish to be seen?"

In general, the building supervisor will wish to be seen as someone who associates with the "right" people in the district. Who the supervisor works with, is seen in the halls with, eats lunch with, or stops in to chat with is important to image. These attending behaviors need to be addressed toward constituents that can be of use to the supervisor as he or she pursues the tasks of the job. One way is to utilize a reputational technique such as that developed by Robert Dahl, Floyd Hunter, or Ralph Kimbrough to uncover the real power structure.[9] Simply by asking people in a variety of roles throughout the district who should be consulted on important issues will provide a pool of common names. Pursuing those identified figures with the same question, and mapping the responses, will eventually lead to a fairly accurate picture of opinion leaders in the district. It may surprise the investigator that such opinion leaders are not always status leaders and are not always within the district itself.

A second way to know whom to associate with is to study the district or superintendent's priorities and see which individuals are engaged with those priorities. These priorities may be pet projects or they may be pressing problems, but the assignment of individuals to deal with them indicates status within the school district. Here, too, a mapping technique can be utilized, linking names with projects to find the common denominators or important people.

At the same time the supervisor must acknowledge that these associations constantly change as administrations and school boards turn over in a school district and as the resource base of the district evolves. The best advice for maintaining associations is to deal in short time frames: bet your money on the horse that's on the track, not the one that's in the barn.

The third major symbolic identification that contributes to the supervisor's image concerns the roles and tasks that are assumed. There are, of course, numerous roles available to the position and the emphasis given to roles or tasks establishes a projected pattern. Such behaviors are usually enacted through regular functions on a day-to-day basis, and can be thought of as combinations. For example, one useful role is identifying concerns (listening, diagnosing, storing, reporting). Another useful role is diagnosing situations (evaluating, judging, deciding). A third might be the consideration of alternative actions (retrieving, planning, managing). A fourth might be directing changes (producing, legitimizing, telling, validating). The roles and tasks selected by the supervisor should be those that will appear harmonious to the arena.

Roles are critical due to their influence on the human systems found in school settings. Havelock and associates suggest a number of roles that might be situationally specific to the needs of a school district and therefore available to the supervisor in image projection:[10]

expert	advisor	retriever
linker	manager	advocate
counselor	trainer	data collector
instructor	modeler	referrer
demonstrator	observer	confronter
diagnoser	evaluator	analyzer

TASKS CALLING FOR HUMAN RELATIONS SKILLS

Because most supervisory work is face-to-face, the practicing supervisor must master the skills of organizing people to work on problems. Supervisors spend an enormous amount of time in group meetings, holding conferences, and generally working with individuals in the organization to improve communication. A beginning point for the study of these many roles is with the nature of communication.

Communication among individuals in organizations is a delicate art requiring, among other things, self-discipline and a cooperative spirit. Spoken English is a complex language which is full of subtleties.

Superimposed on these language patterns are a host of nonverbal clues that can alter the meaning of speech. Add to these dimensions an environmental context, and the result is a communication system that operates at varying levels of effectiveness.

Various social sciences have developed entire languages to describe the intricacies of communication in the American culture and have provided a model of foci in three such social sciences:

Anthropology	*Sociology*	*Psychology*
Cultural behaviors	Role behaviors	Personal behaviors
Acculturation	Interaction	Personality
Implicit meanings	Empathetic meanings	Inferred meanings

Collectively, social science inquiry in the area of interpersonal communication has added immeasurably to our understanding of this complex and important dimension of curriculum improvement.

In any pattern of communication among humans there are at least the following nine elements:

1. What the speaker wants to say
2. What the speaker wants to conceal
3. What the speaker reveals without knowing it
4. What the listener wants or expects to hear
5. What the listener's perception of the speaker will let him hear
6. What the listener's experiences tell him the words mean
7. What the listener wants to conceal
8. What the emotional climate of the situation permits the persons to share
9. What the physical structure of the situation permits the persons to share[11]

Various models have shown communication to be a process of encoding and decoding. A source encodes a message and tries to transmit it to a receiver who tries to receive it and decode the message. Such a transmission between sender and receiver is often distorted by various barriers to communication and by defensive behaviors. Gibb has defined such communication defense:

Defensive behavior is defined as that behavior which occurs when an individual perceives a threat or anticipates threat in the group. The person who behaves defensively, even though he gives some attention to the common task, devotes an appreciable portion of his energy to defending himself. Besides talking about the topic, he thinks about how he appears to others, how he can be seen more favorably, how he may win, dominate, impress, or escape punishment, and/or how he may avoid or mitigate a perceived or an anticipated attack.[12]

Berlo, in a study of human communication, has identified the following four major predictors of faulty communication that can be used by curriculum leaders to anticipate possible communication breakdown:

1. The amount of competition messages have.
2. The threats to status and ego which are involved.
3. The uncertainty and error in what is expected.
4. The number of links there are in the communication chain.[13]

Other barriers to effective communication among people might include any of the following:

1. People use words and symbols that have differing meanings.
2. People have different perceptions of problems being discussed.
3. Members of communication groups possess different values.
4. People bring to discussions varying levels of feeling or affect.
5. Words are sometimes used to prevent real thinking.
6. A lack of acceptance of diverse opinion is present in some communication.
7. Vested interests can interfere with genuine communication.
8. Feelings of personal insecurity can distort communication.
9. Tendencies to make premature evaluations are a barrier to communication.
10. Negative feelings about situations block effective communication.

Group Work

While relationships exist at the dyad, organizational, community, and societal levels, most curriculum development work proceeds at the group level. For this reason, curriculum leaders need to be particularly attentive to group work as a means of promoting better school programs.

Groups can generally be described as two or more people who possess a common objective. As groups interact in pursuit of an objective, their behavior is affected by a number of variables, including: the background of the group, participation patterns, communication patterns, the cohesiveness of the group, the goals of the group, standards affecting the group, procedures affecting the group, and the atmosphere or climate surrounding the group.

Groups perform various tasks that are important to the development of school programs. Among these group tasks are:

1. *Initiating activities* — suggesting new ideas, defining problems, proposing solutions, reorganizing materials.
2. *Coordinating* — showing relationships among various ideas or suggestions, pulling ideas together, relating activities of various subgroups.
3. *Summarizing* — pulling together related data, restating suggestions after discussion.
4. *Testing feasibility* — examining the practicality or feasibility of ideas, making preevaluation decisions about activities.

Group work in educational environments is often ineffective due to various types of nonfunctional behaviors. Leaders should be aware of some of the more common forms of nonfunctional actions:

1. *Being aggressive* — showing hostility against the group or some individual, criticizing or blaming others, deflating the status of others.
2. *Blocking* — interfering with group process by speaking tangentially, citing personal experiences unrelated to the problem, rejecting ideas without consideration.
3. *Competing* — vying with others to talk most often, produce the best idea, gain favor of the leader.
4. *Special pleading* — introducing ideas or suggestions that relate to one's own concerns.
5. *Seeking recognition* — calling attention to oneself by excessive talking, extreme ideas, or unusual behavior.
6. *Withdrawing* — being indifferent or passive, daydreaming, doodling, whispering to others, physically leaving the discussion.

As a group leader, the curriculum specialist should be able to differentiate between those roles and actions that contribute to group effectiveness and those roles that are basically negative and do not contribute to the effectiveness of the group. The following personal characteristics can be thought of as productive and contributing to group effectiveness:

1. Brings the discussion back to the point.
2. Seeks clarification of meaning when ideas expressed are not clear.
3. Questions and evaluates ideas expressed in objective manner.
4. Challenges reasoning when the soundness of logic is doubtful.
5. Introduces a new way of thinking about topic.
6. Makes a summary of points.
7. Underscores points of agreement or disagreement.
8. Tries to resolve conflict or differences of opinion.

9. Introduces facts or relevant information.
10. Evaluates progress of the group.

Roles that can be thought of as negative or nonproductive are:

1. Aggressively expresses disapproval of ideas of others.
2. Attacks the group or the ideas under consideration.
3. Attempts to reintroduce idea after it has been rejected.
4. Tries to assert authority by demanding.
5. Introduces information which is obviously irrelevant.
6. Tries to invoke sympathy by depreciation of self.
7. Uses stereotypes to cover own biases and prejudices.
8. Downgrades the importance of group's role or function.

Sensitivity to such roles allows the group leader to analyze the flow of group work and head off potential distractions to group progress.

Group Leadership

While working with groups, the curriculum leader does not have to restrict his or her role to that of passive observer. It is possible to take steps that will encourage greater group productivity (see Figure 7.2). In any group discussion, the leader has at least six roles which, if pursued, will lead the group toward accomplishment of its objectives. These areas are: presentation of the topic, the initiation of discussion, guiding the discussion, controlling discussion, preventing side-tracking, and summarizing the discussion.

In presenting the topic to be discussed, the leader should suggest the importance of the problem, place the general purpose of the discussion before the group, suggest a logical pathway for the discussion to follow, and define any ambiguous terms to remove misunderstanding. It is useful, where possible, to relate the current discussion to previous meetings or other convenient reference points.

In initiating the discussion, the leader provides advanced thinking for the group. Major questions to be answered are identified and relevant facts and figures are cited. A case in point may be drawn for purposes of illustration. In some cases, it may even be useful to purposefully misstate a position to provoke discussion.

The leader's job in guiding the discussion involves keeping the discussion goal-directed, assisting members in expressing themselves through feedback, and providing the transition from one aspect of the discussion to another. In fulfilling this role, the leader may use direct questions, stories, illustrations, or leading questions to maintain the flow of interaction.

Figure 7.2
Productivity in Group Work

If a group is to be productive, the individuals in question must first become a group in a psychological sense through acquiring the feeling of group belongingness which can come only from a central purpose which they all accept.

If a group is to be productive, its members must have a common definition of the undertaking in which they are to engage.

If a group is to be productive, it must have a task of some real consequence to perform.

If a group is to be productive, its members must feel that something will actually come of what they are expected to do; said differently, its members must not feel that what they are asked to do is simply busywork.

If a group is to be productive, the dissatisfaction of its members with the aspect of the status quo to which the group's undertaking relates must outweigh in their minds whatever threats to their comfort they perceive in the performance of this undertaking.

If a group is to be productive, its members must not be expected or required to attempt undertakings which are beyond their respective capabilities or which are so easy for the individuals in question to perform that they feel no sense of real accomplishment.

If a group is to be productive, decisions as to work planning, assignment, and scheduling must be made, whenever possible, on a shared basis within the group, and through the method of consensus rather than of majority vote; in instances in which these decisions either have already been made by exterior authority or in which they must be made by the group leader alone, the basis for the decisions made must be clearly explained to all members of the group.

If a group is to be productive, each member of the group must clearly understand what he is expected to do and why, accept his role, and feel himself responsible to the group for its accomplishment.

If a group is to be productive, its members must communicate in a common language.

If a group is to be productive, its members must be guided by task-pertinent values which they share in common.

If a group is to be productive, it is usually necessary for its members to be in frequent face-to-face association with one another.

If a group is to be productive, its members must have a common (though not necessarily a talked-about) agreement as to their respective statuses within the group.

If a group is to be productive, each of its members must gain a feeling of individual importance from his personal contributions in performing the work of the group.

If a group is to be productive, the distribution of credit for its accomplishments must be seen as equitable by its members.

If a group is to be productive, it must keep on the beam and not spend time on inconsequential or irrelevant matters.

If a group is to be productive, the way it goes about its work must be seen by its members as contributing to the fulfillment of their respective issue and social-psychological needs, and, by extension, of those of their dependents (if any) as well.

If a group is to be productive, the status leader must make the actual leadership group-centered, with the leadership role passing freely from member to member.

If a group is to be productive, the task it is to perform must be consistent with the purposes of the other groups to which its members belong.

If a group is to be productive, the satisfactions its members expect to experience from accomplishing the group's task must outweigh in their minds the satisfactions they gain from their membership in the group *per se*.

Source: Jon Wiles and Joseph Bondi, *Curriculum Development,* 2nd ed. (Columbus, OH: Merrill, 1984). Used with permission.

In controlling the discussion the leader is concerned with the pace of progress and the involvement of the participants. Among techniques which can be used to keep discussion moving are purposeful negative statements, drawing contrasts between positions of participants, and regularly calling attention to the time remaining.

The discussion leader in a small group can deal with sidetracking in a number of ways. He can restate the original question or problems. He can secure a statement from a reliable group member to head off a rambler. He can request that side issues be postponed until main issues are settled.

Finally, the leader summarizes the discussion. This involves knowing when to terminate discussion reviewing the high points that have been talked to.

Three situations in particular are troublesome to persons new to leading discussions in small groups: the dead silence, the overtalkative member, and the silent member. Any of these three conditions can sabotage an otherwise fruitful discussion period.

A most anxiety-producing situation is one in which there is a complete absence of participation resulting in an awkward silence among group members. While the natural response in such a situation is to speak to fill the conversational vacuum, the leader must do just the opposite. Silence in discussions sometimes means that real thinking is occurring, and this assumption must be made by the leader. Another common impulse is to seek out a member of the group and prod him or her for a contribution. Such a tactic will surely contribute to less participation. When the silent period is convincingly unproductive, the leader should try an encouraging remark such as, "There must be some different points of view here." Failing response, the leader should turn to the process involved with a comment such as "Let's see if we can discover what's blocking us."

Another situation that can ruin a group discussion is an overtalkative member. Such a person, if permitted, will monopolize discussion and produce anxiety among group members. The best strategy in such a situation is to intervene after a respectful period of time with a comment such as, "Perhaps we can hear from other members of the group." In the event that the dominating member still doesn't get the message, the leader can initiate an evaluation of the process and draw attention to the fact that a way must be found to gain input from all members.

A final situation that can be awkward occurs when a member of the group is regularly silent. The leader should recognize that some persons are fearful of being put on the spot and will resent being spotlighted. The leader can, however, observe the silent member and look for signals that he or she is ready to participate. If the member seems to be on the verge of speaking, an encouraging glance or nod may be all that is needed.

In cases where the leader becomes convinced that a member's silence is the result of boredom or withdrawing, it may be useful to confront the member away from other group members with a provocative or challenging question. Whether a member should be forced into a discussion, and whether such an act is productive for the entire group, is a matter of judgment and discretion.

Leaders of small groups should regularly evaluate their own performance following a discussion by asking themselves a series of questions such as the following:

1. Did members contribute to the discussion?
2. Did some people do more talking than others?
3. Are the most talkative persons, and the silent ones, sitting together?
4. Do members talk mostly to the leader or to each other?
5. Was there evidence of cliques or interest groups in the discussion?

Group leaders can sometimes retard creative thinking by regulating discussions in nonproductive ways. Among the most common errors in this respect are:

1. A preoccupation with order throughout the discussion.
2. Stressing too often "hard evidence" or factual information.
3. Placing too much emphasis on history or the way things have been done.
4. Using coercive techniques to insure participation.
5. Suggesting that mistakes are not acceptable.

Two skills that are useful for all small group leaders to possess are that of paraphrasing and brainstorming. In paraphrasing, the leader attempts to restate the point of view of another to his satisfaction prior to continuing discussion. This technique is especially useful in argumentative situations, and often sets a pattern which is followed by other group members.

In brainstorming, the leader introduces a technique that frees the group discussion from previous barriers to speaking. Here the leader sets ground rules which include the following: no criticism of others is allowed, the combining of ideas is encouraged, quality ideas are sought, wild ideas are encouraged. In introducing a brainstorming session the leader hopes to have members "spark" each other and have one idea "hitch-hike" upon another. Brainstorming, as a technique, is recommended when discussions continually cover familiar ground and little or no progress toward a solution to problems is forthcoming.

Finally, leaders of small groups should work to become better listeners. Numerous studies have identified poor listening skills as the biggest block to personal communication. Nicholas has identified ten steps to better listening:

1. While listening, concentrate on finding areas of interest that are useful to you.
2. Judge the content of what is said rather than the delivery.
3. Postpone early judgment about what is being said. Such a posture will allow you to remain analytical if you favor what is being said or to keep from being distracted by calculating embarrassing questions should you disagree with the speaker's message.
4. Focus on the central ideas proposed by the speaker. What is the central idea? What are the supporting "planks" or statements?
5. Remain flexible in listening. Think of various ways to remember what is being said.
6. Work hard at listening. Try to direct all conscious attention on the presentation being made.
7. Resist distractions in the environment by making adjustments or by greater concentration.
8. Exercise your mind by regularly listening to technical expository material that you haven't had experience with.
9. Keep your mind open to new ideas by being aware of your own biases and limited experiences.
10. Capitalize on thought speed. Since comprehension speed exceeds speaking speed by about 3:1, the listener must work to keep his concentration. This can be done by anticipating what is to be said, by making mental summaries, by weighing speaker evidence, and by listening between the lines.[14]

Group Evaluation

Group evaluation is necessary to help assure that the work of a group does not deteriorate. When all members of a group feel responsibility for the group and can evaluate its effectiveness without being defensive, then the evaluation will be most useful to the group. There are a number of group processes one might examine in evaluating group effectiveness. Table 7.1 illustrates eight of these processes.

As a reference to good group work, see Figure 7.3 which provides a planning checklist for conducting an effective meeting.

Conferences

Much of the supervisory day is tied up with conferences that help alleviate problems. Supervisors see parents, teachers, and other district personnel to iron out communication difficulties and solve genuine problems. We treat each of these three primary groups separately because of the nature of communication with each group.

Table 7.1
Group Evaluation Form

GOALS

Poor	1 2 3 4 5 6 7 8 9 10	**Good**
Confused, diverse, conflicting, indifferent, little interest.		Clear to all, shared by all, all care about the goals, feel involved.

PARTICIPATION

Poor	1 2 3 4 5 6 7 8 9 10	**Good**
Few dominate, some passive; some not listened to; several talk at once or interrupt.		All get in, all are really listened to

FEELINGS

Poor	1 2 3 4 5 6 7 8 9 10	**Good**
Unexpected, ignored, or criticized.		Freely expressed, empathic responses.

DIAGNOSIS OF GROUP PROBLEMS

Poor	1 2 3 4 5 6 7 8 9 10	**Good**
Jump directly to remedial proposals, treat symptoms rather than basic causes		When problems arise the situation is carefully diagnosed before action is proposed; remedies attack basic causes.

LEADERSHIP

Poor	1 2 3 4 5 6 7 8 9 10	**Good**
Group needs for leadership not met; group depends too much on single person or on a few persons.		As needs for leadership arise, various members meet them ("distributed leadership"); anyone feels free to volunteer as he sees a group need.

DECISIONS

Poor	1 2 3 4 5 6 7 8 9 10	**Good**
Needed decisions don't get made; decision made by part of group, others uncommitted.		Consensus sought and tested, deviates appreciated and used to improve decision; decisions when made are fully supported.

Table 7.1
(continued)

							TRUST						
Poor		1	2	3	4	5	6	7	8	9	10		**Good**

Poor	**Good**
Members distrust one another, are polite, careful, closed, guarded; they listen superficially but inwardly reject what others say; are afraid to criticize or to be criticized.	Members trust one another; they reveal to group what they would be reluctant to expose to others, they respect and use the responses they get; they can freely express negative reactions without fearing reprisal.

						CREATIVITY AND GROWTH							
Poor		1	2	3	4	5	6	7	8	9	10		**Good**

Poor	**Good**
Members and group in a rut, operate routinely; persons stereotyped and rigid in their roles; no progress.	Group flexible, seeks new and better ways; individuals changing and growing, creative; individually supported.

Parents are the primary clients of the school; they pay for education by their taxes and entrust their children to educators. For this reason, parents often contact the school to voice concerns to the principal. Supervisors are regularly called on to look into these concerns and to work out an amiable solution with the parent. Some typical concerns are listed below.

The curriculum
Dress codes
Request for a specific teacher
Grades and evaluation practices

Discipline at the school
Out-of-school problems
Changes in class assignments
Other students picking on my child

Figures 7.4 and 7.5 provide some general information about possible topics to discuss with parents and obvious do's and don'ts for parent conferences.

Supervisors should think through a parent conference before it occurs because the results of a mismanaged conference can be damaging to the school and the district. In setting up the conference consider the questions on pages 205 and 207:

Figure 7.3
Checklist for a Meeting Leader

ESSENTIALS OF EFFECTIVE MEETINGS

A. Convene on time
B. Good opening/warm-up exercise
C. Well planned agenda (prioritized)
D. Clear roles (leader, recorder, participants)
E. Appropriate environment (comfortable)
F. Materials/equipment
G. No outside interruptions
H. Definite adjournment time

1. PREMEETING CHECKLIST ☐

   A. Precise purpose—objective
   B. Written announcement (time, purpose, location, etc.)
   C. Tentative agenda distributed with vital back up materials
   D. Predetermined adjournment time
   E. Identify audience
   F. Identify materials (visuals, equipment) needed
   G. Who can help? Advise in advance
   H. Plan ingredients—all points to be made
   I. Estimate time for each agenda item
   J. Plan opening
   K. Integrate impact features
   L. Examine texture (variety)
   M. Dry run visuals/equipment

2. ROLE OF CHAIRPERSON ☐

   A. Begin on time
   B. Provide overview
   C. Keep on target
   D. One agenda item at a time
   E. Cut off redundant debate
   F. Neutralize "dominator"
   G. Draw out the "timid/perplexed"
   H. Encourage full discussion
   I. Keep climate relaxed/wholesome
   J. Use rules for brainstorming
   K. Use rules of order
   L. Tap resources of audience
   M. Delegate to "volunteer"
   N. Serve as negotiator, arbitrator, neutral, compassionate listener—shift role
   O. Keep calm
   P. Adjourn on time

Figure 7.3
(Continued)

3. ROLE OF MEETING PARTICIPANT ☐
   A. Do advance preparation
   B. Be on time
   C. Raise questions for clarification—"Gate opening for Expertise"
   D. Demonstrate responsible (attitude/behavior) good manners
   E. Accept share of work—offer to help
   F. Stick to point
   G. Help others to stay on topic
   H. Be sensitive to others' feelings (particularly chairperson)
   I. LISTEN ACTIVELY—LISTENING WITH WARMTH IS CONTAGIOUS

4. POST MEETING CHECKLIST ☐
   A. Minutes or record distributed—24 hours
   B. Clear follow-up assignments and timeline
   C. Evaluation
   D. Next meeting (date/time)
   E. Location
   F. Tentative agenda
   G. Responsibilities

5. MEETING RECORD ☐
   A. Purpose—to provide
     1. Minutes of meeting to participants
     2. Concise, right-to-the-point notes
     3. Opportunity for recorder to be active participant
     4. Basis for summarizing the meeting
     5. Critical elements and decisions made
     6. Immediate dissemination

   B. Objective—to provide
     1. Date, time convened and time terminated
     2. Name of recorder
     3. Names of participants
     4. Specific topics covered
     5. Time spent on each topic
     6. Decisions reached and actions to be taken
     7. Responsibilities for follow up
     8. Deadlines for action to be taken
     9. List of handouts distributed at the meeting

   1. Where will this conference be held? Will the space be comfortable? Will it be possible to have a close interpersonal distance and maintain eye contact?

Figure 7.4
Conference Topics for Discussion

Family Living and Home Background
Learning about normal or other conditions
Learning about adults other than parents living in the home
Learning about child's place in family in relation to other children
Making use of leisure time
Having some definite responsibilities
Dressing and undressing self
Understanding parents' interest, plans, hopes for the child
Understanding parents' influence on child's attitudes
Learning about parents' ideas of acceptable behavior
Learning about parents' methods of discipline
Learning about child's attitude and behavior at home

Emotional and Social Development
Getting along well with others
Having friends his own age
Enjoying group games
Enjoying school
Exhibiting self-control

Accepting criticism
Acting subdued and unresponsive
Being over-aggressive
Feeling secure at home, at school, and to and from school
Exhibiting nervous manifestations
Considering the rights of others
Protecting and respecting property—personal, school, and community
Working and playing well with others
Accepting responsibility
Observing school rules
Displaying leadership qualities

Child's Health
Noting significant illnesses and accidents from infancy on
Noting physical defects—progress in correction
Developing health habits
Exhibiting food idiosyncrasies
Developing proper sleeping habits
Learning about sleeping facilities
Developing recreational habits
Developing muscular coordination
Maintaining good attendance

Figure 7.5
Conference Do's and Don'ts

DO'S	DON'TS
1. When there are several children in the family, consult other teachers in planning conference.	1. Don't talk "down" to parents.
	2. Don't embarrass or offend parents.
2. Create an atmosphere of friendly informality.	3. Don't argue.
3. Show by your attitude that you are sincerely interested.	4. Don't show your personal reactions.
4. Try to understand how the parents feel about their child.	5. Don't listen to complaints about other members of the faculty.
5. Remember that parents are people who have problems, too.	6. Don't listen to gossip about other pupils or their families.
6. Be prepared to understand that there may be more than one solution to a problem.	7. Don't lose your sense of humor even when parents lose theirs.
7. Encourage the parent to tell his side of the story. It releases tension.	8. Don't pass over parents' suggestions for a plan of action.
8. Answer questions directly and in a straightforward manner.	9. Don't appear as one who is passing judgment on the parents' way of life.
9. Admit that you do not have all of the answers.	10. Don't assume that the parents want advice. Wait until you are asked.
10. Explain the philosophy and objectives of the school.	11. Don't make parents feel that you think that they have failed in the upbringing of their child.
11. Find commendable things to tell parents about their children.	12. Don't discuss anything told to you by the parent in confidence.
12. Maintain the "we" relationship to remind the parent that home and school work together.	13. Don't ever give parents I.Q. figures. Instead, give them an idea of the group into which their child falls. ("He is a little slow" or "His intelligence is above average.")
13. Offer plans on a trial basis.	
14. Keep the conference on the question at hand to avoid digression.	
15. Keep your voice quiet and relaxed.	
16. Summarize the conference.	
17. End the conference on a note of confidence and optimism.	

2. How will I use body language (a smile, eye contact, leaning forward to show approval)?
3. How can I greet the parents so that anxiety will be reduced?
4. What message does my appearance send (businesslike, professional, friendly)?

During the conference the supervisor needs to be aware of the parents' feelings. Most parents come to such conferences feeling unequal and, perhaps, defensive. They may fear learning something about their child they don't want to know. The supervisor should not take it personally if parents display anger. The supervisor is a representative of the school.

Supervisors should be careful of their language. Jargon is plentiful in schools (IEP, affective, etc.). Messages should be sent to the parents in small doses and in familiar language. It may help to remain slightly vague (seems, appears, may be) to sooth the communication.

The supervisor should consider the timing and order of the conference. A "we-ness" must be established to have real communication. Advanced thinking about topics and your reaction to those topics will help. Some possible solutions may be thought of ahead of the conference.

Finally, the supervisor must give thought to closure of the parent conference. Many parents will be reluctant to terminate a discussion with a school official. Four common ways to close a parent conference are (1) to mention a "pressing appointment," (2) to inform the secretary to interrupt you at a predetermined time, (3) to send body language that the conference is ending (stand up, change tone of voice), or (4) to press a buzzer near your desk that signals your secretarial staff.

Conferences with teachers differ from those with parents in that the supervisor must, under all circumstances, maintain an open and professional communication with the teacher. Reasons for teacher-supervisor conferences include:

1. Evaluation or review.
2. Curriculum or instructional concerns.
3. Parental complaint or an administrative concern.
4. Union contract or grievance procedures.

The important thing for supervisors to remember in conferring with classroom teachers is that the ultimate object is to improve instruction for students. Teachers are professional, highly educated individuals who practice one of the most difficult roles in our society. In schools, because of the interpersonal nature of the organizations, traditional supervisory practices do not work. Supervisors must approach any teacher conference from the standpoint of establishing a professional relationship and improving practice for students. To become bogged down in power/compliance issues or interpersonal hostility is counterproductive to the ultimate objective of supervision.

In working with teachers through conferencing, supervisors should be aware of the following variables:

1. *Body language* — Gestures, facial movements, eye contact.
2. *Time* — The importance of the meeting is sometimes reflected in when it is scheduled.
3. *The use of space* — Is the supervisor sitting down as an equal or is a desk being used to separate and identify the roles?
4. *Word usage* — How many times do you use the word "I"? Are you top-heavy on superlatives? Is jargon used to mask your real concerns?
5. *Written follow-up* — Is the communication dull, third-person messages that communicate a bureaucratic tone?

Conferencing with other district personnel requires some thinking by the supervisor because of line and staff relationships and the changing nature of the supervision position. When preparing to hold a one-on-one conference, the supervisor should ask himself, "What is the relationship of this individual to the supervision function?" If the relationship is a "line" relationship (one of authority with a direct power connection to a superior) then the communication will usually be task-directed. If, on the other hand, the relationship is "staff" (an assisting role without authority), the communication will take on more of an interpersonal nature.

We make this distinction to reflect the changing nature of supervision in a school setting. Even a decade ago the position of supervisor was an extension of teaching. Today, because of unionization and collective bargaining, supervision is more an extension of management or administration. The modern supervisor must acknowledge this distinction or risk being placed in a compromising position during conferences with either line or staff associates.

The reader may test this distinction by thinking about the following situations:

1. You have had a luncheon meeting with your immediate superior. Upon returning, a friend and staff member in another department wants to know all about what happened.
2. You are in the middle of a conference with a teacher and a call comes in from your superior. The secretary says it is important.
3. You are meeting with staff members about a project and one of the staff members continually interrupts your presentation.
4. A staff member from your unit meets with you to complain about the work habits of another staff member.
5. You are writing an article for publication about your school district and its programs. Should you consult with your superior?

SPECIAL PROBLEMS IN HUMAN RELATIONS

In the initial chapter of this book it was observed that supervision in education is different from supervision in other kinds of organizations because schools deal with a human product. The real measure of the effectiveness of schools cannot be immediately seen or measured. This condition presents some real problems in human relations—problems that must be addressed by the supervisor. Two such special problems are teacher motivation and stress build-up.

Teachers confront the problem of motivation in a number of ways during their careers. One problem is that, until recently,[15] there has been no career ladder in the field of teaching. A teacher enters the profession as a teacher and exits years later still a teacher. In general, experience is neither rewarded nor acknowledged from one year to the next. The old adage that familiarity breeds contempt has some application if the daily teaching routine is allowed to become an insipid routine that stretches out endlessly.

A related problem for many teachers is that most staff development or training opportunities do not discriminate among the inexperienced and experienced teachers. Rarely do school systems design inservice experiences to reflect the growing maturity of the teacher. Said another way, in most school districts there is not a model of teacher growth toward excellence and teachers have no accurate method of assessing their abilities or needs for self-improvement.

A final part of the motivation picture for many classroom teachers is their perception of the position of teacher. A visit to any teacher preparation program will reveal highly curious and eager students who want to teach. However, after three years of teaching, those students will often reveal a slightly cynical attitude about teaching and its requirements. The new teacher is quickly socialized by older teachers and whatever vision, mission, or curiosity he or she possessed prior to teaching is absorbed by the environment and requirements of the job.

These factors, and others, contribute to an overall motivation problem in today's teaching staff throughout the nation and this problem is a direct responsibility of the school supervisor. Helping teachers perceive teaching as a long-term process of growth, building meaningful inservice experiences commensurate with individual needs, and looking for ways to diversify and enrich the teaching role are all challenges to the human relations skills of the supervisor.

A related and serious problem affecting teachers today is that of stress build-up and burnout. The burnout syndrome strikes disproportionately in helping professions like teaching and involves physical, emotional, and attitudinal exhaustion generated by excessive demands on an individual's energy, emotions, or resources. The degree of stress build-up in the teaching profession is reflected by an extensive literature that documents the condition. The actual cause for such burnout seems to be a result of substantial imbalance between environmental demands and the individual's response capability. Common symptoms diminishing the pleasure of teaching include increased drug or alcohol use, greater use of scheduled sick days, fatigue, depression, insomnia, and susceptibility to minor sicknesses.

Historically, our society has associated teaching with low income and limited prestige. Accordingly, the profession has associated a "service orientation" with motivation, and teachers have relied on intrinsic rewards rather than material benefits for job satisfaction. Teachers who believe that they are making a significant impact on the lives of their students find it much easier to sustain a high degree of job satisfaction than teachers who receive little positive reinforcement. Unfortunately, the social message in the media has been that schools and teachers are failing in their role. This lack of appreciation and understanding on the part of the public, plus the miserable extrinsic rewards offered to career teachers, took its toll on the profession in the 1980s.[16]

Supervisors must confront this human relations problem, if for no other reason than to foster instructional quality control. A human organization, like a school, must have fully functioning people if it is to be effective in its mission. Three different checklists are shown in Figures 7.6 and 7.7. These lists may help diagnose teachers who are susceptible to stress build-up, teachers actually experiencing high degrees of stress, and symptoms of teacher burnout. How a supervisor responds to this growing problem in teaching will be dictated by consideration such as environmental factors, school organization, and the degree of supervisory authority at the school building level.

NEW DIRECTIONS

As we move toward a new century, schools will be challenged to do more to help students cope with a technological society unlike any we could envision twenty years ago. In addition, schools have taken over many of the functions once held by the family and other institutions. Questions as to how well schools are functioning may be posed by both those inside the school house and outside the school house. Figures 7.8 and 7.9 provide a perspective on what questions different segments of our society are asking about our schools.

SUMMARY

Human relations skills are foundational skills in school supervision. Because supervisors tend to be communicators and connectors in the

Figure 7.6
How to Tell If You Are a Stress-Prone Personality

Rate yourself as to how you typically react in each of the situations listed below. There are no right and wrong answers.

4—Always   3—Frequently   2—Sometimes   1—Never

_____ 1. Do you try to do as much as possible in the least amount of time?
_____ 2. Do you become impatient with delays or interruptions?
_____ 3. Do you always have to win at games to enjoy yourself?
_____ 4. Do you find yourself speeding up the car to beat the red light?
_____ 5. Are you unlikely to ask for, or indicate you need, help with a problem?
_____ 6. Do you constantly seek the admiration and respect of others?
_____ 7. Are you overly critical of the way others do their work?
_____ 8. Do you have the habit of looking at your watch or clock often?
_____ 9. Do you constantly strive to better your position and achievements?
_____ 10. Do you spread yourself "too thin" in terms of your time?
_____ 11. Do you have a habit of doing more than one thing at a time?
_____ 12. Do you frequently get angry or irritable?
_____ 13. Do you have little time for hobbies or time by yourself?
_____ 14. Do you have a tendency to talk quickly or hasten conversations?
_____ 15. Do you consider yourself hard-driving?
_____ 16. Do your friends or relatives consider you hard-driving?
_____ 17. Do you have a tendency to get involved in multiple projects?
_____ 18. Do you have a lot of deadlines in your work?
_____ 19. Do you feel vaguely guilty if you relax and do nothing during leisure time?
_____ 20. Do you take on too many responsibilities?
_____ 21. Are you constantly volunteering for things without the ability to say "no"?
_____ 22. Are you constantly making excuses or apologies for yourself and your actions?
_____ 23. Do you tend to carry your domestic stresses to work and vice-versa?
_____ 24. Do you feel stress from having the dual responsibilities of family life and a full time job?
_____ 25. Do you tend to feel under pressure about things over which you have little or no control (i.e., state of the economy, nuclear war, family illness, etc)?
_____ TOTAL

INTERPRETATION

If your score is between 25 and 35, chances are you are nonproductive or your life lacks stimulation.

A score between 35 and 60 designates a good balance in your ability to handle and control stress.

If you tallied a score ranging between 60 and 70, your stress level is marginal and you are bordering on being excessively tense.

If your total number of points exceeds 70, you may be a candidate for heart disease.

Figure 7.7
Are You Burning Out?

Check boxes for listings that describe your behavior or feelings.

☐ Increased food, cigarette, and/or liquor consumption.*
☐ Tiredness not alleviated by a night's sleep.*
☐ Increased frequency of colds, flu, or allergy episodes.*
☐ Absenteeism for generalized or vague ailments.*
☐ Elevated blood pressure.*
☐ Grinding or clenching of teeth.*

3 × _____ = _____

☐ Sensations of *deja vu* with work/personal situations . . . the "I've been here before" or "Here we go again" feeling.
☐ Complaints about the sameness of tasks, strong craving for greater uniqueness, variety.
☐ Reduced ability to see uniqueness when it is present.
☐ Language shift to jargon or "labeling" of people.
☐ Lumping consumers/clients/co-workers/public into large undifferentiated groups, e.g. "those taxpayers."
☐ Suppression of feelings resulting in masklike expressions.
☐ Cynical comments about the agency/company/system/department.
☐ Reduced physical or time involvement with consumers/co-workers.
☐ Belief that clients/consumers deserve their problems.
☐ Diffusion of responsibility through staff/neighborhood gripe sessions.
☐ Strong need to conserve energy because "everyone wants a piece of me and there's not enough to go around."
☐ Increased intellectualization of situations, elaborate "explanations" for minor incidents.
☐ Rationalizations of actions (e.g., following gripe sessions, hastily identifying it as a "conference").
☐ Obesity—exceeding healthy weight by more than 20%.

5 × _____ = _____

☐ Cynical or negative feelings toward clients/consumers/co-workers/public expressed in contemptuous or derogatory language, sometimes followed by an attempt to cancel the message (e.g., "Women are dense! . . . Only joking, girls").
☐ Laughing at clients/consumers/co-workers and their problems.
☐ Cynicism about new worker's optimism (e.g., "He'll learn!").
☐ Frequent gallows humor about self, work, consumers, colleagues.
☐ Exaggeration of the border between work and social/personal life.
☐ Exaggerated "going-by-the-book" to short-circuit personal involvement with clients/consumers, public, changing into petty bureaucrat.
☐ Serious doubting of effectiveness ("Do I make any difference here?"), or values ("Is there any point in my life?"), or even the morality of efforts ("Have I helped him/her or just set someone up to get hurt?").

9 × _____ = _____

TOTAL: _____

SCORING: Multiply number of boxes checked in each group by 3, 5, or 9 as indicated. More than 3 items checked in any one category indicates danger of overstress. A total score exceeding 100 indicates a strong need for action.
*Check with a doctor . . . cause may be chemical or physical.

214

Figure 7.8[17]

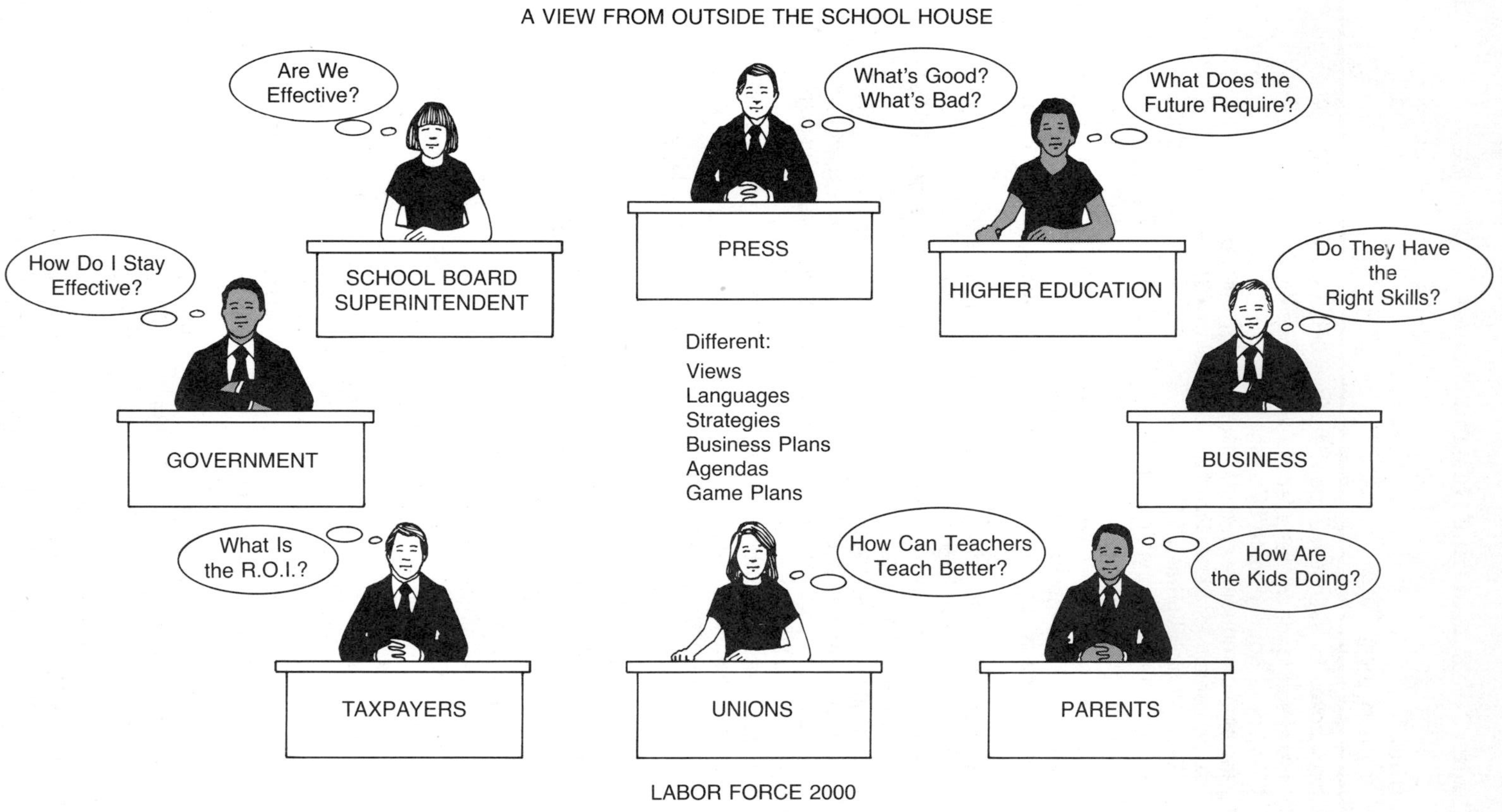

A VIEW FROM OUTSIDE THE SCHOOL HOUSE

LABOR FORCE 2000

Figure 7.9[18]

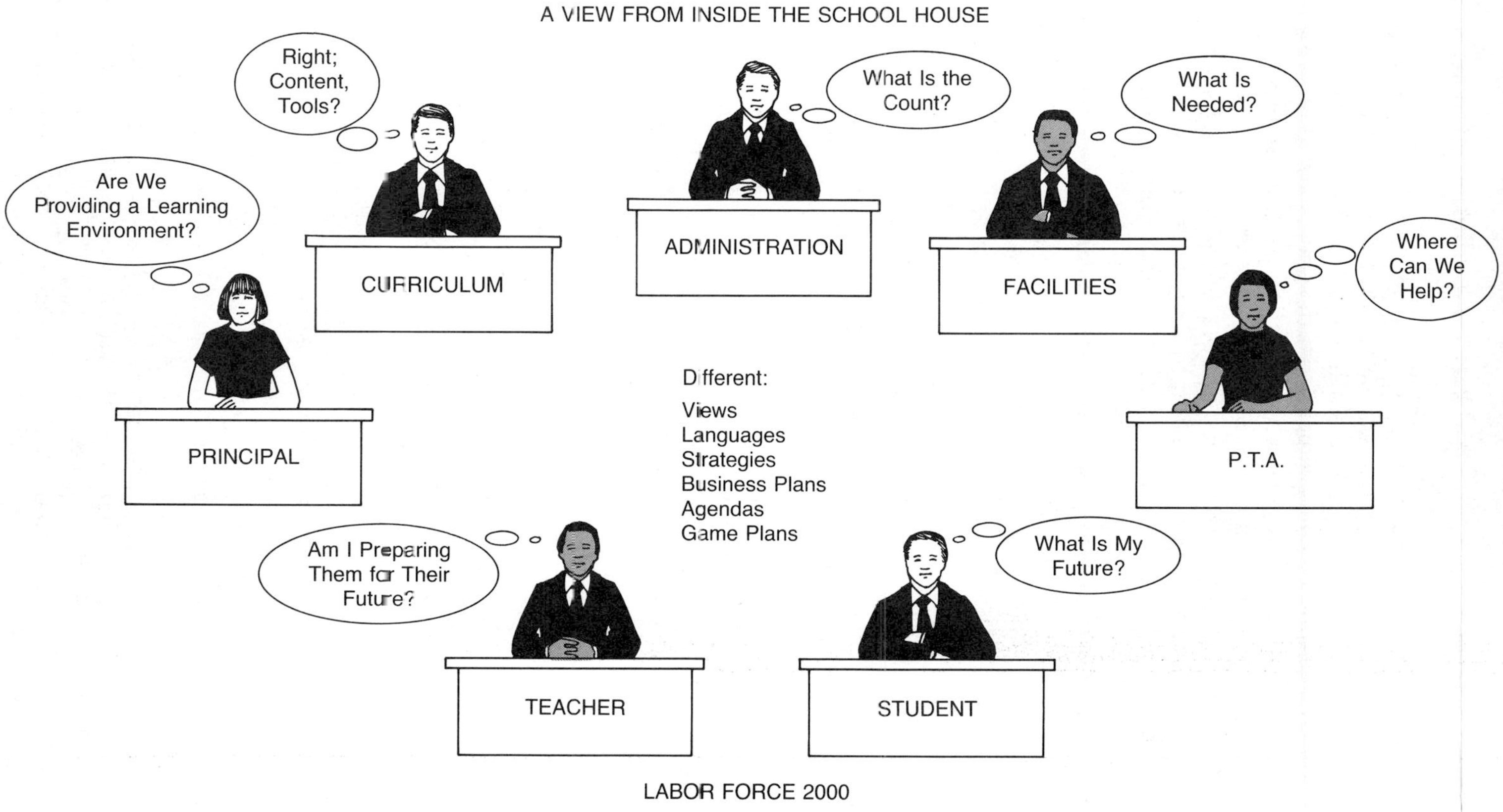

A VIEW FROM INSIDE THE SCHOOL HOUSE

Where Can We Help?

What Is Needed?

P.T.A.

FACILITIES

What Is the Count?

What Is My Future?

ADMINISTRATION

STUDENT

Different:
Views
Languages
Strategies
Business Plans
Agendas
Game Plans

CURRICULUM

TEACHER

Right; Content, Tools?

Am I Preparing Them for Their Future?

Are We Providing a Learning Environment?

PRINCIPAL

LABOR FORCE 2000

215

human network of the school, such skills are essentials for practice. As a "people position," supervision calls for an individual who is comfortable with him or herself and skilled in relating to others.

Three general tasks for supervisors in schools are to create a humane atmosphere, set a positive work climate, and establish an appropriate image for supervision. Supervisors learn quickly that others react to how the supervisor talks, dresses, and works. The supervisor establishes the "feel" of supervision by his or her behavior.

The many human relations skills of supervision include promoting effective communication, working with small groups, and holding conferences with parents, teachers, and district personnel. Special problems in the 1990s include motivating career teachers and the phenomenon of "teacher burnout."

NOTES

1. George H. Litwin and Robert A. Stringer, *Motivation and Organizational Climate* (Boston: Division of Research, School of Business, Harvard University, 1968), p. 100.

2. Ibid.

3. Arthur Combs, ed., *Perceiving, Behaving, Becoming.* ASCD Yearbook (Washington, DC: Association for Supervision and Curriculum Development, 1962).

4. Edward T. Hall, *The Silent Language* (Garden City, NY: Doubleday Books, 1973), p. 100.

5. See "Want Office Status: Remove All Papers From Top of Desk," *Wall Street Journal*, 15 January 1982, pp. 1, 20.

6. Marshall McLuhan, *Understanding the Media: The Extensions of Man* (New York: Mentor Books, 1964), p. 189.

7. Ibid., p. 238.

8. Benjamin D. Singer, "The Future Focused Role Image," in Alvin Toffler, ed., *Learning for Tomorrow: The Role of the Future in Education* (New York: Vantage Books, 1974).

9. Ralph B. Kimbrough, *Political Power and Educational Decision-Making* (Chicago: Rand McNally & Company, 1964).

10. Ronald Havelock, *A Guide to Innovation in Education* (Institute for Social Research, Ann Arbor: University of Michigan, 1970).

11. Kimball Wiles, *Supervision for Better Schools* (Englewood Cliffs, NJ: Prentice Hall, 1975), p. 53.

12. J.R. Gibb, "Defense Level and Influence Potential in Small Groups," in L. Petrullo, ed., *Leadership and Interpersonal Behavior.* (New York: Holt, Rinehart, Winston, 1961), p. 66.

13. D. Berlo, *Avoiding Communication Breakdown*, BNA Effective Communication Film Series.

14. Ralph G. Nicholas, "Listening is a Ten-Part Skill," in *Managing Yourself*, compiled by editors of *Nation's Business*, May 1965, p. 44.
15. Recently, some states like Tennessee and Florida have legislated merit pay plans that attempt to differentiate levels of teaching.
16. *Teacher Burnout: Causes and Possible Cures*, Issues for Education Series (Georgia Professional Standards Commission, 1983).
17. Wiles-Bondi and Associates, Inc. Leadership Seminar Materials, 1990.
18. Ibid.

SUGGESTED LEARNING ACTIVITIES

1. Develop a list of characteristics of a "people person."
2. Using the information given in this chapter, profile a person skilled in human relations. What skills are most important in this role?
3. How might a supervisor send a message of "informality" to teachers and associates on the job? A message of task-orientation?
4. What are the five most important things to know about effective group leadership?
5. What are some strategies that a supervisor might employ to decrease stress build-up in the teaching staff?

BOOKS TO REVIEW

Association for Supervision and Curriculum Development. *Perceiving, Behaving, Becoming*. Washington, DC: Association for Supervision and Curriculum Development, 1961.

Carkhuff, Robert R. *Helping and Human Relations*, vols. I & II. New York: Holt, Rinehart & Winston, 1969.

Combs, Arthur; Avila, Donald; and Purkey, William. *Helping Relationships: Basic Concepts for the Helping Professions*. Boston: Allyn & Bacon, 1972.

Combs, Arthur, and Snygg, Donald. *Individual Behavior: A Perceptual Approach to Behavior*. New York: Harper & Bros., 1959.

Grambs, Jean. *Intergroup Education — Methods and Materials*. Englewood Cliffs, NJ: Prentice-Hall, 1968.

Harris, Ben. *Supervisory Behavior in Education*, 2nd ed. Englewood Cliffs, NJ: Prentice-Hall, 1975.

Johnson, David, and Johnson, Frank. *Joining Together — Group Theory and Group Skills*. Englewood Cliffs, NJ: Prentice-Hall, 1975.

Kindred, Leslie; Bagin, Don; and Gallagher, Donald. *The School and Community Relations*. Englewood Cliffs, NJ: Prentice-Hall, 1976.

Miller, William. *Dealing with Stress: A Challenge for Educators*. Bloomington, IN: Phi Delta Kappa Education Foundation, 1979.

Newell, Clarence. *Human Behavior in Educational Administration*. Englewood Cliffs, NJ: Prentice-Hall, 1978.

Norback, Craig. The Human Resources Yearbook. Englewood Cliffs, NJ: Prentice-Hall, 1989.

Swick, Kevin, and Dutt, R. *The Parent-Bond — Relating, Responding, Rewarding*. Dubuque, IA: Kendall/Hunt, 1978.

CHAPTER 8

Providing Staff Development

INTRODUCTION

Staff development in the 1990s has undergone dramatic changes. The need to rejuvenate mature staff, prepare new teachers lacking traditional courses in teacher education, assist staff in how to deal with disturbed youth, and train teachers to work collegially, are presenting new challenges to those in supervision roles.

HISTORY OF STAFF DEVELOPMENT

Much can be said about the evolution of today's approach to improving the performance of professional educators. To understand better the problems and challenges of planning and developing staff development programs, it will be useful for supervisors to review the history of staff development.

From the early 1900s to the 1930s, educators believed that improving American public schools could be best achieved by having teachers meet certain quantitative standards (teacher certification). The formal concept of instructional program improvement and teaching began with an emphasis on meeting certification requirements. That concept still prevails in public education today. Meeting certification requirements became the primary objective of both teachers and teacher-education institutions. Efforts to help professional educators adjust to social changes and new problems gave way to teachers enrolling in traditional courses required to complete degrees.

During the depression years of the thirties, lack of work opportunities for youth caused many who would have dropped out to remain in high school. There were other youths who could have attended college in better times, but knew high school would be their last chance at a formal education. These new potential high school graduates believed the curriculum irrelevant to their needs and interests and, indeed, to society in general. Pupil unrest caused educators to review the methodology used by teachers and administrators. Progressive educators were beginning to develop new teaching-learning procedures, new and expanded content, and new organizational patterns. Each innovation required practicing teachers to upgrade their knowledge and skills. Because most teachers and administrators had completed all their certification requirements, colleges and universities shifted the focus of staff development to these new-found needs. Thus activities designed to improve teacher performance were now being offered independent of certification programs.

While this development was exciting and offered new insights into the improvement of educational opportunities, it proved to have little success in improving teaching and the curriculum.

Educational leaders such as Ralph Tyler and Hilda Taba reported much later that little impact had been made on improving the educational program for youth. Their findings are summarized in three major generalizations:

1. When programs, systems, strategies and materials are developed in isolation of the educational practitioner, they are likely to become the end rather than the means.
2. When teachers and administrators do not understand the need to change or the basis for change, new programs, strategies, etc., will not occur in the school, regardless of the validity of the research and the soundness of the design.
3. If an educational institution, higher or elementary and secondary, develops and implements programs as ends, clients will be sought to fit the programs rather than continually altering programs to meet the needs and the interests of the clientele.[1]

From the end of World War II into the early fifties, the focus of teacher education once again was on meeting certification standards. An increased birth rate coupled with a teacher shortage forced school districts to employ teachers who were not certified. The lack of long-range planning by both local school districts and colleges of education resulted in a low priority being set for the professional development of teachers already certified.

It was not until the Sputnik years and our entrance into the Space Age that continuous education of teachers, apart from certification status, became a major thrust. Because the United States feared it was lagging behind Russia in producing highly skilled scientists and technicians, new teaching programs in science and mathematics became a priority. High school science programs were being upgraded and training of teachers followed. With help from the federal government and state legislatures, local school districts became responsible for planning and implementing teacher improvement programs. Universities and colleges provided on-site courses and workshops in school districts.

The experience gained from the science and mathematics (and later, social studies and language arts) inservice programs was not lost. Local districts, and more specifically, the practicing educators in those districts, became the focus for staff development. This marked the beginning of staff development. For the first time, educational leaders were asking practitioners three important questions:

1. What does a pupil need to become a successful learner?
2. What programs and services are needed to assure pupils they will be successful learners?
3. What knowledge and skills do teachers need to implement fully the programs and services?

It cannot be implied from the experiences of the late fifties and early sixties that all planners used the results of the questions asked to best advantage. It does say that planners were more concerned about the product of staff development as well as involving teachers and administrators in the development of the product than before. However, both behaviors are considered important to staff development as it is now known.

The 1960s saw professional improvement activities called *"inservice education."* Universities and colleges continued to serve as the primary resources of inservice education with workshops and courses being conducted on campuses and in school districts. During the next two decades, inservice education was considered more and more important by educators and state legislators. The number of school days in a school year was increased to give teachers and administrators more time to plan and participate in inservice activities. In addition, some states began to fund teacher education centers to increase inservice opportunities for teachers.

Specific needs of students were given more consideration during this period by professional educators and lawmakers at both the state and national level. Student needs were identified by category and funds were provided. Examples include programs such as Title I of the Elementary and Secondary Education Act, which was aimed at helping pupils from low-income homes overcome academic deficiencies; Headstart, which focused on school readiness for pre-school students from low-income homes; and P.L. 94-142 (Federal Handicapped Act), which mandated individualized educational programs for handicapped school children. These and other programs, with a requirement for teacher and administrative training, caused local school districts to become more active and independent in inservice training activities.

The 1970s saw a decrease in student enrollment and an over-supply of qualified teaching personnel. Certification was no longer a major focus of inservice activities. However, many states increased teacher certification mandates through such measures as periodic re-certification. These new mandates led to the states encouraging local school districts to provide staff development for recertification. Flor-ida, for instance, allows teachers to select an option of recertification through completing a certain number of workshop hours at the district level or college hours taken through extension courses held in districts or at a university.

Many educational leaders believe the concept of staff develop-ment as we know it today began when local school district planners (responsible for improving performance of teachers and administrators) accepted the mandate to initiate and implement educational change. In turn, local school districts were encouraged to provide training ac-tivities for the purpose of teacher recertification.

Another development in many states was the elimination of the category of *life certificate* from the state certification laws that re-quired all teachers to be periodically recertified. Georgia, for example, required all teachers with a bachelor's or master's degree to be recer-tified every five years after 1981. Those with specialist or doctoral degrees were required to be recertified every ten years.

Beginning teacher programs in a number of states have added even more mandates for staff development. Some states, for example, require all first-year teachers to pass both written and performance tests before they are given regular teaching certificates.

A majority of states have legislated that all school districts must file staff development plans with the state as part of mandated com-prehensive plans.

Staff development emerged at a time when society demanded immediate changes in public schools. As the problems and complex-ities of society increased, local school districts were called upon to deliver more and more services formerly provided by the home and community. Because local school districts assumed these major re-sponsibilities, curricula changes and the upgrading of the skills and knowledge of its teachers became immediate priorities.

Most studies of staff development efforts reveal that the link between staff development and school achievement (both for students and teachers) has failed to materialize. Where teachers are likely to change behavior and use new ideas, the following conditions are found:

1. Teachers become aware of the need for improvement through analysis of their own behavior.
2. Teachers make a written commitment to try new ideas in their classrooms the next day.

3. Teachers modify workshop ideas to fit their classrooms.
4. Teachers try out ideas, observe each other, and report successes or failures to their group. This requires follow-up inservice where ideas can be shared.
5. Teachers learn by doing – try, evaluate, modify, try again.
6. Teachers use a variety of techniques: modeling, observations, and simulations.

The decade of the 1980s continued the conservative trend of the 1970s with many states imposing teacher tests on new teachers entering the profession. Some states tied merit pay to teacher examinations and some attempted teacher tests for teachers already in service, but almost all states dropped such programs in the early 1990s.

Lack of teacher time away from students continued to plague staff developers during the 1980s. Contract negotiations often resulted in higher pay for teachers at the expense of reducing inservice days. With funding tight in many districts, paying stipends for summer training was often eliminated or reduced. In many districts, trading pay for inservice days resulted in teachers receiving as little as 3–4 days of training a year. That training was often spread out over the year with little continuity involved.

BELIEFS ABOUT STAFF DEVELOPMENT

A philosophical base should be established for all staff development programs. A set of procedural guidelines should be built on concepts, values, and theories that professional educators hold to be valid and important to staff development. The state of Georgia outlined the following belief statements for staff development as a part of a major study of teacher training in that state in 1983–1984:

1. All teachers and administrators have a desire to be successful and respected professional educators.
2. The knowledge, attitudes, and performance of teachers and administrators have the greatest impact on the effectiveness of educational programs and services.
3. Professional educators should continuously search for more effective methods of meeting the needs and interests of pupils.
4. The improvement in the proficiency (awareness, knowledge, and skills) of teachers and administrators should be a continuous process.
5. Staff development at the local school district level is the combined responsibility of the district and the individual educator.

6. To be effective, a staff development program must be guided by a systematic plan of action and an integral component of a comprehensive plan for improving the school system.

7. To accurately identify the priorities for staff development programs, the needs of individual teachers and administrators must be considered.

8. Teachers and administrators will show a greater commitment to programs that they help plan.

9. The success of a staff development program will depend heavily upon the amount teachers and administrators are involved in the planning process.

10. Each local school district has needs, priorities, and characteristics that are not common to all other school districts.

11. Staff development programs should be individualized by school district and by school employee insofar as possible.

12. Each local school district should have the autonomy to plan and implement its own staff development program.

13. Certification renewal for local school personnel should be integrated into the staff development program, and should be a by-product of the program, rather than a programmatic entity or prime product.

14. Local staff development programs should be a high priority concern as evidenced by financial resources, time to plan and implement, personnel resources, and verbal and physical support from the leadership at both the state and local levels.

15. If staff development is to be explored, planned, and managed effectively, it must be clearly articulated among all parties having interest and/or an investment in staff development.

16. Teachers and administrators profit most from staff development experience when they are respected, their expertise is valued, their ideas used, and their problems taken seriously.

17. The underlying purpose for staff development is to improve the instructional and service programs of a school district.

18. Staff development should have a direct correlation with the school district's philosophy, goals, and programs.

19. Curriculum development and professional growth through staff development should share a common ground.

20. A systematic program of staff development must be developed in which in-district and out-of-district resources can collaborate to provide leadership and assistance.

21. Educators in designated leadership positions (superintendents, principals, etc.) should have a definite plan for improvement of teaching as one of their primary responsibilities.

STAFF DEVELOPMENT
AND TODAY'S SUPERVISOR

Since the quality of student learning is directly related to the quality of instruction, a major role of supervisors is to help teachers develop the competence to provide improved instruction. While staff development in a school district may take on many different forms, those programs must nonetheless focus on the requisites needed by school personnel to advance the goals of the organization and to enhance staff competence.[2]

Through the 1980s we saw a growing interest in school organizations to improve student performance. National and state reports focused on student achievement as measured by national tests or state assessment tests. Early in the decade, the emphasis in schools was on minimum competence of students. In the middle of the decade the emphasis changed to standards of excellence where average and above-average students were challenged to excel in the sciences, mathematics, and communication skills. "Brain bowls" and "Academic Decathlons" were organized, pitting the brightest students from one high school against those of another high school. Quality of instructional programs seemed to be measured by the number of students in advanced courses and the number of computers at school sites. Lost in the shuffle was the need to develop teacher renewal activities to enhance teaching quality. Other than state efforts (strongly resisted by teacher unions) to implement merit pay plans for teachers and to implement beginning teacher programs to measure competencies of first-year teachers, little has been done to improve the art and science of teaching.

Supervisors today must wrestle with a growing resistance of veteran staffs to "learn new tricks." Union agreements have narrowed full inservice days to as little as three days per year in many school districts. Computers, like their predecessors—teaching machines and educational television—have been seen as one more imposition on teachers' time to teach in the didactic fashion they are so comfortable with in the classroom. Often, computers mean more record keeping for teachers who are already overburdened with diagnostic-prescriptive programs requiring extensive record keeping.

Teacher shortages in critical areas such as mathematics and science have brought on state programs to hire teachers with no formal training in teaching institutions. Many school districts are using out-of-field instructors to teach courses mandated by new graduation requirements in states. These developments, along with the others stated earlier, pose serious challenges for supervisors as they develop staff development programs in their school districts.

If educational organizations are to continue to grow, members of their professional staffs must also continue to grow. Since a prime purpose of supervision is to provide the leadership necessary to promote a continuing climate of improvement, it is vital that supervisors possess the knowledge base and practical skills to carry out that critical function. In this chapter we will examine leadership roles in staff development and outline role expectations and skills needed by supervisors to meet the challenges facing schools today.

STAFF DEVELOPMENT AND INSERVICE

More often than not the terms *staff development* and *inservice education* are used interchangeably. The distinction between the two is a conceptional one. Some would say that while staff development is inservice education, not all inservice education is staff development. Other authors see staff development as basically growth-oriented while inservice education assumes a deficiency in the teacher and presupposes a set of appropriate ideas, skills, and methods that need developing.[3]

We, however, feel that the term *staff development* can encompass *all* activities leading to professional growth. Our definition of staff development is based on the premise that the professional growth of an educator begins upon entry into a teacher-education program and continues until employment ends.

Experiences leading to professional growth (knowledge, skills, attitudes, etc.) can be divided into two categories:

1. *Preservice education*—Formalized teacher education programs designed to help the individual meet employment requirements.
2. *Inservice education*—Programs designed to improve the proficiencies of the practicing educator, which may be under the auspices of the employing school district or at the full discretion of the individual.

With a growing emphasis on alternative certification programs and induction programs, the distinction between preservice and inservice education is beginning to blur.

TEACHER INDUCTION

While the selection of new teachers is often a process external to the school site, the actual induction of the new teacher should be an active process at the building level. The induction of a new teacher into the system represents the best overall opportunity to influence subsequent professional behavior.

Induction can be envisioned as a five-step process which includes community adjustment, personnel adjustment, system adjustment, personal adjustment, and establishing expectations. Until these five sets of tasks are completed by the inductee, the teacher will not be able to direct full attention to the teaching act.

Community Adjustments. This category would include such basics as finding housing, finding schools or child care for children, location of physicians or other special need groups, and a basic "scouting" of the new environment. The school can help in this process by assigning a "buddy" for all new teachers much as the military has done overeseas for years for new personnel.

Personnel Adjustment. High on the priority list of all new teachers is getting on the payroll and receiving benefits for their labor. Often this requires significant time involvement in filling out papers and making visits to designated offices. A simple school check-off list for new teachers and a couple of advance telephone calls to coordinate visits can make this mundane process personal rather than institutional.

System Adjustment. Many new teachers enter into the school system oriented only to their room and how to get their texts and supplies. A very natural and important question in the mind of any new teacher is "how do I fit into the bigger picture?" If you want to orient the new teacher to district goals and philosophy, discipline procedures, or extracurricular duties and expectations, this is the time. What is delivered to the new teacher during induction will influence the individual's perception for years to come.

Personal Adjustment. Like moving into a new neighborhood, the new teacher will be anxious to establish relationships and become known to others. Perhaps schools should invest more on arrival parties than on "going away" parties for teachers. A "buddy" appointment can facilitate this very important task for the new teacher.

Establishing Expectations. Setting expectations for teacher performance can best be accomplished during induction when the new teacher is curious and seeking such information. Sharing evaluation criteria, assessment or visitation schedules, and the role of the supervisor in improving instruction are all relevant topics at this stage of development.

In summary, induction of a new teacher is an opportunity for the supervisor to establish contact, bond with the new teacher, set perceptions of performance expectations, and accelerate the improvement of a teacher's performance in the classroom.

LEADERSHIP ROLES IN STAFF DEVELOPMENT

Supervisors can improve teachers' competencies in a number of ways, but they must be perceived by teachers as a valued resource. Studies have shown that instructional supervisors believe what they do has high value, although the teachers with whom they work find instructional supervision to be of little value.[4] Principals can improve teacher performance, but need to spend more time in the classroom providing direct assistance to teachers.[5]

Thus, those closest to teachers, either in the minds of teachers or in reality, seem to provide little leadership in improving teachers' instructional performance. Teachers are touched only briefly by preservice training. When they find themselves placed in a school setting they often learn their craft in unbelievable solitude inside their cells in the honeycomb of a school. They may get help from a department chair or mentor next door, but often those persons are too busy to be of much help. It is no wonder that teachers see teaching as an individualistic act after having to learn teaching tasks by their own ingenuity.

Leadership in most schools is directed at the daily problems of logistics and management. Record keeping and reporting brought on by accountability mandates leave but precious bits of free time for teachers and they are hesitant to participate in any staff development activity that wastes time. Frequently snatches of staff development touch their lives, usually in brief workshops that feature "inspiring" speeches and demonstrations of discrete skills. In any given year, teachers, on the average, participate in only three days of inservice work and these often include isolated topics and little or no follow-up.[6]

The challenge facing supervisors today in planning for and delivering staff development activities is not insurmountable, but does require skills of building a synergistic environment where collaborative enterprises are both normal and sustaining. Teachers must see a need for staff development activities, be a part of the planning for those activities, and feel a sense of growth and competence by participating in them. Teachers, even veteran staff members, can be good learners. They can master just about every teaching technique and are willing to implement any new instructional program or curriculum they feel is sensible — if the conditions are right. The following sections outline skills and tasks supervisors can use to achieve high quality staff development.

Influencing Teacher Education Training

Although supervisors are responsible for teacher inservice training, they can and should *influence* the training. Supervisors can, for example, collaborate with teacher training institutions by teaching courses at a university or college, serving on college committees, working directly with university supervisors in internship programs, and by serving on teacher education center committees.

Teacher education programs have been under attack for a number of years. Newspapers, magazines, and professional journals have been filled with articles criticizing the state of education in general and teacher training in particular.[7] In 1983, the National Commission on Excellence in Education issued an unprecedented denunciation of the quality of American education. Various state commissions echoed the national report. In teacher education programs, low academic standards and the relevance of such preparation programs for the practical needs of the public schools have been debated.[8]

From a teacher surplus to a teacher shortage, schools have faced a continuing crisis in getting properly trained teachers into the classrooms. Declining enrollments have meant a decreasing need for teachers. However, the number of graduates in education has not kept pace with the need for more teachers, especially in the critical areas of mathematics and science. Compounding the problem of teacher shortfall in the 1980s were increased requirements for high school students. Many of those requirements included additional courses in science and mathematics, thus exacerbating the overall shortages in those two areas.[9]

Other than increasing field experiences and the length of time in teacher preparation programs to include a fifth year, teacher education institutions have done little to change the organization and procedures of such programs. Those programs continue to communicate the myths of teacher education:

Myth No. 1.   *The business of teaching is transmitting knowledge* — This must be the case, for the average teacher education program consists of three years of disciplined coursework followed by one year of professional preparation.

Myth No. 2.   *The best way to prepare for teaching is to be told about it* — This must be true, or we would round up teachers-to-be and run them through a string of courses beginning with a survey and ending with methods.

Myth No. 3.   *Mastery of the skills of teaching is best gained through reading and writing reports* — The incredible procedures found in endless education teacher preparation courses are to read about teaching processes and write papers about things like open education and learning center operation.

Myth No. 4.   *Regardless of their destination, all teachers should be trained the same* — Like the patient described by Mager in Goal Analysis, we line up student teachers for the treatment without ever inquiring about their destinations. A footnote to this condition is that although nearly half the kids in school live in 8 states and most of them in 16 metropolitan areas, most teachers are trained in rural land-grant institutions.

Myth No. 5.   *Children are all alike* — While your individual judgment would tell you this is untrue, we deal with that unitary figment, the average child, almost exclusively. Only recently have we noted a few exceptions such as the mentally and physically handicapped, underachievers and overachievers, the culturally deprived, delayed and nondelayed learners, gifted, dyslexic, emotionally disturbed, disruptive . . . but when we plan for instruction, these "exceptions" seem to evaporate from discussions.

Myth No. 6.   *Most kids you teach will be interested in you and your message* — How quickly university professors and teachers in training forget those we left behind. Of every 100 fifth graders in school, 75 finish high school, 48 enter college, and 23 will graduate.

       Motivation is an elusive commodity to the 75 percent of those who are put out by the system along the way. Many will teach students who have already mentally checked out. Yet, we treat such motivation as a "given" in most courses.

Myth No. 7.   *Most schools are innovative and exciting places* — Many education courses experienced by teachers in training would lead them to believe that the average school is an orgy of innovativeness — open, electric, fluid. To the contrary, as Silberman's survey pointed out . . . and Joseph Mayer Rice's identical accounts at the turn of the last century . . . most schools are conservative and mindless.

Myth No. 8.   *Good teaching is an absolute quality* — Surely this must be so because no one ever mentions that a strict disciplinarian can also be a good teacher. Good teaching is not an absolute quality. Like

leadership itself, good teaching is a situational
phenomenon. Teachers are delivery systems for a
curricular program.

Myth No. 9.   *Teaching is really pretty simple* — All that is
required is to know your subject, know your
methods, and plug in. That may have been true
thirty years ago — today the requirements for
existing are staggering.

Myth No. 10.   *Teacher training ends at graduation* — After all,
many teachers have five year, ten year, or even
lifetime certificates. This must mean that they will
need little support again from teacher training
institutions.

As the national debate over the quality of teachers and teaching
heats up, many policy makers and legislators will be seeking answers
to the critical questions of whether teacher education programs can
attract quality students and whether we can keep them in the field
once they graduate. Supervisors can individually and collectively begin
to exert an influence on teacher education programs. They must insist
on becoming partners in the process of planning and carrying out
teacher preparation programs. They must be master teachers themselves, willing to enter a classroom and work with students and teachers. Finally, they must work to become the premier leaders in their
field so that their voices will be heard and respected.

Assessing Staff Development Needs

Staff development activities should be directly related to instructional
problems and interests of teachers. To learn about those problems and
interests and plan inservice activities, a needs-assessment process
should be used. Surveys of teachers and administrators can be used as
well as collecting other data available at a school or in the school
district. Staff development activities should be based upon docu-
mented need, be highly organized, be sustained beyond one workshop
session, and lead to direct improvement of instruction in the classroom level. Staff development activities should be a part of an ongoing curriculum management plan (see chapter 9) that is a comprehensive plan for managing a school or district curricular and instructional program.

A major point is that staff development activities should lead to
the improvement of student learning. Staff development for the sake
of staff development leads to nothing except a waste of precious
dollars.

Table 8.1
Orange County Public Schools Middle School Teacher Survey May 1984

(To be completed by all seventh and eighth grade teachers and counselors.)

School Name: _____

Teacher Name: _____
                              (Please print.)

This questionnaire is designed to gather data from teachers in Orange County about their teaching experience. Place a check in the appropriate blank to indicate your response.

1. Degree(s) held
    _____ A. B.A. or B.S.
    _____ B. B.A. or B.S. plus 15 hours
    _____ C. Master's
    _____ D. Doctorate

2. Total years of teaching experience
    _____ A. One year or less
    _____ B. Two–four years
    _____ C. Five–ten years
    _____ D. 11–19 Years
    _____ E. 20 years or more

3. Number of years taught in grades 6, 7, 8
    _____ A. One year or less
    _____ B. Two–four years
    _____ C. Five–ten years
    _____ D. 11–19 Years
    _____ E. 20 years or more

4. Certification
    _____ A. Elementary only
    _____ B. Secondary only
    _____ C. K–12
    _____ D. Elementary plus middle school
    _____ E. Secondary plus middle school

5. For the following areas put a check in the blank space if you have current certification in the subject area.
    _____ English
    _____ Math
    _____ Science
    _____ Social Studies
    _____ Reading
    _____ Art
    _____ Music
    _____ Foreign Language
    _____ Physical Education
    _____ Home Economics
    _____ Industrial Arts
    _____ Special Education
    _____ Guidance
    _____ Administration and Supervision

Table 8.1

(Continued)

STAFF DEVELOPMENT CHECKLIST FOR
MIDDLE SCHOOL TEACHERS

Below you will find 31 skills identified as useful in implementing the Middle School concept. From the list, choose the five that you think are most important and necessary for staff development for you and/or your school. Rank them by placing the numbers 1–5 in the appropriate blanks with a "1" indicating the highest priority. For the 31 items, only five items should have a number in the blank space.

_____ 1. Techniques for counseling students
_____ 2. Locating and/or developing appropriate teaching resources
_____ 3. Teaching reading skills in the classroom
_____ 4. Using value-clarification techniques in the classroom
_____ 5. Working with other teachers across subject-matter lines in teams
_____ 6. Planning instructional units
_____ 7. Developing learning centers
_____ 8. Enhancing learner self-concept
_____ 9. Basic classroom management techniques
_____ 10. Record-keeping system in the classroom
_____ 11. Evaluating student progress
_____ 12. Dealing with motivation and discipline problems in the classroom
_____ 13. Teaching for higher thinking and creativity
_____ 14. Promoting effective learning in the classroom
_____ 15. Encouraging learning climates
_____ 16. Individualizing instruction
_____ 17. Grouping and regrouping students for instructional purposes
_____ 18. Developing teacher-made learning materials
_____ 19. Involving students in planning
_____ 20. Understanding culturally-diverse students
_____ 21. Using community resources in teaching
_____ 22. Making classrooms more humane
_____ 23. Counseling students one-to-one
_____ 24. Developing interdisciplinary units
_____ 25. Using audiovisuals in teaching
_____ 26. Preparing teacher-made tests
_____ 27. Use of inquiry techniques in teaching
_____ 28. Use of student contracts
_____ 29. Identifying student learning disabilities
_____ 30. Accommodating special education students in the regular classroom
_____ 31. Understanding characteristics of Middle School students.

The five most important inservice needs for me and/or my school are

1. _____
2. _____
3. _____
4. _____
5. _____

Use the space remaining and the reverse side for any other comments.

Table 8.2
Teacher Survey of Experience and Staff Development Needs

Instrument:	Teacher Survey Form—7th, 8th grade teachers.
Findings:	This questionnaire was designed to gather data from teachers about experience and training. Findings include:

        36% of teachers hold B.S. degree
        58% B.S. or B.S. + 15
        42% Masters Degree
        83% have taught over 5 years
        58% have taught over 10 years
        72% have taught over 5 years in grades 6, 7, and 8
        43% have taught over 10 years in grades 6, 7, and 8

Of 31 skills identified as useful in implementing the middle school concept, teachers indicated the following as their first five choices:

1. Dealing with motivation and discipline problems in the classroom
2. Promoting effective learning in the classroom
3. Working with other teachers across subject matter in teams
4. Teaching for higher thinking and creativity
5. Enhancing learner's self-concept

Implications: Orange County junior high teachers represent a veteran staff. Inservice and staff development should keep providing teachers with the retooling skills needed to carry out an effective middle school program.

One example of finding information about the staff and their needs is to use a district survey form similar to that in Table 8.1. Note that work had already gone into identifying the thirty-one skills useful in implementing the middle school concept. Table 8.2, above, illustrates the results of the survey. One can see that in the conversion from junior high schools to middle schools in the Orange District, the process would involve the retooling of veteran teachers.

Another type of assessment of staff development needs is found in Table 8.3. In this survey, the choices for inservice topics have been narrowed. Also, methods of achieving certain skills and knowledge may be suggested by teachers (e.g., clinical inservice in the classroom or school visits). In addition, times for inservice workshops, as well as types of rewards or incentives, may be suggested by staff members.

District data can be summarized to provide planners with a profile of student needs. Such a profile, as that illustrated in Table 8.4, has great implications for teacher training as well as for school improvement.

Table 8.3
Survey of Inservice Needs

_____

                                                    _____
                                                              NAME

I. I would be willing to participate in the following (check one or more):
   _____ Workshops on listening skills—Interpersonal relations
   _____ Interdisciplinary teaming
   _____ Curriculum development in my subject area—Scope and se-
          quence—Skills checklists—Writing a base or life skills curriculum
   _____ Classroom management—Motivational techniques—Classroom
          interaction

II. I would like to participate in clinical inservice sessions (consultant in the
    classroom with me) where I could get help in the following areas:
    _____
    _____
    _____
    _____
    _____
    _____
    _____
    _____
    _____
    _____

III. I would like to visit certain programs such as:
     _____
     _____
     _____

IV. I would be willing to participate in workshops (check one or more):
    _____ After school hours and evenings
    _____ Friday evening—Saturday morning
    _____ Inservice days only
    _____ During released time when provided substitute
    _____ One-two weeks in summer

V. I'd like to receive the following if possible:
   _____ Inservice points
   _____ Course credit
   _____ Released time substitutes
   _____ Trade-off time
   _____ Stipends for summer writing

_____

Preparing a Staff Development Plan

Since a prime purpose of supervision is to provide the leadership necessary to promote a continuing climate of improvement, it is vital that
supervisors be able to plan and conduct effective inservice programs.

Table 8.4
Summary of General Data

In addition to information about the junior high schools gained through instruments, other data were retrieved from district files and evaluation reports. These data provide a profile of *existing conditions* in the 19 junior high schools of Orange County.

	Low	High
Enrollment range in junior high schools	670	1389
Average daily attendance, (May, 1984) in junior high schools	83%	95%
Absences per teacher per month in junior high schools	.36	1.27
Number of low socioeconomic students in junior high school as a percentage	11%	56%
Ratio of gifted students to other exceptional education students in junior high school	1/104	179/63
Mobility—number of students moving in or out of junior high school during year	33%	70%
Number of students in junior high school experiencing corporal punishment	44	619
Number of students in junior high school experiencing suspension	37	240
Number of students dropping out of junior high school in academic year	0	22
Average score of students in junior high school on CTBS total battery	36	80

Findings: These data confirm that a wide range of conditions and performance exist in the junior high schools of Orange County. The single greatest variable reflected in these data is variance in student population.

Implications: These statistics suggest that the quality of intermediate programs experienced in Orange County School District may depend upon the school attended. Efforts should be made to equalize programs and performance of the individual schools during the transition to middle schools.

There are essential steps in developing an inservice plan. Table 8.5 outlines those steps.

Preparing a staff development plan should include teachers, students, administrators, parents, and supervisors. Local school districts can improve student learning opportunities by improving the educational system and the performance of those who implement it. The following seven premises should guide those involved in developing an inservice or staff development plan:

Table 8.5
A Model for Inservice Education

Conduct an Assessment of Need
- A.   Identify the target learners.
- B.   Determine a strategy for learner needs assessment—goals and objectives, test data, survey data, nature and degree of involvement in inservice project.
- C.   Conduct learner needs assessment.
- D.   Assign priorities to identified learner needs—tasks.
- E.   Collect baseline data regarding target learners.

Make Policy Decision to Initiate an Inservice Project
- A.   Involve target learners, administrators, supervisors in identifying program objectives.
- B.   Designate supervisory personnel (leadership agents) and support personnel to provide leadership for the project.
- C.   Develop budget and process guidelines.
- D.   Set a time frame for the project.
- E.   Design inservice activities, materials, resources.

Develop Evaluative Measures to Assess Developed Inservice Program Objectives and Related Activities
- A.   Design evaluative measures to assess competencies of leadership staff.
- B.   Institute monitoring and formative evaluation regarding inservice project objectives and activities.
- C.   Develop evaluative measures to assess support elements, resources.
- D.   Conduct summative evaluation of inservice objectives, activities, leadership and supportive staff.

---

1. Some knowledge and skills can best be acquired before the teacher enters service, while others can be acquired only after the teacher is in service.
2. The development of curricula and the upgrading of skills and knowledge of teachers and administrators should be a continuous, interrelating process.
3. Curricula and professional improvement programs that are developed in isolation of the educational practitioners become the end rather than the means.
4. Changes in educational programs and strategies will not occur, regardless of the validity of the research and the soundness of the design, unless teachers and administrators understand the need and basis for change.
5. The complexities of society require a system for continually changing programs and services for pupils and the methodology by which they are delivered.

6. Professional improvement programs that are developed and conducted as an end rather than a means will cause clients to be sought to fit the program rather than continually altering the programs to meet the needs and the interests of the clientele.
7. State government is expecting local school districts to become more responsible for professional improvement programs.

Staff development in school districts may occur at four levels in a school district. Figure 8.1 illustrates those four levels and describes those impacted by the staff development.

Planning staff development at these four levels is more successful when the programs are coordinated with the comprehensive plan of the district. A model for a comprehensive plan, the Wiles-Bondi Curriculum Management Plan (CMP) is found in the next chapter.

FACILITATING HUMAN DEVELOPMENT IN STAFF DEVELOPMENT

Supervisors must realize that if a better school program is desired, an environment where teachers can be creative and improve teaching must be facilitated.[10]

Promoting a willingness to try new ideas and techniques in the classroom is an essential step in sparking creativeness in teachers. Supervisors should demonstrate new procedures and provide security for teachers who are willing to try new ideas even if they fail. Constructive experimentation can result in better teaching. Finally, supervisors should be willing to share the heat when experimental programs do not succeed.

Societal demands on public education have resulted in the consolidation of small schools and school districts. As a result, schools and school districts have become complex organizations. Bigger schools and school districts have become further and further removed from classroom teachers. At the same time, teachers' professional organizations have become larger and the leadership of those organizations has become further removed from the needs of the individual teacher. All of these developments, along with an accountability movement, have resulted in school leaders being viewed by teachers as bureaucrats. To help prevent political competition and encourage cooperative behavior between school leaders and teachers, supervisors should encourage a network of educational partnerships between teachers to help solve problems of greatest educational significance. Supervisors who can form those partnerships and are really perceived by teachers and others as willing to share in decision making will help ensure their survival as supervisors. What educational partners are saying to each other is, "I can't be successful without you."

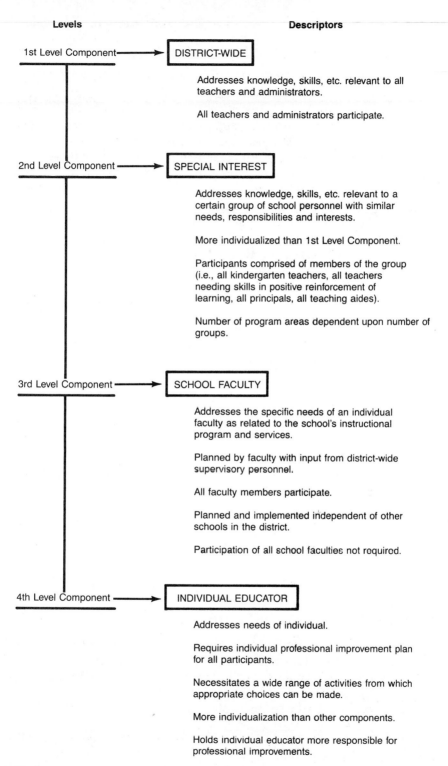

Levels   **Descriptors**

1st Level Component ——————▶ | DISTRICT-WIDE |

Addresses knowledge, skills, etc. relevant to all teachers and administrators.

All teachers and administrators participate.

2nd Level Component ——————▶ | SPECIAL INTEREST |

Addresses knowledge, skills, etc. relevant to a certain group of school personnel with similar needs, responsibilities and interests.

More individualized than 1st Level Component.

Participants comprised of members of the group (i.e., all kindergarten teachers, all teachers needing skills in positive reinforcement of learning, all principals, all teaching aides).

Number of program areas dependent upon number of groups.

3rd Level Component ——————▶ | SCHOOL FACULTY |

Addresses the specific needs of an individual faculty as related to the school's instructional program and services.

Planned by faculty with input from district-wide supervisory personnel.

All faculty members participate.

Planned and implemented independent of other schools in the district.

Participation of all school faculties not required.

4th Level Component ——————▶ | INDIVIDUAL EDUCATOR |

Addresses needs of individual.

Requires individual professional improvement plan for all participants.

Necessitates a wide range of activities from which appropriate choices can be made.

More individualization than other components.

Holds individual educator more responsible for professional improvements.

Figure 8.1
Levels of Staff Development

Changing the Teacher's Work Environment

Teachers in large schools have their own rooms, own students and in many cases, their own instructional programs. They are usually cut off from other teachers and supervisors. Because teachers do not talk with other teachers or with their supervisors, they feel they are invisible and isolated. Schedules for teachers are set by the central office and they are told what they will teach and when they will teach it. Externally developed policies, mandated curricula, and minimum competencies developed at the district or state level, restrict teachers' involvement in making program decisions.

Supervisors can eliminate factors in the school environment resulting in teacher isolation and replace them with a model of collective action by implementing the following steps:[11]

1. Encourage teachers to visit each other to find out what others are doing. Why not teach several periods for a teacher while he or she is observing another teacher?
2. Provide time for professional talk among teachers during faculty meetings. Talk about actions teachers could take to solve instructional problems.
3. Have teachers demonstrate successful teaching techniques to their peers in workshops after school. Keep the sessions focused on a single topic and keep the meetings short.
4. Encourage teachers to work in groups such as teams where common students are taught and common planning time is made available for teachers during the school day.
5. Ask teachers and other staff members to discuss their philosophies about how students are taught, what their school should accomplish, how students should be tested, and how the school environment can be improved. Share research on each of those areas with the group and invite a continuous dialogue about issues that divide the group. If teachers can see that other teachers share their views or at least their views are respected, a feeling of worth will result. Teachers who feel they are respected will continue to work toward collective solutions to school problems.

Teacher Absenteeism and Burnout

Teacher absenteeism and burnout are growing problems in American public schools. As schools become bigger and more complex, and society's problems continue to spill over into the schools, teachers are staying away from school, or leaving altogether.

Studies of absenteeism have shown that

1. Absenteeism increased after the enactment of collective bargaining legislation.

2. Absenteeism has continued to increase despite better pay, smaller classes, and more appropriate assignments.
3. Demographic factors do not have a significant impact on the amount of absenteeism.
4. The highest rate of absenteeism occurs on Mondays and Fridays.
5. High levels of absenteeism occur in school districts where there are low levels of faculty agreement toward goals and policies of the community and school districts.
6. Low levels of absenteeism occur in districts with high levels of community support and policy agreement.
7. Small districts tend to have lower absenteeism rates.
8. Use of personal leave days are almost twice as high for the month of May as the average of the rest of the year.
9. The results of attempts to correlate absenteeism with morale, subunit size, job interdependence, and job involvement are tentative and speculative.

Teacher absenteeism has significant implications for the class-room, school, school district, and community. The mean average number of days absent per teacher due to all paid absences for teachers in 1990 is 8.2 days across all reporting districts. Absences in large school systems (25,000 or more students) is 9.0 days.

When a teacher is absent, there are major costs both instructional and financial. Estimates of costs for teacher absenteeism in the United States range from one to two billion dollars. In addition to paying the cost of a substitute teacher, there are other losses such as loss of time for student programs, loss of instructional time because of ineffective-ness of substitute teachers, and loss of credibility with the public. The administrative time wasted to compensate for a teacher absence also is an important cost. By far, the most significant cost from teacher absenteeism is the effect on the academic performance of students.

Studies have indicated that there are a number of variables as sociated with teacher absenteeism. Those variables can be grouped as: contractual (salary, benefits, leaves); environmental (working conditions, location); procedural (absence policy); and social (interaction of employees with fellow employees). Most studies indicate that as a result of collective bargaining more days off are available and teachers are taking them.

Closely associated with absenteeism is the phenomenon of teacher burnout. Teachers simply get tired, bored, or frustrated with conditions they feel they cannot improve. After about three years, many teachers leave the field. Many only teach a year or two before they quit. The more serious problem is the veteran teacher of seven or eight years who although tenured, burns out and drops out.

DELIVERY SYSTEMS FOR STAFF DEVELOPMENT

Although there is a rich research base to guide the selection of topics for staff development, there is much less research to guide the design of the training process. Critical decisions need to be made about training schedules, activities, and group sizes. We know that long-term training efforts are more likely to succeed than short-term ones. Also, presentation, demonstration, practice, and feedback have been found to be valuable components of staff development delivery systems.

A goal for staff development should be to create a program that enables teachers to share their problems, solutions, and expertise; to put teachers in touch with research on teaching; and to provide teachers with a way to become aware of and consider the effects of their teaching on students.

The following sections represent successful delivery systems of staff development.

Clinical Methods of Staff Development

Microteaching. Microteaching is a process that makes it possible for teachers to participate in an actual teaching situation and receive immediate feedback on their performance. Teaching behavior is defined in terms of specific skills or techniques so that a specific lesson might focus on a single skill. Often, observational systems are utilized to help identify particular teacher behaviors. Other systems are used to look at such teaching skills as the effective use of classroom questions and classroom management.

Microteaching, as a procedure, gives teachers and supervisors the opportunity to identify, define, describe, analyze, and retest certain teaching skills in a lab setting. Teachers can try out lessons on students, other teachers, and supervisors. Through the use of such techniques as films or videotapes, teachers can teach and reteach until a skill is mastered.

Clinical Supervision. The aims of traditional supervision and clinical supervision are the same—to improve instruction. In traditional supervision, however, the supervisor is the instructional expert. In clinical supervision, both the supervisor and teacher are assumed to be instructional experts. The teacher and the supervisor communicate as colleagues, with the teacher identifying concerns and the supervisor assisting the teacher in analyzing and improving teaching performance.

Morris Cogan[12] and colleagues, in the 1950s, initiated a study of supervision that led to the process of clinical supervision. Through a study of graduate students, Cogan found that suggestions on improvement of teaching coming from supervisors often fell on deaf ears. Students were not listening to supervisors because they felt supervisors were not concerned with the same problems the graduate students were experiencing in their classrooms.

In the clinical approach the teacher is not the passive recipient of supervision, but is an active partner whose participation and commitment are critical to the success of the supervisory process. Clinical supervision emphasizes teacher growth and assumes teachers possess the drive and personal resources to improve their teaching. The system is "clinical" because it depends upon direct, trained observation of classroom behaviors.

As a process, clinical supervision helps the teacher to identify and clarify problems, receive data from the supervisor, and develop solutions to problems with the help of the supervisor. Clinical supervision involves more supervisory time than one or two visits to a classroom.

Clinical supervisory techniques offer a number of advantages over traditional methods of supervision. They include:

1. Supervisors and teachers work together toward common objectives.
2. Supervisors can influence teaching behavior to a greater degree.
3. Teachers and supervisors have positive feelings toward the supervisory process.

Clinical supervision involves a five-step process. These five steps are discussed here.

Preobservational Conference. The preobservational conference between supervisor and teacher helps establish rapport between the two, allows the supervisor to get an orientation toward the group of students to be observed, provides an opportunity for the teacher and supervisor to discuss the lesson to be taught and observed, and finally, provides a time for the supervisor and teacher to develop a contract outlining on what aspects of teaching he or she would like feedback.

Observation. The supervisor enters the classroom quietly and tries to avoid eye contact with students or teacher. The observer takes notes during the observation, particularly noting behaviors or teaching methods discussed during the preobservational conference. After the observation, the observer slips out of the classroom as quietly and unobtrusively as he or she entered.

Analysis and Strategy. At this step, the supervisor reviews her or his notes in respect to the contract, analyzing the teaching patterns and crucial incidents observed during the lesson. Often if an observational system has been used, the supervisor can refer to specific verbal behaviors, levels of questions, or classroom management techniques.

After the analysis, the supervisor must consider how to approach the teacher with the suggestions he or she may have developed. The supervisor must consider how defensive the teacher is and how best to approach the conference with the teacher.

Supervisory Conference. During the supervisory conference the teacher obtained feedback on those aspects of teaching that concerned her or him. Specific contract items are reviewed first, with additional feedback on other behavioral patterns later. As a final step in the observational conference, the supervisor may help the teacher plan the next lesson. The new lesson will incorporate the improvements identified during the conference.

Postconference Analysis. The final step in the clinical supervision process is a postconference analysis of the total clinical process. This step is really an inservice process for the supervisor. The supervisor can check to see if the teacher's professional integrity was respected during the conference, if the teacher had time to fully discuss specific contract items reviewed, and if the contract was satisfactory.[13]

The combination of microteaching in a lab setting with clinical analysis of a live classroom holds promise for improving teaching. There are limitations in both the clinical and microteaching designs. The one-to-one relationship between supervisor and teacher is time-consuming and expensive; videotaping equipment is costly. There are also valuable group interaction opportunities that may be lost. Finally, the focus on self found in the clinical design may retard looking outward for new ideas and advice.[14]

Competency-Based Staff Development

Another approach to professional development with a focus on the individual is the competency-based staff development model. In this approach no attempt is made to impose any particular instructional strategy or technique as best for everyone. There are five characteristics of the competency-based model:

1. All staff development efforts focus on the learner (teacher or administrator). Each learner is involved in designating the strategy necessary to develop a specific competency.
2. Instructional modules are prepared to help the teacher or administrator reach his or her professional objective. The instructional objectives are criterion referenced so that the competence attained by a particular participant is independent of reference to performance of

others. Competencies are developed or assessed on three types of criteria: knowledge, performance, and consequences.

3. Each participant sets a target date for attainment of a particular objective viewed as essential to the achievement of a stated competency.

4. Developmental activities occur in a field setting. Simulated conditions are sometimes used to reduce the risk element.

5. Emphasis is placed on exit rather than entrance requirements. Objectives are clearly defined so that all parties know when the objective has been attained.[15]

There have been a number of approaches for identifying both pre- and inservice teacher competencies. Depending on what study the reader reviews, the competencies may be listed as general, specific, or sometimes "critical."

Many states have moved toward competency-based certification for initial certification as well as recertification of teachers. Florida has been a leader in developing competency tests for teachers and demanding mastery of identified teaching competencies. Applicants for initial regular certification must pass a comprehensive written examination. A growing criticism of "too many tests" and the need to fill teaching positions in critical areas is forcing a re-examination of such requirements.

In making the transition from staff development for renewal credits to staff development for professional growth, one would assume that all teaching personnel would be motivated to acquire new competencies or refine present ones. Unfortunately, some teachers do not want to disrupt the status quo. They see change as a threat. Other teachers simply do not have the time or energy to spend time in developmental activities. Teachers are busy people. Primary teachers work an average of 43.9 hours a week; intermediate teachers, 47.8 hours; middle school teachers, 47.1 hours; and high school teachers, 51.1 hours per week. With family and other out-of-school obligations, there remains little time for professional development.

Clinical supervision and other supervisory processes, where informative (not judgmental) feedback is provided participants, are helping teachers and administrators become more supportive of professional development.

To overcome the problem of lack of time for professional development, many school districts are providing an afternoon a week where students are dismissed early or permanent substitutes are hired to relieve teachers of classroom duties.

Those who work with clinical supervision and competency-based staff development recognize that good human relations are the key to the success of both processes. Supervisors must spend considerable time establishing rapport with teachers and administrators.

School-Based Staff Development Programs

School-based staff development programs operate on the following premises: (1) teachers should be involved in the identification and articulation of their own training needs; (2) growth experiences for teachers, as well as for children, should be individualized. If such growth experiences are to be meaningful, they should belong to the learner, not be imposed by someone else; and (3) the single school is the largest and proper unit for educational change.

Florida has been a leader in legislating school-based staff development programs. Gordon Lawrence, in a paper prepared for the Florida Department of Education, presented many findings that support the establishment of school-based staff development programs. Nine of his findings are listed here:

1. Teacher attitudes are more likely to be influenced in school-based than in college-based inservice programs.
2. School-based programs in which teachers participate as helpers to each other and planners of inservice activities tend to have greater success in accomplishing their objectives than do programs that are conducted by college or other outside personnel without the assistance of teachers.
3. School-based inservice programs that emphasize self-instruction by teachers have a strong record of effectiveness.
4. Inservice education programs that have differentiated training experiences for different teachers (that is, "individualized") are more likely to accomplish their objectives than are programs that have common activities for all participants.
5. Inservice education programs that place the teacher in active roles (constructing and generating materials, ideas, and behavior) are more likely to accomplish their objectives than are programs that place the teacher in a receptive role (accepting ideas and behavior prescriptions not of his or her own making).
6. Inservice education programs that emphasize demonstrations, supervised trials, and feedback are more likely to accomplish their goals than are programs in which the teachers are expected to store up ideas and behavior prescriptions for a future time.
7. Inservice education programs in which teachers share and provide mutual assistance to each other are more likely to accomplish their objectives than are programs in which each teacher does separate work.
8. Teachers are more likely to benefit from inservice education activities that are linked to a general effort of the school than they are from single-shot programs that are not part of a general staff development plan.
9. Teachers are more likely to benefit from inservice programs in which they can choose goals and activities for themselves, as contrasted with programs in which the goals and activities are preplanned.[16]

Peer Supervision

Peer supervision as a concept implies that teachers can supervise each other and provide observation, analysis, and feedback to their peers. Peer supervision is still a disturbingly slippery concept for many leaders in the field. In reviewing the term, one does not know whether it is describing a system in which teachers are organized into helping teams under the direction of a supervisor, or whether the total teacher team has the responsibility for the improvement of instruction.

Teacher militancy in recent years has led teachers to demand greater control over their own teaching. Unions have pressed for more responsibility for teachers in providing inservice education, evaluation, and other supervisory tasks. Teacher education center councils, where teachers have majority voting rights, have given rise to renewed efforts to give teachers more control over their destinies. Indeed, teacher organizations have lobbied for controlling access to the profession, selection, and retention of staff members. Because of confusion about the roles of supervisors, evaluation of teachers has become a dilemma for teachers and supervisors. For instance, teachers do not know whether a supervisor's visit is for instructional improvement, administrative evaluation, or both.

There are several drawbacks to peer supervision. As it is defined in many districts, teachers do not know if peer supervision is designed for improvement of instruction, evaluation, or both. Supervisors are also reluctant to share part of their domain of teacher evaluation with teachers. Finally, teachers must have an openness and trust among peers that exists in few places. Tenure laws and declining enrollment mean the prospect of increased numbers of senior teachers. With the security of tenured positions, such teachers may be resistant to supervisory efforts to upgrade instruction. Will peers be able to effect changes on those persons?

Peer supervision does hold promise as an adjunct to a broadly based program for instructional improvement. It is clear that the influence of supervisors in the instructional improvement process can be enhanced by the legitimate involvement of teachers in that process. However, supervisors must provide the linkage necessary between self-directed improvement and improvement that results from formal, organizationally directed supervision.

Teacher Education Centers

The teacher education center concept is a unified approach to the study of teaching and supervision. It is a coordinated program of preservice and inservice experiences planned and administered cooperatively by universities, unions, private firms, governmental agencies, and public school systems.

The teacher center is an approach to inservice education, but not the only approach. Teacher centers supported by federal funds must be governed by a board composed of a majority of classroom teachers. In 1978 the federal government appropriated $8.25 million to create and support teacher centers. Fifty-five local school districts and five universities were awarded grants. Additional funding for teacher centers continued in the years after 1978.

Both the National Educational Association (NEA) and American Federation of Teachers (AFT) have received National Institute of Education (NIE) grants to assist members with teacher center projects. NEA took a different approach than AFT in establishing teacher centers. NEA began teacher center projects in 1977 at fifty-two sites in twenty-five states. AFT did not select sites and develop programs, but chose instead to work through its local affiliates providing help and assistance when requested.

In 1975, a national clearinghouse for teacher centers, the Teachers' Centers Exchange, was funded by NIE and housed in the Far West Laboratory for Educational Research and Development in San Francisco.

Teacher centers can be placed in one of five categories: school district, independent, consortium, legislative, or union. Even though many centers have elements of more than one of these categories, there are unique characteristics of each of the five.

School district centers usually avoid accepting funds from sources outside the district. They remain close to the teachers and conduct workshops, offer graduate courses, and help develop materials for teachers in the district.

Independent teacher centers until recently comprised over 50 percent of all teacher centers; today less than 10 percent are independent. Independent centers receive funds from foundations, business donations, and earned income including that from workshops and sale of teaching materials.

Consortium teacher centers are based on cooperation of a number of groups both in and out of education. Consortium centers operate on the premise that professional growth of teachers involves preservice, inservice, and the surrounding community, and all of those elements are incorporated in consortium teacher centers.

Legislative teacher centers are those established by legislation in a state. Florida is unique in that the Florida Teacher Center Act of 1973 mandated that each of Florida's sixty-seven school districts help sponsor a teacher center. The state legislature set aside five dollars per student to be spent on staff development, with three of those dollars going directly into teacher centers. Several legislative acts after the 1973 Teacher Center Act provided further aid and direction to teacher centers including the sharing of a portion of funds between colleges of education and teacher centers. Florida's teacher centers have been models of cooperation between school districts and the state university system.

Union teacher centers are supported and controlled by an organization representing teachers in collective bargaining. In New York City 95 percent of teachers belong to the AFT and participate in the David Wittes Education Lounge. This center is supported by union dues, and policy is dictated by the union.

Workshops, pre- and inservice courses, studies of teaching and supervision, special programs for paraprofessionals and teachers, development of materials, developing programs for children with special needs, bookmobiles, libraries, and personal tutoring are some of the services provided through teacher centers. Through centers, teachers are being offered a chance to take an active role in decisions affecting their professional growth. Teacher education centers offer a promise for professional growth and improvement of teachers, as well as a challenge to those in supervisory positions to provide new kinds of services in different settings.

Teachers Teaching Teachers (TTT) Model

The Teachers Teaching Teachers (TTT) Model has been widely adopted by large school districts in middle school transitions. By training teacher trainers who work at school sites, outside consultant costs and travel time have been eliminated or greatly reduced in districts using the TTT Model.

In 1989–90 the Dade County, Florida School District implemented an additional planning period during each day for inservice training by staff trainers. Staff training time increased thirty full days a year using this model. Training by peers is not only cost effective, but also relevant, since it allows for immediate feedback at the classroom level.

Inservice for Supervisors

The focus of this chapter has been on the leadership roles supervisors assume in developing effective inservice programs. However, supervisors themselves need professional development. Supervisors have assumed responsibility for their own development by attending seminars, conferences, summer programs, and graduate classes. Professional associations, state departments, and school districts have established supervisory development programs to help supervisors improve their own performance.

Oftentimes, without feedback, supervisors may feel they *are* providing the services teachers desire. A survey of teachers in Tennessee indicated that over 50 percent of teachers surveyed responded that the following services were not usually provided when needed:

1. Involving teachers in district-wide instructional programs.
2. Assisting in developing effective disciplinary techniques.
3. Planning inservice activities.
4. Providing teaching demonstrations.
5. Consulting with teachers on instructional problems.
6. Serving as a two-way communications link with the central office.
7. Helping describe and analyze instructional objectives.
8. Helping define instructional objectives.
9. Helping select appropriate instructional activities.
10. Helping choose methods for evaluating student progress.
11. Aiding in development of curricula.
12. Conducting or directing research.
13. Acting as a change agent.
14. Providing psychological support.
15. Suggesting new ideas and approaches for instruction.
16. Assisting in classroom organization and arrangement.[17]

When supervisors were surveyed, 82 percent of those surveyed reported heavy involvement in most teacher support services such as those listed. It is interesting to note that supervisors had little involvement in teaching demonstrations, helping with student evaluation, or helping with discipline. A large majority of supervisors indicated a desire to increase those services where they had so little involvement.

As supervisory roles change, supervisors must be keenly aware of the leadership roles they must play in the professional growth of teachers. To be effective leaders, supervisors must have both the knowledge and skills necessary to change the behavior of others.

NEW DIRECTIONS

Staff development will in large measure fashion the future culture of the school. How good schools will be as educational institutions—for example, how humane they will be for children from environments that are the antithesis of the "Ozzie and Harriet" families of the 1950s—will largely be determined by how much we invest in our personnel.

In the last decade of this century teaching staffs have become older, problems of students have increased, and newer members are entering the profession in lesser numbers. Over one-half of teachers and sixty percent of administrators will retire in the 1990s, leaving the profession short-handed. Some of the growth states, such as Florida and California, have already taken steps to eliminate the barriers of tests and other increased program requirements for entering teachers that were imposed in the 1980s. Those steps, along with greater pay, will encourage new persons to enter teaching. However, even these steps may be obviated by the fact that lesser numbers of young people are available to enter the work force. Given a choice between teaching and jobs demanding less energy, young people may well choose other professions, thus forcing the education profession to take dramatic steps to increase its numbers.

Our staff development efforts must improve. The 1990 Association for Supervision and Curriculum Development yearbook on staff development highlighted Pink's review of twelve barriers to innovation effectiveness that are common to staff development projects. Paraphrased, they are as follows:

1. An inadequate theory of implementation, including too little time for teachers to plan for and learn new skills and practices
2. District tendencies toward faddism and quick-fix solutions
3. Lack of sustained central office support and follow-through
4. Underfunding the project, or trying to do too much with too little support
5. Attempting to manage the projects from the central office instead of developing school leadership and capacity
6. Lack of technical assistance and other forms of intensive staff development
7. Lack of awareness of the limitations of teacher and school administrator knowledge about how to implement the project
8. The turnover of teachers in each school
9. Too many competing demands or overload
10. Failure to address the incompatibility between project requirements and existing organizational policies and structures
11. Failure to understand and take into account site-specific differences among schools.
12. Failure to clarify and negotiate the role relationships and partnerships involving the district and the local university — who in each case had a role, albeit unclarified in the project.[18]

Staff development, implementation of innovations, and student outcomes are closely interrelated. Because they are interrelated and involve such persistent effort to coordinate, chances of their success are small unless projects are sustained beyond an initial year of operation.[19]

SUMMARY

A primary role of the supervisor is to provide the leadership necessary to promote a continuing climate of improvement. To carry out this role, supervisors must be able to plan and deliver effective staff development programs.

A study of the history of staff development has shown that improving the performance of teachers has moved from merely meeting certification standards to continuous education. Local districts, rather than colleges of education, have become the focal point for staff development. Local staff development programs should be supported by financial resources, have adequate time set aside to plan and implement programs, and include verbal and physical support from supervisory leaders.

A philosophical base for staff development programs should be based on the belief that all teachers and administrators desire to be successful and respected professional educators.

Since the quality of student learning is directly related to the quality of instruction, a major role of supervisors is to help teachers develop the competence to provide improved instruction. Since we have experienced a growing interest in improving student performance in the 1980s, we have emphasized testing of students and, indeed, testing of teachers.

Supervisors can improve teachers' competencies in a number of ways, but they must first be perceived by teachers as a valued resource. Supervisors must be willing to get in the trenches to demonstrate new techniques. They must also involve teachers in the planning and delivery of staff development activities. Collaboration of teachers and supervisors will result in improved staff development programs and lead to improvement of student learning.

NOTES

1. See Hilda Taba, *Curriculum Development: Theory and Practice*, (New York: Harcourt, Brace & World), 1962.

2. Robert Alfonso, Gerald Firth, and Richard Neville, *Instructional Supervision: A Behavior System* (Boston: Allyn and Bacon, Inc., 1983), p. 395.

3. Tom Sergiovanni and Robert Starratt, *Supervision: Human Perspectives*, 2nd ed. (New York: McGraw-Hill Book Company, 1979), pp. 290–91.

4. Arthur Blumberg, *Supervisors and Teachers: A Private Cold War*, 2nd ed. (Berkeley, CA: McCutchan Publishing Co., 1980).

5. American Association of School Administrators, *Teacher Competency: Problems and Solutions* (Reston, VA: The Association, 1980).

6. Bruce Joyce and Beverly Showers, *Power in Staff Development Through Research in Training* (Alexandria, VA: Association for Supervision and Curriculum Development, 1983), p. 1.

7. Gary Clabaugh, Preston Feden, and Robert Vogel, "*Revolutionizing Teacher Education: Training Developmentally Oriented Teachers*," Phi Delta Kappan, Vol. 65, No. 9 (May, 1984) pp. 615–16.

8. Alan H. Jones, "*Teacher Education and the 1980s*," Teacher Education Quarterly, I (Spring, 1983), pp. 1–16.

9. Susan Masland and Robert Williams, "*Teacher Surplus and Shortage: Accepting Responsibilities*," Journal of Teacher Education, 34 (July–August, 1983), pp. 6–9.

10. John Lovell and Kimball Wiles, *Supervision for Better Schools*, 5th ed. (Englewood Cliffs, NJ: Prentice-Hall, 1983), p. 191.

11. Carl Glickman, "*The Supervisor's Challenge: Changing the Teacher's Work Environment*," Educational Leadership, Vol. 42, No. 4 (December 1984–January 1985), pp. 38–40.

12. Morris Cogan, *Clinical Supervision* (Boston: Houghton-Mifflin, 1972).

13. See Charles A. Reavis, *Teacher Improvement Through Clinical Supervision*, Phi Delta Kappa Fastback Series no. 3 (Bloomington, IN: Phi Delta Kappa, 1978) for a thorough discussion of the clinical supervision process.

14. Ben Harris, *Supervisory Behavior in Education*, 2nd ed. (Englewood Cliffs, NJ: Prentice-Hall, 1975), p. 99.

15. Phyllis D. Hamilton, *Competency-Based Teacher Education* (Menlo Park, CA: Pacific Coast Publishers, 1973), p. 4.

16. Gordon Lawrence, "*Patterns of Effective Inservice Education*," monograph (Tallahassee: Florida State Department of Education, 1974).

17. John Lovell and Margaret Phelps, *Supervision in Tennessee* (Knoxville: Tennessee Association for Supervision and Curriculum Development, July 1976), p. 9.

18. W. Pink, "*Effective Development for Urban School Improvement*." Paper presented at the annual meeting of the American Educational Research Association, San Francisco, 1989.

19. Bruce Joyce (Ed.), *Changing School Culture Through Staff Development*, 1990 yearbook of the Association For Supervision and Curriculum Development (Alexandria, VA, 1990).

SUGGESTED LEARNING ACTIVITIES

1. The superintendent has asked you to begin an extensive staff development plan to "improve teaching skills." Many teachers resent the implication that their teaching skills need improvement. You as a supervisor have the task of carrying out the superintendent's order in the face of open teacher dissatisfaction. What steps would you take to overcome hostile teacher feelings?

2. Develop an assessment of needs for a staff development program at your school.

3. Work with a colleague in a clinical supervision setting going through the five steps outlined in the chapter.

4. Develop an action plan to reduce absenteeism and burnout of teachers in your school district.
5. You have been elected to the advisory board of a teacher education center in your state. List the goals you would set for that center and the role you would play to help achieve those goals.

BOOKS TO REVIEW

Borich, Gary. *Observational Skills for Effective Teaching.* Columbus, OH: Merrill, 1990.

Harris, Ben and Hill, Jane. *Inservice Education For Staff Development.* Needham Hts., MA: Allyn and Bacon, 1989.

Jacobsen, David, Eggen, Paul and Kauchak, Donald. *Methods For Teaching: A Skills Approach*, 3rd ed. Columbus, OH: Merrill, 1990.

Joyce, Bruce (Ed.). *Changing School Culture Through Staff Development.* Alexandria, VA: Association for Supervision and Curriculum Development, 1990.

Reynolds, Maynard. *Knowledge Base For the Beginning Teacher.* Elmsford, NY: Pergamon, 1989.

Smith, Wilma and Andrews, Richard. *Instructional Leadership: How Principals Make a Difference.* Alexandria, VA: Association For Supervision and Curriculum Development, 1989.

Stanley, Sarah and Popham, James. *Teacher Evaluation: Six Prescriptions for Success.* Alexandria, VA: Association for Supervision and Curriculum Development, 1990.

CHAPTER 9

Fulfilling Administrative Functions

INTRODUCTION

Modern supervisors help fulfill a number of administrative tasks including setting and prioritizing goals, establishing standards and policies, and providing long-range planning. They should be aware of the functions of each organizational level of the school system (see Figure 9.1). Because of the conditions outlined in previous sections, supervisors today are facing new tasks that may seem peripheral to their assigned roles. Those tasks include helping to negotiate employee contracts, closing schools, and reducing the size of the instructional staff. While most supervisors would choose to avoid some of those administrative tasks, the decision to participate or not is often not theirs.

A school system is made up of many subsystems. Thus, the supervisor must know something of systems theory. Systems theory applied to a school or district setting usually centers on the school or district as a social system in which people interact. A system, then, is a set of interacting parts forming a unified whole. If one part of the system changes, another part of the system will change, or force the deviant element to conform to the existing system. Because it stresses the interrelationships among the behaviors of individuals, systems theory helps us understand how schools operate.

Systems theory suggests that the supervisor has a prime role, along with administrators, in providing leadership in the integration of the system. A structure of positive interrelationships among individuals and groups fosters change and harnesses human resources in carrying out the educational mission of schools.

COMPREHENSIVE EDUCATIONAL PLANNING

Comprehensive school planning ties together all aspects of a school or district into a unified plan for improvement. Those aspects include

255

Figure 9.1
Organization and Function of District Programs

ELEMENTARY SCHOOL	PROGRAM MIDDLE SCHOOL	HIGH SCHOOL
Introduction to School Socialization Beginning Skills Beginning Learnings Introduction to Disciplines Social Studies Science etc.	Personal Development Refinement of Skills Continued Learnings Education for Social Competence	Comprehensive Vocational Training College Pre- paratory In-depth Learn- ings Chemistry Algebra World History American Liter- ature
	Interdisciplinary Learn- ings	Career Planning
	Organization Developmental Skills	
Elementary K-5	Middle 6, 7-8	High School 9-12
K-3 4-5	6-8	
Early Late Childhood Childhood	Transescence	Adolescence

program revision, staff development, evaluation, building needs, and budget. Comprehensive plans include tasks, timelines, and persons responsible for carrying out tasks.

Comprehensive plans incorporate all of the following:

Long-range — three to five years

Based upon in-depth needs assessment

Includes clear set of goals

Provides for program revision, development, management

Ties building needs to program needs

Includes systematic plan for staff development that will reach all teachers, administrators, district personnel, and board members

Has evaluation design that includes both process and product measures

Involves board members, administrators, teachers, students, and parents in development of plan

Is fully interpreted and reported to the general public

Lack of comprehensive planning results in:

Wasted tax dollars

Wrong organizational patterns for schools

Misuse of buildings

Gaps and overlaps in the curriculum

Decline in student achievement

Bored, disinterested, disruptive students

Unproductive staff development

High rate of turnover in board, superintendent, and district and school level administrators

Low morale on teaching staffs

Increased militancy on the part of teachers

Decline in public support for schools

Tools for Planning

A number of planning techniques and management tools are available to supervisors. Supervisors do not have to be experts in each technique, but should have a general understanding of each to use in planning. Effective planning tools for the school supervisor include the following:

Management by Objectives (MBO). In the MBO approach, supervisors and staff set objectives, define individual responsibility in terms of desired results, and use the results to evaluate staff performance. After the supervisor develops objectives, he or she can choose how they will be carried out. MBO relies on individual strengths and intents to carry out objectives vital to the organization.

Planning-Programming-Budgeting-System (PPBS). PPBS is much like management by objectives since both approaches utilize personnel and resources according to agreed-upon priorities. PPBS draws its methods from the systems planning and analysis found in business and economics. Basically, PPBS provides a system for planning and stating objectives prior to developing a review of costs and setting a budget. As a tool in educational planning, PPBS can be useful to the supervisor in developing comprehensive educational plans.

Needs Assessment. Needs assessment is a technique for matching current status with desired goals. Discrepancies between stated goals and present conditions are then identified as needs. The supervisor must choose the right sources for input data. Students, parents, teachers, administrators, and members of the community may all be sources of data. Effective needs assessment requires asking the right kinds of questions and developing suitable questionnaires and surveys. All curricular and instructional planning should be preceded by a needs assessment. The professional supervisor's opinion must not be ignored in carrying out a needs assessment. Needs assessment data are not always value-free and cannot automatically replace a competent supervisor's judgment. Examples of needs assessment instruments and data sources are found in other sections of this text.

Planning, Evaluation, and Review Technique (PERT). PERT is a technique that matches tasks with the exact amount of time necessary to complete tasks. After determining tasks, the supervisor can coordinate events and time schedules with flow charts. This technique facilitates planning by making participants aware of activities and their time requirements.

Checklists. Checklists are practical tools for carrying out basic procedures such as fire drills, bomb-scare evacuations, and other emergencies that allow little time for deliberation.

Zero-Based Budgeting. With this technique, budget planning begins from scratch rather than adding to or subtracting from a previous budget. As with PPBS, this approach bases budgeting on program needs, objectives, and priorities.

The Delphi Technique. This method is used to help groups deal with complex problems. By facilitating communication so that individual and group opinions can be gathered (usually by questionnaire) and analyzed by the group, group consensus can be reached on how to deal with a particular problem. A monitor group is used to analyze individual and group responses. One weakness in this method is that participants in the process often feel manipulated by the monitor group. Individual disagreements sometimes get swept aside by the process.

THE CURRICULUM MANAGEMENT PLAN (CMP)

A plan that utilizes all of the foregoing techniques in an easy-to-follow plan is the Wiles-Bondi Curriculum Management Plan (CMP). This plan has been used successfully with a number of school districts as a tool to implement new organizational patterns, deal with declining enrollment, or to develop a better structure for decision making. The CMP Model is outlined in Figure 9.2.

Figure 9.2
Curriculum Management Plan (CMP)

Components of the Curriculum Management Plan

School and Community. All planning is based on good data. Examples of needs assessment instruments and other means of gathering data have already been presented in previous chapters. The supervisor may often be the key person in conducting a needs assessment of school and community needs. That role involves not only expertise in selecting instruments, but in communicating with students, parents, and other community persons.

With increasing mobility of population, neighborhoods and even total communities often change in student and adult numbers. A plant closing, new residential development, or influx of immigrants can sometimes change the needs of a school or school district overnight. An example is a ring district outside a large city school district that enjoys a generation of college-bound students but fails to cope with the next generation composed of new residents who are not college-bound. Often teachers continue with a strict college-bound curriculum even though it does not meet the needs of the new students or of the changing community.

Philosophy and Goals. Philosophy and goals should be broadly deter-mined by students, teachers, administrators, parents, board members, and community persons. Goals and objectives for schools should be based on identified needs of students and community.

Curriculum. The curriculum of schools is based on needs assessment information and on the philosophy and goals of the district. The cur-riculum should include a defined sequence of content, concepts, and skills to be taught and provide for all levels of learners. There should also exist a balance in the curriculum in personal development, basic skills, and content. District and school leaders should strive for a uni-form, articulated curriculum in grades K–12.

Instructional Program. The instructional program is the process of carrying out the curriculum. It includes a management system to en-sure that skills are taught and the curriculum followed. It also includes materials that are up-to-date and appropriate for all levels of learners – an articulated guidance program to facilitate a smooth transition of students from one school level to the next, and a grading and reporting system that follows the sequenced curriculum.

Organization. Schools may be organized into self-contained classes, teams, or departmentalization when appropriate. Flexible rather than static groupings of students should be employed, and the instructional program organized to ensure a maximum amount of time spent on learning and instruction for both students and teachers. Organization is a means rather than an end of schools. Too often, however, schools use organizational means as ends by nongrading students or team teachers and by failing to train teachers or plan the new curriculum to be implemented.

Staff. Only qualified teachers, support personnel, and administrators should be employed. Job descriptions and responsibilities, clearly spelled out, are essential. Inservice should be based on a needs assess-ment conducted among teachers and administrators with a systematic inservice plan developed, implemented, and sustained for all person-nel. Evaluation of teachers and administrators should then be tied to the improvement of learning opportunities for students.

Facilities. Flexible space must be provided to meet a variety of instruc-tional programs and organizational structures. Facilities, like organi-zation, often are seen as ends rather than means of carrying out pro-

Figure 9.3
Curriculum Management Plan (CMP) Criteria for Inclusion of Programs
in Budget

---

1. Does the program meet an identified need?
2. Does the program support the goals and objectives of the district?
3. Does the program fit within the established curriculum?
4. Can the program be carried out within the existing instructional program or will it require that the existing instructional program be modified?
5. Can the program be carried out with existing staff or will it require new staff or retrained staff?
6. Is the program designed to be carried out within the existing organizational patterns found in the schools?
7. Are facilities adequate to carry out the program or will it require new or modified facilities?
8. Do evaluation and reporting procedures fit district evaluation and reporting procedures?

---

grams. Open space, movable walls, or pods are means of properly using space. Without a definite program to fit the facilities (or teachers trained to use innovative space) little positive change can occur in student learning opportunities.

Evaluation and Reporting. Definite checkpoints should be developed to monitor student progress from grades K–12. Local, state, and national norm-based and criterion-based tests should be used.

A reporting system should also be implemented to give students and parents a clear picture of student progress each grading period. The grading system should match the curriculum and instructional program.

Budget. No program funds should be allocated until each program is filtered through the above screens. A zero-based funding program will force all programs to undergo close scrutiny by district supervisors, administrators, school principals, and board members each year before they are funded in the new budget. Figure 9.3 illustrates the questions faced by a supervisor when introducing a new program.

An instructional improvement plan should be required yearly from all building-level principals and program directors. Development of each plan must include involvement of teachers, students, and parents.

NEW TASKS FOR SUPERVISORS

Some of the new tasks facing supervisors are actually peripheral to their designated role, but are nonetheless central to providing quality education for school children. Four tasks represent the new challenges to supervision: negotiating employee contracts; closing school buildings; maneuvering budgets; and conducting reductions in force of the instructional staff.

Negotiating Contracts

Aside from the rise in union membership, the 1980s may well be remembered for increasingly apparent teacher militancy. In seeking to upgrade their profession, teachers have become more vocal and more likely to use traditional labor methods to achieve desired results — strikes, grievances, sanctions, and collective bargaining. These moves have forced supervisors to assume a more traditional management posture, and many supervisors have been uncomfortable with that role. In a human organization such as a school, with so intangible a product as the education and nurturing of children, adopting traditional labor perspectives has not come easily.

While strikes and grievances have grabbed the attention of the press and public, professional negotiation has been far more important in determining the leadership role of both administrators and supervisors. It will be through professional negotiation that those leaders will communicate with teachers and address the important issues of education. Those in supervisory positions are finding themselves increasingly assigned to management roles such as being a part of the district negotiating team. Regardless of whether they want that role, it is often theirs and they need to know the rules of the game.

We can define professional negotiation as a set of written procedures officially endorsed by both the local school board and the teachers' association for the purpose of establishing a process of communication for matters of mutual interest. These procedures also establish a method of settling an impasse through mediation, if necessary. According to the National Education Association, five basic elements make up professional negotiation procedures:

1. Recognition of the local teachers' association as the representative of the local teaching staff.
2. Specified communication channels to be used by the local teacher association in negotiation.
3. Agreement of both the local teachers' association and the school board to negotiate in "good faith."
4. Establishment of channels for use in settling differences in the event of an impasse.

The question of what is negotiated is a local issue, but the scope of issues has grown during the last decade. A sample list of negotiable issues might include:

1. Teacher salaries
2. Teacher assignments
3. Transfers and promotions
4. Recruitment of teachers
5. Grievance procedures
6. Sabbatical and leave policies
7. Curriculum
8. Class-load formulas
9. Inservice education
10. Personnel policy
11. Nonsalary benefits
12. Collateral duties

The list might go indefinitely; for example, it is not uncommon for a large-city teacher union to negotiate thirty-five to forty-five items in a given session. Figure 9.4 illustrates the issues of negotiation in one school district with about 5,000 students.

When there is a disagreement or impasse in negotiations, there are three acceptable courses of action:

1. *Mediation* – A third party is called in to help both sides settle differences.
2. *Fact finding* – A formal procedure wherein hearings are conducted before a fact-finding panel. While not binding, these hearings result in recommendations that generally carry the weight of public opinion and pressure.
3. *Binding arbitration* – An arbitration committee formed by agreement between the teachers' association and the board, or, as in some states, is compulsory under state law. This committee than makes recommendations to end the impasse.

The kinds of activity involving supervisors in negotiation are too varied to generalize. Depending on the site of the district and other variables, a superintendent may be a chief negotiator, a member of the administrative negotiating team, a consultant to the school board, or a consultant to an outside consultant/negotiator hired by the board. The supervisor may be called upon to be a team member, to advise the superintendent or board, or to act as part of a backup group that analyzes issues and items.

Since most states now have collective bargaining legislation, the administrative role now involves a legal dimension. Coverage of this complex topic is beyond the scope of this book, but supervisors will generally find that most state laws guarantee the right to negotiate, prohibit administrative coercion of teachers, prohibit paternalistic labor practices, and direct resolution of an impasse. One must, of course, understand the restrictions on administrative behavior in one's home state.

Supervisors have important professional interests in the outcome of negotiations. As a leader, the supervisor is responsible for providing the best possible program to educate the district's children. This may mean making tough value-laden decisions about curriculum, instruction, and school management. An overriding concern is to support the

Figure 9.4
Negotiation Issues in a Medium-Sized District

DISTRICT RIGHTS

1. It is understood and agreed that the District retains all its powers and authority to assign, direct, organize and manage to the full extent of the law. This includes but is not limited to the following District Rights:
   a. determine its organization;
   b. determine the kinds and levels of services to be provided and the methods and means of providing them;
   c. establish its educational policies, goals and objectives;
   d. ensure the rights and educational opportunities of students;
   e. maintain the efficiency of district operations;
   f. establish budget procedures and determine the method of raising revenue;
   g. to take any action on matters in the event of an emergency.

ASSOCIATION RIGHTS

1. The Association and its designated representatives shall have the right to make use of school facilities at reasonable hours for Association business when it does not interfere with the educational process. Use of Facilities Request Form must be on file as required.

2. The Association shall have the right to post notices of activities and matters of Association concern on designated bulletin boards, at least one of which shall be provided in each school building in areas frequented by teachers. The Association may use the District mail service and teacher mailboxes for communications to teachers. At the time of distribution, the Association shall furnish the Superintendent or his designee a copy.

3. The Association will exclusively receive time-off from duties for the processing of grievances past Level I of the grievance procedure, Article X herein, for unit members who are designated as association representatives, subject to the following conditions: (a) by no later than 10 days following the signing of this agreement the Association will designate in writing, to the Superintendent, employees who are to receive the time-off; (b) twenty-four hours prior to release from duties for grievance processing, the designated representative informs his immediate supervisor in order that an adequate substitute may be obtained, if such is necessary.

PERSONAL AND ACADEMIC FREEDOM

1. Teachers shall be guaranteed full academic freedom as required by Title V: 80130.

MAINTENANCE OF STANDARDS

1. The District agrees not to reduce or eliminate any specific teacher benefit under this agreement without first affording the Association an opportunity to meet and negotiate with respect to such reduction or elimination.

GRIEVANCE PROCEDURE

1. DEFINITIONS:
   1. A "grievance" is a formal written allegation by a unit member, and/or the Association, who has been adversely affected by a violation of the specific provisions of this Agreement. Actions to challenge or change the policies of the District as set forth in the rules and regulations or administrative regulations and procedures must be undertaken under separate legal processes.

PUBLIC CHARGES

1. Board members receiving complaints about teachers shall notify the site administrator. Citizen or parent complaints about a teacher shall be reported immediately to the teacher by the site administrator.
2. At the discretion of the teacher and/or the site administrator, a conference with the complainant and teacher and/or site administrator, or his designee, may be scheduled
3. If the matter is not resolved at the meeting to the satisfaction of the complainant, he shall put his complaint into writing and submit the original to the teacher, with the copy of the teacher's written response to the immediate supervisor.
4. The teacher, site administrator, or parent may request a conference with the superintendent or his designee, after receiving the written complaint.

STAFF WORKING HOURS

1. Teachers—the length of the teacher work day, excluding a thirty (30) minute duty free lunch, shall be 6½ hours. After consultation between the site administrator and teaching staff, the beginning and ending time of the work day will be determined by the administration. This time frame will conform to the student day as determined by Board policy. The District shall require teachers to attend a maximum of two (2) general staff meetings per month. Nothing shall prevent the administration from scheduling the necessary conferences, departmental, grade level and other small groups meetings within the work day. Effective the 1984-85 school year there shall be 183 teaching days of which at least 180 shall be instructional days. The additional days will be non-teaching days.
2. A teacher shall be entitled to at least one (1) thirty (30) minute duty free lunch period daily, except in case of emergency which affects the health and safety of a student.

Figure 9.4
(Continued)

STAFF WORKING HOURS *(Continued)*

3. Teachers shall be responsible for supervising a maximum of three (3) assigned non-teaching activities per semester outside of the regular work day.

4. Any unit member employed in the Junior High or Senior High and who is assigned to substitute shall receive the hourly rate of substitute pay. Prior to assignment, the administration will make every effort to obtain an outside substitute or volunteer teacher. Failing this, unit members will be assigned by roster on a rotating basis taking into account extenuating circumstances. Last to be used will be service personnel.

LEAVES

1. a. Definition: "Immediate Family" means the father, mother, brother, sister, spouse, father-in-law, mother-in-law, son or daughter, son-in-law, daughter-in-law, grandson, granddaughter, grandmother or grandfather of the employee, the grandmother or grandfather of the spouse, or any relative or person living in the immediate household of the employee.

2. Personal Illness and Injury Leave:

   a. Full-time unit members shall be entitled to ten (10) days leave with full pay for each school year for purposes of personal illness or injury. Unit members who work less than full-time shall be entitled to that portion of the ten (10) days leave as the number of hours per week of scheduled duty relates to the number of hours for a full-time unit member in a comparable position.

CLASS SIZE

1. The following average district-wide class sizes shall be maintained:

Kindergarten	33
Grades 1–3	30
Grades 4–12	33

2. In addition, the above listed class size averages are subject to modification for purposes such as, but not limited to, avoidance of split-grade classes or low enrollment classes, large group or experimental instruction, team teaching limitation because of distribution of pupils by attendance areas or changes in enrollment.

TRANSFERS

1. Definitions
   a. *Transfer:* An administrative change in the movement of a teacher from one job classification, school, or work location to another.
   b. *Voluntary Transfer:* A transfer initiated at the request of a teacher on a voluntary basis.
   c. *Involuntary Transfer:* A transfer initiated by the District.
   d. *Vacancy:* Any teaching position which is unfilled due to the establishment of new teaching positions or by a teacher who leaves the position by promotion, retirement or termination and is to be filled by the District.
2. *Vacancies:* Shall be posted by the District at all work locations for not less than five (5) working days prior to being filled by the District.

CURRICULUM AND INSTRUCTION

1. The District recognizes the right for the Association to consult with the Board's designee in regard to matters relating to educational objectives, context of courses and curriculum and selection of textbooks.

CERTIFICATED EMPLOYEE EVALUATIONS

1. The District management shall evaluate all permanent bargaining unit members at least once every two (2) years and all probationary bargaining unit members at least annually.

IN-SERVICE EDUCATION

1. The District reserves the right to administer all in-service education programs of the District.

TEACHING CONDITIONS

1. The District agrees to provide teachers with typing and duplicating equipment to prepare instructional materials. The District shall provide suitable workrooms for teacher utilization when possible.

Source: Barstow Unified School District, Barstow, California. Used by permission.

267

various educational components equally. Supervisors are also responsible for seeing that an orderly process of education, free from disruption or interruption, is ongoing.

While boards of education must ultimately represent the school system, most boards delegate the responsibility of negotiation to the superintendent, so that the board can maintain a posture as that of a ratifying body. Various estimates suggest that the complete negotiation process, without unusual circumstance, may consume 300 to 400 hours. The superintendent and his/her designates thus need to develop techniques for effective negotiating. Here are some suggestions compiled by the Ohio State Boards Association:

1. *Keep calm—don't lose control of yourself.* Negotiation sessions can be exasperating. The temptation may come to get angry and fight back when intemperate accusations are made or when "the straw that broke the camel's back" is hurled on the table.
2. *Avoid "off the record" comments.* Actually nothing is "off the record." Innocently made remarks have a way of coming back to haunt their author. Be careful to say only what you are willing to have quoted.
3. *Don't be overcandid.* Inexperienced negotiators may, with the best of intentions, desire to "lay the cards on the table face up." This may be done in the mistaken notion that everybody fully understands the other and utter frankness is desired. Complete candor doesn't always serve the best interests of productive negotiation. This is not a plea for duplicity; rather, it is a recommendation for prudent and discriminating utterances.
4. *Be long on listening.* Usually a good listener makes a good negotiator. It is wise to let your "adversaries" do the talking—at least in the beginning.
5. *Don't be afraid of a little "heat."* Discussions sometimes generate quite a bit of "heat." Don't be afraid of it. It never hurts to let the "opposition" sound off even when you may be tempted to hit back.
6. *Watch the voice level.* A wise practice is to keep the pitch of the voice down even though the temptation may be strong to let it rise under the excitement of emotional stress.
7. *Keep flexible.* One of the skills of good negotiators is the ability to shift position a bit if a positive gain can thus be accomplished. An obstinate adherence to one position or point of view, regardless of the ultimate consequences of that rigidity, may be more of a deterrent than an advantage.
8. *Refrain from a flat "no."* Especially in the earlier stages of negotiation it is best to avoid giving a flat "no" answer to a proposition. It doesn't help to work yourself into a box by being totally negative "too early in the game."
9. *Give to get.* Negotiation is the art of giving and getting. Concede a point to gain a concession. This is the name of the game.
10. *Work on the easier items first.* Settle those things first about which

there is the least controversy. Leave the tougher items until later in order to avoid an early deadlock.

11. *Respect your adversary.* Respect those who are seated on the opposite side of the table. Assume that their motivies are as sincere as your own, at least until proven otherwise.
12. *Be patient.* If necessary, be willing to sit out tiresome tirades. Time has a way of being on the side of the patient negotiator.
13. *Avoid waving "red flags."* There are some statements that irritate teachers and merely heighten their antipathies. Find out what these are and avoid their use. Needless waving of "red flags" only infuriates.
14. *Let the other side "win some victories."* Each team has to win some victories. A "shut out" may be a hollow gain in negotiation.
15. *Negotiation is a "way of life."* Obvious resentment of the fact that negotiation is here to stay weakens the effectiveness of the negotiator. The better part of wisdom is to adjust to it and to become better prepared to use it as a tool of interstaff relations.[1]

Finally, the beginning administrator must master the new language of negotiation. Some of the more common terms of negotiation include the following:

Agenda—the agreed-upon list of requests or demands that become items for negotiation.

Agreement—the contract that binds the parties to certain actions for specified periods of time.

Conciliation—use of a third party to help reach an agreement without coercion.

Grievance—an intensified complaint that cannot be settled at an operational level and is referred to a specific grievance process.

Negotiation—a simplified form of collective bargaining where teachers and the school board settle common matters.

Sanctions—severance of a relationship with an agency or withholding services as one step toward applying pressure.

Union affiliation—identification with an organized labor organization for the purpose of entering into negotiations.

Fulfilling Management Roles

Supervisors may find themselves in district management roles and be held responsible for the actions of employees under them. This means the supervisor must know the rules of management and labor. The following are examples of what management personnel can and cannot do:[2]

Some Things Management Personnel Can Do

1. You can remind employees that they are free to join *or refrain from joining* a union without it affecting their work status.
2. You can tell employees that it is unlawful for a union to interfere with their right to refrain from joining a union.
3. You can remind employees that signing an authorization card does *not* require them to vote for that union if an election is held.
4. You can enforce consistently the prohibition against solicitation, including distribution of literature, during the working hours of any employee involved in the solicitation. This includes the employee conducting the solicitation *and* the employee(s) being solicited.
5. You can enforce all rules and regulations impartially, irrespective of union membership or activity.
6. You can discipline and discharge employees for cause, provided you follow existing work rules, contractual provisions and statutory requirements, and take action without regard for union membership.
7. You can assign overtime, as long as it is done without regard for union membership.
8. You can provide employees with facts about the union(s) seeking their support. These facts might include such things as the union's national affiliations, salaries of its officials, or strike statistics.
9. You can explain the dues and fees of union membership (provided that the figures are accurate).
10. You can rebut inaccurate and misleading union communications with the facts.
11. You can tell employees that promised union benefits must be negotiated and that management is not required to accept a union proposal. (You cannot imply that management will refuse to bargain in good faith.)
12. You can express your *personal opinion* as to the reasons for selecting "No Union" in an election.
13. You can post or circulate *unsolicited* statements from employees expressing views on unionization, provided you do not solicit such statements.
14. You can discuss the campaign and related matters privately with other management personnel.

Some Things Management Personnel Cannot Do

1. You cannot promise or grant employees a pay increase, promotion, or other benefit, on the provision that they do not

    join a union or that they vote against representation by a union in an election.

2. You cannot threaten loss of job, reduction of income, or discontinuance of privileges or benefits presently enjoyed, for employees who exercise their right to belong, or refrain from belonging to a union.

3. You cannot actually discharge an employee solely because of his activities on behalf of a union.

4. You cannot discriminate against employees who support a union by intentionally assigning undesirable work or prejudicially transferring them.

5. You cannot intentionally assign work so that those active in a union are separated from those you believe are not interested in supporting a union.

6. You cannot discipline or penalize employees who actively support a union for an infraction that nonunion employees are permitted to commit without being disciplined.

7. You cannot prevent employees from soliciting union membership during their free time as long as such does not interfere with work being performed by others; or prevent employees, off-duty, from distributing union literature in nonwork areas.

8. You cannot ask employees for an expression of their thoughts about a union or its officers.

9. You cannot ask employees about the identity of employee leaders who favor a union.

10. You cannot ask employees about the internal affairs of unions such as meetings, etc. (Some employees may, of their own accord, tell you about such matters. It is okay to listen, but you must not ask questions to obtain additional information.)

11. You cannot ask employees how they intend to vote in a union election.

12. You cannot ask employees at the time of hiring, or thereafter, whether they belong to a union or have signed a union authorization card.

13. You cannot spy on union meetings. For example, parking across the street from a union hall to watch employees entering the hall would be illegal.

14. You cannot conduct yourself in a way that indicates to your employees that you are watching them to determine whether or not they are participating in union activities.

15. You cannot offer to help employees withdraw their union membership.

16. You cannot express or state a preference for one union over another union.

Closing School Buildings

A second major task ahead for school leaders is the selective reduction of physical facilities. The major impact is at the secondary level, when many school districts, particularly those in older and more established suburban areas, will experience declines in junior and senior high school populations. A natural response to this condition will be to consolidate programs by creating middle schools and to close unnecessary buildings.

School budgets are dominated by fixed costs that allow flexibility for cost reduction in only three areas – educational programming, personnel, and facilities. When forced to reduce spending, most administrators select facilities as the area least sensitive to change. Although facility closings may seem a likely way to reduce costs, the experiences of school districts in the 1970s and 1980s suggest a need for caution in proposing and administering these reductions. For one thing, closing a school can be rationalized only when there has been a significant enrollment decline over a relatively long period. Second, savings are not likely to show up immediately on the ledger sheets. Finally, except for certain school activities such as sports, school buildings are a community's most visible symbol of public education. Community identity is often closely tied to a neighborhood structure.

Oddly, real savings from closing a school building are often minuscule. Some costs, such as insurance, continue even after the building is closed; abandoned buildings are more susceptible to physical deterioration; and security measures against fire and vandalism are expensive. There are usually no personnel savings, since teachers and staff are transferred to other sites. The money saved in janitorial services and consumables is simply not impressive on a year-to-year basis.

Closing school sites also involves a political dimension that often surprises school leaders. School buildings represent stability to local neighborhoods, particularly in terms of real estate values. When a proposal to close a local school surfaces, the neighborhood around the school goes through a series of reactions ranging from denial of need to irrational self-serving arguments. It behooves a school leader, therefore, to consider closing a school building only after considerable research into the school's efficiency, performance capability, and alternative uses.

Considering Operational Efficiency. In determining which buildings in the district are most efficient to operate, administrators and supervisors should consider needed capital outlays (such as whether a building needs a new roof or heating system), annual cost of heating/cooling, and the general condition of the facility. A related variable that will prove important in deciding to close a building would be its overall structural safety.

Considering Performance Capability. Among the variables to consider in this category are the previous achievement record of the school (is it known for academic excellence?) and the general cohesiveness of the school's parent group. In cases where a school has a reputation as one of the "better" schools in the district or where parents form an active political coalition, it will be difficult (and perhaps not cost-effective) to close the building. Influential parents will resist such a move and may spur antagonism toward support of public schools in the community.

Considering Alternatives. The third and probably most important category to consider is other uses for the targeted structures. It has been found that the real amount to be saved by closing a school building is determined by its alternative use. The possibilities depend on the geography of the school site and the facility's construction.

Geographical considerations are the location of the site in relation to environmental growth patterns, zoning of the site (it is easier to reuse a building near a commercial area), available public transportation, building costs in the area, and relationships to railways, freeways, or airports that could be considered disadvantages for schools but advantages for businesses.

Factors related to the facility itself are age, structural soundness, special on-site facilities, loading and unloading access points, and possibilities for conversion. When school leaders study possible school closings, they must look at them as structures other than schools. Does the location make the school desirable for outright sale? Can it be converted to office or storage space? Can the building be leased? Could part of the building be rented to other agencies? Experience shows that seeking professional advice from architects and city planners is worthwhile to educators who must project and implement building closings.

Maneuvering School Budgets

A third important task for supervisors in an area of decline is to maneuver school budgets in such a way that the real objectives of education are accomplished. Many new supervisors feel uncomfortable with budgets, believing them to be the responsibility of some business officer at the central office. Nothing could be further from the truth, for in the struggle over preferences, the budget records the outcome of the struggle.

Budgets are governed by either choice or conflict resolution. In other words, budgets reflect values about the priorities of education.

Although words are plentiful, the allocation of scarce resources will reflect the true priorities of school districts.

A beginning point for developing any budget comes from assessing the district's needs and determining a consensus on the mission of the organization. A needs assessment for determining what the district is accomplishing through its programming should be comprehensive (see chapter five for a needs assessment framework). Such a general overview increases the odds of creating an integrated plan for education. The value of a needs assessment to budgeting is that it moves the level of communication about budget items from philosophy to data.

The critical job for the school supervisor is to translate abstract budget concepts such as allocations for facilities maintenance into practical realities *before* budget issues are decided. School boards are presently becoming more influential and claiming legal powers, but are often grossly unprepared to make key decisions. Supervisors must help with such decision making by projecting educational implications of the budget in terms of day-by-day operations and quality control.

It follows that a rational budget plan simply may not reflect political realities. As the professional educator involved in budget projection and preparation, the supervisor might find it necessary to maneuver budget items to best serve school children. The supervisor's role is to defend worthy programs by stressing the negative consequences of eliminating them. In particular, when addressing the board the supervisor should

1. Have a rehearsal (guess the tough questions)
2. Avoid surprises (gain inside information if possible)
3. Have a "plant" (someone sympathetic to frame the correct question at the right time)
4. Paint a portrait (set requests in general frameworks)
5. Know the budget (the bottom line will always be a question of cost and trade-offs)
6. Play the game (sometimes only defeat is possible)

In lobbying for a budget and advocating priorities, certain strategies will work better than others. Effective strategies in an era of decline are to tie requests to long-range planning, present arguments in terms of ratios or percentages to mask the value of requests, tie requests to crisis resolution, and couch requests in cost-benefit language.

As resources decline, pressures on the budget will increase, and the decision making arena will become more hectic. The school supervisor is only one of many trying to influence the outcome of the process.

NEW DIRECTIONS

We had a decade of school reform in the 1980s that included the following:

- ☐ More difficult curricula.
- ☐ "Threshold examinations" for students and teachers that resulted in the child being held back or the teacher not being hired.
- ☐ Choice plans that assumed parents would choose the right schools for their children and shut down bad schools.
- ☐ Restructured schools that give individual schools more control over their destiny.

How well did reform do in the decade of the 1980s?

- ☐ There has been no increase in high school or college graduation rates. In fact, states such as Florida with the highest graduation requirements have the highest dropout rates.
- ☐ There has been no gain in scores for the "lowest third."
- ☐ There has been an increase rather than reduction in youth poverty.
- ☐ Urban school districts have become more segregated with city schools more segregated for Hispanic students than they were for Afro-American students.
- ☐ There has been no increase in equity funding to help students attain higher standards in the forty states that have adopted higher standards.[3]

With decreasing numbers of youth, schools and society as a whole can no longer "write off" young people. The evidence suggests that the educational needs of the United States might be better met by:

- ☐ Focusing attention on the improvement of our bottom third of students.
- ☐ Eliminating retention as a means of quality control.
- ☐ Taking steps to reduce youth poverty estimated at 40 percent in 1990.
- ☐ Providing alternative programs to motivate more youth to graduate from high school and college.
- ☐ Revamping our career education programs to acknowledge the need for large numbers of new workers in the service areas.
- ☐ Providing preschool programs and day care for all at-risk students.

□ Enlarging the talent pool of high achieving students, particularly minority and poverty children.

□ Developing a national health care program for all children, with such programs housed in school buildings.

□ Developing programs for at-risk youth who are at risk from several causes simultaneously, such as family environment, drugs, pregnancy, arrests, and school failure.

□ Developing programs that recognize the increasing cultural diversity of students in American schools.

SUMMARY

Modern supervisors may fulfill a number of administrative tasks including setting and prioritizing goals, developing budgets, closing buildings, and even participating in negotiations.

A school system is made up of a number of subsystems and the supervisor must know something of system theories. The supervisor has a prime role, along with administrators, in providing leadership in the integration of the system. His or her role is to help structure positive relationships among individuals and groups to foster change and harness human resources in carrying out the educational mission of schools.

Comprehensive planning is one of the most important aspects of a school system. The modern supervisor should know various planning techniques that can be utilized to develop and implement comprehensive plans. He or she must also have the skills for helping district and school level personnel achieve the goals outlined in a comprehensive plan.

NOTES

1. David Wiles, Jon Wiles, and Joseph Bondi, *Practical Politics for School Administrators* (Boston: Allyn and Bacon, 1981), pp. 157–58.

2. Florida Department of Education, 1985.

3. Harold L. Hodgkinson, *The Same Client: The Demographics of Education and Service Delivery Systems.* Washington, DC: Institute for Educational Leadership, Inc./Center for Demographic Policy, 1989.

SUGGESTED LEARNING ACTIVITIES

1. Using the Wiles-Bondi CMP Model, take a program area (e.g., mathematics, reading, physical education) and filter that program through all of the criteria for inclusion in the budget. (See Figure 9.3)

2. Outline the guidelines you would use for closing a school building.
3. Working with several colleagues, develop a long-range plan to deal with declining enrollment in your school district.
4. Develop a job description for the principalship of an elementary, middle, or high school.
5. Prepare a report for the superintendent outlining a school improvement plan for your school.

BOOKS TO REVIEW

Narmon, Frederick. *The Executive Odyssey*. New York: Wiley, 1989.

Mohrman, Allen and Resnick, Susan. *Designing Performance Appraisal Systems*. San Francisco: Jossey-Bass, 1989.

Smith, Wilma and Andrews, Richard. *Instructional Leadership: How Principals Make a Difference*. Alexandria, VA: Association for Supervision and Curriculum Development, 1989.

Schwartz, Stuart. *Coping with Crisis Situations*. Englewood Cliffs, NJ: Prentice-Hall, 1990.

Weisbord, Marvin. *Productive Workplaces*. San Francisco: Jossey-Bass, 1987.

PART THREE

PROBLEMS OF SUPERVISION

CHAPTER **10**

Evaluating for Effectiveness

INTRODUCTION

Evaluation is an area of major skill for most school supervisors. It is one of the few fields where leadership can be asserted based on knowledge and competence. Supervisors are regularly involved in evaluation through assessment of programs, processes, and people. The supervisor's leadership effectiveness depends largely on how his or her thinking is organized about the topic. We believe that the growing body of knowledge about schools and teachers can help the supervisor to become a truly effective evaluator.

Why evaluate? This is a question often heard in the field of education—most often from those lacking formal preparation to lead. We know from previous chapters that schools are constructed to aid humans in their development. We know too, that the school's curriculum is a plan or blueprint that reveals an intended pattern of learning. Classroom teachers are the primary deliverers of the curriculum to learners. Supervisors are people who work with teachers and others to improve constantly the students' learning experiences. Evaluation is the basic means by which planned improvement occurs; it is the force that causes constructive change in schools.

The stakes of formal evaluation are high, with considerable resources being directed by the evaluator's decisions. Mistakes or even sloppiness in evaluation can lead to destroyed careers, wasted dollars, and substandard learning experiences for students. The area of evaluation is, indeed, an important function of supervision.

ORGANIZING FOR EVALUATION

Supervisors are generally involved in evaluation activities in four primary areas:

281

1. *Programs* — reviewing the design of school programs to see if they meet, conceptually and structurally, the intentions of planning groups.
2. *Processes* — overseeing operational techniques to assess efficiency and effectiveness of organization.
3. *Products* — summarizing the performance of school programs in terms of predetermined expectations.
4. *Personnel* — analyzing the contribution of people to the planned programs of the school.

These four areas are directly related to one another although, in practice, many supervisors act as if they are isolated dimensions of evaluation. A common evaluation problem in schools, for instance, is the assessment of classroom teachers (personnel) without thorough consideration for instructional design (programs).

Certain evaluation activities are built into the routine of most school districts in the United States. Most districts and schools, for instance, seek accreditation through either a national accreditation association or state accreditation. In many states certain accountability measures have been mandated requiring schools to report data to state agencies in areas such as testing. Most school districts require the annual evaluation of personnel and, in some cases, programs. But, while such requirements may keep a school supervisor busy making reports and conducting evaluations, they rarely improve instructional experiences.

What the supervisor needs to be effective in evaluation is a thorough grasp of the knowledge base of evaluation plus a way of organizing its many dimensions. A starting point is to ask, "What is the purpose of evaluation activity in my school?" A second question might be, "What is the connection between the various evaluation activities in my school?" A third question might be, "How can I as the supervisor begin to tie together these evaluation efforts so that they begin to improve classroom learning?" These questions may lead the supervisor to other questions about learning that become the basis for inquiries into educational research.

Evaluation has at least five general purposes that contribute to the judgment of the effectiveness of a school program:

1. To make explicit the rationale of the instructional program as a basis for deciding which aspects of the program should be evaluated for effectiveness and what types of data should be gathered.
2. To collect data upon which judgments about effectiveness can be formulated.

3. To analyze data and draw conclusions.
4. To make decisions based on such data.
5. To implement the decisions to improve the instructional program.

A more specific outline of this general evaluation function has been provided by Daniel Stufflebeam:[1]

A. Focusing the Evaluation
 1. Identify the major level(s) of decision making to be served (e.g., local, state, or national).
 2. For each level of decision making, project the decision situations to be served and describe each one in terms of its locus, focus, timing, and composition of alternatives.
 3. Define criteria for each decision situation by specifying variables for measurement and standards for use in the judgment of alternatives.
 4. Define policies within which the evaluation must operate.
B. Collection of Information
 1. Specify the source of the information to be collected.
 2. Specify the instruments and methods for collecting the needed information.
 3. Specify the sampling procedure to be employed.
 4. Specify the conditions and schedule for information collection.
C. Organization of Information
 1. Specify a format for the information which is to be collected.
 2. Specify a means for coding, organizing, storing, and retrieving information.
D. Analysis of Information
 1. Specify the analytical procedures to be employed.
 2. Specify a means for performing the analysis.
E. Reporting of Information
 1. Define the audiences for the evaluation reports.
 2. Specify means for providing information to the audiences.
 3. Specify the format for evaluation reports and/or reporting sessions.
 4. Schedule the reporting information.

These efforts to define the purpose and roles of evaluation should lead to a second step in which the supervisor attempts to see the overall pattern of evaluation as a design. In Figure 10.1, the purposes of evaluation are stated. In Figure 10.2, the goals of education are tied to basic data and information sources gathered by a sample district.

A third step in further defining evaluation would be to spell out how these findings or data are to be translated into action steps for improving instruction. In many schools, such a translation is the primary work of supervision and the choice of a medium for reaching classroom teachers is a critical variable for supervisors.

Figure 10.1
Design Outline for School Evaluation

Approach	Focus	Procedure	Questions
Program Design	Conceptual/Structure	Validation of Goals/Purposes	Do we have the kind of program intended?
Program Process	Operational/Technique	Problem Analysis/Checklists	Is the program we have efficient in delivering services?
Program Product	Structured Feedback	Testing and Survey	Does the program work? Are there desired outcomes?
Program Personnel	Observation/Analysis	Review/Redesign	Are personnel making a direct contribution to the planned program?

Figure 10.2
Goals and Evaluation Gathered

GOAL	DATA and INFORMATION SOURCES
I Communication	Educational Quality Assessment Comprehensive Test of Basic Skills Individual Reading Assessment Placement Tests from Reading Series Woodcock Reading Tests Stanford Diagnostic Test
II Mathematics	Educational Quality Assessment Comprehensive Test of Basic Skills California Achievement Test District Mathematics Tests
III Self-esteem	Educational Quality Assessment Teacher Observations Parent/Teacher Conference Tennessee Self-concept Scale
IV Analytical Thinking	Educational Quality Assessment Comprehensive Test of Basic Skills Teacher Observation
V Understanding Others	Educational Quality Assessment Teacher Observation
VI Citizenship	Educational Quality Teacher Observation

THE ROLE OF RESEARCH IN EVALUATION

One of the important contributions of evaluation in school planning is that it introduces the element of rationality into the decision-making process. Said another way, evaluation can minimize the degree of random or superfluous change in schools. Evaluation can reduce some theoretical issues to a decision-making level, and can clearly identify desired outcomes and measure progress toward those ends. Evaluation cannot, however, establish basic principles or assumptions that guide school planning. Answering basic questions about school is the role of research.

Research, unlike basic evaluation or validation efforts, is concerned with discovering basic educational principles. The researcher seeks to develop lawful relationships among a class of problems with a high degree of generalizability. The researcher hopes to establish rules (explanatory statements) about processes that govern common educational activities. Research is called into play in schools when essential differences of opinion exist about a perceived reality.

In terms of our knowledge about teaching and learning in a classroom, our research efforts are primitive. Only in the past twenty years have researchers conducted sound empirical studies that isolate variables and consider teacher behaviors and student behaviors in an environmental context. Some of the major research areas that have emerged are:

1. The impact of context on the teacher's behavior.
2. The impact of the student's background on learning.
3. The individual differences among students in a classroom.
4. The relationship of subject matter to teacher effectiveness.
5. The problem of establishing a cognitive match between teacher and student.
6. The causal impact of student behavior on teacher behavior.

Even something as well-researched as human development continues to produce leads for educators. Consider the following finding of a major research project (1984) at Johns Hopkins University: "Researchers have gathered evidence suggesting that there is a biological basis for mathematical ability in children. The researchers found that children who are exceptional in math are more than twice as likely to be left-handed, six times as likely to have allergies, and five times as likely to be near-sighted as the population at large."[2]

It is obvious that such research, whatever its validity, has overwhelming implications for planners of teaching and learning. The problem supervisors face is that there are literally hundreds of studies available that give leads or hypotheses about learning, but few whose principles of learning are universally accepted. This leaves the supervisor in the posture of gathering, interpreting, and finding research patterns to pass on to teachers and others involved in planning.

RESEARCH ON TEACHING

Serious research on teaching in the United States can be dated from the year 1971 when two researchers, Rosenshine and Furst, summarized a decade of inquiry in the form of eleven hypotheses or proposed principles. The eleven teaching variables were those (suggested by previous research) that appeared to be related to student gains in cognitive achievement. Here are the eleven variables followed by a number in parentheses that indicate how many correlational studies were used in drawing the hypothesis:

1. *Clarity* (7)—The cognitive clarity of the teacher's presentation.
2. *Variability* (8)—The teacher's use of variety during the lesson such as using different instructional materials, tests, or varying the level of cognitive discourse.

3. *Enthusiasm* (6)—Degree of stimulation, originality, or vigor presented by the teacher in the classroom.
4. *Task-oriented Behavior* (7)—Degree to which the teacher is businesslike or achievement-oriented in presentation.
5. *Student Opportunity to Learn Criterion Materials* (4)—Relationship between the material covered in class and the criterion pupil performance. Rosenshine and Furst also identified six variables of secondary importance that suggest significant teacher behaviors in instruction.
6. *Use of Student Ideas and General Indirectness* (8)—Acknowledging, modifying, applying, comparing, and summarizing student statements.
7. *Criticism* (17)—A strong negative relationship between teacher criticism and student achievement. Criticism includes hostility, strong disapproval, or need to justify authority.
8. *Use of Structuring Comments (Advanced Organizers)* (4)—Teacher provides "cognitive scaffolding" for completed or planned lesson.
9. *Types of Questions Asked* (7)—Questions categorized into low cognitive and high cognitive. Questions appropriate to task and group.
10. *Probing* (3)—Teacher responses that encourage the student to elaborate on his or her question.
11. *Level of Difficulty of Instruction* (4)—Student perception of the level of difficulty.[3]

Rosenshine and Furst, pioneers in promoting process-product studies, summarized the existing research in this manner:

The number of studies has been small. Fewer than 25 studies have been conducted on any specific variable such as teacher praise or teacher questions, and these studies are spread across all grade levels, subject areas, and student backgrounds.

The number of investigators in this field is also small. There are no more than twelve researchers or groups of researchers currently studying the relationship between classroom instruction and student achievement. . . .

Although recent studies represent methodological and conceptual expansion of previous work, research on observed teaching behavior is new, sparse, and not always consistent in results. What we have learned to date is offered more as hypotheses for future study than as validated variables for the training and evaluation of teachers. Although practitioners can easily amass a large number of questions on teaching methods for which they would like clear answers, at the rate we are going it will be years before many of these questions are even studied.[4]

The effect of identifying these variables, due to the availability of research funds in the 1970s, was to initiate a search for conditions that would guarantee student learning and effective teaching.

Two massive studies became the foundation for an area of research later known as "teacher effectiveness studies": The Texas

Teacher Effectiveness Project and the California Beginning Teacher
Evaluation Study. The Texas study, employing a process-product design (a teaching process leads to a student product) attempted to determine whether specific teacher behaviors contributed to student
achievement gains as measured by a standardized test. The California
study, by contrast, used an ethnographic (anthropological) approach to
try to isolate general teaching skills contributing to student achievement gains.

In the Texas project, primary researchers Brophy and Evertson
reported:

> The majority of significant relationships with learning gain (Metropoli-
> tan Achievement Tests) scores were negative. In short, we found out
> more about what not to do than we did about what to do. . . . The upshot
> of all this is that teaching involves orchestration of a large number of
> different behaviors which the teacher must have mastered to at least a
> certain minimal level and can adapt to different situations, as opposed
> to application of a few basic teaching skills that are "all-important."
> These behaviors were many and complex rather than few and simple.
> There are no magical "keys" to successful teaching.[5]

The Texas study did find that to increase achievement scores, a
teacher should use strong classroom management, positive rather than
negative reinforcement, possess high expectations for students, and
maintain an optimal level of learning difficulty. Using materials that
are too hard, holding low expectation for pupils, and not responding
to the substance of student questions were all shown to detract from
student achievement gains.

Perhaps more important for teacher education research was the
finding of the Texas study that related teacher behavior to socioeconomic status (SES) of the learner. It was found that the general attitude
of warmth and encouragement was characteristic of successful teachers in low SES schools, whereas "successful" teachers in high SES
schools were not especially warm or encouraging. Such a finding suggests that teaching behaviors that are important to student achievement gains are, to some extent, situationally specific.

Using the more conventional methodology of educational research in the California study, the researchers reported equally dis-
couraging results:

> The history of research on teaching, for example, has been characterized
> by the attempt to find general teaching skills which insignificantly in-
> fluence learning. Did we find any single teaching skill which correlated
> with learning in both reading and math at both grade levels? No such
> skills were found. Performances which correlated significantly with out-
> comes were different by subject matter and by grade level.

This result, if replicated, or if found in comparable studies, is an important one. It indicated that the pattern of effective teaching performances will differ by subject matter and probably grade level. The practical implications of such a conclusion are obvious; the goals of training teachers in the primary grades and the intermediate grades will necessarily be different.[6]

While the California Beginning Teacher Evaluation Study did not isolate a specific teaching skill or set of skills that directly correlated with learning, data analysis of observations did unveil a host of dimensions in which effective teachers (those with high student gains) at both levels (grades 2 and 5, reading) are alike. Berliner reports:

Teachers classified as more effective were found to be more satisfied, accepting, attentive, aware of developmental needs, consistent in controlling classes, democratic, encouraging, tolerant of race and class, flexible, optimistic, equitable in dividing time among students, and knowledgeable of the subject. In addition, more effective teachers provided more structure for the learners, capitalized on unexpected wants, showed more warmth, waited for students to answer questions, promoted students to take responsibility for their work, used more praise, adjusted teaching to the learner's rate, individualized, monitored learning, used less 'busy work,' did not treat the class as a whole, made fewer illogical statements, were less belittling, less harrassing, less ignoring, and less recognition seeking.[7]

A final contribution of the BTES was to suggest a clear linkage between the cognitive styles of teachers and students. Such commonality in "ways of thinking" could mean that students might learn best under teachers with particular cognitive patterns. Stone explains:

Cognitive style is an individual difference variable defined as a consistent mode of information processing. The field-dependence-independence dimension of cognitive style is a continuum, with the field-dependent end characterized by a more global, undifferentiated approach and the field-independent end by a more analytical, differentiated approach to perceptual processing.
This cognitive style dimension has been shown to relate to both how teachers teach and how students learn. Field-dependent teachers tend to prefer teaching situations which allow for interaction with the students, whereas, field-independent teachers prefer more impersonal situations and tend to stress the cognitive aspects of teaching.
The field-dependence-independence dimension of cognitive style also relates to how children learn. Due to their greater social sensitivity, field-dependent children tend to be more adept at learning and remembering materials that have social content, and to be more affected by criticism than field-independent children. On the other hand, field-

independent children are able to impose their own structure on ambiguous or unstructured learning tasks.[8]

The lack of clarity in research about which teacher behaviors elicit which student outcomes was echoed by two basic summaries of research conducted in the 1970s. Robert Soar, a researcher who studied teaching with low socioeconomic Project Follow Through students stated that educational research had an organizing principle but little in the way of prescription for the teacher:

> These findings suggest that an intermediate amount of different kinds of teacher behaviors are best for a particular goal and for a particular group of pupils, but they don't begin to answer the question of the classroom teacher—how much of a certain behavior is best for which goal for which pupil? What we have so far is an organizing principle which can be used by the teacher and the researcher in thinking about effective teaching; we do not have specific answers for the teacher's question. This will require a more detailed research methodology than we have used, but it seems to be a very logical next step.[9]

Soar's "organizing principle" (i.e., certain teacher behaviors are functional for certain types of students) received support from a major review of empirical studies on teacher effectiveness conducted by Medley. Reporting on 289 studies in a 1977 monograph, Medley identified behaviors of teachers that seem effective or ineffective with pupils of low socioeconomic status in the primary grades (Table 10.1).

Another summary by Gage also pointed to desirable teacher behaviors supported by research studies. Clustering studies on teacher effectiveness, Gage makes the following suggestions for teachers:

> Teachers should have a system of rules that allow pupils to attend to their personal and procedural needs without having to check with the teacher.
>
> Teachers should move around the room a lot, monitoring pupils' ... work and communicating to their pupils an awareness of their behavior, while also attending to their academic needs.
>
> When pupils work independently, teachers should ensure that the assignments are interesting and worthwhile, yet still easy enough to be completed by each—working without teacher direction.
>
> Teachers should keep to a minimum such activities as (orally) giving directions and organizing the class for instruction. Teachers can do this by writing the daily schedule on the board, ensuring that pupils know where to go and what to do, and so on.
>
> During ... group instruction, teachers should give a maximal amount of brief feedback and provide fast-paced activities of the "drill" type.

Table 10.1
Behaviors Found to be Characteristic of Effective and Ineffective Teachers
of Pupils of Low Socioeconomic Status in the Primary Grades

Effective Teachers	Ineffective Teachers
1. *Maintenance of Learning Environment*	
Less deviant, disruptive pupil behavior	More deviant, disruptive pupil behavior
Fewer teacher rebukes	More teacher rebukes
Less criticism	More teacher criticism
Less time spent on classroom management	More time spent on classroom management
More praise, positive motivation	Less praise, positive interaction
2. *Use of Pupil Time*	
More time spent in task-related "academic" activities	Less class time spent in task-related, "academic" activities
More time working with large groups or whole class	Less time working with large groups or whole class
Less time working with small groups	More time working with small groups
Small groups of pupils work independently less of the time	Small groups of pupils work independently more of the time
Less independent seatwork	More independent seatwork
3. *Quality of Instruction*	
More "low-level" questions	Fewer "low-level" questions
Fewer "high-level" questions	More "high-level" questions
Less likely to amplify, discuss, or use pupil answers	More likely to amplify, discuss or use pupil answers
Fewer pupil-initiated questions and comments	More pupil-initiated questions and comments
Less feedback on pupil questions	More feedback on pupil questions
More attentive to pupils when they are working independently	Less attentive to pupils when they are working independently

Source: From D. Medley, "Teacher Competence and Teacher Effectiveness," monograph (Washington, D.C.: American Association of Colleges of Teacher Education, 1977), p. 15.

Teachers should criticize, but infrequently, and primarily the academically oriented pupils and those of higher socioeconomic status.

Teachers should optimize "academic learning time"—time during which pupils are actively and productively engaged in their academic learning tasks.

When time is taken for exploration, creativity, self-direction, and games, it should not infringe upon "academic learning time," if achievement is desired.

Characteristics of teacher behavior such as clarity, enthusiasm, and vividness correlate with pupil achievement.[10]

The period between the mid-1970s and the mid-1980s is a curious one in terms of what has happened to this original research on teacher effectiveness and student learning. Whereas in the mid-1970s all of the major researchers were warning that the study of teaching behaviors was at an infant stage of development, in the 1980s that very same research was being promoted by many professional organizations as a dogma. The new labels for the old wine in new bottles are "effective schools research" and "effectiveness teacher research."

In terms of effective schools, the reader is directed to the list of items in six categories that represent a prescription by the leading association of curriculum developers and supervisors:[11]

A. School Climate
   1. Strong sense of academic mission
   2. High expectations conveyed to all students
   3. Strong sense of student identification/affiliation
   4. High level of professional collegiality among staff
   5. Recognition of personal/academic excellence
B. Curriculum
   1. Grade level expectations and standards in reading, math, and language
   2. Planning and monitoring for full content coverage
C. Instruction
   1. Efficient classroom management through structured learning environment
   2. Academic priority evidenced in increased amount of allocated time
   3. Key instructional behaviors (review and homework check, developmental lesson, process/product check, actively monitored seatwork, related homework assignment)
   4. Direct instruction as the main pedagogical approach
   5. Maximizing academic engaged time (time-on-task)
   6. Use of the accelerated learning approach (planning for more than one year's growth)
   7. Reading, math, and language instruction beginning at the kindergarten level
D. Coordination of Supportive Services
   1. Instructional approach, curriculum content, and materials of supplementary instructional services coordinated with the classroom program
   2. Pull-out approach used only if it does not fragment the classroom instructional program, does not result in lower expecta-

tions for some students, and does not interfere with efforts to maximize the use of time

E. Evaluation
  1. Frequent assessment of student progress on a routine basis
  2. Precise and informative report card with emphasis on acquisition of basic school skills
  3. Serious attitude towards test-taking as an affirmation of individual accomplishment
  4. Test-taking preparation and skills

F. Parent and Community Support
  1. Regular and consistent communication with parents
  2. Clearly defined homework policy which is explained to students and parents
  3. Emphasis upon the importance of regular school attendance
  4. Clear communication to parents regarding the school's expectations related to behavioral standards
  5. Increasing awareness of community services available to reinforce and extend student learning

While many of these prescriptions are common sense, many are also terribly misleading in what is being suggested as "essential elements of effective schooling." A structured classroom environment, actively monitored seatwork, and increased amounts of allocated time, for instance, are a prescription for *certain types of learning with certain types of students.* These are not universal prescriptions for effective schools.

Another example at the classroom level is a massive attempt to sell a concept called "time on task" as a research-backed prescription. In a book by the same title, the American Association of School Administrators observe that students spend approximately 12,000 hours in school and that some have more "engaged time" than others. They continue to observe that "since the longer school year correlates with higher achievement," schools need to review their time efficiency. While we, the authors, have no problem with efficiency, we do question whether spending more time on task promotes effective learning. In addition to basic concerns like attention spans of various age groups, the type of learning is an important concern. To teach creative thinking, for example, time-on-task is a dysfunctional concept.

The reader's attention is drawn to this problem with teaching research as a caveat for practice. The difference between the cautious statements of the researchers (Brophy, Berliner, Soar, Gage) and the cock-sure prescriptions of the professional organizations a decade later, illustrates a contemporary problem in educational research. Like a game of "buzz" where successive persons pass on a message, the original message quickly becomes distorted unless the primary information is known and studied. Prescriptions for low socioeconomic students in federal research projects, looking only at gains on standardized achievement tests, have nearly become a general prescription for all students in the United States due to the lack of trained translators who serve in supervisory roles.

We would agree with an observation made a decade ago concerning the status and future of teaching/learning research:

> ... it is difficult to argue with the spirit of Rosenshine's recent contention that the greatest current need is to conduct more research which is designed to link teacher variables with student outcomes. However, studies which attempt to explore further the relationships between student growth and the 11 or so correlates advanced by Rosenshine will be greatly hampered and their value possibly reduced, until serious attention is given to the problem of defining these abstract constructs in terms of low-inference behaviors.[12]

It should be obvious to the reader that research on teacher effectiveness is in an embryonic stage of development. In fact, the past twenty years of inquiry have served only to reveal the complexity of pupil-teacher interaction in a classroom setting and the limitations of our current research methodology.

We seemed to have learned that no single teacher behavior or set of behaviors will universally promote student achievement gains in all subjects. Further, research to date suggests that certain strategies are appropriate for unique groups of pupils, and that the ultimate findings of teacher effectiveness research may call for the matching of teachers and students according to variables as specific as thinking style or personality. The road to prescriptions for classroom teachers by supervisors will be a long one.

THE USE OF RESEARCH AND EVALUATION BY SUPERVISORS

As noted earlier in this chapter, supervisors need to understand fully the role of evaluation in improving instruction as well as the skills that make evaluation work. Most of all, supervisors need to be able to tie the efforts of research and evaluation directly to activities that improve instruction at the classroom level.

In seeking the big picture of evaluation, supervisors should also understand the basic precept that good decisions are based on good information. To obtain good information, the supervisor must do assessments, conduct testing, and establish a research program that answers basic questions about improving instruction.

The needs assessment, shown in Table 10.2, provides the super-

Table 10.2
Sources of Data About an Instructional Program

A. Pupil performance
   1. Standardized tests—teacher-made tests
   2. Pupil grades
   3. Dropout data
   4. Pupil attendance
   5. Observation of pupil performance
   6. Inventories—skill continuums
   7. Observations of teaching-learning situations in the classroom
   8. Degree of student attention and involvement

B. Questionnaires—polls of opinions of pupils, teachers, parents
   1. Polls of parents regarding the success of certain school programs
   2. Group interviews with students, parents, teachers about the success of curriculum innovations
   3. Attitude surveys of students about certain programs
   4. Comparison of attitudes of pupils and teachers toward contrasting programs
   5. Systematic questionnaires, rating sheets, and interviews with small random samples of students

C. Follow-up studies of learners
   1. Success at the next grade level
   2. Continuation of schooling
   3. College success
   4. Success at work
   5. Application of skills learned, interests generated in school—e.g., participation in lifetime sports, the arts

D. Examination of learning materials
   1. Examining learning materials to see if they are feasible and practical for use by teachers in the schools—accuracy and soundness of materials
   2. Determining if costs of materials are too great
   3. Checking materials to see if they are at the right level for students
   4. Determining whether teachers get special retraining in order to understand and use new materials
   5. Matching materials to students' interests, needs, and aspirations—relevancy of materials

Source: Jon Wiles and Joseph Bondi, *Curriculum Development*, 3rd ed. (Columbus, OH: Merrill, 1989). Used with permission.

Figure 10.3

Comparison of Schools by Variables That May Influence Instruction

RANGE

Enrollment — 670 (Winter Park) — 1389 (Liberty)
A.D.A.* 83% (8th Apopka) — 95% (7th Maitland)
Teacher Absence Ratio — .36 (Glenridge) — 1.27 (Union Park)
% Low SES* — 11% (Glenridge, Conway) — 56% (Howard)
Gifted/Other Special — 1/104 (Carver) — 179/63 (Glenridge)
Mobility In/Out — 14 Schools over 40% — Howard at 70%

Corporal Punishment	44–619
Suspensions	37–240
Expulsions	1– 22
Dropouts	3– 22
Grade Distribution Pattern	5 Extreme Negative
CTBS Range	(Carver) 36–80 (Maitland)
Total Battery	

Source: Orange County, Florida schools:
*ADA – Average Daily Attendance
SES – Socioeconomic Status

visor with many sources of data about existing conditions. In such a general assessment, all aspects of the instructional program are reviewed and contrasted with opinions of those supporting the program to find where consensus and discrepancies are located. It may be helpful for the supervisor to look at a number of schools in the same district to see what kind of variables might be responsible for school performance (Figure 10.3). Follow-up studies may be conducted to examine how the product of education looks once it leaves the school environment.

Testing is an area that dominates the time of many school-based supervisors, but many never see testing in its proper perspective. The primary purpose of testing in schools is to receive feedback on the effectiveness of the instructional program. The results of the total testing pattern provide much better clues about what is happening in the classroom than the scores of the individual students.

In Figure 10.4, the reader views a comprehensive testing design showing the general needs assessment conducted to gain instructional information. Figure 10.5 shows the overall performance of a district, grades 1–12, against the norms of a national standardized test. Figure 10.6 uses test data to follow a class through the years of the middle school on the Metropolitan Achievement Test. Each of these three examples indicates the level at which the supervisor should review testing programs. To view testing as the measure of one teacher's worth, as is done in some school districts, is to ignore 95 percent of the variables influencing such a score.

Figure 10.4
Needs Assessment Plan: Testing Component

Data	Population	Source or Instrument	Description of Data Collection Procedures
4. Achievement			
a. Reading	Grades: 4,5,6, 8 & 11.	Iowa Test of Basic Skills.	All reading achievement will be reported in grade placement and will be the results of achievement test administered pre- and post- during the 1983–1984 school year.
	Grades: 2 & 3.	Gates-McGinitie Reading Test.	
	Grades: 4,5,6, 8 & 11. Same students for eight years.	Iowa Test of Basic Skills.	The reading achievement of one class will be tracked for eight years from the fourth grade to the eleventh grade. Data will be reported in grade placement for five years.
b. Language Arts	Grades: 4 & 8.	Iowa Test of Basic Skills.	Language arts achievement data will be reported in grade placement and will be the results of achievement test administered during the 1983–1984 school year.
	Grade: 11.	Test of Academic Progress.	
c. Mathematics	Grades: 4,8,& 11.	Iowa Test of Basic Skills.	Same procedure as for language arts. The data will be the results of the 1983–1984 testing program.
5. Self-concept			
a. Primary	A 30 percent random sample of grades 1–3.	"When Do I Smile."	Population will be selected using the table of random numbers. The instrument will be administered to the population by one person by reading each item. The data will be reported in percent of response for each item.
b. Elementary and High School	A 30 percent random sample of grades 4–12.	Coopersmith Self-esteem Inventory.	The Coopersmith will be administered by one person at the elementary school and one person at the high school. Each item will be read to the students. Since the Coopersmith consists of four major subtests, the data will be reported in percent of responses for each item divided by the subtest.

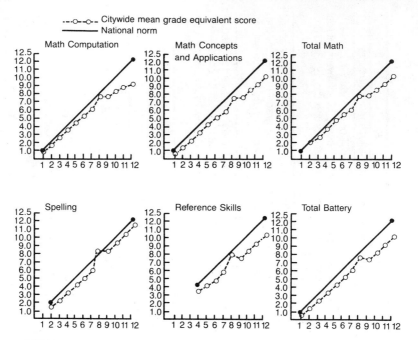

Figure 10.5
District Performance Versus National Norm

Supervisors should also make it their business to be knowledgeable about major tests given in their district to assess and place students. Listed here are some of the more widely used tests in American schools:

Intelligence Tests

Wechsler Intelligence Scale for Children (WISC)—Consisting of twelve subtests, ten of which are used to calculate the intelligence quotient. Mental age equivalents are figured from performance. Ages six to sixteen.

Stanford-Binet Intelligence Scale (3rd Revision)—A scale or ladder-of-tasks approach with many levels. A scoring guide defines acceptable or unacceptable answers. Used in many districts to find or qualify gifted students. Ages two and over.

Slosson Intelligence Test for Children and Adults — Provides a mental age for humans from .5 to 27 years and also uses a ratio I.Q. Has been criticized because of language dependence in early years.

Otis-Lennon Mental Ability Test — A group-administered test for levels kindergarten to grade twelve. Test is considered more

Figure 10.6
Three-Year Progress of a Single Class in Reading and Math

Metropolitan Achievement Test: Mean Percentile by Subtest in Reading and Math

Table 1 — Growth of 1978 Sixth Grade Class Through the Eighth Grade

	Reading			Math			
	Word Knowledge	Reading Comprehension	Total Reading	Math Computation	Math Concepts	Math Problem Solving	Total Math
1978 (6)	46	50	46	48	40	46	50
1979 (7)	52	48	50	46	40	40	44
1980 (8)	44	48	48	50	48	40	48

Table 2 — Growth of 1978 Seventh Grade Class Through the Eighth Grade

	Word Knowledge	Reading Comprehension	Total Reading	Math Computation	Math Concepts	Math Problem Solving	Total Math
1978 (7)	50	44	46	46	40	46	44
1979 (8)	40	40	40	44	48	36	46

Table 3 — Growth of 1979 Sixth Grade Class Through the Seventh Grade

	Word Knowledge	Reading Comprehension	Total Reading	Math Computation	Math Concepts	Math Problem Solving	Total Math
1979 (6)	46	50	50	48	40	46	46
1980 (7)	56	50	54	46	40	40	44

Source: East Baton Rouge Parish School District

299

accurate in later years because of the reasoning needed to respond to questions.

Achievement Tests (Group administered)

Comprehensive Test of Basic Skills (CTBS)—Designed to measure the level of attainment of language, number, and problem-solving skills required for academic study and for everyday needs outside of school. Scoring reported in reading, language, mathematics, reference skills, science, and social studies. Grades K–12.

Iowa Test of Basic Skills—A comprehensive measurement of growth in the fundamental skills crucial in current daily learning activities and future educational development. Grades 1.7–3.5.

Metropolitan Readiness Test—Provides measures of prereading skills in Grades K–1. Subtests include auditory memory, rhyming, letter recognition, visual matching, school language, listening, and quantitative language.

California Achievement Tests—A general battery of achievement in reading and mathematics. Grade range 1.5 to 12. Five levels of achievement measured.

Supervisors should distinguish between norm-referenced tests (examinee's performance against normative group), achievement tests (student has acquired knowledge or skills intended), and criterion-referenced tests (the status of the examinee with respect to a well-defined class of behaviors). Supervisors should be aware that each of these types of tests intends to test something different, and that the various types are appropriate according to the kind of curriculum that is in place.

Supervisors should also be aware that in many school districts in the 1990s the pressure of school boards or parents to show score performance on achievement tests has distorted the curriculum. This phenomenon usually occurs when no one in the district takes the leadership role in defining the meaning of testing and interpreting such tests to the Board and public.

Finally, standardized testing implies that people can and should be compared with one another. This is a philosophical distinction that sometimes is not self-evident to those who write the goals for the educational program.

In the use of both research and evaluation, a special language exists among specialists. Some of the more important terms are defined in Figure 10.7.

Figure 10.7
General Terms Used in Evaluation

Content Validity: The degree to which a measuring device is judged to be appropriate for its purpose, for example, the degree to which it is congruent with a set of instructional objectives.

Correlation: The tendency for corresponding observations in two or more series to have similar positions.

Criterion-Referenced Measurement: Measurement designed to assess an individual's status with respect to a particular criterion or standard of performance, irrespective of the relationship of his performance to that of others.

Criterion Validity: Characteristically, the degree to which a particular measure, such as a test of intellectual ability, correlates with an external criterion such as subsequent scholastic performance in college.

Distractors: These are the alternatives or wrong answers in a multiple-choice or comparable test item.

Formative Evaluation: The evaluation of an instructional program before it is finally completed—that is, the attempt to evaluate a program to improve it.

Item Analysis: Any one of several methods used in revising a test to determine how well a given item discriminates among individuals or different degrees of ability or among individuals differing in some other characteristic.

Item Sampling: The procedure of administering different forms of a test (characteristically, shorter forms) to different individuals, thereby reducing the time required for testing.

Norm-Referenced Measurement: Measurement designed to assess an individual's standing with respect to other individuals on the same measuring device.

Percentile (centile): The point in distribution of scores below which a certain proportion of the scores fall. For example, a student scoring at the seventieth percentile on a test would have exceeded the scores of 70 percent of those taking the test.

Reliability: The accuracy with which a measuring device measures something; the degree to which a test measures consistently whatever it measures.

Standardized Test: A test for which content has been selected and checked empirically, for which norms have been established, for which uniform methods of administering and scoring have been developed, and which may be scored with a relatively high degree of objectivity.

Summative Evaluation: The final evaluation of a program in which the results of the program are characteristically compared with results of comparable programs in order for selection to be made among competing instructional programs.

Validity: The extent to which a test or other measuring instrument fulfills the purpose for which it is used.

SCHOOL-WIDE EVALUATION PLANNING

Evaluation in any school must be comprehensive if it is to serve its primary purpose of improving student learning experiences. Since the operation of a school should be based on the objectives of the curriculum, it makes sense that evaluation, too, should be tied directly to the goals and purpose of the program. This means that all aspects of the school program should contribute to the major concepts that are found in a program design.

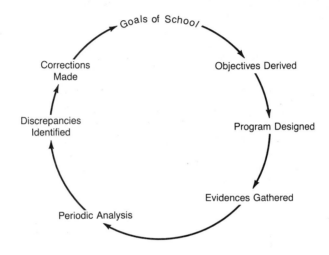

One way of viewing evaluation is as a corrective mechanism or feedback loop in the curriculum cycle. The goals of the school are represented by objectives which, in turn, create the basic program design. Student learning experiences, for instance, are structured into activities that have clear objectives and expectations. As the program is implemented, these expectations are either met or not met. Evaluation helps clarify any discrepancies between the expected outcomes and the actual performance. At that point, evaluation guides the adjustments to the program to allow a fuller correspondence between expectations and outcomes. In some cases, feedback may suggest a revision of basic goals and purposes.

Another way to approach school evaluation would be to use evaluation as a means of "validating" program goals and objectives. In this approach, evidences are gathered to justify specific facets of the program and these facets or subsystems collectively comprise the evaluation program. Examples of such subsystems are student performance, teacher effectiveness, program design, resource utilization, facilities usage, policies and regulation, parent and community feedback, and staff development programs.

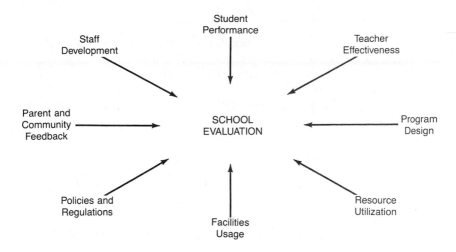

Using this approach, a concern for any one area of the program would trigger a review of other areas. For example, if student study skills proved deficient in testing, other areas could be explored for probable cause—i.e., deficient materials, additional teacher training, or inadequate facilities.

By combining these two ways of viewing evaluation, the supervisor can develop a system of assessing the school programs and taking corrective action where necessary. Some guiding questions in each of these areas are provided for the reader's consideration:

Program Design

1. Is the program concept consistent with the overall philosophy of the district and its leaders?
2. Does the program articulate (fit) with preceding elementary, middle, or secondary programs? Is there a consistent follow-through in other programs?
3. Are resources dedicated to this program commensurate with other programs found in the curriculum?
4. Is there an internal consistency to this program such as a set of objectives that provide structure?

Facilities Usage

1. Does the physical location and allocation of space reflect this program's priority in the curriculum?
2. Are learning areas within the space consistent with the instructional intent in delivering this program to students?

Policies and Regulations

1. Are some policies and regulations essential in allowing this program to function fully?
2. Are there rules or policies that in fact contradict the spirit of this program?
3. Is there a better way to handle policy-formation and enforcement in operating this program?

Resource Utilization

1. Is there a clear relationship between the allocation of resources and funds and the curricular objectives of this program?
2. Are resources available to support innovative instructional approaches or to promote desired changes?
3. Is there an established procedure for assessing future resource needs and planning for their acquisition?

Student Performance

1. Is student evaluation in this program both systematic and continuous?
2. Is student evaluation perceived by teachers as a measure of the program's success?
3. Are parents involved in the evaluation of the student and program?
4. Is student evaluation directional, indicating where improvement is needed?

Teacher Effectiveness

1. Is program improvement based on input by the instructional staff?
2. Is teacher-evaluation tied directly to program improvement?
3. Have the talents and abilities of teachers been fully explored in terms of contributing to this program?
4. Are there any unplanned organizational or administrative constraints on teaching styles in this program?

Staff Development

1. Are monies budgeted for staff development tied to the needs and goals of this specific program?
2. Do teachers have the opportunity to critique current staff development efforts?

3. Can it be shown, through evaluation, where staff development in the past has improved this program?

Parent-Community Feedback

1. Are members of the community involved in the formulation and maintenance of this program?
2. Are members of the community kept informed about any major changes contemplated or implemented in this program?
3. Does a communication vehicle exist that effectively shares the accomplishments of this program with parents and community?

Each of these components of a school-wide evaluation system is important to both program improvement and program performance. Each major area is interrelated to and crucial to other areas.

EVALUATION IN THE CLASSROOM

The bottom line for all supervisory evaluations is the assessment of classroom teaching. It is at the classroom level that the supervisor will ultimately learn of the effectiveness of the school programs.

There are three major ideas that govern the evaluation of teachers in the classroom: (1) the teacher needs to see himself or herself as part of the curriculum, not apart from it; (2) the teacher needs to understand the intent of the planned program as well as its structure; and (3) the teacher must clearly perceive evaluation and staff development as part of a program improvement effort. Each of these ideas is treated more fully here.

Curriculum and Instruction

For years it has been held that teaching is an art. More recently, teacher effectiveness research has pursued the idea that the teaching act is comprised of a series of interrelated acts or skills that contribute to effectiveness. In truth, both of these positions are probably valid . . . to some degree. The judgment of teaching through formal classroom evaluations is totally dependent on a model of the aims of teaching. A teacher who is personable or entertaining may be an instructional delight without contributing significantly to learning. By contrast, a teacher who grinds through a curriculum without spirit or understanding may be equally ineffective as a teacher. Evaluation of classroom instruction must be based upon some understanding of what is supposed to happen to students in the learning experience that is planned.

The beginning point for classroom evaluation is helping the teacher see himself or herself as an extension of the curriculum. Instruction is the implementation of the curriculum, and the teacher is the instrument by which the curriculum is delivered. At the lowest level this would mean that the teacher is not a free agent who teaches what is familiar or interesting to him or her. At a higher level, this would mean that the teacher is always conscious of what is supposed to happen to the student and how teaching contributes to that end.

There are many lists of teacher behaviors that go into school-based teacher evaluation forms. Here is a list of eight categories that could be used to construct such an instrument. The critical question is which of these performances actually contribute to the purpose of the curriculum?

I. Dependability
   A. Punctual.
   B. Reliable.
   C. Fulfills duties.
II. Human Relations Skills
   A. *Helps development of positive self-images in learners.* Praises. Listens, making students feel important. Elaborates and builds on the contributions of students. Relates to students on an individual basis. Provides opportunities for successful experiences.
   B. *Works effectively with different social/ethnic groups.* Relates well to students, parents, and staff from different ethnic and socioeconomic backgrounds.
   C. *Demonstrates skills in various kinds of communications.* Enunciates clearly and correctly. Adjusts voice and tone to situation; large group, small group, and individuals. Listens accurately to pupils and staff. Recognizes nonverbal statements. Adjusts language and content to students' age level.
   D. *Helps students become independent learners.* Helps students identify personal goals. Facilitates individual exploration. Provides opportunities for diversity. Offers alternative paths to skill acquisition.
   E. *Facilitates students' social interactions and activities.* Helps in special activity: field trip, play, games, and PTA.
   F. *Works effectively as a team member.* Gets along with staff. Assumes responsibility for tasks as a team member.
III. Managing the Classroom
   A. *Maintains a safe environment.* Follows safety regulations.
   B. *Maintains physical environment conducive to learning.* Arranges room with books, materials, and learning stations that produce a stimulating academic environment. Decorates

room reflecting students' ages and interests. Maintains room lighting and temperature as comfortable as possible.

C. *Maintains socioemotional environment conducive to learning.* Uses students' mistakes as sources of new learning. Respects rights of individuals. Enthusiastic about class work. Sense of humor. Uses competition to allow for the success of many. Provides opportunities for students to share experiences and feelings. Provides opportunities for cooperation.

D. *Involves students in the management of the classroom.* Delegates responsibility of housekeeping tasks to students. Involves students in decision making concerning the identification, implementation, and enforcement of classroom regulations. Matches management duties with students' needs as an opportunity for personal enhancement.

E. *Manages disruptive behavior appropriately.* Implements rules and procedures consistently. Standards of behavior are public and professionally justifiable. Attends to disruptive behavior individually and privately. Maintains control.

F. *Designs procedures for handling routines in the class.* Gets class started within 5 minutes of signal and finished on time. Establishes procedures for hall passes, lunch count, storage of materials. Keeps register accurately. Scores, reviews and records grades properly.

IV. Planning Instruction

A. *Selects appropriate learning goals and objectives.* Develops units and daily lesson plans that include appropriate learning objectives.

B. *Demonstrates skills in organizing learners for instruction.* Organizes different size groups of students for various instructional purposes.

C. *Selects appropriate teaching strategies.* Lecture discussion; lecture demonstration; lecture; inductive; individualization; group investigation; open classroom; simulations; programmed instruction.

D. *Skillful in selecting and preparing resource materials.* Selects and prepares resource materials for lessons. Utilizes a variety of printed and electronic media.

E. *Involves students in design of the instructional plan.* Seeks students' suggestions in the designing of the instructional plan. Provides opportunities for student choices.

F. *Demonstrates skill in evaluating the instructional plan.* Provides a rationale for instructional plans. Establishes criteria for attainment objectives. Evaluates effects of the instructional plan.

V. Implementing Instruction

    A. *Relates instruction to the world of the learner.* Relates learning objectives to students' perceptual world. Teaches at students' level in terms of language, examples, and activities. Deals with content in a problem-solving context. Provisions are made to learn by "doing" rather than listening only. Points out implications of material learned for students' career development.

    B. *Skillful in use of various teaching strategies.* Lecture discussion; lecture demonstration; lecture; inductive; individualization; group investigation; open classroom; simulations; programmed instruction.

    C. *Applies group dynamics techniques.* Uses different group management and leadership styles when working with large groups, middle size groups, and small groups of students.

    D. *Skillful in the individualization of instruction.* Diagnoses individual levels of proficiency; prescribes appropriate activities; selects appropriate materials; manages learning procedures.

    E. *Skillful in the use of A-V equipment and computers.* Operates overhead projector, opaque projector, recorder, movie projector, slide projector, ditto machine, mimeograph, CAI.

    F. *Skillful in the use of multimedia resources.* Incorporates printed and electronic media into learning activities.

    G. *Demonstrates skills in questioning and responding.* Asks questions at various levels of cognitive taxonomy. Phrases and times questions appropriately. Elicits student participation through questions. Uses rapid fire questions to move students into work. Uses questions as means of success for all learners. Builds new questions on students' answers. Challenges and probes through questions. Responds to answers by reinforcing or abstaining from judgment as the activity prescribes.

    H. *Demonstrates skills in value-clarification techniques.* Raises questions in the mind of the students to prod them gently to examine personal actions, values, and goals.

    I. *Evaluates and modifies his/her own performance.* Gathers self-evaluation data through VTR or audio tape playback, student oral and written feedback, supervisor feedback. Identifies areas of strength and weakness and formulates plan for improvement specifying criteria for accomplishment. Implements plan and evaluates and report results.

VI. Knowledge of Subject Matter

    A. *Demonstrates adequate general academic preparation.* Makes accurate statements and allusions to related fields of knowledge outside areas of specialization. Exhibits broad academic preparation.

B. *Demonstrates knowledge of areas of specialization.* Well informed, and skillful in field(s) of specialization.

VII. Assessing and Evaluating Students

    A. *Recognizes individual personalities/learning styles.* Designs and implements curriculum plans that provide for alternative learning styles and different cognitive and affective make-up.

    B. *Demonstrates diagnostic skills.* Skillful in the analysis of learning tasks. Determines student's level of proficiency in content area(s).

    C. *Skill in selecting and devising formal evaluation instruments.* Writes tests utilizing variety of types of items, appropriate to content area and student's level.

    D. *Skillful in devising and using informal evaluation procedures.* Uses informal evaluation techniques to assess progression in learning such as: interview, case study, analysis of student performance data.

    E. *Skillful in providing feedback to students and parents.* Devises formative evaluation events: teacher evaluated, learner/parent evaluated.

VIII. Professionalism

    A. *Seeks to improve own professional competence.* Reads professional journals. Attends professional meetings. Visits other programs and teachers. Seeks and utilizes professional feedback.

    B. *Is accountable for professional actions.* Dependable. Fulfills responsibility of the professional teacher: planning, implementing, validating instruction, maintenance tasks, playground duties, and other tasks.

    C. *Demonstrates skill in professional decision making.* Possesses a rationale for professional action. Produces evidence to justify professional decisions. Evaluates the consequences of actions.

    D. *Demonstrates awareness of strength and weaknesses.* Identifies teaching roles and strategies most and least suited to own style. Identifies personal human interaction style and its effects in professional work. Identifies own value system and how it relates to teaching.

    E. *Behaves according to an accepted code of professional ethics.* Works to fulfill institutional goals. Bases public criticism of education on valid assumptions as established by careful evaluation of facts and hypotheses. Refrains from exploiting the institutional privileges of the teaching profession to promote partisan activities or political candidates. Directly uses information about students; refrains from unprofessional comments. Avoids exploiting the professional relationship with any student. Deals justly and considerately with each student.

F. *Seeks to improve the profession.* Participates in professional organizations. Prepares plan for improvement of the profession to be implemented during first year of teaching.

Figure 10.8
In-class Teacher Evaluation Form

BASED ON RESEARCH

Begins instruction promptly	———	———	Starts unevenly/ interruptions evident
Provides orientation to lesson	———	———	Does not use advanced organizers
Addresses material in orderly manner	———	———	Materials do not appear sequenced
Maintains academic focus	———	———	Sidetracks to unrelated subjects
Conducts ending review	———	———	Does not summarize lesson
Modulates speech in class	———	———	Uses monotone or constant pitch
Shows enthusiasm verbal/ nonverbal	———	———	Appears bored or uses sarcasm
Emphasizes important items	———	———	Does not differentiate material for student
Asks directional questions	———	———	Uses multiple questions as if one
Gives corrective feedback to students	———	———	Ignores or responds harshly to student ideas
Provides praise when appropriate	———	———	Avoids or overuses praise in instruction
Uses correct grammar/ spelling	———	———	Makes frequent academic errors
Assigns and corrects homework	———	———	Provides inadequate homework feedback
Maintains discipline and order	———	———	Unable to stop misconduct/establish order
Displays evidence of creativity	———	———	Little sign of teacher personality/creativity

---

Teacher observed	Date observed	Observer signature

If the supervisor were to construct such an evaluation instrument solely from the research on teacher effectiveness reviewed earlier in this chapter, it might look like Figure 10.8. Again, the instrument of evaluation can be justified only by the curriculum and its overall intent.

Curriculum Intent

Another important concept in classroom evaluation is the intent of the curriculum, which is quite distinctive from the organization or structure of the curriculum. What do we really want to happen to the student because he has experienced this instruction? This question guides the teacher's behavior and must be built into the evaluation of that teacher's performance.

Included in this consideration are such things as the organization of the classroom, the teaching style employed, and the balance between cognitive and affective emphasis. While most classrooms are square or rectangular spaces, concerns such as the arrangement of furniture and the type of objects in the room communicate to the student a message about learning. Even the way a student is allowed to move is dictated by classroom arrangement.

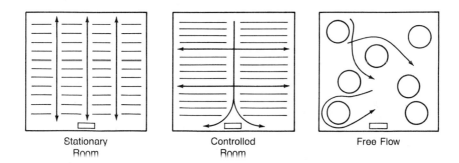

| Stationary Room | Controlled Room | Free Flow |

The actual teaching style employed by the teacher should correspond to the objectives of the curriculum. Theatrics are not needed in teaching algebraic formula, but may be helpful in showing how civil rights legislation works in a social studies class. Some of the nonverbal categories that contribute to teaching affect and style are listed below:

| Kinesics: use of body actions | Proxemics: use of space or distance | Haptics: use of touching behaviors | Oculesics: use of eye movement | Vocalics: use of voice | Environmental factors: use of the physical environment |

As the teacher understands the intent of the planned curriculum, he or she can adjust the emphasis of teaching behaviors to meet the expectations for student outcomes.

Staff Improvement

A third major idea for evaluation in the classroom is that the act of evaluation and accompanying staff development efforts are directed toward an improved instructional program for students. As the teacher understands and relates to the curriculum and its intent, evaluation can begin to be perceived as a fine-tuning of the delivery mechanism rather than a judgment of the teacher's worth.

While we have directed most comments about the role of staff development to the treatment in chapter eight, we think it is useful to introduce an evluation model that borrows heavily from management-by-objectives procedures found in business. This model involves teachers and rests on the assumption that to be rational, goals must be understand by all involved in the supervision process. Unlike the traditional "deficiency" model of evaluation so commonly found in schools, this model seeks to build the teacher into the evaluation process and, hopefully, clarifies the role of staff development in the process.

The Alternative Supervision Model consists of six major steps that lead to the activation of a supportive system of instructional assessment:

1. During released time within the school day, staff members collectively identify key performance/problem areas in instruction according to the goals of the system in which they work. These areas are then ranked by the staff as to importance. Supervisors might use a "ranking" device to identify the "key" areas.
2. Staff members collectively describe behaviors that, as a composite, indicate the optimal (desired) performance or solution in each area from item 1. The descriptions, as a whole, form an exemplary instructional profile. This profile is disseminated to all persons affected by the supervisory process.
3. At an agreed upon time, the supervisor observes the instructional performance of the classroom teacher to record and assess the current condition of instruction in each of the teacher-determined areas from item 1. The observation period is followed by a conference between the supervisor and teacher during which an agreement is reached concerning present "realities" in each area and the method of observation. The product of the conference is a shared perception of "what is" by both teacher and supervisor.

4. Viewing the instructional pattern of the classroom teacher as a totality, the supervisor and teacher conduct a "discrepancy analysis" to identify those areas where performance deviates most from desired conditions. At this point, the behaviors that mediate between the actual and desired state in "priority" categories are identified. Accuracy of both teacher per- formance *and* observer viewing are discussed.

5. In the "priority" areas the teacher, with the assistance of the supervisor, sets improvement goals. The supervisor sets ob- servational goals at the same time. These goals describe an- ticipated changes in behavior on the part of the teacher and the supervisor, the evidence that will be accepted as proof of improvement by both, and a time by which the desired changes will occur.

6. On the date identified in item 5, the supervisor returns to the classroom to observe and "validate" the progress of instruc- tional improvement and observation. At this time, also, new improvement goals are set (Figure 10.9). By this means, class- room instruction and observational technique are continually being upgraded toward the ideal profile with emphasis directed toward eradication of the greatest deficiencies.

The supervision-by-objectives model has any number of distinct advantages over the predominant pattern of supervision found in most

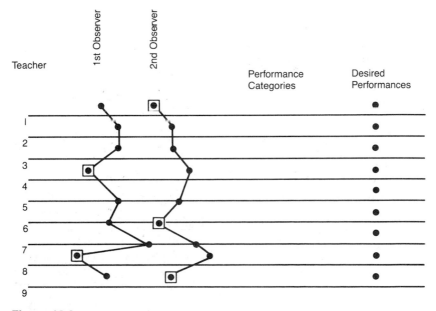

Figure 10.9
Supervision-by-Objectives

school districts. Primary among these advantages is that the model constrains the supervision process toward the improvement of classroom instruction by focusing on jointly agreed upon performances rather than intangibles. Not only does this method give the supervisor and teacher a common language for discussions, but it also allows for communication outlets in case of superordinate-subordinate role impediments.

The model is also advantageous because it directly involves the supervisor *and* teacher in defining and monitoring the growth of each. Such an internal, normative change strategy should significantly lower the threat level normally associated with supervision.

For the supervisor, the method can be a manager of time and resources, and a useful device for identifying common staff points of insecurity and development needs. The process is continuous and therefore should be relatively nondisruptive in nature. Where fully implemented, the model could stimulate the sharing of expertise among system teachers and supervisors in a self-reinforcing manner.

The supervision-by-objectives model is most appropriate for supervisory activity in rapidly changing instructional environments. Beyond assisting teachers who are struggling to master new techniques and educational approaches, the model has potential as a communication device with utility in the classroom with students. At the district level, the supervision-by-objectives model may prove useful for a superintendent working with building principals who have different needs and concerns.

To be effective during instructional improvement, supervision must promote both trust and clear communication about directional progress. The supervision-by-objectives model offers an objective, fair, and productive means of assisting instructional improvement. That, in turn, means an improved program of education for students.

NEW DIRECTIONS

Research on evaluating for teacher effectiveness has resulted in more questions than answers. While there are those who profess that teacher evaluation is a science, the evidence suggests that such evaluation is more an art than a science. A tragedy of wasted hours using instruments that were not valid and observers who were not reliable characterized teacher evaluation in the decade of the 1980s. This is particularly true in states with mandated use of state instruments.

The evaluation process remains ambiguous, as evidenced by a review of the literature where one finds authors' diverse perspectives on a variety of issues.[13]

Questions from the 1970s and 1980s still remain. Should evaluation be used to determine merit pay and tenure? How is evaluation tied to further staff development and training? Should evaluation focus on teaching competencies or on student achievement? How should student achievement be defined or measured? What factors beyond school contribute to student achievement or lack of it? Who judges the evaluator's ability to evaluate? Who should be involved in the evaluation process? Should students and parents be involved? Finally, who are evaluations supposed to help—teachers, students, administrators, or the courts?

Other issues remain, such as when and how the evaluation process should take place and how to handle bias.

It appears that evaluating for effectiveness, for both teachers and programs, will not go away. There is no substitute for leadership in evaluation and the modern supervisor must be involved in the process of evaluation each step of the way.

SUMMARY

Evaluation is one area of school performance where supervisors can demonstrate leadership through knowledge and competence. In school settings, evaluation is the primary means by which learning experiences for students are upgraded. Four areas of evaluation—programs, processes, products, and personnel—dominate most of the evaluative activities of supervisors. To be effective in the evaluation role, supervisors must organize these activities into an approach that is consistent and known to others.

The role of research in evaluation is puzzling to many new supervisors. Research, unlike evaluation, helps identify those meaningful relationships in teaching and learning that can be generalized to most situations. Establishing such key principles is not easy in education due to the many variables, and current research on teaching effectiveness has been badly overextended in the professional literature. At this time, such research can only suggest instructional patterns that seem to work with certain types of learners.

Supervisors should be particularly knowledgeable about testing because such instruments are regularly used in many districts to define instruction. Certain standardized intelligence and achievement tests are almost universal in schools today.

Supervisors are encouraged to think of evaluation at the school level as a cycle tied to curriculum development. Questions that relate certain planning variables to that curriculum are provided for the reader to study.

In the classroom, the supervisor should strive to help the teacher see instruction as an extension of curriculum planning, to understand the thrust or intent of the curriculum being taught, and to begin to see evaluation and staff development as methods of improving the curriculum as it is delivered to students. A six-step supervision-by-objectives model that eliminates the "deficiency orientation" of much classroom evaluation is presented for the reader's study.

NOTES

1. Daniel Stufflebeam, "Toward A Science of Educational Evaluation," *Educational Technology*, (June, 1968), p. 33.

2. Lee Dembart, "Researchers: Evidence Implies Biology, Math Linked," *Los Angeles Times*, 15 Jan., 1984, p. 11-A.

3. Barak Rosenshine in *Research in Teacher Education: A Symposium* (Englewood Cliffs, NJ: Prentice-Hall 1969), pp. 43–51.

4. Barak Rosenshine, "Recent Research on Teaching Behaviors and Student Achievement," *Journal of Teacher Education*, 27 (Spring 1976), p. 61.

5. Jere Brophy, as reported in Gary Borich, *The Appraisal of Teaching* (Reading: Addison-Wesley, 1977), pp. 79–89.

6. Frederick MacDonald, "The Effects of Teacher Performance on Pupil Learning," *BTES Phase II* (Princeton, NJ: Educational Testing Service, 1975), pp. 368–69.

7. David Berliner, "Impediments to the Study of Teacher Effectiveness Research," *Journal of Teacher Education* 27 (Spring 1976), pp. 5–6.

8. Meredith K. Stone, "Correlates of Teacher and Student Style," in *BTES Phase II 1973–74* (Princeton, NJ: Educational Testing Service, 1976), p. 13.

9. Robert Soar, *Follow-Through Classroom Process Measurement.* (Gainesville: University of Florida, 1971), p. 10.

10. N.L. Gage, *The Scientific Basis of the Art of Teaching*, (New York: Teachers College Press, 1977), pp. 15–18.

11. Association for Supervision and Curriculum Development, 1985.

12. John J. Kennedy and Andrew J. Bush, "Overcoming Some Impediments to the Study of Teacher Effectiveness," *Journal of Teacher Education* 27 (Spring 1976), p. 16.

13. Sarah Stanley and James Popham, *Teacher Evaluation: Six Prescriptions For Success* (Washington, DC: Association of Supervision and Curriculum Development, 1988).

SUGGESTED LEARNING ACTIVITIES

1. Assume a teacher has asked you why you must come into her classroom to evaluate performance and why so many days are wasted on inservice activities. What is your response?

2. Explain why inconclusive primary research on teacher effectiveness has become so prescriptive in the 1990s.

3. What are some ways that a supervisor might get teachers more interested in research at the classroom level?

4. In Figure 10.3 a wide range of conditions are shown for schools in one school district. Should the supervisor be concerned about this? Why?
5. How can the supervisor gain control over the misuse of testing in defining the school curriculum?
6. Describe strategies for getting teachers to see evaluation as a way of improving instructional opportunities for students.

BOOKS TO REVIEW

Archbald, Doug and Newmann, Fred. *Beyond Standardized Testing*. Reston, VA: NASSP, 1988.

Chiarelott, Leigh, Davidson, Leonard, and Ryan, Kevin. *Lenses on Teaching*. Philadelphia: Holt, Rinehart and Winston, Inc., 1990.

Corey, Stephen. *Action Research to Improve School Practices*. New York: Teachers College Press, 1983.

Eggen, Paul and Kauchak, Donald. *Strategies for Teachers*. Englewood Cliffs, NJ: Prentice-Hall, 1988.

Elbrow, Peter. *Embracing Contraries: Explorations In Learning And Thinking*. New York: Oxford University Press, 1986.

Goodlad, John. *A Place Called School*. New York: McGraw-Hill, 1984.

Jackson, Philip. *Contributing To Educational Change: Perspectives On Research And Practice*. Berkeley, CA: McCutchan Publishing, 1988.

Stanley, Sarah and Popham, James. *Teacher Evaluation: Six Prescriptions For Success*, Alexandria, VA: Association of Supervision and Curriculum Development, 1988.

CHAPTER 11

Politics in Supervision

INTRODUCTION

In this book we have identified the primary purpose of educational supervision as the improvement of instructional experiences for students in school. It has been suggested that there are many leadership roles that might be utilized by a supervisor to be effective, and that *where* supervision is practiced sometimes determines the choice of that role. In this chapter we will focus on the school environment — an environment that is increasingly political in nature — and help the reader in assessing this important variable in supervision. It is believed that such an understanding is critical to successful leadership in the 1990s.

When we use the term *political environment* we mean a setting that is influenced by forces. The more foces acting to influence a school and its operation, the more political that setting. In the 1980s many school settings were highly political and this atmosphere had the effect of distorting normal supervisory activity.

It is competition that is making schools political — competition for control of schools, competition for scarce resources, competition for the primacy of values in the school setting. While the nature of political activity in schools is not new, the degree of influence has been greatly accelerated by changing societal conditions.

Battles for control of schools are everywhere. Professional educators fight among themselves to determine the nature of the curriculum (classic versus individualized). Management is pitted against labor to determine the control of student instruction. Educators fight the public in the courts, in elections, and in the legislatures for the definition of education and its purpose. Often the issues of confrontation are far removed from the real issues at stake.

Conflicts, too, over resources have been accelerated by the crises of school funding in the 1990s. Many districts have experienced drastic curtailment of revenue resulting in struggles for survival among areas of study. The "back to the basics" movement of the 1980s was essentially an economic issue since returning to a minimal school program is a direct way to provide tax relief.

The struggles over values have been increasingly evident. Sometimes a single issue polarizes a community—community schools, sex education, humanism, or evolutionary approaches to biology are examples. Because schools are "normative" by nature, it can be expected that values confrontations will continue to occur in schools.

The upshot of this aggressive competition in schools is the rise of political behaviors that detract from the overall effort of professionals to educate students. If educators and the public situate themselves in opposing camps or align with special interest groups trying to dominate the control, resources, or values in schools, the historic method of operating schools is alarmingly disrupted. Through the years public schools have operated within a consensus opinion to provide a general education for all students. The introduction of political activity on the scale seen in the 1990s demands that the supervisor understand this new phenomenon if he or she is to function effectively in improving school programs.

SEEING THE SCHOOL ENVIRONMENT

Recent educational literature dealing with political activity in schools provides a wealth of information about the subject.[1] These resources offer "ways of seeing" that begin to connect the nature of the environment with the behaviors of the supervisor who must practice within that setting. Three such "handles" for understanding are power configurations in organizations, the various groups of players in the organization, and the use of budgeting as an instrument of influence in schools.

Earlier in this text educational organizations were described as "flat" because they contain so few layers of bureaucracy. While the organization of school districts is remarkably similar throughout the United States, the power structure within such organizations is usually quite dissimilar. In Table 11.1 Kimbrough[2] identifies four stereotypic power configurations found in organizations. The primary difference between the four types outlined by Kimbrough is the degree of stability found in the operation. If there is a single chain or pyramid of power leading to the superintendent, for instance, communication and issue resolution will be predictable. If, by contrast, there is considerable competition for "being in charge," then the pattern of communication and issue resolution is less predictable.

It is vital that the supervisor look beyond the simple organization

Table 11.1
Types of Power Structures

Monopolistic Elite	Multigroup Noncompetitive
1. Single pyramid of pervasive power 2. Issues contained, 80-100% overlap 3. Communication up and down within group	1. Two or more pyramids which share power 2. Minor issue competition, 70-80% overlap 3. Communication to guarantee consensus
Competitive Elite	**Segmented Pluralism**
1. Two or more pyramids in competition for power 2. Major competition on issues, 50% or less overlap 3. Communication with satellites, little with competitors	1. No stable pyramids of power 2. Issues determine power arrangements, no overlap 3. Little communication, function of issue

chart for the school district to determine how power is really distributed within the organization. If the status leaders are also the real leaders, politics will be minimal and the supervisor can trust the official map of how things happen. If, however, the supervisor detects multiple sources of power and organization that are highly competitive, there may be nonconventional ways of getting things done in the district.

Because American education is essentially local-controlled, there are always many players in the school environment. Some, however, are more important than others from the perspective of a supervisor trying to improve instruction. Among those groups demanding the most attention by the supervisor are members of the board of education, central office personnel, key community groups, and various teacher organizations. Each of these groups interacts with supervisors in value-laden and potentially competitive areas of operation.

School board members, despite eloquent expressions of a desire to serve all citizens, are typically representative of certain social, economic, or political groups. The supervisor can best think of an individual board member as part of a political interest group that sought election for some purpose. Time is well spent reviewing the voting records and board meeting minutes to see what issues were important to individual members. It is also instructive to watch board members during meetings to find clues of power alignments. Who gets along with whom? Does the board member ever intervene on behalf of individuals, specific schools, or instructional issues?

Another key group to know well is the central office staff, where the supervisor most often is a member. In stable school districts with little distortion in communication and decision making, personal loyalty will be directed upward from subordinate to superordinate. If political conditions have produced coalitions or competing power groups, however, administration will be more situational than predictable and loyalty will be to issues, not offices.

A third important group of players to know is the various community groups that interact with the schools including parents, students, and organized interest groups. In particular, the recently formed political action committees (PACs) bear watching because these groups now regularly attempt to influence instructional decision making. Ranging from ultraconservative to reactionary, these groups use organization and money to influence schools. Figure 11.1 lists some of those organizations now active in American education.

The extent to which these community groups will want to intervene in educational decision making will shock some new supervisors. Since each group represents a set of values that they wish to defend or insert into the curriculum, and since there are so many special interest groups today, almost any topic is a possible source of confrontation. In one list of "hot" topics, a group of the fundamental right attacks a broad range of school subjects (Figure 11.2).

A final key group for the supervisor to know well is the various teacher groups that now represent the instructional force. Nationally, approximately 2.5 million teachers belong to an organized union and these professional organizations are vitally involved in instructional decision making as the result of negotiated contracts. Teacher empowerment has resulted in increased stakes.

Modern supervisors must be thoroughly knowledgeable about the collective bargaining process and the terms of their local contracts. Such a contract spells out in legal language just what rights management and labor possess, as well as the exact procedures to resolve any source of conflict or disagreement. In the 1960s when such unions were gaining strength, most of the contracts dealt with extrinsic rewards such as salary and working conditions. In the 1990s, by contrast, contracts are quite specific about teacher involvement in curriculum development and inservice design. Obviously, the supervisor as a representative of management who goes into the schools to work with teachers must know the rights and limitations of the local contract. Figure 11.3 outlines the subtle changes during the past twenty-five years, while Figure 11.4 lists some of the items now negotiated that affect instructional improvement.

A last major variable that will help the supervisor to see the environment in which he or she practices is the budget and how

Figure 11.1

NEW RIGHT GROUPS (a partial listing)

Today's New Right is a combination of the old right-wing establishment and many more newly organized groups, ranging in Ideology from ultraconservative to reactionary. Most of the groups have common ties (mailing lists, advisors, members of coalitions, and the like) while others may have only common Ideology. The following listing of New Right (NR) groups includes research organizations, political action committees, "think tanks," lobbying groups, action organizers, and fund raisers.

AAUCG—Americans Against Union Control of Government

ACU—American Conservative Union

AF—America's Future

ALEC—American Legislative Exchange Council

AAOBS—American Opinion Book Stores (John Birch Society front organization)

AOSB—American Opinion Speakers Bureau (JBS front)

CAVE—Citizens for Another Voice in Education

CEAFU—Concerned Educators Against Forced Unionism

CES—Committee for Economic Strength

CFTR—Citizens for the Republic

CLYF—Conservative Leadership Youth Fund

CSFC—Committee for the Survival of a Free Congress

CUE—Council for a Union-Free Environment

CURE—Citizens United for Responsible Education

CV—Christian Voice

CVF—Conservative Victory Fund

EF—Eagle Forum (Phyllis Schlafly's group)

ERA—Education Research Analysts

FCM—Fund for a Conservative Majority

GOA—Gun Owners of America (originally anti-gun control, now supports general NR candidates)

GOLD DUSTERS—"Gold Dust Twins" (Jay Van Andel and Richard DeVos of AMWAY Corporation, a door-to-door sales organization)

HF—Heritage Foundation (founded by Joe Coors of Coors Beer)

ICEPS—International Center for Economic Policy Studies

ICR—Institute for Creation Research

IEA—Institute for Educational Affairs

ILS—Institute for Labor Studies

JBS—John Birch Society

KG—Kingston Group (strategy group which includes: ACU, ALEC, CFTR, CSFC, CV, CVF, NAM, NCPAC, and TCC)

KKK—Ku Klux Klan

LIRE—Lincoln Institute for Research and Education

LITE—Let's Improve Today's Education

LL—Liberty Lobby

MM—Moral Majority

MOTOREDE—Movement to Restore Decency (JBS front)

NAPE—National Association of Professional Educators

NAM—National Association of Manufacturers

NCAC—National Christian Action Coalition

NCEE—National Congress for Educational Excellence

NCPAC—National Conservative Political Action Committee or National Conservative Public Affairs Council (both have same mailing address)

NPLW—Network of Patriotic Letter Writers

NRTWC—National Right to Work Committee

NSCEE—National Schools Committee for Economic Education

NTU—National Taxpayers Union

PSRC—Public Service Research Council

PWC—People Who Care

RAVCO—Richard A. Viguerie Co. (computerized NR mailing lists)

RR—Religious Roundtable

STOP-ERA—Phyllis Schlafly's anti-Equal Rights Amendment organization

TCC—The Conservative Caucus

TRIM—Tax Reform Immediately (JBS front)

YAF—Young Americans for Freedom

YNT—Youth Needs Truth (JBS front)

YPA—Young Parents Alert

Figure 11.2
Objectionable Educational Terminology Identified by One Fundamentalist Group

Academic Freedom
Acceptance
Accountability
Achievement Motivation Program
Active Listening
Actualization
Adlerian Therapy
Affective Domain
Affective Teaching
Agents of Change
Alternative Behaviors
Alternative Economic Systems
Alternative Lifestyles
Analysis
Anthropology
Armenianism
Attitude
Attitudinal Behavior
Awareness
Behavior
Behavior Modification
Behavioral Objectives
Behavioral Outcomes
Behaviorism
Beliefs, Deeply held
Black Studies
Body Language

Capping Off
Careers Education
Carnegie Foundation
Center For War:Peace Studies
Change Agent
Child-Centered Learning
Child Development
Choosing Freely
Citizenship
Client-Centered Therapy
Clinician
Common Good, For the
Communicating
Communication Skills
Community Education
Community Schools
Computerized Instruction
Conditioning
Conflict
Confluent Education
Conjoint Therapy
Consciousness
Consensus
Coping
Counseling, Group
Creative Expression
Creative Life Management

Creative Listening
Creative Thinking
Creative Writing
Creativism
Criticism
Culturally Deprived
Decision Making
Deeply Held Beliefs
Democracy
Democracy, Participatory
Diagnostic Approach
Diagnostic Clinician
Disconnectedness
Discovery Method
Discussion Groups
Domain Affective
Drug Education
Emotional Growth
Emotions
Encounter Groups
Enlightenment
Esalen Institute
Ethics
Ethnic
Eupsychian Network
Experimental Program
Expression, Nonverbal

Fabianism
Facilitator
Family Life Education
Feedback Mechanism
Feelings
Foundations:
  Carnegie
  Ford
  Kettering
  Mott
  Rockefeller
Ford Foundation
Free Schools
Gaming Techniques
  (e.g. Mood Masks, Amnesia,
  Chairs, One-Way Glasses, Dear
  Granny Letters)
Gestalt Therapy
Global Community
Global Economy
Global Man
Global Perspective
Global Resources
Good of the People, For the
Group Consensus
Group Counseling
Group Criticism

Group Discussion
Group Dynamics
Group Facilitator
Growth, Human
Growth, Self
Hawaii
Hawaii Master Plan
Helping Relationships
Human Development
Human Dynamics
Human Growth
Human Potential
Human Relations
Human Resources
Human Sexuality
Human Themes
Humanism
Humanistic
Humanities
Humanized Learning
IALAC (I Am Loveable and Capable)
Identity
Illuminati
I-Message
Individualized Instruction
Inductive Method

Innovative Program
Inquiry Method
Inservice Training (for Teachers,
  Administrators, etc.)
Interact
Interaction
Interdependence
Internalization
Interpersonal Relations
Journals (Private or Surveillance)
Kettering Foundation
Laboratory Method
Learning Clinician
Learning How to Learn
Learning through Inquiry
Learning to Learn
Listening Skills
Magic Circle
Mastery Skills
Measurable Objectives
Measurable Outcomes
Mental Health
Messianic
Middle Schools
Modular Scheduling

Figure 11.2
(Continued)

326

Moral-Free Teaching
Morals, Teaching without
Mott Foundation
Multicultural Studies
Multiethnic Studies

NEA Peace Studies
Nihilism
Non-Directive Therapy
Non-Traditional Roles
Non-Verbal Expression

Objectives, Measurable
Occult
Open Classroom
Open Concept Classroom
Open Design Classroom
Operant Conditioning

Parent Effectiveness Training (PET)
Parenting
Peace Studies (NEA)
Performance Budgeting
Planning, Programming & Budgeting
    System (PPBS)
PPBS (Planning, Programming &
    Budgeting System)
Prescriptive Teaching
Preventive Mental Health
Private Journals

Problem-Solving
Programmed Instruction
Progressive Education
Psychometrist
Psycho-Drama
Psycho-Politics
Psycho-Therapy

Questing

Racism
Reality Therapy
Receiving
Reinforcing
Relativism, Scientific
Relevant Curriculum
Risk-Taking
Responding
Rockefeller Foundation
Role-Playing
Roles, Non-Traditional

School Health Education Studies
    (SHES)
Schools Without Failure
Schools Without Walls
Scientific Relativism
Secular
Secular Humanism
Self-Acceptance

Self-Actualization
Self-Adjustment
Self-Analysis
Self-Awareness
Self-Concept
Self-Criticism
Self-Evaluation
Self-Examination
Self-Growth
Self-Help
Self-Hood
Self-Identify
Self-Image
Self-Judgment
Self-Morality
Self-Understanding
Sensory
Sex Education
Sex Information in Education
    (SIECUS)
Sharing
SHES (School Health Education
    Studies)
SIECUS (Sex Information in
    Education)
Situation Ethics
Social Development
Social Growth

Social Interaction
Social Problems
Social Values
Socio-Drama
Socio-Grams
Stereotyping, Sex
Street Schools
Surveillance Journals
Synthesizing

T-Group
Taxonomy
Teacher Effectiveness Training (TET)
Therapy, Adlerian
    Client-Centered
    Conjoint
    Gestalt
    Non-Directive
    Reality

Third-Force Psychology
Three-Tier Curriculum
Transactional Analysis
TA for Tots
TA for Kids
TA for Teens
Transfer Leadership
Trust

Understanding
Utopianism

Values
Values Clarification
Values Continuum
Values, Social
Valuing

Weltanschauung (World View)
Western Behavior Sciences Institute
Will of the People
Witch Craft
Whole Child Development
World Goodwill
World Overview
World View

Source: Reported in the Newsletter of the Center for Democratic Action as compiled in *The School Bell*, a publication of the John Birch Society. Dallas, TX, Fall, 1982.

Figure 11.3
Changes in Management/Labor Relations in Schools 1965–1990

1965	1990
1. Board could act unilaterally without consultation with its employees.	1. Consultation with employees required under the good faith assumption.
2. Mutuality of interests and interdependency assumed.	2. Mutuality of interests and interdependency, plus divergency of interests and needs, are assumed.
3. Grievances and other personnel matters sometimes overlooked.	3. Grievances and other personnel concerns are considered important, and provisions are made in writing to handle them.
4. Much taken for granted.	4. Nothing taken for granted.
5. A day's work in teaching often puzzling to determine.	5. A day's work in teaching and responsibilities specifically defined.
6. One-way communications.	6. Two-way communications
7. Narrow sphere of bargaining, often confined to economic matters only.	7. Parties may elect to bargain on a broad scale.
8. Superintendent represented teachers to the board and the board to teachers.	8. Both parties represented by expert representatives of their own choosing.
9. Board always had last word.	9. Impasse procedures provided; neither party can be allowed to paralyze the bargaining process.
10. Courts finally resolved disputes; losers paid costs.	10. Third parties called in to intervene in resolution of disputes; costs shared equally.
11. Good faith not mandated.	11. Good faith bargaining mandated and assured legislatively and by written agreement.
12. Written personnel policies lacking specificity.	12. Written agreements set terms and conditions of personnel administration
13. Divergencies between policy and practice often left unexplained.	13. Constant dialogue permits discussion of divergencies of policy to practice.

Figure 11.4
Possible Items Open to Negotiations

Salary schedule	Terminal leave pay
Various benefits	Teacher transfer policy
Class size	Teacher involvement in textbook selection
Committee work	Teacher participation in budget development
compensation	Procedures for handling discipline problems
Summer school salary	Participating in teacher evaluation
Duty-free lunch	Procedures for attending professional
Paraprofessional help	meetings
Leave policies	Professional work days
School holidays	Attendance of teacher at scheduled staff
	development

money is handled within the district. As Aaron Wildavsky has observed:

> Human nature is never more evident than when people are struggling to gain a larger share of funds or to apportion what they have among myriad elements. . . . If politics is regarded in part as conflict over whose preferences will prevail in the determination of policy, the budget records the outcome of the struggle.[3]

As a rule of thumb, approximately 5 percent of any local school's budget is uncommitted and therefore discretionary. The supervisor can learn a great deal about what real priorities are simply by identifying how those extra funds are distributed among the many possible causes.

The organization of fiscal matters in a district is also a key to the distribution of power and the relative stability or instability of the total organization. Are budgets developed "top-down" from the superintendent's office or is the budget development process a grass roots phenomenon? Key terms such as *incremental approach* or *PPBS* (program planning and budgeting system) tell you that the budget is highly structured. Other terms like *lump sum* or *a zero based budget* tell you that the budget is not centralized and therefore control does not really exist in this important area.

Looking at power structure alignments, community groups, and the way the budget is handled in the district will provide the supervisor with invaluable information about how the environment may affect his or her behavior in improving school programs. Two critical pieces of information to be gained this way are: 1) determining whether this is a stable or unstable organization and 2) determining the nature of boundaries within the organization.

In stable environments, the supervisor will find that the various players normally act as representatives of their particular groups or roles rather than as independent individuals. For example, a department chairman in a high school will defend his department according to the expected role. In a stable organization, such predictable behavior will reward all players because loyalty is the key value. Conflict will be minimal and the ways of settling differences will be established.

Supervisors who practice in a stable school district will do best for themselves and the students by going along with the established groups, power structure, and budgetary rules. Ultimately, the supervisor and the programs he or she advocates will be rewarded by loyalty and team playing. To challenge a stable organization on an issue is to risk being excluded from decision making and resources.

If, however, it appears that the school district is unstable, the supervisor must prepare to become politically involved to promote better school programs. In unstable environments, trading is the name of the game. Supervisors must participate to gain their fair share of resources and must also be prepared for shifting coalitions of players according to specific issues or needs. Above all, in an unstable school district, the supervisor cannot count on using title or borrowing power from the status leaders, but must instead figure out who has the power and how things really get done.

A second concept that is important to the supervisor operating in a less-than-stable organization is that of *boundary*. Boundary tells the supervisor where he or she can and can't operate safely in the district and how to proceed when advocating a specific change. Several questions can help establish the supervision boundaries on the job. First, ask yourself how many resources are guaranteed to you for your work because of your position. Second, in making decisions, how often do you need to check with someone else before proceeding. Finally, ask yourself what the chances are that someone (a superior, a board member) can reach in and overturn your actions or decisions. Boundary, then, is a measure of your autonomy to act as a supervisor to improve instruction. In stable organizations, boundary is reflected by organizational charts and job descriptions. In an unstable school district, boundaries are established by experience.

PROMOTING CHANGE DURING INSTABILITY

Throughout this chapter we have alluded to the many school districts that are presently unstable in their make-up and operation. This condition results from a number of factors: fiscal stress, labor relations, legal accountability, political pressure, and work overload. In too many districts the supervisor will find himself or herself underfunded, outmanned, hemmed in by external expectations and requirements, and possibly at the center of a stressful management-labor relationship. Yet, the tasks of supervision must be accomplished; instruction must be constantly upgraded and improved for students.

It is important, therefore, that the school supervisor understand the nature of change in an unstable environment. During the 1960s, change in schools came about because of planning and the application of resources. In the 1990s, change can only occur if it is carefully planned and understood. The simple application of resources will not guarantee planned change if the system being targeted is distorted by political factors. There are certain general understandings about the change process that each supervisor should be familiar with and incorporate into his or her thinking regarding instructional improvement.

One of the most fundamental lessons about change in schools is that it occurs in stages and that different members of the organization will participate in different stages. A change effort, particularly in instruction, is never an all-or-nothing venture and suggests a strategy for working with others. Figure 11.5 presents a classic illustration of those affected by any change proposal. The supervisor should focus his or her energies on those individuals who, for whatever reason, want to change. In stable or unstable organizations there are always innovators who want to be creative and will support changes. Others, the early adopters and the early majority will support change as it benefits their needs. In an unstable environment, it will pay the supervisor to know what those needs are through observation and study.

A first lesson here is that the supervisor should never invest significant energy or resources in persons who are not ready to change. To bring about change, there is a tipping point for adoption and once that point is reached the momentum will carry the change over the top. The tipping point is achieved by building a working majority.

A second lesson is that the best way to overcome a "show me" stance by disbelievers is to do so. Whenever possible, the use of demonstration or pilot programs is preferable to discussion, pronouncements, or pleas. This strategy is especially useful in a highly unstable

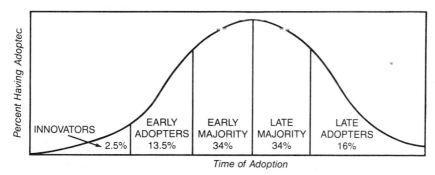

Figure 11.5
Adoption Curve of Planned Change

Source: Reprinted by permission from *Adoption of New Ideas and Practices* by Herbert F. Lionberger © 1961 by The Iowa State University Press, Ames, Iowa, 50010.

school district because in such an environment there is a constant search for stability and success.

A third lesson is that unless the supervisor can get those who are responsible for implementing a change to really "own" it, the change will not be lasting. In an unstable district, the true concern will be what has to be given up to achieve change rather than an elaborate rationale to justify a certain decision.

A fourth lesson is that change in schools occurs in natural patterns over time. Institutions go through evolutionary patterns of growth, stability, and decline. At a certain stage of decline there is an institutional need for temporary reform and change. Supervisors must feel the cyclical nature of this change and introduce ideas when the time is most appropriate.

A fifth lesson is that there really is not too much original change in education. There is, however, a lot of borrowing. Supervisors strive to improve instructional programs and to recognize that most of the ideas are already in practice somewhere.

A sixth lesson is that time constraints and resource shortages are definitely related to people's willingness to try something new. If the supervisor is practicing in an unstable environment where crises are the operational reality and shortages force competition at every turn, it will be natural not to change unless such change can guarantee an improved condition.

A seventh and final lesson is that change under fear or threat resembles an inverted U. A medium level threat will promote somewhat conservative tendencies among the target population, while extreme fear or threat will cause unpredictable responses to proposals for change.

As the supervisor studies the change process in a specific environment, he or she will begin to build theories about how to overcome a resistance to change—change needed to improve instruction. Goodwin Watson, an early student of the change process in schools, provides the following observations about resistance to planned change:

1. Resistance will be less if administrators, teachers, board members, and community leaders feel that the project is their own—not one devised and operated by outsiders.
2. Resistance will be less if the project clearly has wholehearted support from top officials of the system.
3. Resistance will be less if participants see the change as reducing rather than increasing their present burdens.
4. Resistance will be less if the project accords with values and ideals that have long been acknowledged by participants.
5. Resistance will be less if the program offers the kind of new experience that interests participants.
6. Resistance will be less if participants feel that their autonomy and their security are not threatened.

7. Resistance will be less if participants have joined in diagnostic efforts leading them to agree on the basic problem and to feel its importance.
8. Resistance will be less if the project is adopted by consensual group decision.
9. Resistance will be reduced if proponents are able to empathize with opponents to recognize valid objections, and take steps to relieve unnecessary fears.
10. Resistance will be reduced if it is recognized that innovations are likely to be misunderstood and misinterpreted, and if provision is made for feedback of perceptions of the project and for further clarification as needed.
11. Resistance will be reduced if participants experience acceptance, support, trust, and confidence in their relations with one another.
12. Resistance will be reduced if the project is kept open to revision and reconsideration if experience indicates that changes would be desirable.
13. Readiness for change gradually becomes a characteristic of certain individuals, groups, organizations, and civilizations.[4]

Another way that the practicing supervisor might begin to focus on the change process is to analyze the probability that the proposed change will succeed. Jon Wiles, following a study of this question in a major research project, developed a chart (Table 11.2) that might serve as a beginning point of analysis. Also provided (Table 11.3) for the reader's study is a description of change in a middle school that incorporates the primary stages of change as an organizer.

By "typing" the organization being served, by identifying real boundaries for practice, and by thinking about how change might fit in the organization, the supervisor acknowledges and plans for the political dimension that exists, in some degree, in all school systems. This need to plan ahead is summarized as follows:

> . . . the role of leading or governing in the school is not fixed or stable in the traditional sense. Neither bureaucratic stipulation of authority (legal rules, delegated formal authority) nor descriptions of professional expertise will explain how leadership *actually* operates in the local school. Both formal authority and professional orientation provide some guidance concerning the management of a particular school, but neither describe the dynamics of governance. The leader's role is defined by the issue and the choice situation.[5]

LEGAL DIMENSIONS OF PRACTICE

One last force that strongly influences supervisory practice in the 1990s is the legal rights and responsibilities of school leaders. In particular, the liabilities of practice are an influential factor in modern

Table 11.2
Educational Innovation Probability

	High Risk →				→ Lower Risk
Source of Innovation	Superimposed from outside	Outside agent brought in	Developed internally with aid	External idea modified	Locally conceived, developed, implemented
Impact of Innovation	Challenges sacrosanct beliefs	Calls for major value shifts	Requires substantial change	Modifies existing values or programs	Does not substantially alter existing values, beliefs or programs
Official Support	Official leaders active opposition	Officials on record as opposing	Officials uncommitted	Officials voice support of change	Enthusiastically supported by the official leaders
Planning of Innovation	Completely external	Most planning external	Planning processes balanced	Most of planning done locally	All planning for change done on local site
Means of Adoption	By superiors	By local leaders	By Reps	By most of the clients	By group concensus
History of Change	History of failures	No accurate records on	Some success with innovation	A history of successful innovations	Known as school where things regularly succeed
Possibility of Revision	No turning back	Final evaluation before committee	Periodic evaluations	Possibility of abandoning at conclusion	Possible to abort the effort at any time

Role of Teachers	Largely bypassed	Minor role	Regular role in implementing	Heavy role in implementation	Primary actor in the classroom effort
Teacher Expectation	Fatalistic	Feel little chance	Are willing to give a try	Confident of success	Wildly enthusiastic about chance of success
Work Load Measure	Substantially increased	Heavier but rewarding	Slightly increased	Unchanged	Work load lessened by the innovation
Threat Measure	Definitely threatens some clients	Probably threatening to some	Mild threat resulting from the change	Very remote threat to some	Does not threaten the security or autonomy
Community Factor	Hostile to innovations	Suspicious and uninformed	Indifferent	Ready for a change	Wholeheartedly supports the school

Shade the response in each category that most accurately reflects the condition surrounding the implementation of the middle school. If the "profile" of your school is predominantly in the high risk side of the matrix, substantial work must be done to prepare your school for change.

Source: Jon Wiles, *Planning Guidelines for Middle School Education* (Dubuque, IA: Kendall-Hunt, 1976), p. 30.

Table 11.3
Outlining the Stages of Instructional Change

	Present Condition	Awareness Stage	Experimentation Stage	Adoption Stage	Desired Condition
	Stage 1	Stage 2	Stage 3	Stage 4	Stage 5
The School Philosophy	Either no formal statement or a written document on file in the school office.	School staff share beliefs, look for consensus, restate philosophy and objectives in terms of expected behavior.	Staff begins use of goals as guide to evaluating school practices. Begin to involve students and community in planning.	Philosophy and goals used to shape the program. Formal mechanism established to monitor program and decision making.	Philosophy a living document. Guides daily decisions. The program a tool for achieving desired educational ends.
			The Learning Environment		
Use of the Building	Only uniform instructional spaces. Little use of the building spaces for educational purposes.	Some deviation from traditional space utilization (classroom learning center). Possibly a complete demonstration class for bright ideas.	Limited building conversion (knock out walls). Begin to identify unused spaces. Planning for large learning spaces.	Development of a comprehensive plan for use of grounds and building. Total remodeling of spaces.	Talor-made learning environment—all spaces used to educate. Building facilitates the learning intention.
Use of Materials	Classrooms are dominated by a grade-level text. Library with a limited offering. Used as a study hall for large groups.	Use of multi-level texts within classroom. Materials selected after an analysis of student achievement levels. Suplemental resources made available to students.	Diverse materials developed for the students. Resource centers established. Cross-discipline selection of materials. More multi-media used. Some independent study.	Materials purchasing policies realigned. Common learning areas established as resource centers. More self-directed study built in.	Diversified materials. Something for each student. Integrated subject materials. Portable curriculum units (on carts). Heavy multi-media. Active learning centers.

Use of Community	Little or no access to school. Information about programs scanty. Trust low.	Some school program ties to community. Token access via PTA and media. School perceived as island in neighborhood.	Preliminary uses of community as learning environment. Identification of nearby resources. Use of building for community functions.	Regular interchange between school and community. Systematic communication. A network of services and resources established.	School programs outwardly oriented. Community seen as a teaching resource. Systematic ties with services and resources around school.

Instructional Organization

Staffing Patterns	Building teachers isolated in self-contained classrooms. Little or no lateral communication or planning present.	Limited sharing of resources. Some division of labor and small-scale cooperation in teaching. Informal communication about student progress.	Regular cooperative planning sessions. Some curricular integration via themes. Students rotate through subject areas. Problems of cooperation identified.	Interdepartmental organization. Use of common planning time. Administrative support such as in scheduling. Use of philosophy as curricular decision-making criteria.	Teaching staff a "team" working toward common ends. Staff patterns reflect instructional intentions. Administration in support of curricular design. Coursework integrated for students.

Table 11.3
(Continued)

	Present Condition	Awareness Stage	Experimentation Stage	Adoption Stage	Desired Condition
	Stage 1	Stage 2	Stage 3	Stage 4	Stage 5
			Instructional Organization *(Continued)*		
Teaching Strategy	Some variety but lecture and teacher-dominated Q-A session the norm. Homework used to promote day-to-day continuity.	Observation of other teaching models. Skill development via workshops. An identification of staff strengths and weaknesses. Some new patterns.	Building level experiments by willing staff members. "Modeling" of ideas. On-site consultant help made available for skill development.	School day divided according to the teaching strategy employed. Faculty evaluation of the effectiveness of new ways after a trial period.	Great variety of methods used in teaching, uses of media, dealing with students. The curricular plans determine strategy.
Staff Development	Staff development is global, rarely used to attack local needs and problems. Occurs as needed.	Staff identifies inservice needs and priorities. Philosophy assists in this process. Local staff skills and strengths are recognized.	Staff development realigned to serve needs of teachers. Opportunities for personal growth are made available.	Formal procedures for directing staff development to needs established. Staff development seen as problem-solving mechanism.	Staff development an on-going process using available resources. An attempt to close theory-practice gaps.

Administrative Conditions

Organization of Student	Uniform patterns. One teacher, 30 students in six rows of five in each row in each period of each school day.	Understanding that organization of students should match curricular intentions. Some initial variation of group sizes in classroom.	Limited organization to facilitate the grouping of the students. Begin use of aides and parents to increase organizational flexibility.	Full administrative support for a reorganization of students. Building restructed where necessary. An increase in planning for effectiveness.	Group sizes vary according to the activity planned. Full support given to eliminate any problem areas.
Report of Student Progress	"Progress" is defined narrowly. Letter grades or simple numerals represent student learning in the subject areas.	Recognition of broader growth goals for students. Use of philosophy to evaluate the existing practices.	Experimentation with supplemental reporting procedures. Involvement of student and parents in the process.	Development of a diverse and comprehensive reporting procedure for student progress.	Descriptive medium used to monitor individual student progress. Broadly focused evaluation. Team of teacher, student, and parents involved.
Rules and Regulations	High degree of regimentation. Many rules, most inherited over the years. The emphasis on the enforcement and on control. Staff and students identify essential rules. Regulations matched against the school philosophy.	Rules and regulations streamlined. Used as a teaching device about life outside of school. Increased student self-control.	Greater use of student and staff input into the regulation of the school environment. Rewards built-in for desirable performance.	Moving toward minimal regulation and an increased student self-control. Regulations a positive teaching devise.	

339

Table 11.3
(Continued)

	Present Condition	Awareness Stage	Experimentation Stage	Adoption Stage	Desired Condition
	Stage 1	Stage 2	Stage 3	Stage 4	Stage 5
Administrative Conditions *(Continued)*					
Discipline	Reactive pattern ranging from verbal admonishment to paddling and expulsion. Reoccurring offenders.	Staff analysis of school policies. Shift of emphasis to causes of the problems. Some brainstorming of possible solutions.	Establishment of a hierarchy of discipline activity. Begin implementing preventive strategies.	Design of curriculum programs to deter discipline problems. High intensity program for regular offenders.	Program of the school eliminates most sources of discipline problems. The procedure for residual problems clear to all.
Roles of Participants					
Student Roles	Passive recipient of knowledge. Instruction is geared to average student. Reactive communication with the teacher.	Investigation of new student roles by teacher. Limited hierarchy of trust established in the classroom. Needs and interests of student investigated.	Groundrules for increased student independence set. Student involvement in planning. Role of student connected to philosophy of the school.	Periodic staff review of student roles. Roles linked to schoolwide rules and regulations. Philosophy guides role possibilities.	Students involved in planning and conducting the program. Increased independence *and* responsibility. Use of "contracts" to maintain new understandings.

Teacher Roles	Defined by the subjects taught. Perceived as the source of all knowledge. Other roles peripheral.	Perceiving roles suggested by the philosophy. Roles accepted at verbal level. Limited experimentation with new roles.	Investigation of new roles—trying on new relationship. Goal-setting for individual teacher. Skill development through in-service.	Administrative reorganization for role support. A sharpened planning and action skills needed to serve the student accfording to the philosophy.	Teacher role is defined by student needs. Teacher the organizer of the laerning activities. Teacher talents used more effectively.
Principal Roles	Solely responsible for school operation. The "boss." Enforcer of all rules. The linkage to all outside information and resources.	Awareness of role limitations. An awareness of real leadership potential. A setting of role priorities.	Limited sharing of decision-making in area of curriculum. Limited joint planning with the faculty. Review of existing policy according to the philosophy.	Role perception changes to manager of resources. Emphasis on development (active) rather than on order (static). Increase in curriculum leadership functions.	An instructional leader. Administrative acts support the curriculum program. Philosophy guiding decision-making. Built-in monitoring system for evaluating building level progress.

Source: From "Development Staging—In Pursuit of Comprehensive Curriculum Planning" by Jon Wiles, *Middle School Journal* 6 (September 1975): 7–10. Used by permission.

supervision. *Black's Law Dictionary* defines liability as "the state of being bound or obligated in law or justice to do, pay, or make good something." Said another way, supervisors must be aware of both what they must do on the job in a legal sense as well as the limitations on their practice found in the law. Until very recently, supervisors and other administrators seemed largely indifferent to the legal principles applicable to public schools.

In most states, the law differentiates between those persons who serve as officers of a school district and other employees. The school board members are universally protected in all states by a cloak of immunity from direct liability. Sometimes superintendents are also protected. Below that level, however, school employees are responsible in a legal sense for their actions or negligence. This concept is extremely important for supervisors since they work directly with teachers. Teachers, more so than principals, are the subjects of most legal action in schools.

As a state agency, the school board delegates certain duties to its employees, such as teaching, supervision, and maintenance. It is a governmental function to educate our youth, and the school board assumes the responsibility for fulfilling this function. In this capacity, however, the board does not create a relationship of master and servant. Public officers are not liable for the negligence of subordinates unless they cooperate in, or direct or encourage, an act about which someone complains. Charges of negligence, therefore, are most often heard at a lower level of operation.

Negligence is any conduct that falls below the standard established by law for the protection of others against unreasonable risk of harm. In general, such conduct may be of two types: 1) an act that a reasonable man would have realized involved an unreasonable risk of injury to others; and 2) failure to perform an act that is necessary for the protection or assistance of another and that one is under a duty to perform.

The law prohibits careless action. Failure to use care, skill, preparation, or warning may be interpreted as negligence. It is negligence, for instance, for a supervisor to permit a teacher to engage in an activity that is under his control if he knows or should know that the person engaging in this activity could cause harm to others.

The first test for determining liability for negligence is "foreseeability." If a reasonably prudent person could have foreseen the harmful consequences of his actions, disregarding the foreseeable consequences makes one negligent.

In particular, supervisors are vulnerable for various legal actions in any area where the rights of students or teachers are infringed upon. Examples of student rights include the right to be educated, the right to not be discriminated against on the basis of race or sex, the right of privacy in school record-keeping, and the right of free speech. Teacher rights also include free speech and expression, the right not to be discriminated against because of age, and the right of confidentiality in matters such as personnel evaluation.

What all of this means to the supervisor who is already operating in a political environment full of tripwires, is that he or she must learn about the law. No other leadership role in school interfaces with so many other roles, and for that reason the odds of facing a negligence or liability charge are increased. In the new world of school legality, it is important to learn the language. A glossary of common legal terms is included in Figure 11.6 for the reader's review and study.

TOWARD REALISTIC PRACTICE

In the choice to include this chapter in a basic book on school supervision, we are telling the reader that theory and practice are not always identical on the job. School districts do have distorting influences that affect the supervisor in his or her attempt to improve learning opportunities for students. The supervisor should acknowledge these conditions and plan for them.

The message for the reader is that being able to analyze the practice environment is an important skill. If the supervisor can accurately assess conditions that may influence supervisory activities, then they can be anticipated. In the 1990s, supervision is not as orderly as it was twenty years ago, but the goals remain constant.

We close this chapter with two prescriptions gleaned from the literature on political behaviors in schools. One prescription is for a form of direct supervision where practice is in an undistorted (stable) bureaucratic setting. The other, by contrast, is for an indirect style of supervision that better fits an unstable condition where politics is an everyday reality.

The Direct Supervisor

1. Set unmistakable goals
2. Supervise the work more than the worker
3. Demand perfect compliance to the essential rules and ignore violations of nonessential rules
4. Reward sparingly but punish much more sparingly
5. Give praise and criticism in private and understate it
6. Listen to complaints sympathetically; never complain in turn
7. Defend the faith—the manager is the natural custodian of the organization's sacred symbols and moral character

Figure 11.6
Glossary of Legal Terms

Ad valorem: "According to the value"; a tax or duty assessed in proportion to the value of the property.

Appellant: Party, be s/he plaintive or defendant at the lower court level, who upon losing at the lower level brings an appeal.

Appellee: Party, be s/he plaintive or defendant at the lower court level, who is put in the position of defending the decision upon its appeal. It should be noted that the same party may become "appellant" and "appellee" at successive stages of the litigation.

Certiorari: "To be made certain of", the name of a writ of review for a case falling in the discretionary area of the Supreme Court's appellate jurisdiction, requiring an affirmative vote of four Justices.

Class Action: An action brought on behalf of other persons similarly situated.

Concurrence: An opinion separate from that of the majority filed by one or more Justices who agree(s) with the general result of the majority decision, but who choose(s) to emphasize or differentiate the reasoning or grounds for the decision.

De facto: "In fact"; actually occurring.

De jure: "By law"; occurring as a result of official action.

Dissent: An opinion that disagrees with that of the majority and is handed down by one or more members of the Court.

Dismissal: Decision without opinion by the United States Supreme Court in the mandatory area of its appellate jurisdiction that summarily disposes of the case because of the procedural status of the parties or the issues e.g., mootness, standing, or lack of substantial federal question.

Due process: The regular course of administration of justice through the rules and forms that have been established for the protection of private rights in courts of law.

Enjoin: To require a person by an injunction to perform or to abstain from performing some act.

344

Ex post facto: "After the fact"; a law passed after the occurrence of an act which retrospectively changes the legal consequences of the act.

Ex rel: "Upon information of"; legal proceeding that is instituted by the Attorney General or other appropriate official in the name of and on behalf of the state, but on the information and the instigation of an individual who has a private interest in the matter.

In loco parentis: "In place of parents"; charged with a parent's rights, duties and responsibility. In the case of a teacher, this is a condition applying only when the child is under the reasonable control and supervision of the school.

In re: "In the matter of"; designating a judicial proceeding, e.g., juvenile cases, in which the customary adversarial posture of the parties is deemphasized or nonexistent.

Incorporation: Evolving doctrine by which the United States Supreme Court has applied a substantial part of the Bill of Rights, e.g., First Amendment, to the states and thereby public school officials via the Fourteenth Amendment.

Infra: "Below"; cross reference to a fuller citation appearing subsequently in the document.

Inter alia: "Among other things."

One-judge opinion in chambers: Special ruling issued by a Supreme Court Justice under unusual circumstances and thus not carrying full precedential effect.

Moot: An issue that is not considered by the Court because it no longer contains a live dispute of the sort proper for a judicial decision. A moot case seeks to determine an abstract question that does not arise upon facts or rights existing at the time.

Parens patriae: "Parent of the country"; referring to the states as having sovereign power of guardianship over persons under a disability, such as minors and insane persons.

Per Curiam: "By the Court"; an opinion concurred in by several/or all the members of the Court but without disclosing the name of any particular Justice as being its author.

Figure 11.6
(Continued)

Police power of state:	The power vested in the legislature to make and establish laws, statutes, and ordinances that would be for the good of the state and its people. This power extends to all areas of health, morals, safety, order, and comfort of the people.
Prima facie:	"On first appearance" or "on its face"; evidence that is presumed to be true unless rebutted by proof to the contrary.
Remand:	"To send back"; action by an appellate court to send the case back to a lower court for further proceedings.
Standing:	Status as a proper party before the Court as determined by the Court; requires an actual injury or immediate interest in the action at hand.
Statute:	A law enacted by the legislative branch of the federal or state government.
Sub nom:	"Under the name of"; designation for the change in the name of either party (or both parties) in the course of the litigation, e.g., upon the death of one of the parties during the appellate process.
Supra:	"Above"; cross reference to a fuller citation appearing earlier in the document.
Summary affirmance:	Decision without an opinion by the United States Supreme Court in the mandatory area of its appellate jurisdiction that gives binding effect to the lower court's decision but which does not have as much precedential value as a full opinion by the Court on the merits. Thus, the Court feels less constrained to overrule summary affirmances than full opinions while it expects lower courts to follow both equally. The jurisdictional statement filed in the parties' briefs to the Court, rather than the lower court opinion, must be the focus of any inquiry regarding the scope and meaning of the summary affirmance.
U.S. Reports:	Official reports of the United States Supreme Court decisions, as contrasted to parallel citations of unofficial reports of the decisions that are available through Shephard's and other such reference volumes.
Void for vagueness:	Constitutional infirmity when a law is so unclear that it does not provide the specificity required by due process, thus making it void.

8. Protect the differentiated status of subordinates (e.g., seniority)
9. Take infinite pains to do the job right
10. Retain the final control

The Indirect Supervisor

1. Find and hold the purse strings. Curricular and instructional decisions affect allocation patterns like everything else.
2. Rely on personal and professional relationships with teachers and other subordinates to gain adequate information.
3. Do your homework and "roam the streets." Without the luxury of direct, firsthand knowledge of actual operations the principal must make extra efforts to find out what is going on.
4. Develop detailed plans and projections and, *above all*, refrain from attempting the impossible. Individuals and subunits of the school need to know their own expectations and that of others. Be open about this. Set goals that lie within reach and waste little effort on rhetorical exercises about the unattainable.
5. Reorganize drastically or not at all. The indirect supervisor cannot tinker or fine tune a person or department/program cluster. If an operating unit gives an unsatisfactory performance and cannot be improved the principal should make every effort to disband or remove it. If corrective measures are beyond the power of the principal then isolate and leave the problem alone.
6. Respect successful operations that are productive, even if some aspects of their efforts seem crazy or unnecessary. All humans practice what Veblen called the "conscientious withdrawal of efficiency." The principal should focus upon results.
7. Innovate boldly, but not often. As noted earlier all change efforts are costly, time consuming, and likely to meet resistance or generate unintended effects. Since all efforts are potentially dangerous, go for broke. The best hedge against failure is extensive consultation and gaining consensus among key actors of the school arena.

NEW DIRECTIONS

The Four C's

A new era of school reform and restructuring is changing the face of American education. Most noticeable are the four "C's":

Cooperative learning among students — Learning outcomes promoted by cooperative learning include higher achievement and increased retention; more positive accepting relationships with peers regardless of ethnic, sex, ability, social class or handicapping, and greater collaborative skills and attitudes necessary for working effectively with others.

Cooperative teaching — School organizations that utilize cooperative teaching — whether they are elementary schools with grade level teams, middle schools with interdisciplinary teams, or high schools with department teams — produce a working environment that results in higher teacher satisfaction and student learning.

Cooperative leadership — School-site management, teacher empowerment, and shared decision-making signal an end to top-down bureaucratic management of schools. Where teachers feel ownership in school decisions, morale will improve and student learning environments will be enhanced.

Cooperative relationships between school and community — Cooperative relationships between schools and community have resulted in increased support for schools. Many schools have been adopted by businesses or agencies who have provided needed funds, volunteers, tutors, equipment, and other means of support.

During the 1970s, the public blamed schools for what was wrong with youth. In the 1980s, the public and parents blamed themselves, but still expected schools to find solutions. In the 1990s, the schools and community are joining hands in a "we can do it together" relationship.

Supervisors will find themselves involved in all four "C's." New skills will have to be developed, especially in working with community persons as they enter our schools in greater numbers.

Teacher Empowerment — The Collaborative School

Collaboration was a topic seldom mentioned in the effective schools literature of the 1980s, but it appears in the 1990s in a growing number of publications. Evidence is accumulating that the nature of the relationships among adults who live and work together in schools has an important influence upon the school's quality and character and on the accomplishment of its students.[6]

Collaboration in schools does not occur easily. One is reminded of the school with a sign on the teachers' room: NO STUDENTS ALLOWED. When asked about that message, a teacher replied that the sign contained two messages. The first message was the written message. The second message was an unwritten message: NO TALK-ING ABOUT TEACHING IN THE TEACHERS' ROOM. That expe-rience points out the difficulty of developing collaboration within a school. It also points out the isolation and fragmentation that char-acterizes teaching in many schools.

Reversing that situation is the challenge of supervisors, teachers, and administrators. After decades of overreliance on bureaucratic rules and regulations, school environments that isolate teachers, evaluation systems that fail to facilitate instructional improvement, and lack of involvement of teachers in decision-making, there is much to be done in school environments.

Prestigious groups such as the Carnegie Task Force on Teaching As a Profession and the National Governors' Association have called attention to the need for alternative structures which accord teachers greater respect as professionals, induce teachers to work with one an-other, more closely with administrators, and with supervisors on school improvement.

The collaborative school is not new in theory or practice. Re-search on effective schools and evidence of successful practices from the business world have highlighted the advantage of consultation and teamwork.

Elements of the collaborative school philosophy can be summa-rized by the following:

☐ The belief (based on effective school research) that the quality of education is largely determined by what happens at the school site.
☐ The use of a wide range of practices and structures that enable teachers and administrators to work together on school im-provement.
☐ The belief that teachers are professionals who should be given the responsibility for the instructional process and held ac-countable for its outcomes.
☐ The belief that instruction is most effective in a school envi-ronment.

School improvement efforts have resulted in new models of col-laboration involving lead teachers, school improvement teams, peer coaching, and team coaching. Mentor programs that stimulate collab-oration among faculty members is facilitating professional develop-ment in a number of school districts in the country. An example of a teacher mentor program is the Charlotte-Mecklenburg (N.C.) School District's Teacher Career Development Program.

Another model for collegial professional development is the teacher support team — a school-based cadre of professionals who provide systematic support and assistance to individual teachers.

Many important ideas originating in business and industry have been adopted by educational institutions to enhance their effectiveness. One technique from William Ouchi's "Theory Z" application is the quality circle. The quality circle consists of a small group of people (6–12) with a common work interest, meeting for about one hour every week. Facilitators train the members of the circles in group process and problem-solving techniques. Encouragement is offered by administrators. Following training, the quality circle members work to identify, document, and recommend solutions to problems.

Many teachers have leadership qualities. Empowering teachers allows the school to tap these qualities for the benefit of the school. Teachers are also more likely to use those leadership qualities when they are applied to problems of practical concern to them, than when they are applied to problems of concern only to the principal.

Another comprehensive strategy for school improvement that encourages collaborative practice is organizational development (O.D.). Organizational development is aimed at improving the ability of the subsystems of a school district to change themselves.

Time and resources to change school environments for collaborative endeavors remains a problem. Finding time for teacher growth obviously involves increased costs. According to the National Governors' Association report, *Time for Results*, schools typically spend about one-tenth of what private industry devotes to development of personnel.[7]

The argument for collaboration in schools is straightforward. Teaching and learning can be improved by a collaborative endeavor in which teachers work closely with one another and with administrators and supervisors. The teacher as a solitary craftsperson no longer fits the needs of a changing society.

SUMMARY

The environment of a school district has a direct bearing on the practice of supervision. In the 1980s, conditions such as finance and legislation increased competition for control, resources, and the primacy of values in schools. The 1990s are beginning to see a shift of control of schools back to school sites.

Supervisors who can "see" their practice environment and adjust their behavior to accommodate political conditions will be more effective. Three handles for understanding the political dimensions of the school district are power configurations in the organization, various "players" who interact, and how the budget is managed. These factors, and others, will tell the supervisor about the stability of the district and where the real boundaries for practice are to be found.

Promoting change in an unstable environment is difficult, yet the task must be accomplished if instruction is to be improved for students. We presented a number of lessons about change for the reader's consideration as well as several instruments for assessing change in a school environment.

Legal dimensions of education today influence and distort supervisory practice. Supervisors are particularly vulnerable to legal problems of negligence because they oversee teaching practices and stand at the crossroads of responsibility in schools.

In closing the chapter, we suggest that two global strategies — direct and indirect supervision — are appropriate according to the nature of the practice environment.

NOTES

1. See David Wiles, Jon Wiles, Joseph Bondi, *Practical Politics for School Administrators* (Boston: Allyn and Bacon, Inc., 1981).
2. Ralph Kimbrough, *Political Power and Educational Decision-Making* (Chicago: Rand McNally, 1964), pp. 38–39.
3. Aaron Wildavsky, *The Politics of the Budgetary Process* (Boston: Little Brown, 1974), p. 4.
4. Goodwin Watson, *Concepts for Social Change* (Washington, DC: National Training Laboratories, National Education Association, 1967), p. 22.
5. Jon Wiles, "State-of-the-Art in Administration," a position paper for Georgia Professional Standards Commission, 1983, p. 16.
6. Stuart Smith and James Scott. *The Collaborative School: A Work Environment for Effective Instruction*. Eric Clearinghouse on Education-1 Management. Univ. of Oregon, NASSP, 1990.
7. National Governors' Association. *Time for Results: The Governors' 1990 Report on Education*. Washington, DC: Center for Policy Research and Analysis, 1990.

SUGGESTED LEARNING ACTIVITIES

1. Develop a list of areas in which struggles for control might exist in an unstable school district.
2. If there is no visible pyramid of power (segmented pluralism), how should the supervisor proceed to improve instruction?
3. What are some of the areas in which supervisors might find themselves in conflict with the teacher unions?

4. Why do the authors suggest that supervisors invest their time on people ready to change rather than those opposed to change proposals?
5. Using the probability chart (Table 11.2), develop some action steps that a supervisor might take in high-risk areas to lessen that degree of risk.
6. What general rule-of-thumb do you think a supervisor might use to avoid charges of negligence in practice?

BOOKS TO REVIEW

Campbell, Roald, et al. *The Organization and Control of American Schools,* 5th ed. Columbus, OH: Charles E. Merrill Publishing Company, 1985.

Blanchard, Kenneth and Peale, Norman. *The Power of Ethical Management.* New York: William Morrow, 1988.

Clancy, John. *The Invisible Power.* Lexington, MA: Lexington Books, 1989.

Fullan, Michael. *The Meaning of Educational Change.* New York: Teachers College Press, 1982.

Greiner, Larry and Schein, Virginia. *Power and Organization Development: Mobilizing Power to Implement Change.* Reading, MA: Addison-Wesley, 1988.

Ichilov, Orit. *Political Socialization, Citizenship Education, and Democracy.* New York: Teachers College Press, 1990.

Ouchi, William G. *Theory Z.* Reading, MA: Avon Books, 1981.

Slavin, Robert. *Cooperative Learning: Theory, Research and Practice.* Englewood Cliffs, NJ, Prentice Hall, Inc., 1990.

Wiles, David, Wiles, Jon and Bondi, Joseph. Practical Politics for School Administrators. Boston: Allyn and Bacon, Inc., 1981.

CHAPTER 12

Case Studies in Supervision

AREA I—HUMAN DEVELOPMENT
Case A

It all started with a simple phone conversation in which a teacher had voiced concern about the harshness of grading patterns in the seventh grade math department. Many teachers, the supervisor was told, were teaching exclusively to the advanced students in their courses and letting the others "sink or swim." As a result, the teacher reported, students were failing left and right.

The next day the supervisor went to the school office and pulled the grading records for the seventh graders. The pattern that emerged was shocking; 47 percent of all seventh graders were receiving D's and F's in mathematics. Worse, a similar pattern existed in seventh grade and eighth grade English. No wonder our dropout rate in the high school is 35 percent, thought the supervisor!

After speaking with the principal, who was also unaware of the grading pattern, it was decided to speak with the faculty at the next scheduled meeting about the grading pattern that had been found at the school. The presentation was primarily statistical in nature, with the supervisor hoping that the faculty would also be surprised. They weren't. As one faculty member put it, "The real world is all about failure. Some people are winners and some losers. Our slogan is save the best and shoot the rest, ha ha."

Questions:

1. What do we know about human development that has a bearing on an instructional practice such as grouping or grading?
2. What, if anything, should the supervisor do to correct this rather disturbing attitude?

Case B

It was unusual for a supervisor to be summoned by a building faculty, but that was essentially what was happening. Of course, officially the principal had requested that the supervisor come to a monthly faculty meeting to talk about emotionally handicapped students who were being mainstreamed into the regular classroom for part of the day. A few discreet phone calls, however, had revealed the dangerous tenor of this meeting.

For the regular faculty at the school, all mainstreaming was viewed as an imposition. The students required extra attention. They tended to slow down the whole class with their specialness. None of the special students were quite so disturbing as the EH kids who could explode in a moment and disrupt an entire class. Apparently, this very thing was happening too frequently at the school and the faculty wanted to establish "a different program" for special education.

Questions:

1. What "givens" exist that must regulate the posture and behavior of the supervisor in this meeting?
2. What issues are at stake in this process of defining the program for special students?
3. What basic approach should the supervisor take to disarm the emotional nature of this meeting?

AREA II – CURRICULUM DEVELOPMENT

Case A

During a routine process of mapping the curriculum of an intermediate school, the supervisor ran across something new. A social studies teacher in an eighth grade team produced a map for the year with only one topic area – "Stonehenge."

In the conference that followed, the teacher was emphatic that Stonehenge was a legitimate topic for teaching world history. "All history," she reported, "is simply symbolic samplings of the events of man. Stonehenge is comprehensive in that it covers the art, the science, the religion, and philosophy of the Western culture. It is as relevant today as ever," she concluded. The teacher would not hear of covering a textbook and therefore "diluting" the meaning of this important event.

Questions:

1. If you were the supervisor in this case, what important things would you want to communicate to this teacher? List these

points and prioritize them with numbers 1, 2, 3, and so forth.
   2. What, if any, issues of academic freedom might exist in this case?

Case B

As a new supervisor in this district, your immediate task was to organize the science textbook adoption procedure for the year. A plan for review and adoption was sent to each building principal along with a timeline and state-adopted list. Arrangements had been made for a districtwide display of texts that might be chosen. All that was before receiving the Benson memo.

Benson was the most senior principal in the district and an opinion leader as well. Benson had been straight to the point in his correspondence. "We have *always* selected our books at the building level in this district and we would not like to see this local autonomy infringed upon." Additionally, Benson went on to mention that tradition had the representatives from the book companies hosting little "wine and cheese" parties for the faculties and that these were very popular in the individual schools.

Questions:

   1. What are the major issues in this case?
   2. If the supervisor found that Benson was indeed very influential, what things should be fought for and what things overlooked?
   3. Describe this process from a pure "curriculum" perspective.

AREA III—INSTRUCTION
Case A

The supervisor had to admit that the meeting with the teacher had been less than satisfactory. If this conferencing was supposed to lead to better classroom instruction, something was missing! The supervisor had followed the state-mandated process, step-by-step, but the teacher hadn't responded in the "textbook" manner.

The whole evaluation program was based on teacher effectiveness research that identified key skills of teaching like "advanced organizers" and "questioning techniques." Following several observations, the supervisor and the teacher were to sit down and analyze the performance of the teacher and to set goals for improvement. Instead, the teacher had challenged the validity of the skills observed saying they were based on composite studies drawn from a "skewed" population of effective school characteristics. The teacher had sounded very knowledgeable and was known to be taking a research course at a nearby university.

Questions:

1. What should the supervisor do given this communication impasse?
2. How would the supervisor's behavior be affected if it was found that the teacher was correct in her observations about the evaluation tool?

Case B

It was a common complaint from the teachers in the district. For the second straight year a survey had identified "motivating students" as the highest priority for staff development activities. The problem was, what did the teachers really mean by "motivating?"

A recent needs assessment in the district had turned up some interesting facts about instruction. At all levels from the fifth grade up, teachers lectured better than 80 percent of the time. The standard routine was didactic, with homework problems serving as the application of the day's topic. The same needs assessment had indicated that students favored a variety of interactive instruction techniques over lecture and odd-and-even homework problems. The supervisor felt that the answer to motivation must lie in this kind of data about classroom instruction.

Questions:

1. What are some of the more common theories about why students are not motivated in school today? What is meant by motivation?
2. What is the most effective way the supervisor might present this needs assessment data to the teachers?

AREA IV – HUMAN RELATIONS
Case A

Never in her wildest dreams had the supervisor expected a full auditorium for a school-sponsored meeting. How could people get so excited about textbooks? At issue was a proposal from the Parents for Decency group to remove approximately fifty books from the school library because they were felt to be pornographic. Other parents came out of the woodwork to react to this proposal.

The frightening thing about the meeting had been that rather than opposing the proposal, each group of parents seemed to want to remove other books for other reasons. One group was concerned with sexism in textbooks. Another group thought that the library had too many books insensitive to the needs of minority children. Still another group was anxious to review all books for "humanism."

The principal and superintendent attended the meeting but refused to engage the people stating that books were an instructional concern and that the staff (supervisor) would develop a procedure for getting people together to air their concerns.

Questions:

1. What is the best way to get people to communicate about controversial issues related to schooling?
2. Outline a plan of attack for developing this procedure.

Case B

It was surely a case of discrimination if she had ever seen one. Prior to becoming a supervisor she had heard that schools were a man's world. True, most administrators were men, but who could ever have guessed how invisible a woman supervisor could be in a meeting among men. It was just as bad trying to speak out in a face-to-face conversation with the administrator. Whenever she said something, the administrator just looked away. It was infuriating!

The worst part was that, when she raised the issue with the superintendent, he acted genuinely surprised and said, "I doubt that he was doing it on purpose."

Questions:

1. What are some of the more common snubs that men give women supervisors in a school setting? Members of minority groups such as blacks?
2. How might a woman supervisor in a school setting bring this behavior to the attention of her male counterparts in a meaningful way?

AREA V – STAFF DEVELOPMENT
Case A

Without any sort of assessment to determine the needs of the faculty, the new curriculum assistant decided that *everyone* needed an inservice program in writing behavioral objectives for lesson plans. He set up the date for a workshop (without consulting any of the faculty) for a Saturday from 8 A.M. to 4 P.M. The principal of the school endorsed the inservice program and at the next faculty meeting stated that all faculty members would be required to attend. When many of the faculty members complained that they had already had a course involving writing objectives during their graduate work at the university, they were told that all the staff would attend so that the lesson plans would be the same for each teacher. Very angry about this demand, the teachers sought a grievance through their professional organization.

Questions:

1. What are the first steps you would take to head off the grievance?
2. Outline a needs assessment process you would use to determine inservice needs of the faculty. What information is needed?
3. What face-saving techniques would you employ to help the curriculum assistant and principal overcome their decision to carry out the present inservice program?

Case B

The superintendent and board have decided that the present grades 7–9 junior high school will be converted in two years to a grades 6–8 middle school. The conversion is one of necessity to cope with declining enrollment rather than developing a needed program for middle grades students. The faculty and community have already raised questions about a middle school. The faculty is a veteran staff that likes the junior high school and sees little need to change their secondary teaching styles to accommodate the younger middle school students.

Over the years, the community has changed. There are a number of single-parent homes and the mobility rate of students in the middle grades (students entering and leaving school during the school year) exceeds 35 percent. In addition, there are a number of students who are over age for their grade and an even greater number who are below grade level in achievement.

Your assignment, as a supervisor, is to develop and implement a staff development plan to carry out a successful middle school program.

Questions:

1. Outline a two-year staff development plan for the middle school staff. What tasks and timelines would you use?
2. What sources of information would you use for a needs assessment of faculty inservice needs?

3. What strategies would you use to get the "old dogs" to learn the new tricks necessary for middle school teaching?

AREA VI – ADMINISTRATIVE TASKS
Case A

As a supervisor, you have been engaged in long-range planning for your subject area for a number of years. Recently, the superintendent asked you to chair a committee charged with developing a comprehensive plan for the entire district for the next five years. Curriculum revision, building needs, staff development and budget needs, as well as others to be identified by your group, are to be addressed in your plan. The superintendent has requested that timelines and persons responsible for carrying out tasks be identified in the comprehensive plan. She has also suggested that community persons be actively involved in the development of the comprehensive plan.

Questions:

1. What aspects would you include in the comprehensive plan?
2. Who would you suggest as members of the planning committee?
3. What planning techniques and management tools would you employ in developing the comprehensive plan?

Case B

An unsettling feeling came over Sylvia as the superintendent continued his budget report to supervisors and administrators. So this was what a conservative board meant. They were really serious about cutting 15 percent of the local district budget by next year. Never had anyone in the room thought that a basic budget could mean this. Sylvia leaned forward to catch the superintendent's summation: "And so I'm asking for the assistance and cooperation of each of you in meeting this contingency. You will be asked to assess the drop of enrollment last year and adjust your staff patterns and material budget accordingly."

The following week Sylvia received the district's much-dreaded envelope that showed her fair share of budget cuts to be $79,000. Material reductions would not cover the deficit. Teaching positions would have to be eliminated.

Sylvia now knows that any cut in staff will necessarily affect the curriculum available to students. She plans to visit principals and the Assistant Superintendents for Business and Curriculum. She is tempted to see the superintendent and some friends on the board to try to get some relief from the budget reduction mandate.

Questions:

1. What information should Sylvia arm herself with before pleading her case?
2. What risks will Sylvia take if she makes an "end run" to the superintendent and board members to gain relief from budget cuts?
3. What contingency strategies should Sylvia use in case budget figures are amended at the last minute to give her back funds?

AREA VII–EVALUATION FOR EFFECTIVENESS
Case A

Miss Morris is a well-known figure at Southland High. She should be, for this fall marks the thirtieth year she has been teaching in the Home Economics program. It is hard to believe that she represents the example "homemaker" of tomorrow. She is always sloppy and her hair is never neatly groomed. Even boys notice her disheveled appearance when they see her in the halls. It seems that the faded lace on her slip shows beneath her dress quite frequently. But this doesn't seem to bother Miss Morris at all. She shuffles to her class at a snail's pace and relishes the last drag from her cigarette before the final bell rings.

Class is automatic for Miss Morris. She has read her notes so many times that they are now old and yellow. Sometimes, however, she doesn't instruct but talks to her pupils of when she was a young girl living in Cleveland, Ohio. Her stories are so worn that students write letters while she dreams of days gone by. When Miss Morris does instruct, she strictly follows her outline and lectures throughout the entire class period. She rarely uses available facilities and seems to ignore the questioning minds of her students.

Even though Miss Morris heads the Home Economics program, she never instigates committee meetings; nor is she receptive to the enthusiastic ideas of the newer teachers. She has held her position for the past ten years, and she feels she could really tell these young idealists about the problems of education. There has been neither appreciation of her hard work nor recognition—monetarily or otherwise. At this point, Miss Morris's only desire is to complete five more years of teaching so she can retire and go back to Cleveland to live out her remaining years.

A new principal has informed the superintendent that he intends to do something about Miss Morris. He asks for help from the district office. The superintendent asks you, as Miss Morris's supervisor, to respond. He wants to support the new principal at Southland, yet suggests that fewer waves will be made if Miss Morris can improve her performance rather than be terminated.

Questions:

1. Miss Morris is obviously a marginal teacher who has "gotten by" for years. What can you as a supervisor do, if anything, to improve the performance of Miss Morris?
2. What issues would you face if you recommend the termination of Miss Morris's employment?
3. Outline an incentive plan for teachers like Miss Morris to participate in staff improvement programs. How would you sell your plan to teachers? To the board?

Case B

As part of the curriculum change to accommodate the middle school philosophy, guides were set up for the various disciplines. The science program was designed to give general subject area topics to each grade level. A general science background was to be provided in the sixth grade, biology was to be covered in the seventh grade, and the physical sciences, chemistry, physics, meteorology, and astronomy, were to be studied in the eighth grade. No one textbook was to be used as the basic book for any grade level; rather, there were several books that were suggested as having good material for various specific topics. As a first year teacher in this system Mark James was at a loss as to how to teach. The county office had provided him with a basic cognitive outline for the seventh grade level. However, Mark had realized after the first week of classes that the content was more than the majority of his students could handle. After consulting with his department head Mark was disappointed to find little help. The basic backbone, biology, had already been given to him, he was told. The department head stated that this system was the best for personal freedom in teaching. Mark argued to no avail that some structure was needed. As a first year teacher he felt handicapped and frustrated with the system. At a county science meeting Mark voiced his concern about this problem and nearly all the other teachers present seemed to agree with him.

Questions:

1. As district science supervisor, what steps would you take to resolve the concerns of teachers about the effectiveness of the new science program?

2. In what ways could you help first year teachers like Mark become more effective teachers?
3. How would you assess the effectiveness of the new program other than listening to the complaints of teachers?

RESOURCES FOR SUPERVISORS

Because supervision in an educational setting is not always clearly defined, procedures and techniques are often improvised. Supervisors often must find their own means of solving problems. For this reason, supervisors should be aware of the wealth of resources available to them through agencies and professional organizations. Some of these general resources follow.

NEWSLETTERS

ASCD News Exchange
Association for Supervision and
  Curriculum Development
1250 N. Pitt Street
Alexandria, Virginia 22314

Department of Classroom
  Teachers
News Bulletin
National Education Association
1201 16th Street, N.W.
Washington, D.C. 20036

Educational Product Report
Educational Products
  Information Exchange
  Institute (EPIE)
386 Park Avenue, South
New York, N.Y. 10016

Educational Researcher
American Educational Research
  Association (AERA)
1126 16th Street, N.W.
Washington, D.C. 20036

Educational Recaps
Educational Testing Service
Princeton, New Jersey 08540

Education U.S.A.
National School Public
  Relations Association
1201 16th Street, N.W.
Washington, D.C. 20036

NASSP Newsletter
National Association of
  Secondary School Principals
1201 16th Street, N.W.
Washington, D.C. 20036

National Elementary Principals
National Elementary Principals
Department of Classroom
  Teachers
1201 16th Street, N.W.
Washington, D.C. 20036

SLANTS
School Information and
  Research Service (SIRS)
100 Crochett Street
Seattle, Washington 98109

DIRECTORIES

*Current Index to Journals in
  Education (CIJE)*
CCM Information Corporation
909 Third Avenue, New York,
  New York 10022

*The Directory of Publishing
  Opportunities*
Academic Media
Cordura Corporation
32 Lincoln Avenue
Orange, New Jersey 07050

*Directory of Special Libraries
  and Information Centers*
Gale Research Company
The Book Tower
Detroit, Michigan 48226

*Directory of Educational
  Information Services*
Division of Information
  Technology and
  Dissemination
Bureau of Research
U.S. Office of Education
Washington, D.C.

The Education Index (authors
  and titles in education)
The H.W. Wilson Company
950 University Avenue
New York, New York 10452

Encyclopedia of Associations
Gale Research Company
The Book Tower
Detroit, Michigan 48226

REFERENCE BOOKS

Dictionary of Education
Edited by Carter V. Good. New York: McGraw-Hill, 1959. Definitions
  of educational terminology.

Digest of Education Statistics
Available from U.S. Government Printing Office, Washington, D.C.
  20402. A statistical abstract of American education activity.

Encyclopedia of Educational Research
Fourth ed., edited by Robert L. Ebel. New York: Macmillan, 1969.
  Describes research findings on broad range of topics in education.

Handbook of Research in Teaching
Third ed., edited by Merlin C. Wittrock. New York: Macmillan, 1986.

Handbook of Research on Teacher Education
Edited by W. Robert Houston. New York: Macmillan, 1990.

The International Encyclopedia of Teaching and Teacher Education
Edited by Michael J. Dunkin. New York: Pergamon Press, 1987.

National Society for the Study of Education Yearbook (NSSE)
Published by the University of Chicago Press. An in-depth treatment
   of an educational concern each year. More information from NSSE,
   5835 Kimbark Avenue, Chicago, Illinois 60639.

The World Yearbook of Education
Available from Harcourt, Brace, and Jovanovich, New York. Provides
   articles on various topic areas in education by year.

INFORMATION SERVICES
ERIC (Educational Resources Information Center)

ERIC is a network of information centers by topic areas established
by the United States Office of Education. ERIC disseminates research
findings and other resource materials found effective in developing
school programs.

   ERIC publishes a monthly catalog, *Resources in Education* (RIE).
Reports in RIE are indicated by an "ED" number. Journal articles that
are indexed in ERIC's companion catalog, *Current Index to Journals
in Education*, are indicated by an "EJ" number.

   Most items with ED numbers are available from ERIC Document
Reproduction Services (EDRS), P.O. Box 190, Arlington, VA 22210. To
order from EDRS, call 1-800-227-3742 for price information.

ORGANIZATIONS AND ASSOCIATIONS
Citizens' Organizations

Council for Basic Education
725 15th Street, NW
Washington, D.C. 20005

National Congress of Parents
   and Teachers
1715 25th Street
Rock Island, Illinois 61201

SRIS (School Research
   Information Service)
Phi Delta Kappa Research
   Service Center
Eighth and Union Streets
Bloomington, Indiana 47401

National Coalition for Children
6542 Hitt Street
McLean, Virginia 22101

National Center for Middle
   School Materials
P.O. Box 16545
Tampa, Florida 33687

Educationally Related Organizations and Associations

American Association for
Higher Education
One Dupont Circle, NW
Washington, D.C. 20036

American Association of
School Administrators
1800 North Moore Street
Arlington, Virginia 22209

American Council on
Education
One Dupont Circle, NW
Washington, D.C. 20036

American Educational
Research Association
1126 16th Street, NW
Washington, D.C. 20036

American Vocational
Association, Inc.
1510 H Street, NW
Washington, D.C. 20005

Association for Supervision and
Curriculum Development
(ASCD)
1250 N. Pitt Street
Alexandria, Virginia 22314-
1403

Childrens Television Workshop
One Lincoln Plaza
New York, New York 10023

College Entrance Examination
Board
888 7th Avenue
New York, New York 10019

Council for American Private
Education
1625 I Street, NW
Washington, D.C. 20006

Council of Chief State School
Officers
1201 16th Street, NW
Washington, D.C. 20036

International Reading
Association
800 Barksdale Road
Newark, Delaware 19711

Joint Council on Economic
Education
1212 Avenue of the Americas
New York, New York 10036

National Art Education
Association
1916 Association Drive
Reston, Virginia 22091

National Association for
Education of Young Children
1834 Connecticut Avenue
Washington, D.C. 20009

National Association of
Elementary School Principals
1801 North Moore Street
Arlington, Virginia 22209

National Association for Public
Continuing Adult Education
1201 16th Street, NW
Washington, D.C. 20036

National Association of
Secondary School Principals
1904 Association Drive
Reston, Virginia 22091

National Council of Teachers
of English
1111 Kenyon Road
Urbana, Illinois 61801

National Council of Teachers
of Mathematics
1906 Association Drive
Reston, Virginia 22091

National Education Association
1201 16th Street, NW
Washington, D.C. 20036

National Middle School
  Association
P.O. Box 968
Fairborn, Ohio 45324

National School Boards
  Association
800 State National Bank Plaza
P.O. Box 1496
Evanston, Illinois 60204

National Science Teachers
  Association
1742 Connecticut Avenue, NW
Washington, D.C. 20009

Ethnic and Minority Organizations

Bilingual Education Service
  Center
500 South Dwyer
Arlington Heights, Illinois
  60005

National Council of Negro
  Women, Inc.
1346 Connecticut Avenue, NW
Washington, D.C. 20036

National Indian Education
  Association
3036 University Avenue, SE
Minneapolis, Minnesota 55419

National Organization for
  Women (NOW)
1424 16th Street, NW
Washington, DC. 20036

Federal Agencies

National Institute of Education
1200 19th Street, NW
Washington, D.C. 20208

National Science Foundation
5225 Wisconsin Avenue, NW
Washington, D.C. 20015

Office of Education
Office of the Assistant
  Secretary
Room 3153
400 Maryland Avenue, SW
Washington, D.C. 20202

Organizations for Children with Special Needs

ACLU Juvenile Rights Project
22 East 40th Street
New York, NY 10016

American Academy for
  Cerebral Palsy
University Hospital School
Iowa City, IA 52240

American Association for the
  Education of Severely and
  Profoundly Handicapped
1600 West Armory Way
Garden View Suite
Seattle, WA 98119

American Association for
  Gifted Children
15 Gramercy Park
New York, NY 10003

American Epilepsy Society
Department of Neurology
University of Minnesota
Box 341, Mayo Building
Minneapolis, MN 55455

American Foundation
for the Blind
15 West 16th Street
New York, NY 10011

American Medical Association
535 North Dearborn Street
Chicago, IL 60610

American Psychological
Association
1200 17th Street, NW
Washington, DC 20036

Association for the Aid of
Crippled Children
345 East 46th Street
New York, NY 10017

Association for Children with
Learning Disabilities
2200 Brownsville Road
Pittsburgh, PA 16210

Association for Education of
the Visually Handicapped
919 Walnut Street
Philadelphia, PA 19107

Bureau for Education of the
Handicapped
400 6th Street
Donohoe Building
Washington, DC 20202

Council for Exceptional
Children
1920 Association Drive
Reston, VA 22091

Institute for the Study of
Mental Retardation and
Related Disabilities
130 South First
University of Michigan
Ann Arbor, MI 48108

Muscular Dystrophy
Association of America
810 7th Avenue
New York, NY 10019

National Association for
Retarded Citizens
2709 Avenue E, East
P.O. Box 6109
Arlington, TX 76011

National Association of Social
Workers
2 Park Avenue
New York, NY 10016

National Committee for Multi-
Handicapped Children
239 14th Street
Niagara Falls, NY 14303

President's Committee on
Employment of the
Handicapped
U.S. Department of Labor
Washington, DC 20210

PROFESSIONAL ORGANIZATIONS
AND JOURNALS

Association for Supervision and Curriculum Development (ASCD)
National Education Association (NEA)
Phi Delta Kappa (PDK)
National Elementary Principals Association (NAESP)
National Association of Secondary School Principals (NASSP)

American Educational Research Association (AERA)
National Middle School Association

Among other functions, these professional organizations produce excellent journals that allow educators to communicate with one another over a broad range of concerns. The following journals are thought to be valuable resources for those persons engaged in supervision work:

Academy of Management Journal
American School Board Journal
Educational Administration Quarterly
Educational Forum
Educational Leadership
Educational Technology
Elementary School Journal
Harvard Educational Review
Journal of Research and Development in Education
Journal of Secondary Education
Learning Magazine
Management Review
Middle School Journal
NASSP Bulletin
National Elementary Principal
Phi Delta Kappan

Name Index

Subject Index

The Authors

Jon Wiles (left) and Joseph Bondi (right) are professors of education at the University of South Florida. As a writing team, they have co-authored fifteen major texts in the areas of supervision, curriculum, administration, and middle schools. In addition to *Supervision: A Guide to Practice*, texts for Merrill (an imprint of Macmillan) include *The Essential Middle School, Principles of Administration*, and *Curriculum Development: A Guide to Practice.*

Dr. Wiles and Dr. Bondi have served in a variety of educational roles—as teachers, school and college supervisors and administrators, and researchers. As consultants with their firm of Wiles, Bondi and Associates, they have worked in forty-five states and ten foreign countries.

Both authors received their doctoral degrees from the University of Florida.